GENERAL REUB WILLIAMS'S MEMORIES OF CIVIL WAR TIMES

Personal Reminiscences of
Happenings That Took Place from
1861 to the Grand Review

Edited and with
an Introduction by
Sally Coplen Hogan

HERITAGE BOOKS
2015

HERITAGE BOOKS
AN IMPRINT OF HERITAGE BOOKS, INC.

Books, CDs, and more—Worldwide

For our listing of thousands of titles see our website at
www.HeritageBooks.com

Published 2015 by
HERITAGE BOOKS, INC.
Publishing Division
5810 Ruatan Street
Berwyn Heights, Md. 20740

Copyright © 2004 Sally Coplen Hogan

All rights reserved. No part of this book may be reproduced or transmitted in any form or by any means, electronic or mechanical, including photocopying, recording or by any information storage and retrieval system without written permission from the author, except for the inclusion of brief quotations in a review.

International Standard Book Numbers
Paperbound: 978-0-7884-2517-2
Clothbound: 978-0-7884-6161-3

For my husband, Jerry, whose love and
support made this book possible.
And for my parents,
Adrian and Mary K. Coplen.

CONTENTS

Preface	v
Introduction	vii
Chapter 1 The Great Conflict Begins	3
Chapter 2 1861 Skirmish at Dam Number Four	15
Chapter 3 Imprisoned at Richmond, Virginia	31
Chapter 4 Home to Recruit for the 12th Indiana	47
Chapter 5 Battle of Richmond, Kentucky	57
Chapter 6 Incident at Holly Springs	79
Chapter 7 Playing Jokes on Grant and Sherman	93
Chapter 8 Battle at Lookout Mountain	111
Chapter 9 Winter Camp at Scottsboro, Alabama	131
Chapter 10 Fighting Against General Joe Johnston	143
Chapter 11 Battle for Kennesaw Mountain	165
Chapter 12 Moving Toward Atlanta	175
Chapter 13 Atlanta Campaign	195
Chapter 14 Indiana Conspirators Trial	211
Chapter 15 Marching to Columbia, South Carolina	225
Chapter 16 Columbia Burns	239
Chapter 17 Raid on Florence, South Carolina	249
Chapter 18 March to Raleigh, North Carolina	259
Chapter 19 At Raleigh	279
Chapter 20 Grand Review May 1865	289
Epilogue	303
Bibliography	313
Index	315

PREFACE

These Civil War memories were written by General Reuben Williams and were published by the General in the two Warsaw newspapers that he was editor of and owned. *The Northern Indianian* and the *Warsaw Daily Times* ran the articles weekly from January 3, 1903 to July 21, 1904[a] The account is very interesting and moving but difficult to read in the microfilmed copies of the old newspapers. Knowing the General's remembrances would be of great interest to many persons, I transcribed the copy, editing the redundancies that were a part of the original text. These redundancies occurred at the beginning and end of each article as the General would introduce a new article by briefly summarizing the previous weeks information, and end the article with a hint of what next week's article would contain. The dates, anecdotes and facts have all been preserved as the General related them.

It must be remembered that General Williams never intended to qualify any of his experiences as fact. His intent was to inform people who had grown up since the war of what it was like to be involved in the greatest struggle that our nation had ever known. His hope was to show the importance of the ordinary soldier, the one who had to fight in the trenches and had dealt most directly with the extreme hardships of war. He wanted to relate instances of camp life, battles, and personalities that he had been a part of and had witnessed. His remembrances may vary from the accepted accounts of events of the Civil War that have been written by historians. Reub Williams's writings deal, perhaps, more kindly with certain personalities of the war than might be justifiable, but Reub Williams relates his information from a first hand knowledge that he realized was small in scope. He stated throughout his account that he was relating what he saw and what he experienced and that historical accounts might differ from his, but "this *Memories of Civil War Times* is what I witnessed".

Since *General Reub Williams's Memories of Civil War Times* was written forty years after the actual event and entirely from memory, it is certain to contain some facts and information that is in error. Some substantiation of the facts can be offered in the form of letters that were written and published in the *Northern Indianian* during Reub Williams's involvement in the war that are dated during the years 1861 to 1865. There are many such letters that were printed and relate the same information as he wrote forty years later. Perhaps the insights and eyewitness accounts

---

a The Northern Indianian, January 8, 1903 thru July 21, 1904
   Warsaw Daily Times, January 3, 1903 thru July 16, 1904

that Reub Williams offers to us are correct or perhaps they are softened by Reub Williams's loyalty to the Union cause and his esteem for some of his superior officers. Perhaps his account would cause certain incidences of the war to be reevaluated and perhaps rewritten, but that is for historians to undertake. I present this account, as Reub Williams did, to help the reader understand the hardships and sufferings that the ordinary soldier had to endure.

I hope you enjoy reading *General Reub Williams's Memories of Civil War Times* as much as I have.

Sally Coplen Hogan

INTRODUCTION

Warsaw, Indiana is honored to have had such a man as Reub Williams to represent our community so bravely and justly in the war to save the Union. The story of his involvement in the Civil War is insightful and moving. All throughout his life he was an asset to our city and helped to form its early character having arrived here in 1845 twelve years after the treaties with the Indians were ratified, opening the lands for settlement.

The following biographical sketch was written by George I. Reid and was published in "The Encyclopedia of Biography of Indiana"[b]. General Williams declared that it was more nearly correct than any of the many that have appeared.

"One of the best-known men of Northern Indiana today is General Reub Williams, of Warsaw, editor of two newspapers. He has been a resident of the place for half a century and rendered as valuable service to the community as any of its citizens. General Williams sprang from a patriotic stock. His grandfather, Jeremiah Williams, served with credit in the volunteer forces of Maryland as a member of the Continental army during the Revolution. His father, Reuben Williams, was a soldier in the war of 1812, attained the rank of sergeant, and was a member of the guard in charge of the British prisoners taken by Commodore Perry on Lake Erie, in their march from the lake shore through Ohio to Chillicothe, then the state capital. He himself maintained the family standard of patriotism by honorable and distinguished services in the Union army during the Rebellion.

"He was born in 1831, in Tiffin, Ohio, where his father had settled immediately after the second war with England. This first twelve years of his life were passed in his native place and he came to Warsaw with his father's family in 1845. Having an independent turn of mind, and appreciating the burden carried by his father in supporting a large family on meager resources, he resolved to be self-sustaining. After spending a single term in the private seminary conducted by Mrs. Jane Cowan, and a shorter term under the tutelage of Joseph A. Funk, he became a voluntary apprentice in the office of the Whig organ of Kosciusko County. The paper was conducted by Andrew J. Bair, with whom young Williams remained four years, until he acquired a practical knowledge of 'the art

---

[b] Reid, George I., Encyclopedia of Biography of Indiana, Century Company, Chicago, 1895

preservative of all arts.' For a brief period thereafter he published the Warsaw Democrat, and then started out as a journeyman printer to see something of the country. He traveled over several states, paying his expenses by setting type in newspapers offices while en route. He spent considerable time in Iowa and from that state was recalled to Warsaw upon the organization of the Republican Party.

"The members of the Republican Party in Kosciusko County wanted an organ able to advocate its principles and defend its policy. Many of them knew the boy who had learned the printer's trade in Warsaw and became a publisher before he was a voter. They recognized his sprightliness and enterprise. They were satisfied that he would be successful as an editor, and for this he returned home. Associating himself with G. W. Fairbrother, he began the publication of *The Northern Indianian* in 1856. The paper was aggressive and vigorous from the beginning. As its editor, he soon exhibited the peculiar qualifications essential to pronounced success in journalism. The paper became a power in politics and a recognized agency in advancing the interests of the county within a few years. But the opening year of the Rebellion fired the patriotism of Reub Williams and he exchanged the tripod for the battlefield.

"Williams performed his services gallantly in the field, and the rank of General was bestowed upon him by brevet near the close of the war. The appointment of brigadier general was conferred by the President in Washington and his commission delivered to him by General Logan. A resume of his military service, covering a period of more that four years, is unnecessary to attest his bravery. He was connected with the important operations and engagements of the armies of the southwest, including the siege of Vicksburg, Jackson, Mississippi; Kenesaw Mountain, Mission Ridge, Atlanta, Jonesborough, Bentonville and scores of skirmishes. He took pride in the discipline and bravery of his regiment. He was complimented in a personal letter from General Sherman for the regiment's soldierly bearing, and the boys were equally proud of their commander.

"He soon resumed editorial control of *The Northern Indianain* which has been continued to the present time, with one or two short intervals. In 1881 he began the publication of *The Daily Times* at Warsaw. In 1866 and again in 1870, he was elected clerk of court of Kosciusko County, serving for eight years. For a few months, on the importunate solicitation of prominent Republicans of the state, he took charge of *The Fort Wayne Daily Gazette*, but could not be induced to abandon his first love in journalism and remove his residence to Fort Wayne. Afterwards for the space of seven months, he held the position of deputy second comptroller of the United States Treasury, but resigned in order to resume his editorial work in Warsaw.

"His old paper, *The Northern Indianian*, is one of the most influential and widely known of its class in Indiana. It established his reputation as an editorial writer. His style is crisp, snappy and forceful. He was united in marriage, April 5, 1857, with Miss Jemima Hubler, daughter of the late Major Henry Hubler, a veteran soldier of two wars—Mexico and the Rebellion. They have reared five sons and one daughter.

"General Williams is held in high esteem by members of the press on account of his ability, long service, uniform courtesy and kindness. His faith in God and good men is a part of himself and is a fountain of unselfishness within. He is naturally reserved in speaking of himself, as all sensitive souls are, but to his comrades he was ever open, frank, cordial and tender. His bravery, loyalty and fidelity won the affection of Governor Morton, and no military commander who went out of the state enjoyed the confidence of the great war-governor more unreservedly."

> I heard the ringing bugle call,
>   the drums that loudly beat,
> And country-folk were gathering
>   in throngs on every street.
> In thoughtful mood, the farmers
>   with comely country dame,
> The joyous lads and lasses,
>   from far and near they came;
> While portico and balcony,
>   housetop and window-bars
> Were decked with loyal mottoes,
>   with waving stripes and stars.
> I asked a passing soldier—young, fair,
>   erect and strong—
> The meaning of the muster,
>   and all that loyal throng;
> He gracefully saluted,
>   then proudly he did say
> "Why the Twelfth Indiana
>   are off to the war today!"
>   —Anonymous

Sally Coplen Hogan

October 7, 2003
Warsaw, Indiana

GENERAL REUB WILLIAMS'S MEMORIES OF CIVIL WAR TIMES

CHAPTER 1

The Great Conflict Begins

Breathes there a man with soul so dead
Who never to himself has said,
"This is my own, my native land!"
Whose heart has ne'er within him burned
As home his footsteps he has turned
From wandering on a foreign strand?
If such there breathe, go, mark him well;
For him no minstrel raptures swell,
High though his titles, proud his name
Boundless his wealth as wish can claim
Despite those titles, power and pelf
The wretch concentered all in self—
Living, shall forfeit fair renown,
And doubly dying, shall go down
To the vile dust, from whence he sprung
Unwept, unhonored and unsung.
                                -Sir Walter Scott

Very many times since the war I have been solicited and urged by the surviving veterans of that period to write a book on the subject. In all probability this comes from the fact that almost my whole life has been spent in the newspaper and printing business, and thus the idea has obtained that I was, in consequence, particularly prepared to undertake such a work. For many years past I have perceived the necessity of something of the kind relating to soldier-life during the ever-memorable period of the civil war—the daily and inner life, so to speak—instead of a history of the war or accounts of the battles, sieges, etc., and hence in the following account the reader should understand that only incidents, anecdotes and happenings, that a perusal of which might interest the reader will be undertaken. If I can interest the young and rising generation to take an interest in the history of their own country—especially those who were quite small or who have been born since the stirring days from 1861 to 1865—I will have accomplished at least a portion of the object in view. This wartime account will be written of scenes, incidents and anecdotes that came under the writer's observation and is written from memory.

Hundreds of books have been written of the Civil War and many more will yet appear. Biographies of the prominent generals of the war have been voluminous—all of them, perhaps, of deep interest and worthy of a place on the shelves of the libraries, both public and private. Few of them portray the life of the soldier—the every-day life of the man in the ranks; the man who carried the musket and to whom, after all, the final victory must be attributed. I desire to say that I shall tell the facts as I saw them, and the private soldier shall receive his full share of the glory won in the greatest war of modern times. I am fully aware that the same act looked at by two or more individuals does not appear precisely the same to the one who may give his view of whatever the subject might be. This often comes for the reason that whatever it may have been was looked at from a different point of observation. Of necessity I shall be compelled to use the personal pronoun to a greater extent than it would be were there any way to avoid it.

I feel confident that those who have grown to manhood's estate since that period do not remember the wonderful excitement that almost instantly prevailed with the start of the war. Indeed, even a vivid and faultless description of the uprising—for, in the truest and broadest sense of the word, that is just what it was—written by the finest descriptive author the country has ever known, could not do justice to the subject. Those who have been born since the war have often heard the story detailed, yet it is doubtful whether the most glowing description could convey a true picture of the excitement that swept over the land like a tornado, and I often think that the facts would not be believed even were they most successfully and eloquently set forth.

I have often entertained the idea that a body of troops—a regiment, for instance—was something like a family on a large scale, and the point is, at least, not wholly inappropriate. In time, after it was fully organized and the men of each company became acquainted with one another, it assumed the character of a family by the daily association of one with the other. The commanding officer of a regiment took the place of the father of the family, and in the same way he saw that the wants of each were supplied; that each member of the family was well clothed, well fed and especially that their arms were in good condition. In time, too, such a feeling grew into the minds of the men composing it, and the esprit du corps finally obtained, that they espoused the quarrels of the command, should there be any, and defended its members regardless of the company to which they belonged, in the hitches that sometimes occurred, just like a family of sons would espouse the cause of one another. It must be understood that there was a good deal of rivalry existing between different regiments of the same corps, division, and even in the same brigade. There were some occasions when the officers had all they could do to prevent an appeal to arms originating in quarrels between the enlisted men of separate commands.

The Great Conflict Begins

The real outbreak of the civil war started on the plains of Kansas two years prior to the firing on Fort Sumter. Under John Brown and Jim Lane the Border Free State men were determined that slavery should be an illegal measure in the new territory. On the other hand, under the lead of various individuals, the Missourians with the slogan of Senator Douglas's captivating scheme of "squatter sovereignty"—thrown out as a bait to secure his nomination for the Presidency in 1860—were equally determined that the Missouri Compromise had been abrogated, and that slavery should extend all over the territory lying west of and adjoining the state. Thus the war was on and many men on both sides lost their lives previous to the fateful 12th day of April 1861, when Fort Sumter was fired on by the South Carolina militia under the orders of Gen Beauregard.

As early as December, 1860, the Governor of South Carolina had called the Legislature of the State together at Columbia, the capital of the State, and this body at once passed the ordinance of secession from the brotherhood of States that had existed from the ratification of the present Constitution till that time, although the same State made an abortive attempt to get out of the Union back in the thirties. Andrew Jackson, the then President of the United States, at once sent word to the leaders of the movement that he would hang every mother's son of them if they persisted in their attempt. Jackson's prompt action succeeded in quieting the question for the time, but the embers of secession continued to smolder even though they had been fairly well covered, and broke out again in the December previous to the time for this newly-elected President, Abraham Lincoln, to take his seat in the March following.

The excitement of the time grew at a rapid pace. State after State in the South followed the example set by South Carolina, and finally "Old Virginia" remained to decide, although Maryland, Kentucky and Missouri were kept from following South Carolina's lead by the presence of Federal troops. Each one of these States set up a sort of "bogus" or "shinplaster" State government, which like a traveling circus, was kept on the move, and none of these ever secured a permanent abiding place.

On the 12th day of April 1861, Fort Sumter, occupied by about two hundred Federal troops under the command of Major Anderson, was fired upon. This attack occurred a little over a month after Abraham Lincoln had taken his seat as President of the United States. History shows very plainly that had President James Buchanan supplied the troops in the harbor of Charleston properly, Fort Sumter could have held out for a considerable time. There are those who declare that with prompt action on his part in sending supplies and two or three naval ships, the fort might have been held clear through the war by the Federal instead of Confederate troops. Be that as it may, the fort was fired upon on the 12th day of April 1861, and surrendered on the 14th, the garrison being permitted to march out with flying colors and drums beating, and thus "the war was on."

The next day, April 15, President Lincoln called for seventy-five thousand troops to "suppress the insurrection" that had broken out in the seceded States, and then there was an uprising! In all those intervening months from the date of Lincoln's election until the surrender of Fort Sumter, public feeling was at fever heat, and grew in extent from day to day and week to week. Here in Warsaw, Indiana (my home) public feeling took on an intense character. The people were so greatly aroused and the news of the day was in such great demand that the writer issued a small daily journal giving the latest dispatches concerning the Southern uprising for two weeks preceding the firing on Fort Sumter. I well remember the day the news of the surrender was announced. The office was then on the third floor of a downtown building. There must have been eight hundred or a thousand people around the corner, and as fast as the little paper was printed it was flung out of the upper windows to the throng below where it was eagerly seized and zealously fought for and torn up in the excitement to procure a copy. The establishment was then only supplied with a hand press, and the work of supplying such an excited, tempestuous and maddened crowd, proceeded quite slowly. The lower doors of the office had to be locked and guarded to keep the building from filling up with the excited populace.

The dispatch announcing Lincoln's call for seventy-five thousand men reached Warsaw at about 11 o'clock a.m. on April 15, 1861. The writer had hand bills printed at once, calling a meeting of the citizens of the town and county to be held in Empire Hall, a building of that period which was able to accommodate an immense crowd. Billy Williams, (citizen of Warsaw, Indiana who became a congressman and later the charge de affairs to Paraguay and Uraguay under President Garfield), delivered one of his inspiring speeches and the names of fifty men were signed to the paper for forming a company under the call of the President. Another meeting was held the next evening and at least a hundred and twenty-five men were added to the list. They were to serve for three months, and no doubt the short time required was quite an inducement to many men who felt that they could serve for that length of time and give that much to their country at any rate.

The company here (Warsaw, Indiana) consisted of Henry C. Hubler, as captain, the only man in the place who had ever had any military training, he having belonged to an independent company in Pennsylvania, where the militia law was excellent, as it was all over the Eastern States. A. P. Gallagher, who had served as a private soldier in the Mexican war, was elected first lieutenant. As we had no other guide at that time to go by but Hardee's tactics, two second lieutenants were elected. Reub Williams was selected for second lieutenant and Andrew Milice was chosen as sub-second lieutenant. The mustering officers, however, failing to recognize the position of sub-second lieutenant, Milice was appointed a sergeant.

After the company was mustered the writer became the captain of the company, following the promotion of Captain Hubler to the majorship of the regiment, thus making a vacancy. Milice was appointed the second lieutenant, while the writer went up to Hubler's place.

In the call for seventy-five thousand men to "suppress the insurrection in the South," President Lincoln had apportioned the number of regiments that each State was expected to furnish, there being six required from Indiana. Governor O. P. Morton at once issued his call for these six regiments. It should be understood that a regiment at that period consisted of seventy-seven men and officers to a company, and thus a regiment would be composed of seven hundred seventy men. Added to this was the "field and staff officers," consisting of a colonel, lieutenant-colonel, major, adjutant, quartermaster, a surgeon and one assistant surgeon. A month or more later, when the first call for regiments for "three years or during the war" was made, Congress had raised the number composing a regiment to one thousand forty men and officers. Companies consisted of one hundred-one men each. Under Governor Morton's call only four thousand six hundred twenty men and officers were required to fill the six regiments first called out. For this number twenty-two thousand men offered their services. Companies boarded trains in many instances without orders and arrived at Indianapolis to be cared for without even letting the Governor know they were coming.

After the company was formed fully ten days—perhaps longer, as time flew fast to those who were so eager to receive orders to come to the State capital—elapsed before it could secure an order to proceed to the State capital. In fact, owing to the reason that the companies raised near Indianapolis rushed in upon the Governor, without orders, it began to look as if our services would be dispensed with entirely. However, Colonel J. B. Dodge, at that time treasurer of this county, went to the capital in order to have the company accepted. A more delighted lot of young men has seldom been seen, when Captain Hubler received a telegram the next day directing him to entrain for the State capital.

The company left for Indianapolis, going by way of Fort Wayne, thence to Peru, and thence to the capital, the only route the north part of the State had except the longer and still more roundabout way via Wanatah, Lafayette and from the latter place to Indianapolis. I have already stated that up to the time the company from this place arrived at Indianapolis, the term of enlistment remained three months; but the wisdom of Governor Morton, and his fitness for the position he held was illustrated by his permitting so many companies to come to the capital. It was at that time uncertain what Kentucky would do, for while there were plenty of Union men in that State, all of the State officials, or nearly so, were favoring secession. Certainly Governor McGoffin favored secession, and should that State be dragged out of the Union as Tennessee was, there would be danger all along the southern border of Indiana.

Foreseeing this, about the first thing Governor Morton did after receiving the President's demand for six regiments was to call the State Legislature in extra session. In view of the danger along the Ohio River, about the first thing the Legislature did was to call out six regiments of State troops to serve for one year. The Governor rightly considered that the overflow of the six regiments of three month's men would fill up these extra regiments quickly. Such certainly would have been the case only Congress passed the law for three hundred thousand men to serve for "three years or during the war." This had a tendency to prevent the filling up of all six regiments of State troops and only the Twelfth and Sixteenth were mustered into the State service, and thus became the very first regiments in all the country agreeing to serve for a longer time than three months.

Many men who were left after the company from this place was mustered in, went into various other regiments, and it is quite likely that nearly all of the regiments from Indiana enlisting under this first three years' call contained more or less men from Kosciusko County. I know that I was greatly surprised on one occasion after the war while in Adjutant-General Terrill's office to find that there were thirty-six men in the Eighteenth regiment credited on the muster rolls to Kosciusko County. The cause for this scattering of men from this county is thus accounted for, as the Eighteenth was scarcely known in Northern Indiana.

When one looks back at this early period of the war, how little did any of us know or even dream of the wonderful immensity, which it was to assume? In the Southern States the remark that "one Southern soldier was the equal of any seven north of Mason and Dixon's line" was common. On the other hand, we had here at home many who declared "that it would only be a breakfast spell for the North to subdue the rebellion." Both were wrong, and at the same time even a conservative statement on the subject could not have been but a mistaken one. Many homes were to be made desolate, many children made orphans, and many wives to journey along life's highway alone for the reason that a fond and loving husband was the occupant of some unknown grave among the pines of Georgia, or in the desolate valleys of Old Virginia. In fact every State in the Union was to have graves whose occupants wore either the blue or the gray.

Perhaps, history cannot show an instance where a government was so utterly unprepared to either begin a war to defend itself or carry one on. For years the "fire-eating" leaders of the South—the Yanceys, the Toombses, the Wises, had been at work in preparing the slave-holding States for a dissolution of the Union, and the setting-up of a confederacy, whose corner-stone should be slavery. In fact, the second section, I think it is of the constitution of "The Confederate States of America," provided for slavery so clearly and so free from ambiguity that it would never leave any question of doubt upon the subject. Quietly, but surely, the South was getting ready for the contest for years before their leaders had worked the people of their section up in a way that the vast majority would sustain the effort to divide the Union when the time came to strike.

Under Buchanan's administration, the then Secretary of the Navy, Floyd, under the power given him by his position, had so widely scattered our navy that but a few of the better ships were within reach of the new administration when Lincoln took his seat as President of the United States. The War Department of the government had been also stripped of arms. When the opening of the war came with the firing on Fort Sumter, there were not enough muskets to arm one man in ten who had offered their services. In the South in almost every county, at least in the Gulf States, independent military companies had been organized and armed for several years previous to the memorable and fateful 15th of April, 1861. Both Maryland and Virginia contained a number of these, at least partially drilled, armed companies.

How different it was here in Indiana when the war broke out. There were not over four independent companies in the State. The militia laws of the State were so defective that scarcely any aid could be secured from the State government. I remember that a year or two preceding this breaking out of the war that a military tournament was held at Crawfordsville, where Lew Wallace, as captain had kept a company of soldiers at Wabash. Captain Charles Parish was the head of a similar company; and Captain Simon Buckner, of Louisville, Kentucky the commanding officer of another, and these three companies only, attended the tournament at Crawfordsville.

All three of these captains possessed a taste for military matters. Gen. Lew Wallace had served in the Mexican War, and I think Parish also, and both responded to Governor Morton's call for troops at once, and each of them, as might have been expected, became prominent in the war. Lew Wallace became a Major-General; and Charles Parish became the Colonel of a regiment on the Union side, while Buckner entered the Confederate service and was in command when the rebel forces afterward surrendered at Fort Donelson, as a Major-General. Floyd, the Secretary of the Navy, who had scattered the United States ships to the four winds, slipped out of the Fort the day preceding, fearing that if captured by the Federals, there might be a reckoning with him. He, previous to leaving, turned the command of the Fort over to General Buckner and made his escape. After that Floyd seemed to have sunk out of view even in the South. At least, his name was seldom heard of to any extent, after he made his escape from Fort Donelson.

Governor Morton had all that he could do to find arms for the six regiments called for from Indiana. By using every kind of musket offered—the Harper's Ferry, the Belgian, some of the old style of Springfield rifles, etc., he got his quota filled. The troops were hastened to West Virginia as fast as cars could be furnished to carry them. Here is where the far-seeing wisdom of Governor Morton showed itself. He felt sure that the three months term would expire ere the war, which he felt would last for years, would have only begin. Thus out of the surplus of men in Camp Morton, Camp Sullivan, etc., when the call for three years troops came in addition to the two State regiments organized, the second call was soon filled from among those who failed to get into any of the three months' regiments. Consequently, the second quota for Indiana was quickly filled by his splendid management and equipped fairly well, he having by "hook or crook," secured a sufficient number of guns to arm them all.

The first duty that fell to the command to which the writer belonged, the Twelfth Indiana Infantry, was at Evansville, on the Ohio River, away down in the southwest part of the State, a region known for many years as "The Pocket." Two pieces of artillery were added, and men detailed from the regiment to manage them—although these were men enlisted as infantry. The duty of the troops at that point was to blockade the Ohio River and prevent supplies of all kinds of war material from passing southward to be used by the Confederate army. It was almost a daily occurrence to stop one or more steamboats. Some of them were carrying cargoes that might be considered contraband of war. This class of goods was taken possession of, but in most instances, the owner of the goods could establish his own loyalty, and fully explain the real destination and ownership. Thus in most instances most of the cargoes were returned to the owners. This kind of duty continued up till July 21, 1861 (the day of the first Bull Run disaster). On that Sunday evening Colonel John M. Wallace, who commanded the Twelfth, received a telegram from Governor Morton, stating that cars would be at Evansville that evening for the purpose of transferring the regiment back to Indianapolis. Early in the forenoon of the following day, Monday, the train arrived at Indianapolis and the proposition was submitted to the members of the regiment to be transferred to the United States service. This was complied with at once, not a man refusing as he might have legally done, perhaps, and the next morning, Tuesday, we left to aid the defense of Washington.

The members of the regiment had been so busily engaged in being transported from Evansville to Indianapolis, and in transferring their allegiance from the State to the National government, and in receiving clothing, arms, etc., that they had not time to observe how wildly the country was excited over that first battle of the war—a struggle that, compared with some that were to follow, amounted to nothing more than an ordinary lively skirmish. The killed and wounded in all only amounted to something over four hundred and the fight itself might be classed as a "stand-off". It was, however, much nearer to Washington than to Richmond, the respective capitals of each side, and the stragglers of both sides found themselves either in Richmond or Washington. It is said that on Monday evening there were stragglers from a Zouave regiment back at their homes in New York City.

At any rate there was no little fear for Washington City, and in looking back at the situation today, had the army under Beauregard been older troops and free from the excitement that prevails in all first battles, the city might have been captured by a forward movement on the part of the rebel leader. While it was really a drawn battle the Confederates held the ground and made the most of it. Maps of the struggle were lithographed and sent broadcast all over the Southern States, and the struggle was hailed as a certain indication of future success and the establishment of the "Southern Confederacy." On the side of the South the first Bull Run had the effect to crush out the strong Union sentiment that was visible at many points, particularly in Western North Carolina and in Eastern Tennessee as well as in smaller numbers at many localities in almost all Southern States.

In the North the effect was to arouse the people to an immensity the struggle was to assume. The orators, who announced that the suppression of the rebellion "would be a mere breakfast spell," took a new view of the situation. The first battle showed that the South was terribly in earnest, and plainly showed that the Confederacy at the start was better prepared for war than was the North. A deep and determined feeling took hold of every patriot in the land, who felt that the government of "The Fathers" must be preserved. The news of the battle of Bull Run awakened the people of the North to a degree that nothing else could have done.

Hence the passage of the Twelfth Indiana through the country on its way to the defense of Washington City was a continued ovation from the passing of the first small village to the east of Indianapolis, on through Richmond, Indiana, Columbus, Ohio, and on into Pittsburgh, and the State capital and the smaller towns of Pennsylvania, the regiment was greeted by one and all with wild acclaim. Even along the line of the railroads in the country, the people had assembled at the crossroads to greet, to welcome and to cheer the Hoosiers. At Richmond great stacks of sandwiches, coffee, ice water, cakes, cigars, etc., were donated to the soldiers. If anything not in sight was wanted, all that was needed was to make the want known and it was or would be supplied. At Columbus, Ohio, perhaps two thousand young ladies had assembled in a body to cheer the oncoming regiment and when the train slowly entered the depot, these young ladies broke forth in a patriotic song prepared for the purpose.

And so it continued clear through to Baltimore. At Pittsburgh, Pennsylvania, the ladies had prepared a regular meal where the entire regiment could be seated while it devoured a portion of the plenteous food that was so patriotically and generously provided. It was at Pittsburgh that the ladies organized an association, the intention of which was to provide a full meal for any and every soldier that might pass through that place during all of the protracted struggle. I well remember seeing over the great dining hall, these patriotic women had fitted up for the purpose, even several years after the war, the statement over the door, the precise number of meals that had been provided for all passing soldiers in letters of gold just as they should have been. I cannot remember the exact number, but it was large beyond two millions. Think of that! Instead of a "breakfast spell," as at first thought, it afterward required many a dinner and supper and even an odd lunch thrown in for good measurement in the four years that followed.

At Baltimore came orders to send the regiment to Harper's Ferry, Virginia, where General N. P. Banks, of Massachusetts, was assembling a large force to checkmate the advance of a rebel army into Maryland. Maryland had been held fast to the Union side through the efforts of its loyal Governor Hicks. We derailed outside of the town that had already mobbed a Federal regiment on its way to the defense of Washington. At that time, and in fact clear through the war, fully a mile and a half intervened without a railroad connection and it was necessary then to march all troops through the city as well as to transfer all freight, arms and supplies of every kind by wagon. The city was tunneled after the war, and now passengers can go to Washington without even seeing Baltimore, by passing under its streets and houses.

As the regiment had to march through the streets, and in view of the fact that there were still many of its citizens who sympathized with the Confederate cause, our Colonel, John M. Wallace, ordered the soldiers to load their muskets in the suburbs of the city, but of course not to fire under any circumstances without orders. While it was a very natural thing to do, yet owing to the lack of discipline in the ranks at the time, I have many times thought what a fortunate thing it was that no soldier allowed his musket to go off by accident during that passage. Everybody who passed through the war now knows that if a single gun had been fired fully a dozen more would have followed, and hence there would have been trouble! General Ben Butler had taken command of the city at that time and the regiment was not even scoffed at in any way, but on the contrary, the Union sentiment had become so strong that at several points along the line the soldiers were lustily cheered; quite a different reception than the one the Massachusetts regiment received a few weeks earlier.

The soldiers that were assembling under General Banks at Harper's Ferry were of the first call for three hundred thousand three-year troops, and consequently their ranks were full, each one of the ten companies containing its one hundred and one members, with the field and staff additional. In consequence of their full numbers, compared with our own little lightweight regiment of seven hundred, an Eastern regiment looked like a full brigade beside it. Besides, the Twelfth, as were all the first Indiana troops, were clothed in a uniform of Kentucky-jeans, consisting of a round-about pants with a hat that the boys soon nicknamed "camp-kettles," vastly inferior to the full United States Uniform with which the Eastern Army was equipped.

Soon after arriving at Harper's Ferry, John W. Wallace resigned his position. This advanced Lieutenant Colonel William H. Link to the place vacated. George Humphreys became Lieutenant Colonel, and Captain Henry Hubler was appointed Major. This made a vacancy in the Warsaw Company, to which the writer was selected, jumping over Patrick Galagher, the First Lieutenant, as Captain. This also allowed Andrew S. Milice to become Second Lieutenant, who after serving the allotted time in the Twelfth, became captain in the Seventy-fourth Indiana Infantry, following the promotion of C. W. Chapman as Colonel of the regiment. Captain Milice was severely wounded at Chickamauga, and was compelled to resign in consequence.

When Link assumed the command of the regiment new life was infused into it at once. He, too, was grieved over the disparity of the number of men in his regiment as compared with the full regiments with which his own was associated. This grew on him to such a degree, as did also the ill-looking, ill-fitting and rather gawky uniforms of the Twelfth that he secured an order to send a recruiting party back to Indiana to procure enough men to fill the regiment up to the maximum of 1,040. The party was also to procure new uniforms and to secure a band. All of the regiments with which the Twelfth was associated had full bands of twenty-six instruments. The recruiting party was to consist of a sergeant and one private soldier from each company with a commissioned officer in command of all of them. The writer of these war time memories was placed at the head of this party, and immediately left Harper's Ferry for Indianapolis.

On arriving at the State capital and reporting to Adjutant-General Laz. Noble, one of the most competent assistants to Governor Morton, who gave us all possible assistance, and as the regiment had been made up from the State at large, the recruiting party had the whole State to draw from. The term of enlistment was for the uncompleted term of one year, and as the regiment had served for about five months, the call I made was for seven months. As all other recruiting was for three years it can be seen that the term offered by my party for seven months became quite popular. It was only a brief time after the party got to work that the list showed an enlistment of considerably over two hundred. I also had the good fortune to secure through its leader, a man by the name of Lasher, a full band, instruments and all. The band's home was at Peru and after it was mustered in, I took it back to the regiment and nearly three hundred men.

This large body of recruits was furnished transportation for Washington, where it was expected to join its command. Like the original regiment it was also headed off at Baltimore. The regiment had been ordered during my absence to Sharpsburgh, which a year later became a central point of the battle of Antietam. The recruits were received with great rejoicing. Nearly every one of them had personal friends in the regiment, who cheered them greatly in introducing them to soldier life. Among these recruits was a young fellow about seventeen years old, with whom the writer had a rather pleasant episode before leaving the State for our destination.

The boy's mother could scarcely be induced to give her consent to let the boy go at all. She heard that I had promised to appoint him as a musician after we got to the regiment and let him learn to blow a fife or bugle, or beat a drum. The reader can perceive how surprised I was to receive a note from the mother of this boy on the evening of the day that the detachment was to leave for the East at 2 o'clock a.m. In this note she said: "Captain Williams, I jest heard yister'day that my boy was to be made a musician of some kind. Do you think I want a son of mine to go about in the army blowin' a fife or a bugle, or poundin' on the leather head of a drum? I did not like to let him go at all, but having consented, I want him to be a soldier and carry a gun, and to learn to use it to a good advantage, too. Jest you consent to let him carry a gun, else I'll come and take him home with me on the return train." Of course I consented, and I only mention this incident to show the true patriotism that not only prevailed everywhere, but dominated the women to a wonderful degree. This woman was anxious to have the war over, and as she afterwards stated, that her idea of war was to give every man a gun and make him use it, too. Drums, fifes and bugles she said were good enough in their place, but neither one would count much in a fight. There were thousands of just such women whose hearts were as tender as those of the gentlest, but she reasoned that a son of hers must do something to help suppress the rebellion and end the war so he could get home all the sooner. All of these incidents occurred before any of the great battles of the war were fought. The homes in the land whether cottage or palace in either the North or the South had not as yet felt the affect of the war.

CHAPTER 2

1861 Skirmish at Dam Number Four

When through the shuddering Southern air
   Men heard the boom of Sumter's guns:
When flashed the tidings everywhere,
   "Columbia calls her noblest sons."
He left his dear young wife and child,
   His peaceful home, the sword to wield;
His happy home to face the wild
And awful horrors of the field.
—Eugene J. Hall

Twelfth Indiana regiment, after it was recruited up to the maximum number of 1040, was detailed to picket the Potomac River from Harper's Ferry up to Williamsport. This necessitated the breaking up of the command as a body, and the stationing of the various companies at different points along that historic stream. The headquarters were at Sharpsburgh, Maryland, a town located a mile or more from the river with Shepardstown on the opposite side in Virginia. At some points two companies were stationed, and at others only one. Four companies and the newly recruited band were held at Sharpsburgh, while companies E and K were sent up the river to what was known as Dam No. 4.

The Ohio and Chesapeake Canal ran along the eastern shore, and this important public enterprise was supplied with water by dams built across the Potomac River. At Dam No. 4 a portion of the stream was diverted into the canal. As the canal ran through a mountainous country, of necessity, these dams were numerous. I think their full number was twenty-two, and all of them were built of stone. They were of the most durable character, and of course had to be unusually strong for the Potomac sometimes rose as high as fourteen feet in twenty-four hours. With the rush of such a body of water, it is easy to perceive that in order to withstand a flood, these dams had to be not only durable but also exceedingly strong and well built in every way.

At the beginning of the war, it was a favorite idea of the Confederate authorities to destroy these dams—some of them at any rate. They reasoned that the principal supply of coal was furnished to Washington City by this canal, and to destroy its usefulness as a feeder to the Federal capital, was a pet measure with the Jeff Davis' government. The destruction of a few of the dams that supplied the canal with water would be all that was required. In order to carry out this idea a full division of Confederate troops, as early as November 1861, under the command of "Stonewall" Jackson occupied Winchester. He sent a brigade to Martinsburg, Virginia, and held that point quite close to the Pennsylvania line about the time that Companies E and K of the Twelfth Indiana took up their station on the Maryland side to protect and defend Dam No. 4. Very soon after arriving with the recruits, I found myself, along with Captain Draper, of Company K, assigned to this duty, with Major Henry Hubler in command of the two companies. Company A was stationed about a mile and a half below us on the river, in order to prevent a surprise by the enemy fording the river below the dam where the water was shallow.

All at once Major Hubler received intelligence from a Union man on the Virginia side that the rebels were preparing to attack and destroy the dam, the structure that it was the duty of these three companies to guard. The Federal troops had only been in their position near the dam for a short time when this news was received from the citizen. The approach of Stonewall Jackson with a full division of troops caused no small amount of flurry on our side of the river. It was with considerable trepidation that the authentic information was received. This information was in addition to the news already possessed by Major Hubler that the dam was to be destroyed. Major Hubler had received the information in a letter from a prominent gentleman by the name of Resin Shepard, the family for whom the Shepardtown was named, who was known as loyal to the Federal government.

During the night of the tenth of December this letter came, having been smuggled over the river to Major Hubler, commandant of the Dam No. 4 post, which contained the information that Jackson's full division was really on the way to attack the dam. Mr. Shepard was an out-and-out Union man, but the pressure of the rebel forces under "Stonewall," and the continuous roaming about that section of Virginia of Ashby's Confederate regiment of cavalry, mostly raised in that neighborhood, compelled him to keep very quiet in whatever he did. He was already suspected of being in communication with the Federal army under General Banks, whose headquarters at that time were at Frederick, Maryland. Shepard had a brother whose feelings were entirely enlisted in the Confederate cause. The report was very general on our side of the river that the brother had uniformed and equipped a full regiment for the Confederate army with every requisite except muskets, and it is more than probable that the story was true. I had it myself from several Union Virginians, who had visited our camp at the dam.

Both these men were well off and in espousing different sides they only showed how families were divided in the earlier part of the war. This was not only so in the South, but prevailed to a greater extent in the North than was generally known, especially among the "Border States," where relatives lived on both sides of that imaginary division known as "Mason and Dixon's line." Quite often during the war I have had persons ask me after their capture if I knew of this or that person who lived at Indianapolis or Lafayette, or whatever the point might be, they claiming them sometimes as relatives, sometimes mere acquaintances, but anxious to hear from them.

Shepards's letter was carefully worded so that if it fell into the hands of a Confederate soldier it could not be traced to its author, as it was signed by a fictitious name previously arranged between himself and Major Hubler, when the troops first took up their station at the Dam. Of course, the news of the advance of the rebel troops created no small amount of excitement in our camp, composed of troops that had never yet met an enemy. Early on the morning of December 11, 1861, every Federal soldier on our side of the river was up early and scanning the opposite side for the appearance of the enemy.

As the day wore on the impression began to prevail that the whole thing was a ruse, that no enemy was near, and that no intention to destroy the dam existed in the minds of any save those on the Virginia side, actuated by fear or false reports. This absence of an enemy that was reported, even in writing, and from a man of known Union sentiments, could not be reconciled. Major Hubler was confident that Mr. Shepard, who he had met two or three times, was not intentionally deceiving him. His reputation in the section of the country in which he lived for truthfulness and honesty was too well substantiated to believe there was any deception about the matter.

Firmly believing this, Major Hubler decided to send a squad of men over the river above the dam on a tour of investigation, and I was ordered to take command of the scouting party. We had a rowboat above the dam, and the scramble to join the party was very great. Nate B. McConnell was crowded out just as the boat pushed away from the shore, else he would have borne his part in the ill-luck that afterwards befell the party. The boat was so small that even the seven men that got away were crowded in the shaky, leaky affair. As it was, Sergeant James McGuire, Oliver Hubler, Timothy Robbins, Robert S. Richhart (who afterwards became the captain of a company in the Twelfth Indiana Cavalry) and Lemuel Hazzard, who became Captain of I company of my own regiment after it was reorganized when its term of a year expired, with a man from K company whose name I cannot recall, and Henry Wescot, who in like manner became the First Lieutenant of I company on the reorganization, composed the scouting party.

The orders were to be very cautious and careful for the reason that if we should happen on a squad or a company of Confederate cavalry, there would be but little chance for escape. The party was instructed not to go farther than a mile from the river and to be very watchful. On the opposite side of the Potomac was an extraordinarily high and steep bluff—probably a rise of two hundred feet or more. By zigzagging, this bluff could be and was scaled. On reaching the top, where there was an old-fashioned "worm" fence, the party stopped for a time and scanned the surrounding country, which, except the bottom of several ravines that ran into the Potomac River, could be readily seen from our vantage point. Nothing in sight had the appearance of an enemy. It was a bright, cold morning and at one time I saw something glisten in the distance. I surmised it to be the glint of a gun-barrel, but as only two Negroes with a team gathering corn fodder could be seen, I concluded that what I had seen and thought might be a gun, was just the sun shining on the bright wagon-tire.

There was a hewed log house in an open field a few hundred yards inland, and where—as we had previously known—an old lady and a young woman made their home. This home was surrounded by a wheat field, the growing crop being a couple of inches high. I had determined in my mind not to go further than to this house, and in obedience to orders started for the river. On reaching that point and inquiring of the woman whether any Confederate soldiers had been seen in that quarter, and receiving a negative reply, I ordered the men to fall back to the river. About this time Tim Robbins concluded to see if his Springfield rifle would carry a ball into a little cross-road village called "Hard Scrabble." It only contained a general store, a blacksmith shop, and when the Federal government held sway—a post office. The gun had scarcely been fired when a party of at least fifty mounted men made their appearance, emerging from a ravine that had kept them hidden until the officer in charge concluded to see what the firing of the gun meant.

Of course I ordered the men to retreat as rapidly as possible back to the fence from where we had overlooked the country. I am confident that the party would have made the few hundred yards to the fence but for the fact that all of us sank to our ankles in the soft ground, thus not only impeding our speed, but making it a very laborious, breath-consuming race. As we had gone past the log house a short distance, I was confident that the officers in command concluded that there was a body of soldiers inside the house, and on turning my head I discovered that he had taken time to dismount and was conversing with the inmates. Had it not been for this I am sure the party would have been captured sooner. A few of us got quite near the fence we had left. It was our intention; if we did so, to roll down the bank as best we could, and thus permit our own two companies to stop the pursuit at that point by volley after volley from the other side of the river.

Unfortunately the soft ground wearied us to such an extent that of sheer necessity our speed was relaxed to such a degree that we were headed off when some of us were within a couple of rods of the fence. Besides the officer in command of the Confederates, now fully assured that he was not leaving a hidden enemy at the house, came up and by his presence pressed the pursuit to a greater degree of speed. It was men on foot against others on horseback, the difference being almost wholly in favor of the enemy, and it is not at all surprising that we were overtaken. Squads of Confederates, upon hearing the firing, were coming in from every side. Henry Wescott, who afterwards fought in the reorganized Twelfth, and was mortally wounded, dying of lock-jaw at the hospital after the battle of Richmond, Kentucky, would have lost his life at that time, I feel sure. Wescott was leading us all in the race, when a Confederate soldier coming from another direction, rode right up behind him, unslung his carbine and was about to blow his head off, when I hollowed his name. He turned and took in the situation so quickly that the soldier's fire went wild, and before he could do anything more the entire party was surrounded and surrendered.

During the entire race for the fence shots were fired at us not only from the pursuing party but also from other detachments of six, ten or a dozen or more, and bullets struck the ground in many places. At the onset we returned the fire of the first party we saw, and at least two of the Confederates were knocked out of their saddles, one of whom was severely wounded in the breast as I could plainly see. The horses of both were flying over the field, of course, riderless. The distance with which the Springfield musket would carry was well illustrated on that occasion. The troops we had left on the opposite side of the river could see the advance of the Confederates through the ravines long before my party did. Major Hubler ordered the troops to fire, scarcely believing the enemy could be reached. But it is a fact that although the distance from the firing lines on the Maryland side was scarcely less than a mile, the balls from the muskets of our own men fell not only among the immediate troops that were pursuing us, but amongst us as well. Afterwards in the Atlanta campaign, a volley from the rebels, also using the Springfield musket, as was afterwards ascertained, carried over a mile and mortally wounded a man, the distance being measured after the "Johnnies" fell back. These pieces may have been, and doubtless were, elevated to a considerable extent when fired in both instances.

The entire party, of course, was captured and as soon as we surrendered, it was easy to see that Stonewall's division had reached the vicinity, for very soon all of Ashby's entire regiment of cavalry had assembled around us, consisting of over a thousand men. No one belonging to my party was injured in the least. That we should all escape thus, has been a great mystery to me; for, from the time the fight commenced up to the time we yielded, extending over nearly a half mile of ground, there could not have been less than four hundred rounds fired at us. The bullets whistled on all sides, fell at our feet, passed between us and over us, but no injuries were sustained by anyone.

On coming up, Colonel Ashby directed a Captain by the name of Baylor to detail a detachment of fifteen men with himself in command, and take the prisoners to Martinsburgh, Va., where a brigade of Confederate infantry was stationed. As the party was conducted through the village of Hard Scrabble, we found at least two brigades of Confederates there, with probably twenty newly built boats, evidently to be used to transfer a portion of troops to the Maryland side in the hope of surrounding and capturing Major Hubler's command. There were also four guns. These were to be used in shelling the Federal camp across the river and to attract the attention of our side while the Confederate infantry crossed in boats above the dam and Ashby's cavalry forded the Potomac below it.

The plan was a good one and I have always been satisfied in my own mind that but for sending my party across the river in the forenoon prevented a capture by surprise, for it was not Jackson's intention to cross that day, but to make a night attack. This having been frustrated, the rebels put in their time on the 11th in firing into our side with both artillery and musketry fire and then abandoned the attempt in the evening. Major Hubler had also received reinforcements. In the meantime Captain Baylor conducted us prisoners to Martinsburg, where we arrived a short time before dark. Since the war I met Captain Baylor at Kansas City and we talked over war times with great satisfaction, both of us having commanded brigades in the after years that followed.

The arrival of the party of prisoners at Martinsburg created no little excitement in that very important place on the line of the Baltimore and Ohio railroad. I allude to it as important for the reason that it was the place where there were located the shops of the road and where following the "First Bull Run Battle" the Confederate government was enabled to secure many locomotive engines. At the time it was reported that they captured ninety engines, but I conclude this to be greatly more than the facts. That they did secure a great number is, however, true, and what is more, they were a godsend to the Confederacy, for engines were not only scarce within the limits of the Confederate States, but also none could be secured from abroad after the blockade was established. And it was very doubtful whether there was a shop within the lines of the seceded States that could turn out a brand new engine.

All the Southern shops could do was to repair broken and disabled locomotives, and for this purpose the Tredegar Iron Work, located at Richmond, Virginia, was the central point for repairing engines. Looking back at the war, it can be seen that the constant depreciation and wearing out of locomotives; the destruction of railroads by tearing up the rails; the blowing up of bridges along the lines; and the breaking down of long lines of trestles, was at all times a serious blow to the Confederacy. The Federals learned the trick of heating and twisting the rails, thus putting the rails in a condition that no machinery within the Confederate lines could straighten or repair them. The rails were useless for railroad purposes and this destruction went on constantly after the first battle of the war. The engines secured at Martinsburg were placed on trucks. There was a good pike road from that place to Winchester and Strasbourg where they were hauled by horses and ox-teams to the latter place then placed on other roads and taken via Manassa Junction to Richmond and thence south to where they were most needed. The intelligent reader can readily perceive how seriously the transfer of troops and supplies was impeded by the wholesale destruction of everything connected with railroads. The demolition of the railroads and also their motive power had as much to do with the shortening of the war as the inability of the Confederate soldiery to continue it.

We prisoners arrived at Martinsburg an hour or so before dark. I have already stated that a brigade of infantry belonging to Stonewall Jackson's division was stationed at that place. Although the town was nine miles distant from Dam Number 4, the people had heard the artillery fire throughout the afternoon. Members of the brigade were anxious to learn the cause and the result of any engagement and hence the arrival of Captain Baylor and his prisoners created much excitement among the people. As the news spread, a large number of citizens gathered on the streets anxious for intelligence of any kind. The arrival of several "Yankee" prisoners was an incident that had never occurred before.

The point that amused us most was the fact that none of the landlords of hotels in that place would care for us prisoners and take Confederate money for pay! There was a strong Union sentiment in all that section of Virginia. The majority of the people refused to recognize the new money; but the presence of a Confederate brigade closed the mouths of many people against refusing to use Confederate money in their business. So that after being turned away from three public houses, the fourth finally acceded to Captain Baylor's request and agreed to furnish the prisoners with food and lodging in exchange for Confederate money. It should be stated that the destination of the party of prisoners was Winchester, the headquarters of Stonewall Jackson' division where the General was conducting his operations against the dams.

Captain Baylor had decided to remain at Martinsburg all night and proceed at an early hour the next morning to Winchester, a distance, if I remember right, of forty miles. After dark the hotel was surrounded by hundreds of people all anxious to get a peep at the "Yankees," and as the crowd enlarged the noise and confusion outside increased, also. After supper the prisoners assembled in the hotel parlors and were very kindly treated by those who called. Several citizens and quite a number of Confederate officers belonging to the brigade that was encamped in the suburbs of the town came to see us. Of course the curiosity to see the prisoners became very great and among the callers were a number of ladies who, added to the regular boarders there, made quite a crowd in the large parlor. There was also a piano in the parlor and a young lady, to whom I had been introduced, who claimed her home as Alexandria, Virginia a town near Washington, was invited to play and sing something. The very first thing she selected was "Yankee-doodle came to town on a little pony," and as the selection fitted my own case so closely, she came over to where I sat and apologized, declaring there was nothing personal in the words. She afterward rendered "Oh, say can you see by the dawn's early light?" as a salve to my wounded feelings, if they had been ruffled.

All this time the crowd outside had been accumulating, and as usual under such circumstances the rougher element was beginning to get in the ascendant. I stepped to the window and could hear many threats of mobbing us and I could also see that some of the young fellows, generally boys from about sixteen to twenty, were well prepared with stones and some of them with eggs, which they intended to use upon our party. I called Captain Baylor's attention to the matter and, although he had intended to have us remain over night he decided right then to change the program and get out of the place as soon as possible. Like all old-fashioned taverns, in Virginia, there was a barn and barnyard connected with the house. His plan, he told me, was to place a wagon in the barnyard, very quietly and put the six men into it, giving to myself a horse. All this he conducted so quietly that not one of the large yelling crowd in front of the tavern either knew of or expected the movement. The crowd was growing larger and larger all the time, especially with those who would delight in stoning Captain Baylor's prisoners, and I could perceive that the latter, although determined to do his duty, and protect his prisoners, was growing quite nervous over the situation. He told me that he had procured a half dozen mounted men, which, added to his own guard of ten men, made a very respectable guard for the party.

When everything was in readiness, the men were placed in the wagon and told to lie down until they got outside of town. I mounted on a very handsome and spirited, although small, mare, and Captain Baylor gave the order to start on a dead run, the mounted men bringing up the rear. The move was so well executed that the howling crowd in front of the hotel never knew what was up until the wagon shot out into the main street, the continuance of the pike road to Winchester. The mob hallowed and hooted for some time, but only a few small boys followed us and they only for a short distance. I was then, and I am still, thoroughly convinced that but for Captain Baylor's skillful movement the party would certainly have been mobbed, perhaps some of them killed, or at least hurt. It was also a wise move for us not to stay all night, for in all probability the crowd would have greatly increased during the night. After we got safely beyond pursuit on the fine highway, on several occasions, I was tempted to make a dash for liberty by turning my horse and taking the road back at full speed.

Of course, I would have had to take my chances of a volley from the guard, but on the other hand, unless they hit me or lamed my horse I reasoned that I could be beyond their reach before they could reload for a second fire. Then came the thought that, as I was the only commissioned officer present, it would be unfair to desert the men I had brought over the river. Still, I was tempted, and it is quite likely if I had thought I could have found the way back to the Potomac River without passing through Martinsburg, where I would be almost sure to meet Confederate soldiers, I would have made the attempt.

The longer the idea of escape was deferred, the narrower became the chance, of course, so I allowed it to depart from my mind. The night was a beautiful one, clear and cold, with bright moon. The well-kept pike made traveling easy. Just before daylight the party approached Winchester. The town was made historic during the Revolutionary war, as the region where General Morgan organized the Mounted Riflemen. The Rifleman rendered efficient aid to General Washington, and arrived at his headquarters directly after the investment of Boston and confined the British army within the town limits, which greatly cheered Washington. In the suburbs of Winchester, we passed though a large body of Confederate troops, their tents shining white on both sides of the road in the splendid moonlight.

Just as Captain Baylor's command in charge of us reached the encampment, I heard him order his bugler to play something. The bugler at once struck up the then popular air of the Confederacy of "Dixie's Land," and what is more he played it so well that I at once knew that he was not a novice on the instrument. What is more, in the still, cold, morning air the sound reached far and wide and awoke the sleeping camp. When the camp discovered us they gathered along the highway on both sides so fast that we had to press through a big line of spectators, all of who had to be informed that Captain Baylor had "brought in a batch of Yankee prisoners." Of course, this announcement induced hundreds more of the men of the camp to come out to see the "Yanks," as we were the first captives they had seen. As a result the road into town was so impeded by them that Captain Baylor found it difficult at times to pass through the constantly growing crowd.

This, however, was finally accomplished, and the gentlemanly and kind-hearted officer reported at General Stonewall Jackson's headquarters for further orders. The party of prisoners was taken to what had been the "Sons of Temperance Hall" previous to the war. Into this large building we were turned only to find it already full of men in confinement for offenses of a military nature. Two of them were accused of desertion from the Confederate army and were awaiting their trial, and others, the charges against whom were of a less grave nature. Captain Baylor apologized to me for putting us into such a pen, and promised his assistance in getting us better quarters during the day if possible. This, however, he failed to do, although I am satisfied that he would have done so if he could, for he was a perfect gentleman. But of course, in Winchester just then, there were many officers who outranked him and whose word, instead of his, was law.

Day had not fully dawned when Captain Baylor left us. I was quite sorry to see him go as I thought quite probable that whoever took command of us henceforth might, in all probability, be a very different sort of a person. Along about 8 o'clock in the morning a commissioned officer and a sergeant, as I saw by the chevrons on his arm, came into the room and looked us over, calling for the late arrival of "Yankee prisoners" to show themselves. It should be understood that there were nearly a hundred people in confinement in the room into which we were placed, and amongst them there was not a single one with a blanket nor were the quarters supplied with anything on which a man could rest except the bare floor. Of course my party was lightly clad, having left their overcoats in camp before crossing the river. For myself, in standing before a campfire a few days before our capture, I had so badly burned one of the tails of my uniform coat that I had it converted by an expert tailor into a roundabout by taking off both tails. The coat not only looked well, but also was really an improvement. However, it was not a warmth-giving garment, but it was the one I had on when I was taken prisoner, and I felt the need of those tails" very badly during those cold December days.

The officer placed us in line and told us that we could receive our rations through the sergeant. This officer called a Negro to him. We prisoners stood in line; the darkey cut each of us a piece of fresh beef and gave us some crackers. He added what I thought at the time was a quarter of a pound of tea, a dish that our soldiers learned to forego, but instead was coffee, an article that the soldiers took to like fiends in the later part of the war. There was a very large, old-fashioned fireplace in the end of the hall and the officers told us that we could cook our meat there. There were but two stewing pans for all the party, and, of course, those had to be used by turns, save those who could relish their meat by cooking it on the coals or on the end of a stick. A colored man seemed to take pity on me and when it came my turn to use the pan he offered to cook my piece of meat for me, which he did, and for which I thanked him. I am fully aware that these are small matters to write about, but the biggest war of modern times was made up of small events, and bigger ones will come as the story progresses and the war grew more and more fierce.

We prisoners landed at the guardhouse at Winchester, Virginia, a place that was in all its glory as a typical Southern county seat. Later it was almost destroyed by the wear and tear of war. After the long delayed breakfast, we seven prisoners began to mix up somewhat with our fellow prisoners, all of whom having more or less curiosity to see us Yankees and to hear us talk. We were not long in discovering that there were three of the regiment to which we all belonged, though of different companies which were stationed at Sharpsburgh, Maryland. I at once perceived the danger these men were in for they were in Virginia without orders, and of course, if the news came to the Confederate authorities, they could and would very probably be tried as spies. I told my men by all means not to recognize these men in any way as old acquaintances. And cautioned the men not to recognize us for there was a real danger for them should the fact be ascertained that they were Federal soldiers and belonged to the regiment that was patrolling the Maryland side of the Potomac. One of these men's names was Wildman and another Strauss. Both were from Noble County, Indiana. The remaining one was a German whose name I never knew. Upon the completion of the year's service for which time the regiment was to serve, this same Wildman became a captain in the One Hundred and First Indiana Infantry, and made a brave and gallant officer, remaining in the service till the close of the war.

I feared greatly for these men during our brief occupation of the Winchester Sons of Temperance Hall as a guardhouse, and I may as well dispense of the incident concerning them now, as to bring it up in its regular order. All three of them made their escape from the guard-house after we seven prisoners were conveyed to Richmond, the capital of the Confederacy, as we learned through the Richmond journals after we arrived there, and all three of them made their way back to the regiment. At the time they seemingly did not know of the danger they were in until informed by my party. In fact, they had been arrested at Winchester and for a couple of days drilled with the militia there, and by violating some command of their officers they had been arrested and conveyed to Winchester for trial—the fact of their being Federal soldiers being unknown. All of us legally captured prisoners felt greatly relieved and were greatly pleased to read of their escape a couple of days after our own arrival at Richmond. All of the journals of that place giving a fairly good account of their escape, which they accomplished by cutting up a blanket into strips and by tying them together letting themselves down from the second story unknown to the guard.

But to return to our own affairs as connected with the guardhouse. At about eleven o'clock in the forenoon and after we had breakfasted, an officer came into the room in which we were confined and asked for Captain Williams. I told him that I presumed that I was the individual whom he was seeking. After asking me if I was the commander of the squad of Yankee prisoners brought in by Captain Baylor, I told him I had been, but all of us were at present, it seemed, under the command of somebody else. He informed me that I was to accompany him to General Jackson's headquarters. At that early period in the war Jackson was not so generally known by the sobriquet of "Stonewall", as was afterward the case. He won that name in the first battle of Bull Run, when General Bee, of the South Carolina troops, pointed him out and called on his men to see how Jackson's brigade stood like a stone wall. The expression was seized upon by some newspaper reporter, perhaps, and the synonym of "Stonewall" clung to him ever after.

On arriving at Stonewall's headquarters, which were located in a neat, old-fashioned brick house with wide spreading lawns stretching away from it in several directions, I was taken into the room occupied by him and asked to take a seat. Another officer was present that I afterward learned was General Preston, and if I remember correctly was from Kentucky, and who was then serving as Stonewall's adjutant general. I did not have to wait long until General Jackson began interrogating me, and for which a more appropriate term would probably be, "pumping me." Fortunately, I was aware that he was a West Pointer, had belonged to the regular army and had served during the Mexican war, and consequently I was able to be somewhat on my guard. As I remember the conversation, I am confident in my own mind that Stonewall did not get ahead of me to any great extent in the battle of questions and replies that followed.

At the very start I resented being called a "Yankee" and told him that none of my ancestors were New Englanders and that both my father and myself were born in Ohio. "Oh, well," said he, "we call all you folks Yankees." I insisted so strenuously against the term that I noticed it tickled the adjutant-general sitting by, considerably. I had made up my mind to tell him the truth, when I felt that he was sufficiently well informed to catch me up if I didn't, and when I could deceive him a little, to do it on a magnificent scale. So when he asked me how many troops General Banks, of our army, had under his command on the opposite side of the Potomac, I told him that it was understood to be eighty thousand! At the time Banks was in command of thirty thousand. When he asked me in what kind of money the troops had been paid. I told him gold, and so the first troops were, the greenbacks not coming into use until the autumn of 1861. At any rate as I was not present on payday at Indianapolis, I afterward received my dues in gold. Much of his conversation was of a desultory, commonplace character. All at once he asked me how many troops Indiana had in the field. I told him that the State had just organized and filled out its sixtieth regiment. That surprised him greatly, and it seemed to make him somewhat indignant also; "for," said he, "the Confederates had been led to believe that they would receive a good deal of help from that State and Illinois." Of course, I only replied to questions, never asking any and very many that he asked were of a trifling nature.

I had been there, perhaps, a half an hour, and during a portion of that time Stonewall was engaged in writing. All at once he again asked, "How many troops did you say that General Banks had?" I replied by saying that it was understood by all who seemed to be well-informed that he was at the head of eighty thousand men. He then asked why I came over into Virginia? I replied by saying, "I received an order to do so, and of course, obeyed it." "Do you know," said he, "what I think ought to be done with you invaders, and all like you?" "I do not," I replied. "Well," said the General, "you ought to be taken right down into that meadow there and hung." I replied by saying "That would be pretty rough and decidedly unpleasant for me, young as I am, too!"

My interview being over I was conducted back to the guardhouse, and some of the enlisted men of my party were sent for to go through the same sort of a sweatbox. I found an opportunity, however, to caution them against telling Stonewall anything that would be of value to the Confederacy, and requested them to stick to my own story, that Banks was in command of eighty thousand men, and afterward they told me they did so. Since the war Stonewall Jackson has been extolled as a very religious, conscientious, conservative man. There was a story that he engaged in prayer for a full week before making up his mind as to which side he would take. It can now be perceived that it was the wrong choice for him. Seeing him on that occasion, I set him down as a high-tempered, hotheaded, vindictive sort of a fanatic. I arrived at this verdict at the only interview I ever had with Stonewall Jackson, and I am firm as to the conclusion still. At any rate the Lord did not answer his prayer, evidently differing with him!

At that period Winchester was not connected with the outside world by rail. When we were captured a line of busses and stages were in operation from the old town to Strasbourg, where these vehicles made railroad connections for Manasas Junction. How much further it went west of Strasbourg, I do not know. As it was nearing dark an officer informed us that we were ordered to Richmond, where we would be confined with the first Bull Run and Ball's Bluff prisoners, in a tobacco warehouse. Afterwards this warehouse became famous as "Libby Prison"—a name that has sent many a shudder through the hearts of men and women here at home, who had sons there in confinement. After the war, it was bodily removed to Chicago as a showplace.

The party of prisoners was all placed in an old-fashioned omnibus. I had purchased a shawl, an article all the fashion for men just preceding the war, for which I gave seven dollars in gold to a Confederate sergeant, willing to sympathize with me to that amount owing to the loss of the tails of my coat as previously narrated. He came very near getting all the gold I had with me, too, but the shawl was a very comfortable addition, and in consequence I decided to mount to the seat by the side of the driver with a man with a musket on the other side of me.

By the time we got started it was dark, and if I mistake not it was thirty miles to Strasbourg, and then twenty miles to Manasas Junction, where the Confederate army of Virginia was encamped between that place and Alexandria at that time. We were to leave Manasas at seven or eight o'clock the next morning by rail for Richmond. This would compel us to arrive at Manasas several hours before the train would leave for our destination. It was a cold night, yet with my shawl and sitting between the driver and guard, I got along pretty well. The road was a good one and the driver disposed to get along at a good gait. Darkness came on so dense, however, that it soon became impossible to see more than the horses, everything at the side of the pike road fading and falling away into deeper gloom. We had crossed one or more covered bridges—all bridges in the South were covered over—and in going over the first one I remember that in putting up my hand I brushed a timber at right angles from the bridge. Like a flash it came over me that I might make my escape by just pulling myself up on to this crosspiece, let the bus pass out from under me then crawl to either side and let myself down on the bridge. There I would await developments till morning, and after that find my way to the Potomac River.

By the time that this idea was reached in full, the bus passed out of the other end of the bridge and I resolved to await the opportunity at the next one and let circumstances govern me, whether to make the attempt, or not. But when the next bridge was reached, and although I held up my hand I failed to find a cross-stringer. The guard was sleepy, that I already knew; there was a good deal of Union sentiment in that part of Virginia, and I might have found assistance at some of the cabins in hiding me away for a time, and afterward some one to pilot me to safety. All these ideas passed through my mind, and I really believe I would have made the attempt to try the plan had I been able to touch a similar timber at the second bridge.

On reaching Manassas Junction after taking the train at Strasbourg, we found the station perfectly dark and the prisoners all of them chilled to the bone. For myself, I was shaking as though from an ague-fit, and was all in a tremble with cold. There was a big stove in the passengers' room, but it did not seem that there had ever been a fire in it. We were to remain there several hours to await the starting of the train for Richmond. I had a silver quarter in my pocket and offered it to a roust-about looking young man if he would build a fire in the stove. He went out and I could hear him breaking up boards, or whatever he could find. He found a considerable amount of pitch pine and he soon had a fire that carried us prisoners clear to the other extreme. We went from shaking cold to steaming perspiration, which compelled us to go out in the chilly air to cool off.

We were finally off for Richmond and the entire party was the object of great curiosity on the part of everybody who saw us. The road we traveled went by way of Gordonsville, and at the latter place we prisoners came very near getting into a difficulty that promised at one time to be very serious. The two deserters to whom I referred in an early part of these scribblings were on the train and in fact on the same car. They were an exceedingly saucy and abusive pair, and were insolent with everybody. On arriving at the depot at Gordonsville an aged Irish apple woman was plying her vocation and these two "Louisiana Tigers" picked her out for their raillery, and soon had the high-strung old woman giving tit for tat at repartee—none of it fit for ears polite. All at once the crowd discovered the Yankee prisoners on board, and the volleys of stones, pieces of brick and chunks of wood soon knocked out the glass of the car-windows. The whole attention of the crowd was transferred from the two guilty villains to us entirely innocent prisoners. If it had not been for a few citizens on the same car interceding for us through a Confederate officer, who had a few men under his command operating as a provost guard, I have no doubt we would have been seriously hurt. The old woman, herself, turning her ever-growing anger to the "Yanks was loudest of all in her demand to "kill the villainous nigger-lovers, and d—d abolitionists!" The officer and guard soon quieted the disturbance, but we barely escaped injury.

MEMORANDUM FROM PRISONER OF WAR RECORDS.

(This blank to be used only in the arrangement of said records.)

No. ....

NAME: Williams, Reuben

RANK: Capt.

ORGANIZATION:
- No. of Reg't: 12
- State: Ind.
- Arm of Service: Inf.

INFORMATION OBTAINED FROM:
Reg't...
M. R.
O.R.
Pub'd

Captured at Nr. W. Mt. Dec. 11, 186-, confined at Richmond, Va., Dec. 13, 186-.

Admitted to Hospital at .... 186 , of ....

where he died ....

Paroled at Richmond, Va., Feb. 22/23, 1862, no further information, the carrier reported at Camp Parole, Md., 186-.

Again Capt'd Richmond, Ky. Aug. 30/62, Paroled Richmond, Ky. Aug 30/62.

Copied by ....

CHAPTER 3

Imprisoned at Richmond, Virginia

Do we know what a land
God hath placed in our hand
To be made into star-gems or crushed into sand?
Let us feel that our race,
Doomed to no second place,
Must glitter with triumph or die in disgrace!
That millions unborn,
At night, noon and morn,
Will thank us with blessings or curse us with scorn,
For raising more high
Freedom's flag to the sky,
Or losing forever the Fourth of July!
—*Will Carleton*

The party reached Richmond, the Confederate capital, as the shades of the late afternoon were falling. It was in the middle of December and the days were approaching their shortest. The weather had been murky all the day and night fell upon us so quickly that on arriving at our destination, the prison was already lighted up. We prisoners, and a portion of the guard, were ushered into the prison office presided over by Major Gibbs, a sedate, gentlemanly officer. He was under the command of General Winder, who was in charge of all the prisons in the South, located then at Charleston, South Carolina, Salisbury, North Carolina, Richmond, Virginia and at other points. Andersonville had not yet been established, nor was that terrible spot in the James River, right in the city of Richmond, where many a Federal soldier afterwards pined his life away, known as Belle Isle.

Here I was separated from the rest of the prisoners, they being assigned to other tobacco warehouses located in different parts of the city. I was conducted to a large room on the same floor as the office there to find myself in the company of seventy-one officers ranging from Colonels down to Second Lieutenants. Nearly all of the officers had been captured at Ball's Bluff. Captain Isaac Hart, quartermaster of the Twentieth Indiana was captured on board the little steamer "Fannie"; a vessel attached to what was known as the Burnside Expedition.

I at once became an object of interest to everyone of those prisoners who were so anxious to hear from home that even what brief intelligence I could convey to them was listened to with deep attention. The entire evening was spent until nine o'clock at least, the hour that the prison rules compelled the shutting off of gas and the compulsory retiring to whatever sort of bed the prisoners might be in possession of. In this officer's room the rules had been adopted to divide the entire number into "messes of six". It so happened that there was a vacancy in the one known by the name of the "regular mess." It was composed of officers belonging to the regular army, and who were, at the breaking out of hostilities, stationed in Texas, under General Twiggs, of the United States Army, who basely surrendered them as prisoners of war to the Confederacy.

The prisoners, in order to preserve their health as far as it was in their power, had drawn up and signed a set of rules governing the sanitary features of the prison to which every officer had attached his name. While I was a prisoner there, the rules were religiously obeyed and lived up to by every one of the inmates of the big room. The sink was located at the west end of the long building and fortunately for the prisoners it was connected with the city waterworks. We were able to preserve cleanliness, which as the war progressed and prisoners became so numerous on both sides that there was scarcely floor space for them all to lie down at night and cleanliness became an impossibility. The rules forbade the playing of cards or games of any kind on Sundays. There was a chaplain among the prisoners, belonging to a Maine regiment so that religious services were held every Sunday forenoon. The speaker was always sure to have every one of the seventy-two of his audience present. There was no way, though there might have been the strongest desire, to avoid being present.

The rules governing the inmates called for one to be selected by the members to act as a 'caterer" for the week beginning every Sunday morning and ending the following Saturday. The Confederate government furnished us with salt, pepper, Texas beef and bread that was baked in ovens established especially to supply the prisoners. To add to this bill of fare other edible articles were to be acquired by the caterer and on Saturday evening he would make out his expense bill. This bill was promptly paid and varied according to the liberality or closeness of the individual in charge for each particular week. I was pleased at the time of being assigned to this "regular mess" for I had lain awake many nights in camp studying army tactics in hopes of learning to lead more efficiently. These gentlemen who were my fellow prisoners were West Point graduates, and I was able to absorb a great deal of military information from them that I would not otherwise have been able to. Hence I regarded it as a schooling that was of value to me.

I had not been there over two weeks when it came my turn to act as caterer. The question of small change became a great one on both sides immediately after the war started. Gold and silver actually disappeared entirely by the beginning of the second year. Consequently businessmen, cities and small towns all issued their fractional "scrip" for use in making change. Many first-class business houses did this, and what is more it passed, grumblingly, it is true, but nevertheless it was made to serve the purpose.

I had during my time at the prison learned that a First Lieutenant, who belonged to the Fourteenth Brooklyn regiment, by the name of Gramman, was an expert with a pen as any one I had ever known up to that time. For he could do almost anything if given ink and a pen, even to drawing a very fine individual likeness of any one he attempted. I discovered that Lieutenant Grumman had so perfectly counterfeited one of the local businesses "scrip" that it could only be told from the genuine by the closest inspection. I resolved to try to pass it during my first week of mess catering. In addition to the mess of six, a private soldier selected by some member of the mess had been detailed to wait on the table, wash the dishes, and see to things generally. These soldiers delighted in being selected for this detail for the reason that they lived on much better food when attached to an officers' mess than otherwise, as a result applications for the position were far greater than the number of positions.

I had a quantity of Gramman's scrip and as we were allowed to do our own marketing at the prison door through our mess boy, I met with ready success. Negroes were in the habit, as well as white men, of bringing oysters to the door referred to for sale to the "Yanks". This they did at twenty cents a quart. The consequence was that during my week of catering the mess was supplied with that delicious bivalve at every meal; fried for breakfast, raw or stewed for dinner and just as you pleased for supper. All of these oysters and other delicacies were paid for through our mess-boy with Grumman's scrip. Consequently when Saturday night came and members of the mess expected to pay a much larger sum than usual, having had oysters every meal, they were thunderstruck to find it even a little less in amount than the former week with no oysters. Not one among them knew to this day, not even the mess-boy who paid it out, that the scrip was a prison enterprise.

I have already stated that I was quite short of money, after paying out my seven dollars in gold for a shawl, so on the morning following our installation into Richmond tobacco warehouse, afterwards known as "Libby Prison," I wrote to Schuyler Colfax, who was then speaker of the house. I requested that he send me a fifty-dollar gold piece by express and draw on Mrs. Williams at Warsaw for the amount. Within four days the gold piece arrived, on which there was a charge of one dollar and fifty cents to the express company for bringing it a distance of seventy-five miles. Prices had already begun to go up and what is more just about that time the Confederacy ceased to issue coffee as a ration to their army. I don't know how the Confederate soldier took it being deprived of his coffee, but had it been done by the Washington government, such a howl would have gone up that would have compelled its restoration no matter what the cost. I sometimes think the war would have been considerably prolonged but for coffee. In a worn-out, played-out, wearied-to-death soldier, a cup of coffee went far-and –away ahead of a full meal in restoring him to his normal condition. A Federal even yet cannot conceive how he could have survived what he passed through, but for that restoring, consoling, strengthening, and stimulating beverage. That the war made us a nation of coffee drinkers is quite likely. Coffee helped, and very materially, helped to crush the rebellion. I sold my fifty-dollar gold piece for ninety dollars in Confederate money. This was an early period in the war when the Richmond markets were still fairly well supplied with everything that went to sustain life. We lived "like fighting cocks" during all of my stay, something over four months.

On entering the prison, I found an old man by the name of Pancoast, who was approaching seventy years of age. The old gentleman "kinder took to me on sight."
We became closest of friends and remained so during all my time of confinement. While some of the officers in the big room were supplied with cots and blankets, there were others who had just a cot (a piece of coarse tow cloth, stretched over a frame on which to lie down at night). Others, like myself, had nothing at all, so at night I lay down on the bare, plank floor, with my seven-dollar shawl under my head. It was late December and I had wished often that I had not been forced to alter my coat into a roundabout by cutting off the tails for the added material would have helped to keep me warm.

The daily grind of prison life was at times almost insupportable. I made, while there, some of the most pleasurable acquaintances of that ever-glorious four years. The war brought out the truest patriotism known to mankind. For a good many years I kept up a correspondence with quite a number of my fellow prisoners. When the National Encampment was held in Washington City, I inserted a notice in the Washington Star requesting that if there were any one of the four who nightly took their places at the table for a game of euchre, they should call at my rooms at the National Hotel. I had no idea at the time that even one of the other three might call. All of the great battles of the Army of the Potomac were still to be fought when we were released from prison in Richmond, following the rebel disaster at Fort Henry and Donelson. The notice was inserted with the hope, rather than the belief that it might bring the meeting of two or more old comrades whose friendship was first formed in that Richmond tobacco warehouse. Later the warehouse was the scene of so much want, suffering and death, and incarceration of a soldier there caused so much mourning, misery and sorrow in many a bright and sunny Northern home.

Behold on the next day at the hour fixed in my notice in the Star, I heard what I at once knew was the stumping of crutches in the long hall leading to the room occupied by myself. On stepping to the door I perceived a man coming with only one leg left, the other off above the knee. It was a man by the name of Vassal, of Boston, whom I had known in prison as a member of the Twentieth Massachusetts regiment. It was a pleasant meeting, although the man I now met was grizzled and gray and not at all the cheerful young fellow to whom I had bidden good-bye in Washington City upon our release from the tobacco warehouse at Richmond. He had lost his leg in the battle of the Wilderness, but had up to that time passed unscathed through many of the very hard battles that had preceded the engagement that had so badly crippled him. He was a few years younger than I was. We had kept track of each other up to a few years previous to the Encampment we were then attending. The meeting was in every way a pleasant one, yet feelings of thankfulness overflowed me to the Great Giver of all good that He had permitted me to come out of the wonderful struggle without a scar or a scratch. When I once more bade my friend a second, and most likely a last, good-bye, tears came to my eyes. The tears were not so much of sorrow for the maimed condition of my old prison companion, but of gratitude to God that He had permitted me to come home with a whole body when the war was over.

Life in the tobacco warehouse in Richmond, early in the war, was not what it became as the war progressed. Men on both sides felt their contention wholly right while the reasoning of the other was that it was wholly and entirely wrong. In consequence of this feeling as well as from the large accession of prisoners following the first year of the war, almost every month witnessed a change for the worse in their treatment. Before the war came to a close General Winder, who had full and complete charge of the entire prison affairs of the South, came to be known as almost a demon in human form because of the treatment he accorded those who were so unfortunate as to be transferred from the well-clothed, well-fed ranks of the Federal army into his keeping by the fortunes of war.

With the beginning of 1862, it was plainly perceptible that with a rigid blockade all along the coast that supplies would grow less and less in the Confederacy as the war was protracted. I have already stated that the ration of coffee was eliminated from the Confederate soldier's bill-of-fare as early as December, 1861, and as the weeks and months progressed, other articles grew so scarce as to become unknown as a ration. The scarcity of whatever the article might be accounted for it's absence. During my incarceration in "Libby" or in the building, which afterwards came to be called by that name, it was principally the irksomeness of prison-life that was so hard to bear, and the "homesickness" that followed such a state of existence. In the room into which my lot was cast, all of the seventy-two being commissioned officers, on that account were permitted to purchase any supply or article whatever that was not contraband of war. As a consequence we lived well during the four months that we were in confinement.

All these favors were restricted as the war progressed. The privilege of buying supplies was forbidden and all prisoners were put on a diet that would barely sustain life. A hearty, vigorous prisoner on being captured would become a walking skeleton, with a hunger that was never satisfied until he again returned to the Federal lines either through a parole, an escape, or an exchange. The terrors of "Belle Isle"; the agonies of "Libby," and the incarnate treatment bestowed upon prisoners in that hell on earth, "Andersonville," have all been written up. All over the country one can still come across an invalid soldier, the foundation of whose ailment was laid at one of these life-destroying stations.

On my arrival at the prison the one great theme of conversation every day, every night, at all times in fact, was "exchange". "When will our government demand an exchange of prisoners" was the one great tropic of conversation. It should be borne in mind that the first Bull Run prisoners were captured on July 21, 1861, and here it was the middle of December and yet no attempt at an exchange had been made. These young fellows were not aware of the fact that an exchange of prisoners would be a partial recognition of the Confederacy which up to that time nothing even squinting in that direction had been officially uttered. In my letter to Speaker Colfax asking him to send me a fifty-dollar gold piece, already referred to, I also entered upon the theme of exchange. I urged that something be done to relieve those to whom prison life, if protracted, meant death. In his reply he spoke so favorably about the measure that I suggested to every officer in the room to write to his own member of Congress urging upon the government to do something on the question.

This was done and the swooping down upon Congress with these missives had a wonderful effect. Members of Congress suggested many plans and some bills were introduced on the subject. But we prisoners were to receive our freedom from an entirely different source. The capture of Fort Donelson and Fort Henry near the mouth of the Tennessee River in Kentucky so frightened the Confederate authorities, that the rebel war department concluded to parole all who were held prisoner in Richmond. When the great Federal victory in that west was announced in Richmond, through the morning papers, the enlisted men occupying the two floors that were filled to overflowing above us, went wild. They cheered. They sang. They hung out imitations of the old flag made out of some colored window curtains, which they found and improvised, into flags.

About fifteen thousand prisoners were captured by the Federals at the two forts mentioned. This victory placed the "boot on the other leg," and the prisoners kept up their rejoicing over the victory until the prison authorities sent an officer with a guard to suppress the "disorder". Many of us prisoners believed that the Confederate authorities privately feared that there might be an uprising. There was a large union sentiment among the people in Richmond then, and throughout the war, that was of concern to the Confederate State. There was a scare in Richmond over the Confederate defeat in the west. The next morning the *Dispatch* of that place announced that fact that there were over four hundred applications to the Jeff Davis government for permission to go North after word of the fall of the two forts. The *Dispatch* urged the government to grant all passes that were applied for on the grounds that it "would be better to get rid of the cowardly sympathizers with the Abe Lincoln government!"

Evidence of the large Union sentiment in Richmond was also evident by the fact that on Sundays from early dawn to sunset an immense crowd of people, ranging from one to three thousand surrounded the prison. Nothing more delighted these people than to evade the guard who marched back and forth along the street in front of the big building and exchange a few words with a "Yankee prisoner". This was sometimes risky, as there were some guards who would readily probe them with their bayonets since conversation with the prisoners was not permitted.

My time in prison was not all gloom at this early period of the war by any means. Among the seventy-two fellow officers in the room occupied by myself, were a number of young fellows full of life and vigor. They seemed to take it on themselves as a duty they owed to the rest to make fun for those predisposed to despondency. Their jokes, jests and the pranks they played upon one another helped to wile away time that but for their efforts would have hung heavily indeed. Also my time in confinement was on several occasions enlivened by the somewhat frequent attempts on the part of the prisoners to escape. These attempts by the private soldier and the officers were the source of much merriment on our part when the news reached us of their adventures. Among these, the escape of Col. Charles A. DeVilliers, of the Eleventh Ohio regiment was remarkable for its skillful contrivance and for the devices use in defeating all efforts at detection.

Col. DeVilliers was captured on the Kenawha River on July 17th, 1861 with some other officers of General Cox's brigade. DeVilliers was taken prisoner before the first Bull Run, and of course was there in confinement when my party reached Richmond. He was a splendid fellow, of a nervous temperament, and a thoroughly drilled and accomplished soldier. It was to him that a number of us prisoners became indebted for instructions in sword exercise, of which he was a master. Knowing this, a class of officers was made up to take lessons under him in that branch of military tactics. Consequently, we were given permission to get a dozen or two of lath, and some one, expert in the use of a pocket knife, gave these lath the shape of what is known as the straight sword.

Under the Colonel's instructions we went to work in such a way that it was not long until some of us became quite expert in the handling of these wooden swords. And it was splendid exercise for men in confinement. For myself I can say that the exercise developed strength of wrist, shoulders, and an agility of foot. We also felt that we would not always be prisoners and wished to become worthy soldiers. We sent out and bought two dozen "Hardee's Tactics,"--the mode at that time in use by both armies, although our side was about to change the drill at the time. DeVilliers delighted in teaching us and when the time came for us to come out of prison we knew a great deal more than when we were incarcerated.

DeVilliers, being somewhat acquainted with the practice of surgery, was detailed by the Confederate surgeon in command of the prison hospitals to assist in taking care of the sick and wounded prisoners at the Richmond hospital. In this capacity he enjoyed the freedom of the city on his parole of honor until on one occasion he grew tired and for some reason surrendered his parole. He returned to close confinement in the officers' quarters. He afterwards sold at auction several articles of his military clothing and a short time afterward DeVilliers escaped from prison. How he escaped from prison was never known although it was pretty certain that some officer knew, for at roll call when his name was called it was promptly answered, and the sergeant of the guard was kept unaware of his absence. This was kept up for four days until the guard discovered the absence of the prisoner.

It was conjectured by some of our prison officers that the Colonel had fled in the disguise of a Confederate officer. It was surmised that two Confederate officers assisted in his escape who supplied him with a fleet horse on the outside of the city and who furnished him with pistols, a carbine and food with which to pursue his journey which was at night. After his escape became known to the prison officers, great efforts were made by the rebel authorities to recapture him, if at all possible, and scouts were sent out in all directions. DeVilliers bent his course toward Norfolk, but before his departure, and being of French descent, previous to leaving Richmond, he provided himself with an outfit so that he could represent himself as a mendicant Frenchman desirous of getting out of "ze damn countree and back to his beloved Paree!" McGruder was the Confederate General at that time in command of Norfolk and by feigning illness the mendicant got himself admitted to the hospital there to await developments. In some way he had secured a white-haired wig and a pair of green-glass goggles. During the daytime the hospital authorities permitted the old and infirm Frenchman to wander about the town wherever he chose, he only speaking in French.

Keeping his disguise in this way the Colonel concluded he had been there long enough to establish the claim of a real mendicant. He determined to apply to the commanding officer for permission to go to Fortress Monroe under a flag of truce in order, as he put it, that he might embark for his dear old home in France. The pitiful story of the venerable Frenchman and his urgency to return to his home which he had left before the rebellion broke out, and the accommodating spirit of the Confederates manifested just at that time to both France and England, induced General McGruder to grant the request through charitable motive, but only after two weeks' of persistent effort on the part of DeVilliers.

At last the "flag of truce day" arrived and the rebel boat steamed out to meet that of the Federals in open water. Quite a number of friends DeVilliers had made while at Norfolk were on the Confederate boat who assisted the poor infirm old Frenchman (at the venerable age of thirty-five) on board and bade him an affectionate adieu. No sooner had DeVilliers reached the deck of the Federal steamer than he coolly cast off the pack he had been carrying, wig, and green goggles. After thanking the officers for their politeness, he shouted a loud huzzah for the Stars and Stripes and gave the Confederates the pleasing information that they had just parted with Colonel DeVilliers, of the Eleventh Ohio Infantry. DeVilliers was soon afterwards promoted to Brigadier-General.

Escapes from the prison were quite numerous during the times I was there, but unfortunately the prisoners were caught in making their way to the Union Lines. They were returned to prison where in a number of cases their escape was as yet unknown. The friends of the escaping soldier answered to his name at every roll call during his absence. There was no difficulty in breaking out of the tobacco warehouse, but getting out of the country was a different matter entirely. It was not difficult at all to evade the guards of the prisons, who while not meaning to disobey their officer or the orders governing the prison, often became negligent of their duties and permitted whoever was intent on making an escape to grow familiar. The guard never dreamed that "the Yank" with whom he was conversing was only laying his plans with an object in view, that is, to lull the guard into confidential conversation and when his attention was diverted elsewhere, perhaps purposely by a comrade, the latter would quickly walk past the guard. It was only a few feet until the prisoner could turn the corner of the building and be out of sight. While his disappearance might be noted, the other prisoners would crowd around the guard to attract his attention for a brief moment until the escape had been made. The guard would even cease to think of the individual with whom he had been talking.

It was well known and much commented upon in the newspapers of the North that Congressman Ely, from the Rochester district, New York with a number of prominent men had gone from Washington to witness the first battle of Bull Run, and was unfortunately captured. He was an inmate of the prison when I arrived there. It is very probable that there are but few who will now remember the incident. General John A. Logan, too, was then serving his district in Congress from Illinois. He had served in the Mexican war, but voluntarily took up a musket and accouterments to serve in the struggle as a private soldier. He soon afterwards resigned his position in Congress, was appointed the Colonel of one of the Illinois regiments then in progress of formation by Gov. Dick Yates.

Ely was unpopular amongst the rest of the prisoners and I found quite a feeling against him on my arrival at the tobacco warehouse. It grew out of the fact that he had informed the rebel authorities in charge of the prisoners of an attempt to escape. This caused prison regulations to be greatly circumscribed, and a more careful watch was undertaken. A number of favors previously enjoyed by his mess-table had been withdrawn. It was said that in order to curry favor with the rebel officers in charge of us he made this disclosure to them. What the Confederate officers thought of him for doing this I cannot say, but there was a widespread dislike for him amongst the Federal officers and enlisted men.

Among the seventy-two officers in the room to which I was assigned on reaching Richmond a majority were young men. A number of them were about my own age and quite a number of Second Lieutenants being still younger. There were a number of Colonels. Old and gray-headed, amongst these was Colonel Coggswell of what was known as "The Tamany Regiment," of New York and Colonel Henry Lee of the Twentieth Massachusetts. Quite a number of men holding the rank of colonel were sent to Charleston, South Carolina, Salisbury, North Carolina, and other places.

One could go a long way and mingle with many crowds and then fail to find as companionable a set of men as I found in Libby prison as soon as I became acquainted with them. Nearly all of them were from Pennsylvania and the New England States, the latter largely predominating. I wrote earlier of an old gentleman by the name of Pancoast who was among the oldest in the room. He was one of perhaps a half dozen private citizens who had been arrested on various pretexts and were inmates of the same room.

Pancoast was a wealthy iron dealer, whose home was near Romnery, where one of the very first skirmishes of the war occurred. Colonel Lew Wallace at the head of the Eleventh Indiana captured the town very early in the war. Pancoast was a Quaker and operated a large bloomery where he made pig iron and was arrested for his Union sentiments. He, as I said earlier, took a very kindly interest in me from the first night we arrived.

Perhaps the most pleasant and agreeable gentlemen amongst the rest was a young man by the name of W. C. Harris, who was a First Lieutenant in Baker's California regiment, who was taken at Ball's Bluff. An attachment grew up between Lieutenant Harris and myself that made us fast friends and this friendship was maintained for many years after the war through mutual correspondence. He possessed a fine college education and after we became intimates he showed me several pages of manuscript that he had prepared concerning the capture of Ball's Bluff, and the consequent events that had occurred since he had reached Richmond as a prisoner.

I at once discovered that his articles were written in a very agreeable, and at times, eloquent, and always racy style. I urged him to keep on at his writing and when we were released to have them printed in book form. At first he scouted the idea, but I kept on insisting and he final determined to follow my advice, on the ground that being a newspaper man I ought to know whether such a book would sell or not. So he sent to his home in Philadelphia and got a ream of what is known as tissue writing paper. On occasions I assisted him, sometimes furnishing a sketch of a few pages for his forthcoming book on my own account.

Both of us were at work upon the proposed book when Fort Donelson fell, the victory leading straight up to our release on parole. Harris then got frightened about being able to get this manuscript out of the prison, for it was practically certain that all the prisoners would be searched previous to their transfer to the United States "flag of truce boat," at Fortress Monroe. I told him I would get it through. I had a Massachusetts's overcoat that I had bought from a soldier in the prison. Robert S. Richhart, of Warsaw, Indiana, then the steward of our mess, at my suggestion sewed the manuscript up in the lining of the back of the coat and it passed the guards without any trouble whatever. Here I would like to relate Mr. Harris' description of the way in which the prisoners celebrated Christmas, 1861, which will assist in showing his racy style. It is taken from the pages of the book and is as follows:

"We determined to enjoy Christmas as far as possible, so on Christmas Eve active preparations were made for the celebrations of the day. Sundry sly nudges and knowing twinkles of the eye bade the writer glance towards the nearest mess table. On it lay a turkey, bunches of celery, cranberries, four pies, and half a dozen contraband bottles. An unusual bustle among the stewards gave token of a mighty feast on the morrow. The old darkey who runs the errands for the officers was big with importance. He passed in and out every few moments and it was evident that "Yankee" gold was gladdening the hearts of Secessia . Gliding on with unusual merriment, the evening closed, according to our "Hoosier," with "hearty good songs and jolly good stories from merry good fellows."

The morning opened with sixty voices greeting, "A happy Christmas!" Bright faces and glad voices seemed to illumine the old walls for they looked less chilling, and gave back our shouts with a clearer tone than before. As the hours rolled on, turkeys were prepared for the adjacent bakery, cranberries put on to stew, and busy stewards were seen flying about, bustling over their manifold household duties. The morning sped on with narrative and reminiscences. This one and that one, each and all had personal sketches of an old Christmas spent at home. Rich scenes of frolic and rollicking incidents, told with impetuous gayety, or the quiet enjoyment of a home Christmas at the family board, surrounded by a cherished and oft-remembered group of loved ones. Many officers invited to their Christmas dinner a non-commissioned officer of their company. As we sat around the mess table, covered with tin crockery and steaming with our costly meal, we presented a perfect picture of democratic luxury. What cared we for prison walls? Had we not turkey for dinner? What if gold was at fifty percent premium, did not ours pass at prison bars and yield us six bottles of "contraband"?

After the tablecloth (which consisted of four copies of the Richmond Enquirer) was removed, we pledged our country, our cause, our friends, and loved ones. Arising from the table, the hours as usual were passed in conversation, reading, etc. But it soon became apparent that Christmas was being celebrated outside, as well as within the walls. The report spread though out the room that our guards were in an intoxicated state and that few were able to discriminate properly between friend and foe. Such a condition of this caused much amusement. We crowed to the window to get a sight of the muddled sentinels. We laughed until weary at the ludicrous idea of being guarded by the drunken soldiers of Secassia. In a few moments a brother officer whispered to the writer, "Taylor's out". A moment elapsed and again, "Wallace is out". A short interval later, "McPherson's out". Escapes kept coming until the writer believed that the whole building would be deserted. He did not relish the idea of being the sole occupant of the immense prison. So he drew on his heavy coat, passed to the outer door, motioned to the sentinel, with all of a Confederate officer's hauteur, to lift his musket, which was done, and walked out to once again breathe free air.

Thoroughly at a loss where to direct his steps, and knowing it to be impossible to escape during mid-winter, he wandered up Main Street, looking around him and feeling like a countryman upon his first visit to a great city. He walked through the streets adjacent to the warehouse, and saw crowds of peep, clouds of darkeys, drunken soldiers, a rainbow group of Confederate officers, a fat woman, and a silver half-dollar with a crowd around it. But fearing that his unceremonious walk, if known, might compromise the future privileges of his brother officers, he bent his steps toward the prison, where with a magisterial motion of the hand he caused the musket to give way. He passed into the familiar halls having been absent one hour. One by one the excursionists returned, but it was not until eleven o'clock at night that all were again under the protection of the drunken guards.

During the evening a Federal officer, who is noted for quaint drollery and waggish humor, approached the sentinel at the door and proposed to stand guard, stating that he desired the soldier to purchase for him a canteen of liquor. To our astonishment, the proposal was accepted. Amid the chapter of startling Christmas events must be recorded that fact that the Federal prisoners of war in Richmond were guarded on Christmas, with the consent of a Confederate sentinel, by a United States officer, a prisoner of war. In a short time the guard returned and was liberally endowed with the "contraband" that he had so patriotically earned. Many will think it singular, that with the loose system of guard mounting, that we did not escape, and by traveling through the country, reach the Federal lines. It must be borne in mind that it was mid-winter. Richmond was one hundred miles from any United States forces and the route taken would have been through the enemy's country. Travel must be at night and through woods and not on frequented roads. The weather was so severe that sleep in the open air would have been impossible. The country was filled with fugitive slaves and constant patrols of every avenue of escape. Christmas closed with much quiet enjoyment. We had the usual pastimes: cards, backgammon, checkers, etc. and the inseparable concomitant of Christmas sports—eggnog. And such eggnog it was made without milk!"

The capture of Forts Donelson and Henry, the main defenses of the Confederates at the mouth of the Tennessee River, or near it, opened up by way of that river a vast region of the Confederacy. In fact, within only a few days thereafter the United States' gunboats penetrated the Southern States as far up as Florence, Alabama. The boats would have gone much further; save for what is known as "Mussel Shoals" prevented the passage at that point. Gunboats, it must be remembered draw a great depth of water on account of their armor and heavy guns. It was not so strange that the Jeff Davis government was terribly frightened over the capture of the two forts and at the ease by which the Yankees went up the Tennessee River a couple of hundred miles or more afterward.

In fact, the effect of the great victory was to flank Nashville, the capital of Tennessee, and compel its evacuation. I remember that before the close of the war I got hold of a book racily written by a Frenchman who had joined the Confederate army as an officer. It gave a description of the widespread disorder that prevailed in Nashville after the country was thrown open to the advance of the Federals. The French officer had held a position in a Confederate cavalry regiment and had become so disgusted with the service on the Confederate side that he resigned his commission and afterwards published the book. A copy of this book fell into my hands in the fall of 1863. But I deeply regret that it was lost on "The March to the Sea," for its criticisms of the mob that took possession of Nashville and literally tore the place to pieces for two or three days was a piece of very vivid writing. Reports that the Federal army was on its way to Nashville came to the citizens, frequently causing the most exaggerated form of pandemonium. The mob, as is frequently the case, took to robbing and soon fire was added to the miseries of private citizens. All the stores and groceries in the town were robbed and many of them gutted of everything they possessed. Even men belonging to the Confederate army became part of the mob and were mutinous, riotous and disobedient, according to the Frenchman's story. I would be willing to pay a pretty big price for a copy of the lost book, because it was written from a perfectly impartial standpoint. It fearlessly discussed the cause of the war, and criticized fearlessly and openly the Confederate officers and their failures. It predicted very correctly the final result—the overthrow of the Confederacy, and the immense cost in life, in suffering and in property.

I have never talked to any prisoner of our side who did not in his heart believe that had McClellan with the Army of the Potomac made a general advance toward Richmond at the time, the panic being so great both in Richmond and Nashville and vicinity, that the Confederates could have been persuaded to end the war. Had an advance been made, the Union sentiment in the South would have asserted itself under such men as Brownlow, Andy Johnson and many other prominent Union men, and made the Confederate rear unsafe by the destruction of railroad bridges, blowing up of tunnels, etc. The subject was quietly talked of in places and greatly feared on the Confederate side. However it all worked out for the best, for had a compromise occurred following the first Bull Run, slavery would have been preserved and the result would only have staved off the war for a term of years to be fought out at a later period.

On the 19th day of February 1862 we were informed that the Confederate Secretary of War had issued an order releasing all the Federal prisoners in the South. Coming as this information did through the commandant of the prison, we hailed it with hearts filled with joyous, although subdued, emotion. There was an almost disbelief in many a man that the long cherished hope for freedom was, after many weeks and months, to be finally realized. It was difficult to comprehend that their distant and loved homes in the land of our flag would see them free once more. The commandant of the prison could give us no information as to the day or the hour of our release. "It may be tomorrow or not till next week," was his usual reply to the deeply earnest questioners. Many of the prisoners immediately packed their few belongings and stowed them away into carpetbags, boxes, cotton bags, or whatever "makeshift" bags they could rig up. Every countenance in the big room was illumined by the glad tidings of our long sought release.

Two days passed and hearts became almost sick with hope deferred, but at last on the morning of February 22nd, Washington's birthday, we were informed by the prison commandant that the flag-of-truce boat would leave that evening at 6 o'clock p.m. for Fortress Monroe. Then came the general preparation of all hands, and the big tobacco warehouse was to be left without an inmate except Samuel A. Pancoast, the old gentleman frequently referred to as having been arrested for his Union sentiments.

All of the baggage of the prisoners was gathered into a corner of the room under directions of a prison officer. Small trunks, bags, boxes, bundles, and parcels were all piled up. Among these I put my overcoat with a string around it, and it was my intention if the Confederate officers in their search of the prisoners and their baggage discovered the now greatly valued manuscript and trouble arose out of it, I would just disown the coat. I could prove it by the fact that I was from Indiana and did not use, nor could I own, a Massachusetts overcoat. In that event the manuscript would have been lost, of course, but fortunately a search of baggage was not made because the Confederate officers were perfectly certain the prisoners had no means of purloining anything contraband of war.

A few weeks before our government had obtained the favor of the Confederate authorities to send some clothing, shoes and underwear to her own soldiers in confinement. They were most of them captured during July, and many of them while the weather was warm had cast off much of their apparel, so that those in confinement were badly in need of warmer clothes. A supply had but recently been delivered to the prisoners, and they put in the forenoon of the day putting on their new clothes and in trading one with another until "a fit" for the bargainer was secured. This done, they commenced throwing their discarded clothing out of the windows. There were fully a hundred Negroes in the street when this began, but before it was over there were probably a thousand colored people among whom were a good many whites. These persons wrestled and scuffed for the old garments and to us onlookers the scene was exceedingly ludicrous. When one Negro would stoop to pick up a piece of clothing another one would butt him over and in the struggle that followed secure the garment himself only to be similarly tumbled to the ground. This continued all the afternoon, and I am confident that such an act could not have occurred with any other class of people without ending in a dozen or more "knock-downs," bloody noses, or severe injuries. But the uniform good humor of the colored people prevented them from losing their temper in a single instance.

The night before our release the Union officers in some way or other succeeded in sending a parole form among the prisoners. This form was signed as a precautionary measure, fearing that they might be induced to sign a parole that might mean more than our own government would sanction. The following is a copy of the oath taken by one and all, officers as well as enlisted men.

"We the undersigned, in the service of the United States, prisoners of war, pledge our word of honor, that we will not, by arms, information or otherwise during the existence of hostilities between the United States and the Confederate States of America, aid or abet the enemies of the said Confederate States, or any of them, in any form or manner until released or exchanged. Given at Richmond, Virginia, this 22nd of February 1862."

During all the afternoon, there was a constant addition to the number of people that crowded the street in front of the "Old Tobacco Warehouse". The rumor had leaked out that the "Yankees" were to leave them that evening. There was great curiosity to see the "Yanks" start on the march for the steamer that was lying in the James River to convey them to Norfolk that evening.

Six o'clock finally came, and as I passed out of the door I grasped the warm hand of Mr. Pancoast, who had refused to take the oath of allegiance to the Southern Confederacy. He was the only remaining occupant of a building that on all its floors had just contained over a thousand men. Tears were standing in the grand old gentleman's eyes as I bade him goodbye. A half-hour previously I had bestowed upon him my cot and its accumulation of six blankets, and a pillow I had bought as a gift for him. I had also bestowed upon him sixty dollars in Confederate money.

I may as well add right here that this true-blue Virginian—bear in mind that he was said to be worth a million dollars and over when the war began—was still confined in Richmond for two years after the event just related. He was finally freed from prison only in time to permit him to reach his home at Romney and die. Through prisoners who had been released from Libby afterward I kept in touch so far as information was concerned for that length of time. Frequently he was offered a release if he would take the Confederate oath of allegiance, but his steady reply was, "No, I was born and lived under the flag which Washington and his heroes won the independence of the United States, and as I have not got a long time to stay, I will not dishonor my few remaining years by doing a thing so repellant to my feelings and so false to a country under which I have so greatly prospered until this unholy war began."

I wrote to his relatives in Philadelphia following the war and ascertained from Dr. Pancoast, a very prominent physician of that city, that the Confederates permitted him to go home so that he might die among his friends, and he lived but a few weeks after reaching there.

CHAPTER 4

Home to Recruit for the 12th Indiana

When freedom calls in thunder tones,
    Far sea to sea replies,
And God the cause of freedom owns
    And thunders from the skies.
The highest law is freedom's word,
    And where her sons have bled
Each wind-swayed reed becomes a sword
    To strike oppression dead.
Holy her cause and he who fights,
    Contending for a clod
Where freedom, mourns her ruined rights,
    A Hero is to God.

—Frank L. Stanton

It was a dreary, cold, disagreeable, wet, sleety night, and as the steamer was greatly crowded, many of the men were compelled to use the deck with no covering whatever. Since they had been under shelter for months this exposure sat very hard on them indeed. We arrived at Norfolk and moved out into the Hampton Roads where the Confederate steamer, carrying a white flag, met the steamer George Washington, also flying white colors along with the handsomest flag the world contains, the glorious "Stars and Stripes." How those prisoners cheered, and cheered again! On board the George Washington there were piles upon piles of ham sandwiches, and colored people were dishing out all the coffee the men could eat and hold. On passing Newport News all the soldiers there, over five thousand, were lined up to give us three cheers, while fully a dozen men-of-war vessels manned the yard-arms with "Jack Tars" in honor of our home coming. That is the way we got back and set our feet once more on the soil of—"God country."

Fortress Monroe was under the command of General Wool, a Mexican war officer, who gave us a most generous reception. Arrangements were made for the returning prisoners to go on board the big steamer that was to convey us to Baltimore. The men were to make it their home as long as they remained in Hampton Roads. Of course, all of the enlisted men were entitled to and did receive their rations on board the big steamer. The officers in charge had also arranged to have their rations cooked for them. They were served in the large dining room of the vessel in detachments, as all could not be served at once. The orders for the boat were to start on its northward journey through the Chesapeake Bay at about six o'clock in the evening of the day of arrival, which left the prisoners with nearly a full day to examine the great fortress.

The whole day was spent in examining everything that came in view. A great many of the returning prisoners, both officers and men, had never been inside of a fort before. Besides, away back during President Jackson's administration, it had been determined to build an island well out from the fort, on which to mount an independent battery. From Jackson's time until the breaking out of the war, each succeeding administration to a greater or less extent, according to the means provided by Congress, never entirely ceased in sending ship-load after ship-load of stone. These stones went into the creation of the proposed island called the "Rip-Raps," because some stones were dropped by whole cargoes one on top of the other and allowed to find their own location at the bottom. It was a Herculean task, but when the prisoners visited that place on their homeward-bound journey, the stone had begun to show above the water. I heard an officer who had been stationed there a long time say that an area above water was about the size of a big town. After the Civil War broke out, the work of forming the island was greatly accelerated. In the fall of 1862, six or eight months after our visit, a big gun cast at Pittsburgh, said to be the biggest cannon ever manufactured at that time by any nation, was placed in position on the "Rip-Raps. The cannon was called "The Union" and if I remember correctly, its weight was ninety thousand pounds.

After a most interesting day spent in looking about and in making the acquaintance of many officers of the Fortress, a large number of whom belonged to the regular army, and after attending a reception given by General Wool to the returning officers among the prisoners, we went aboard our steamer. It was an all-night run to Baltimore and we arrived there about eight o'clock the next morning. There was little sleep on board the big steamer as men and officers were so overjoyed at being released from prison. The night was spent in a social way; the memory of which no doubt comes pleasantly back to many of the survivors of that genial, merry company as it does to me. Alas, there may be few, very few indeed, of that happy company still living, for nearly all of the great battles were still to be fought. The steamer was packed with men full of youth and vigor and filled with patriotic enthusiasms. They had so earnestly enlisted, heart and soul in the great cause for which they were fighting, but I doubt if a corporal's guard, of that whole ship's load, is alive today.

On reaching Baltimore it was my intention to proceed to Washington City, only about forty miles distant to procure a leave of absence then to proceed to my home. At Baltimore I turned over to William C. Harris his manuscript, (the manuscript that I had managed to smuggle out of the Confederacy safely). Harris was so overjoyed that he at once went to a military store, not far away, and bought me a present of an officer's sash.

The sash cost him twenty-five dollars. When it is understood that a very handsome one could be procured for ten dollars, it can be perceived that it was a beautiful one. Harris procured an ordinary pass and went to his home in Philadelphia. I never saw him again but we kept in touch through letters from 1863 to 1867. When I ceased to hear from him through the mails, I had a "personal" published in several of the Philadelphia dailies inquiring for his whereabouts, but no response was ever received. I am sure if living he would not have broken off our correspondence, for we became almost like the Siamese twins in our private life as long as we were together.

When Harris reached Philadelphia, he at once went to work to get out his book. Although it was a small one, selling in bound form for a dollar, it was the very first book that the war subject had produced. It sold rapidly, as of course, all those who had been confined as prisoners bought a copy on sight. It was published by the late George Childs, for so many years the editor and owner of the Philadelphia Ledger, and a great friend of General Grant. Harris wrote me in one of his letters that Childs had offered him four thousand dollars for the copyright of the book and he had accepted it. Pretty good pay for about six or seven months in prison.

The great body of prisoners arriving at Baltimore were either sent to camps to await exchange or given furloughs to their homes. The enlisted men were given a furlough for thirty days and the officers given a twenty-day leave with the privilege of additional time, unless in the meantime, they were exchanged. For myself I went to Washington City. My regiment at that time, under General Banks, was making the first advance of the Union army into Virginia. They were crossing the Potomac at Williamsport and Harper's Ferry. The troops were moving in such a way as to concentrate at Winchester, which was taken in March 1862.

At Washington I called on Speaker Colfax of the House to thank him for so promptly complying with my request to send me a fifty-dollar gold piece to the Richmond prison. I had known him previous to his entry into Congress as the editor of the St. Joseph Valley Register, of South Bend, Indiana. He seized me by the arm at the entry door of the House and hurrying me into the congressional chamber, he succeeded in getting me considerably frustrated. Every member of the House was solicitous to see and converse with one who had been in prison, and was fresh from the Confederate capital. On all sides the members closed around me. Mr. Colfax would introduce me, and over and over I repeated the story, briefly, of course, until it became so wearisome I discovered an egress and swiftly passed out of the House and was soon down on Pennsylvania Avenue at the hotel. I resolved never to permit such a reception from the "big-guns" of the country, as I did then. Why, the members of Congress wanted me to go up in the Speaker's stand and tell the story of my imprisonment! Many times since there have been crowds that have tried to get me to make a speech, but none of them have ever succeeded. And every time I have been called on since that period, I think of my escape from the capitol at Washington.

I only remained in Washington for a few days, and then came to my own home. I remained in Warsaw for a few weeks, and then concluded to revisit my regiment, which was at Winchester. Upon arriving at Winchester by a railroad that the army had rebuilt from Harper's Ferry to Winchester, it was learned that the regiment had been gone for a full day and was probably twenty or twenty-five miles away. It seems Stonewall Jackson had been prowling about the country southwest of Winchester and General Nate Kimball, of Indiana, in command of the Federal forces, had been giving Jackson a severe drubbing a few miles outside of town. It was the only time, I have heard many officers say, that Stonewall Jackson was worsted up till his death, which occurred at the battle of Chancellorsville. In consequence of this fight, General Abercrombie's brigade that the Twelfth belonged to had been ordered to Snickers Gap toward Manasas in the hope, perhaps, of getting on Stonewall's flank. Those of us attempting to rejoin the Twelfth, stayed overnight in the same town, where in December last, as prisoners of war, we had stayed a few days in an old "Sons' of Temperance Hall". This time we stayed at a hotel and paying our own bills avoided being given some "stringy beef" and bread and being treated as if we were dogs.

At an early hour the next morning, we started out to catch up with our regiment. We plodded on all day long, occasionally meeting a Federal courier, evidently carrying dispatches from General Abercrombie to General Kimball. But we could get no information as to how far the troops we were seeking were ahead of us. As the war went on we found it to be simply out of the question for anyone to find out where his command was by inquiring. Not being accustomed to marching, several of the party became foot-sore. Almost at dark we crossed the Shenandoah on a bridge and ascending a long hill, we could plainly see a gap in the mountains, Snicker's Gap.

Right at the summit of the gap was a small village called Snickerville, which was named, after the gap of Snicker. All of us were worn out and there were no signs of catching up with the troops we were searching for. Just after dark, I discovered a citizen of the village, and in talking with him I ascertained that the troops we were seeking must be camped about ten miles further on. This was discouraging, for two of the party were already lame. We were fully aware of the danger in staying in Snickerville, but determined we must spend the night, as we were too tired to move foreword. For a shelter we took possession of an empty two-story house. There was no strategy in selecting a two-story house, but after we did so, we perceived that it would be decidedly to our advantage to occupy the second story, which was reached by a narrow stairway. We all had revolvers and in case of an attack the stairs could be easily defended. There were five of us in the party, which would suffice to put up a pretty good fight if were we attacked during the night.

Whether there really was an attempted attack upon us during the night I have never been quite satisfied. There were quite a number of men hanging around the building for an hour or more. During this period, Dan Hamlin, who was trying to ascertain whether we were surrounded by enemies or not, forgot the banisters that surrounded the upper floor of the stairway had been broken down. He walked right off the second floor and fell to the floor beneath. He fell with such a crash that the rest of us heard three or four individuals running through the brush in full flight. As we were in enemy's country, and in the identical region that afterwards was roamed over and dominated by Mosby's Guerillas till the close of the war, it can be perceived that a party of some kind was arranging to attack us. Hamlin's crashing down to the floor below caused such a great noise as to frighten them away. They evidently feared that they had been discovered.

Hamlin's ankle was so severely wrenched that he was quite lame, but at daylight we started in the hope of catching up with our troops. After about ten hours of rapid marching, as rapid as could be made with Hamlin's lameness, we overtook the command, which had stopped for dinner. As dinner ended, an order reached the Colonel to retrace our way back to Winchester, over forty miles, with all possible haste. We retrograded to Snicker's Gap, where our orders were countermanded and we were directed to proceed to Manasas Junction, the original plan to be carried out.

The Northern people were filled with excitement following the driving of the army under General Banks back to Harper's Ferry and Williamsport. General Lee had assembled a large army in front of the Federal forces, overpowering them in numbers, at least for a time, causing a despondent feeling to prevail among the people in the Northern States. There were but two Indiana regiments that had finally accepted the call of the State Legislature to serve as State troops for one year—the Twelfth and Sixteenth Indiana Infantry. These two regiments, after the battle of the first Bull Run were turned over to the United States service, served the remainder of their time in the Army of the Potomac, and at the end of their service were mustered-out. The two regiments sought, but were refused permission to reorganize "for the war".

But owing to the military reverses that so soon followed, both regiments were directed to reorganize under the terms then applying to all troops "for three years or during the war". The order, dated the latter end of May 1862, was issued by Governor Morton.

Directly following the issuing of the order for the reorganization of these two regiments came an order from President Lincoln for Indiana's quota for "three hundred thousand more". Governor Morton proposed in his call to fill the quota for this body of men by assigning a regiment to each of the congressional districts of the State. This would amount to about eleven thousand infantry for the State at large. In addition there were several batteries and also a number of cavalry regiments. I refer to these points for the purpose to explain that the organization of two regiments, the Twelfth and the Sixteenth, proceeded slowly. The commissioners of every county in the State became solicitous, of course, to recruit the congressional district regiments and hence, they discouraged the raising of troops for any other purpose than to fill the call by districts. As a consequence those engaged in the effort to reorganize these two regiments found unusual impediments in their way.

In Kosciusko County, myself assisted by Samuel Boughter, Ed Webster, Lemuel Hazzard and others, had gone immediately to work to raise the company expected from this county. I had already taken forty men to Indianapolis, where they were in camp with Mr. Boughter in charge. Mr. Boughter had been a sergeant in the original Twelfth Indiana; he was assisted by Webster and Hazzard. The commissioners of Kosciusko County had met and offered a bounty of twenty-five dollars for every man who would enlist in the congressional district regiment. This was a severe blow to me, as I had fourteen recruits at the moment in a hotel in Warsaw, the Wright House. I perceived that I must get them to Indianapolis before they ascertained that the commissioners were discriminating against them as to bounty. I rushed them off to Indianapolis during that night before they had learned of the bounty offered. The Congressional District Regiment that was formed was the Seventy-fourth Indiana Infantry.

After landing my recruits at Indianapolis, I returned to Warsaw and had a "heart to heart" talk with the county auditor, Joseph A. Funk. He saw the great injustice that was being done to me. He also was aware that I had expended nearly every dollar I had in aiding and helping to reorganize the Twelfth. Mr. Funk decided that all who enlisted in the Twelfth should also have the twenty-five dollar county bounty. The fear of a draft by the government accelerated the filling-up of the district regiments greatly. The Twelfth not only secured its full company for the reorganized command, but it also contained a second one from this county composed of the overflow from the district regiments, which became Company I in the new Twelfth, commanded originally by Captain Samuel Wells.

Very few of the original Twelfth's officers made any attempt to assist in reorganizing their companies. Full regiments from every district were needed and promotions from the ranks of the enlisted men of the disbanded Twelfth were quite numerous. It is a fact that every regiment in the State, organized at that time, had quite a number of officers in it who had been enlisted men in the original Twelfth. Consequently the influence of these men upon their relatives and friends to enlist in the regiments in which they belonged was a great hindrance to the reorganization of the Twelfth. This left for several weeks only two officers who were actively working to reorganize the Twelfth, Colonel William H. Link and myself. For myself I had come home from the first year with about eight hundred dollars in demand notes—in other words, just the same as gold. Before the regiment was fully reorganized, I had expended every dollar of this and borrowed three hundred more. The money was used to pay for the thousand and one expenses involved in the reorganization, and for quite some time it was doubtful if the Twelfth would ever be reorganized. However the threat of the draft, and the advance of the Confederate armies into Kentucky through Cumberland Pound, and other gaps in the Cumberland range, made enlisting very rapid. In some instances recruits had to be refused as all the commands called for under the proclamation of the President were full.

At the beginning, little opposition to the war to save the Union had been openly expressed, but by the close of 1861 and all through 1862, those who had voted the Democratic ticket in the North had become faultfinders and grumblers. Some even at that early period began to openly espouse the cause of the South. It is positively astounding that with so large an opposition in the north, that the Union cause succeeded as well as it did. As the years of the war progressed this opposing element grew stronger and much bolder in its hostility to Lincoln and his administration.

From early in May until the Twelfth Indiana Infantry was reorganized and mustered into the service, I was constantly engaged in recruiting. I enlisted many persons individually and after my own company was full I would assign these men to the company in camp that needed them the most that is to those who had the fewest number so as to enable them to reach the minimum number and permit the muster in. I remember standing at the old Palmer House corner in Indianapolis and enlisting as many as twenty or thirty men by eight o'clock in the morning. I lost no time in having the United States mustering officer administer the oath required so that they could be held, as all of them were strangers to me.

Considerable tact was required in handling new recruits. It was not at all uncommon for a squad of young men to come to Indianapolis, ostensibly to enlist, but on reaching the city—probably the first time they were ever in a large place—some of them would suddenly decide that they did not want to enlist after all. I remember one of the excuses they would most frequently make was that they would not be stripped in order to be medically examined. This was required by the medical staff as early as the middle of 1862. They would declare that they would not undress to be examined before anybody! I would generally overcome this suddenly conceived excuse by deriding them for their lack of pluck and would end up offering to go before the medical examiner and strip off all my clothes with them. In almost every instance this method would succeed. And I know I am safe in saying I have taken off my clothes in this way and received the administration of the oath required of all soldiers as frequently as four to six times in a day. The recruits could see that I was an officer and they would reason that if an officer would put himself on an equality with them in this way, he, above all others, was the man to enlist with. I have often thought I was the most "sworn in" officer in the Union Army and that few had sworn to "support the President in all his behests," oftener than I did in all those four years.

The regiment was reorganized and mustered in about the middle of August 1862, in the Old State House Square at Indianapolis. I had supposed that Colonel Link would see to it that I should be made the Major of the regiment on its reorganization, although never a word had passed between us upon the subject. I was astounded on the evening of the muster-in to receive a commission from Governor Morton sent to my headquarters at the Oriental House, appointing me Lieutenant Colonel. Next to Colonel Link himself, I had been most active of all in assisting in the reorganization, but I never looked beyond a Major's commission. Commissions were issued the same day to Samuel Boughter, as Captain, Alonzo Hubbard as First Lieutenant and Ed H. Webster as Second Lieutenant. The commissions received by these men gave me much pleasure for all three of them had assisted greatly in reorganizing the company to which they belonged.

The next day following the "mustering in" of the regiment, I left Indianapolis for my home in order to procure a horse. Silas W. Chipman, who was a good judge of horseflesh and knew all the good ones in the county, was commissioned to procure me a suitable animal. During my brief absence from Indianapolis the regiment had received marching orders and took the cars for Cincinnati, there to be sent to any given point thought to be the most in need of troops. General Kirby Smith with the Confederate veterans of Pea Ridge and an army of thirty thousand had come through the Cumberland and Pound Gaps into Kentucky. A larger force of Confederates under General Bragg was marching on Louisville with the Federal army retiring before him and sometimes almost alongside of them. The two armies apparently were racing for the same objective point—Louisville.

On reaching Indianapolis, I ascertained that the Twelfth had proceeded to Lexington, the capital of Kentucky. I had no difficulty in procuring a car for my horse's conveyance and I had in my employ Jacob Merriman, a hired man to take care of him. We arrived at Lexington in a couple of days only to learn that the regiment had been sent to Richmond, Kentucky, the first county seat east of the capital.

In Lexington, I found a number of members from different companies of my own regiment, who for various reasons had been left behind. All of them were solicitous to go along with me when they learned that I intended to proceed to Richmond the next day. Charles R. Cruft, of Terre Haute,

Indiana, was in command of the Federal troops in the city of Lexington, and had about eight thousand men under him. Lexington at that time contained all of the supply wagons except those containing ammunition, which had been sent to the troops at the front. Hundreds of officer's trunks were in storage and there was nothing left for me to do but to follow the procedure of the others and leave my baggage there also—something that I have regretted all my life since for aside from a double suit of officer's uniforms, fatigue and full-dress, the latter a present from Stephen Bond, a well known banker in Fort Wayne, there was the very handsome sash that was the gift from William C. Harris for saving his manuscript at Libby prison.

| H | 12 | Ind. |

Reuben Williams

Col., Co. ......, 12. Reg't Indiana Inf.

Appears on a

Detachment Muster Roll

of the organization named above,

for Oct 31/62 to Feby 28 1863.

Station Indianapolis, Ind.

Present or absent Present

Stoppage, $ 100 for

Due Gov't $ 100 for

Remarks: Taken prisoner on the 20" of Dec/62, paroled Dec 20/62. Not exchanged. Detailed by Lt Col Bomford S.O. No 185, dated Mch 14/63 to recruit. Has pay due from Oct 31 to Nov 7/62 as Lt Col; since that time pay due as Col. Mustered out as Lt Col, & mustered in as Col Nov 7/62.

CHAPTER 5

Battle of Richmond, Kentucky

Hark to the sound! There's a fore on the border—
A foe striding on to the gulf of his doom;
Freemen are rising and marching in order
Leaving the plow, the anvil and loom.
Rust dims the harvest sheen
Of scythe and of sickle keen;
The ax sleeps in peace by the tree it would mar;
Veterans and youth are out,
Swelling the battle-shout,
Grasping the bolts of the thunders of war!
—T. Buchanan Read

General Lew Wallace had been in command in central Kentucky, but was given a command with headquarters at Cincinnati. General Nelson, a loyal Kentucky officer, had been placed in command of the troops in the fields. Under Nelson, the next in command was Brigadier General Mahlon D. Manson, of Indiana. The troops had been assembled at Richmond to retard and delay the advance march of the Confederate General Kirby Smith. To oppose Kirby, General Manson had at Richmond less than five thousand men, all of them fresh from the fields, workshops and counters of Ohio and Indiana. They were generally quite young men with no experience whatever as soldiers, hundreds of whom had never fired either a revolver or a gun in all their lives. It was this small body of troops that were to meet General Kirby Smith's thirty thousand veterans in the heart of Kentucky. It should also be borne in mind that in the last few days of August 1862 the weather was exceedingly hot and there was a scarcity of water throughout the area. Every farmhouse was provided with cisterns to catch and hold the water that was drained into them from rains. But at this time even the deeply sunken wells had given out and there was scarcely sufficient water for drinking and cooking purposes of that small army, let alone for the livestock—the horses and mules.

As I stated earlier, upon reaching Lexington there were many men from the Twelfth regiment who were very solicitous to accompany me to Richmond and after gaining permission from General Cruft, I gave my consent for them to go with me. There were probably seventy-five men who went along. Some were from other regiments as well as my own, but all were anxious to rejoin their commands.

Richmond was fully twenty-five miles distant from the State capital and due east, consequently the shades of night were falling at the close of a long August day when we reached our destination. The enlisted men soon found their respective companies and I reported to regimental headquarters only to learn that Colonel Link, the commanding officer of the Twelfth, had been assigned to command a brigade in the battle that was expected on the morrow. Because of this, I was compelled to take command of a full regiment. The responsibility almost appalled me. I had had considerable experience as the Captain of a company and I doubt if any of the volunteer forces had studied the tactics more assiduously than I had done, but this education was all for company movements. On the night of reaching Richmond I found I was to take command of ten companies. Ten companies, too, that had not as yet seen a full day's drill, and had never stood up in line of battle, or even on dress parade. The responsibility was so great that I did not sleep much that night after the meager repast of coffee, crackers and bacon.

I was aroused at four-thirty the next morning with an order to be ready to march at five-thirty. It should be remembered, too, that I had never before seen more than three or four of the companies composing the ten companies of the regiment, as I had gone home from Indianapolis just as soon as the organization of the regiment had been completed. That evening was the first I had seen them. After breakfast consisting of the same bill-of-fare as the previous supper, the bugle sounded and we took up the line of march to the eastward. Colonel Metcalf's Kentucky cavalry had developed the fact that the Confederate Army was advancing in heavy force on several roads. We were an unorganized, undisciplined force of less than five thousand men who were expected to prevent the Confederate Army from moving forward.

I should judge that we had moved about five or six miles when a halt was ordered for some cause and I had received directions from Colonel Link, to place the Twelfth in a line facing the east and along a rail fence. I at once perceived that there was a cornfield somewhat to my right as well as to the front. As it was the last day of August the corn stood up at its full height. The thought passed through my head that the Confederates might utilize this cornfield, which was a large one, to cover a flanking movement. But just then the rebels in our front, principally cavalry, opened up with four or five shots from what "our side" afterwards came to call a "jack-ass battery." These kinds of guns were taken to pieces and carried on several mules, proper panniers having been arranged for the purpose. The gun itself, I believe, was carried between two mules; the wheels on another and the ammunition on still another. They were used considerably by the Confederates during the early part of the war. The first shot struck the fence behind which my command was stationed and several men were hurt by the flying rails. The third shot struck the pummel of my saddle, cut the bridle reins out of my fingers and so bruised the withers of my horse that the blood slowly oozed from the wound. As he was a very spirited animal I had all I could do to remain on his back while I was trying to quiet him.

Colonel Link and myself were the only field officers on the immediate ground and it was evident that the Confederate army was engaged in making a wide flanking movement, the objective point being Richmond and its supplies. But there seemed to be no head to our army so we remained there for some time awaiting orders. I had ridden to a point where I could look through the long rows of corn from whence I could see a body of men moving to our right. I hastened to Colonel Link and told him what I had seen. He replied by saying it must be some of our own men. While I could not contradict him, I insisted on him going to a point where we could take a look through the rows of corn. He did so, but as neither of us was in possession of "field-glasses", we could not make out whether they were our own men or the enemy. We rode back and Colonel Link decided to have us fall back into a skirt of timber to await orders and events. We stopped immediately behind the cornfield. During this time the rebels were using the standing corn as a cover and on the south side of the field was a road. After the Confederates turned the corner of the cornfield, they crept along this road until within easy gunshot, and poured into us a most fatal volley. This was followed by other volleys as fast as they could reload their guns. Of course the men of the Twelfth returned the fire, and after awhile held the enemy sufficiently in check. We began the retrograde movement back to Richmond as we had been ordered to do some time earlier before the attempt was made to fall back.

As the movement to the rear began, John McCulloch, the noted correspondent of the Cincinnati Commercial, interviewed me for a brief moment. In his article on the battle, published about a week later, he stated that at the time he was writing, the Twelfth Indiana was the only Federal regiment on the field that had preserved its organization. It was wholly intact and unexcited when he came up with it.

The day was a fearful one and all in all I hark back to what is called the battle of Richmond, Kentucky, as one of the severest in which myself and my regiment were engaged in during the war. The regiment had gone out in the early morning with a breakfast insufficient to stay the appetite of a single one of the men in the command. The day was a blistering hot one and neither man nor beast had even a sip of water. The suffering of the men must have been great. All of them were new to the service and none of them were accustomed to marching or to carrying the impediments with which a soldier is loaded. After the first contact with the enemy there was not a moment in which there was not a skirmish or a more pretentious struggle in progress all over the field. Many skirmishes were fought by small detachments and at other times involved the whole regiment. The Confederate General was continuing his flanking movement, and being superior in numbers, he threw most of his cavalry between Richmond and Lexington.

Probably an hour before sundown most of the Federal army had fallen back and assembled along the eastern side of the town of Richmond where it was determined that a last stand should be made. Sometime in the afternoon, General Nelson and his staff appeared upon the scene. He had heard of the fight in progress through couriers sent to him at his headquarters in Nicholasville, a village perhaps twenty miles distant. He rode along the lines in the endeavor to encourage the men. After the final disposition, late in the evening, I saw him no more.

My horse had sustained a second injury in the first volley the regiment had been involved in at the edge of the timber. A musket-ball had stuck the animal low down in the belly, cutting a small piece out of my trousers and boring a hole through the saddle girth. It must have hurt him seriously for in his plunge he threw me straight up in the air so that when I came down there was no horse to light upon. The horse had run away and Jacob Merriman, the young man employed to care for the animal had found him, tied him to a fence and came forward to the battle line to ask if I wanted to use him. The skirmishers were just beginning, so I informed Merriman that I would remain on foot and that he should stay with the horse until the contest was over, and then hunt me up.

After the line had been formed for the last stand, Merriman came up to me and asked if he should bring my horse up to me. My instructions were for him to move back toward Lexington with my horse until after the encounter with the Confederates had ended. He had evidently obeyed his instructions but neither the young man nor the horse was ever seen alive again. The young man's remains were never found, although an extended search was made the next day. The body of the horse with his entire rump torn away, by either a solid shot or a shell from a rebel battery, was found on the Lexington Pike, about a mile west of Richmond. It was presumed that Merriman had gotten that far and may have been killed with the same shot that so terribly mangled the horse. But this is only a surmise, as Jacob Merriman's body was never seen afterwards. I had owned the horse about a week and as I rode through Lexington after taking the animal from the cars, a Kentuckian bartered with me to take three hundred dollars for him. I didn't do it, but Uncle Sam after the war allowed me just half that sum— one hundred-fifty dollars for the horse.

Following the departure of Merriman with my horse to the rear, the Confederate forces moved forward upon the thin and weak line the Federals had formed. The line extended partly through the Richmond cemetery and south of that among some forest trees. It was evident from the start that the Confederates had determined to take the town at any hazard, for their army moved forward three lines deep and in some places four deep. They ran right over our skirmishers, although the Federals held their line for some time, (quite a long time when it is considered how outnumbered they were).

Over in the cemetery there seemed to be a weak spot in our lines and it was retreating slowly before the heavy onset of the enemy. To remedy this and to check the retrograde movement of the men, Colonel William H. Link, with a portion of his brigade, dashed over to the wavering point. In so doing Link received a musket ball in his hip that shattered the thighbone. He died from the effects of this wound about ten days later. A monument to his memory stands in the beautiful Lindenwood cemetery at Fort Wayne, Indiana where he lived previous to the war. He was a brave and gallant soldier who had served in the Mexican war. His career as Colonel of the Twelfth Indiana Infantry was extremely brief and his death came so quickly after the regiment was organized that there were many men and even some officers who scarcely knew him when they saw him.

For myself, I can truthfully say that the battle of Richmond was the most trying one of the many that it was my lot to pass through. Few men who had served in the Twelfth, except in Company F, knew who I was. I did not know on sight some of the captains of the companies of my own regiment. And having never before attempted to maneuver a battalion, I felt inadequate. I deeply felt the responsibility of handling ten companies instead of the one, which had been the previous limit of my command. I can only say that vigilant and vigorous study of the tactics by night, and the drill that we had inaugurated while prisoners at Richmond, under the competent direction of Colonel DeVilliers, was of great service to me when responsibilities had to be undertaken.

The forces that made the last stand in the outskirts of Richmond were literally swept from the field by the on-rushing charge of the Confederates, three, four, and sometimes five lines deep. The Federal line was formed on the east and south sides of the town, and consequently fell back in their retreat by the pike road leading westward to Lexington.

I had been on foot from the time my horse threw me in the first contest with the enemy in the grove of timber. I was completely exhausted, having had nothing to eat during the entire day, nor a drop of water. In the immediate rear of the line of the last stand were open fields, and near the middle of one of them were two stacks of wheat or rye. I was so exhausted that I made up my mind to get back to them and seek their great bulk for protection from the oncoming enemy. As I started, a boy, Dennis Murphy, had been a Five Point New York orphan (a few years before the war began orphans from Five Point were brought to my hometown of Warsaw and placed with the families of farmers and others of the vicinity). The boy had enlisted in what, after my promotion, became Captain Sam Boughter's company. He was about fifteen years of age at the time. Both of us had taken protection behind one of the stacks referred to, and by peeping around we could easily see the Confederate lines advancing, preserving their lines in very good order.

Murphy was a wild sort of a boy and all at once he made the remark to me, "Colonel, they are coming like hell and I'm going to take a shot at 'em." Before I could check him, he stepped out from behind the stack and fired his musket right into the advancing rebel lines that were only a few rods away.

After Murphy's shot I determined to endeavor to get to a seminary we had passed earlier that was located between where we made our last stand and the town. Earlier in the morning it had been taken, by order of General Manson, for the Federal hospital. Murphy was of the same mind and together we arrived safely at the hospital.

I got some refreshments from the surgeon in charge and ate a sandwich that did me a vast amount of good. I began to look around for the means to prevent my capture for a second time. Directly across the street from the hospital was a very large cornfield. Past this I could see not only a large farmhouse, but also an old-fashioned well sweep. Water was the great cry of both sides engaged in that day's fight and fearing that I might be again taken to Richmond, Virginia, I ran across the street, climbed the stake-and-rider fence and entered the cornfield where I was completely hidden from view. I lay down for a short time, but in my thirst for water that well sweep was continually in my thoughts. I got up and passed through the field of corn determined to get some water even though I was captured in the attempt. The well was on the opposite side of the house from where I came out into the open, but I could see the sweep extending above the roof.

I passed through a gate, turned the corner of the house and there, less than ten feet away, stood a Confederate soldier who had drawn a bucket of water. His gun was leaning against the well curb and my first thought was to make a dash for it and through its help make him a prisoner. Just at that moment he took the gourd from his mouth and asked me if I wanted a drink. After I took the gourd, he picked up his gun and trudged away over toward the Lexington pike, where the pursuit of the Yankees was in progress, leaving me in full possession of the well.

There was no sign of a living person about the big house. Its occupants evidently had been frightened away by the nearness of the daylong battle. The sun by this time was sinking low in the west and I had had such good luck in avoiding capture thus far that I was considerably encouraged. It came into my head that if I could place the Kentucky River between myself and the rebels, I could yet escape and join the eight thousand Federals that held Lexington. The river was almost midway between Richmond and Lexington, so after being invigorated by all the water that I could drink, I determined to make the effort. I had probably gone nearly a half a mile from the farmhouse when I came to the brink of a very deep but narrow ravine. On the opposite side I could perceive a small body of horsemen.

One of them discovered me and called out, "Halt!" Of course I obeyed at once. Then the horseman directed me to come over to the other side of the ravine. I asked him whose cavalry he belonged to, not knowing but that it might be my own. He replied, "To Kunel Stahn's ragiment". His very pronunciation showed me that I was in the presence of a detachment of rebels.

Obeying his order for me to cross over to his side, I commenced the descent into the ravine. These gullies during heavy rains and floods are always as cleanly swept at the bottom of all sorts of debris, and are as solid as a barn floor. When I got to the bottom I discovered this and also that it was quite dark down there, so I took to my heels and ran with all the might left to a man already nearly "played-out". I ran for perhaps a half-mile and in that way I eluded "Kunnel Stahn's ragiment". I was greatly fatigued and almost wholly worn out, but I was greatly encouraged by the good luck that had thus far attended my attempt to escape capture. I continued in the ravine for some time and when I came out found that I was only a short distance from a very excellent pike road. I later learned the road was called the Nicholasville pike.

It was now dark and I continued my journey to the west in the hope of reaching the Kentucky River and crossing it before daylight. I was pushing forward as fast as a man in my condition could, when all at once in making a slight turn in the road, I caught up with someone, who, after some talk I discovered to be Captain Hueston, of G company, of my own regiment. Of course we joined company, both of us intent upon getting over the Kentucky River as soon as possible. Some minutes after midnight the Captain and myself made a long descent down a ridge, at the bottom of which was a small stream. The surrounding trees made it quite dark. It was so dark in fact that when we reached the bottom we ran right into a detachment of Louisiana cavalry and were immediately captured. We were within but three miles of the river and perhaps safety.

The Louisiana detachment consisted of about fifty men. There were several spare horses and we were mounted on them. After perhaps an hour of steady marching, the command halted and we were ordered to dismount. We found, to our surprise, that we were in a large cleared space of about an acre in size, surrounded by thick cedar and other shrubbery. There, in this opening, were about two hundred of our own men who had been captured in small squads, and during the remainder of the night several other small lots of men were brought in. General Manson, the immediate commander of our forces in the battle of the day before was there when we first arrived. He had been captured in the early part of the evening the day before, and was quite severely wounded. This was my first meeting with him after joining his forces at Richmond, although I knew him well and had frequently met him at Indianapolis. The wound was in his left hip, but fortunately no bones were broken or even touched.

I had been given by Governor Morton a number of letters to carry to officers in the field. One of them was a long letter to Colonel William H. Link, of my own regiment, two to General Manson, and my own commission as Lieutenant Colonel of the Twelfth. I had had no opportunity to deliver them since I reached the command, as it was about to engage in a contest with the enemy. Ending as the contest did all of these letters and documents were in the side pocket of my coat, and as I lay there on the ground the thought entered my mind, "what if I am searched in the morning? The letters may," I reasoned, "contain matters intended only for private ears," and right there I concluded to get rid of them. So while lying on my back, supposedly asleep, I took my penknife and dug a deep hole right under me. I deposited all the papers in my pocket into the hole and covered them up. I pressed the ground all about them as hard as I was able to do. As it was dark, I could not distinguish my commission as Lieutenant Colonel from the rest, and hence it was buried with the others. I have often wondered if those documents were ever found; if they were plowed up in the years that have elapsed since that weary August night in 1862.

About six o'clock in the morning we were ordered to prepare to march. What our destination was, we did not know. Not a particle of food was given to us, but there was a good-sized stream alongside the road we traveled so that water was plentiful. But there are times when too much water and no food become unpleasant as a regular diet. I was well on in the second day without any food save what I got from the hospital—a sandwich made of two pieces of "hard-tack" and a slice of bacon. The column in charge of us seemed to grow larger and larger as we winded our way back to Richmond, which we reached at about ten o'clock that morning. We were halted in front of the public square that packed full of Federal prisoners. It was a terribly hot day and there was not a shade tree of any kind inside the enclosure, nor anything else that would cast a shadow as big as a man's thumb. I could see it was the intention to place all of us prisoners in that square also. In a minute I made up my mind that I would not be one of the number, if any sort of a ruse would prevent it. I believe I would have even told a downright lie right there and then rather than to become one of that crowd suffering in the broiling, blistering sun. I had no plan and can only remember that I was determined not to enter that public square at any hazard.

Quite a number of our party had passed through the double gate with a guard on each side. A sergeant stood near the gate and when it came my turn to go in I said to one of the guards, "I want to see General Kirby Smith, the commander of these forces." "You will have to ask the sergeant of the guard," the guard replied. The sergeant came up, and of course he could perceive that I was an officer. I repeated my demand to see the commanding officer of the Confederate forces on matters of importance, and that I must see him in person. "All right," said the sergeant, "come this way." I was almost thunderstruck with surprise at the success that had thus far attended my ruse. I only hoped it would continue to be as successful after General Smith's headquarters were reached. As luck would have it, the general's headquarters were just across the way in a hotel. The commander-in-chief of the Confederate forces occupied the commodious parlors.

There must have been a dozen or more of staff officers in the room, all of them quite busy. I was taken straight to the General. The sergeant told him that here was an officer who wished to see him. I saluted him, made a lame sort of a joke about our defeat of the day before and told him that I had come to secure the favor of a personal parole so that I could pass about the town until the regular parole was made out and signed. "Certainly," said General Smith. "Adjutant make out a personal parole for this officer confining him to the town proper." It was soon done, and when the Adjutant General handed it to me, I spoke to General Smith saying, "I had hoped the parole would permit me to visit the battlefield of the day before, where I felt sure there were a number of men from my regiment." "All right," said the general, "make out a new permit and give Colonel Williams permission to visit the points he wishes." "I ought to have an ambulance," said I, "in case I find some of our wounded men, or even your own, General, so that I can bring them to the hospital." "Give him an ambulance, also, Adjutant, there are plenty of them since yesterday," he replied with a smile, and I bowed myself out.

After securing some crackers and raw bacon at the hospital, I was on my way to the point where we had met the enemy the first time. I found Harmon Beeson of F Company and Lieutenant Henry Wescot of I Company on the battlefield. Wescot was suffering from a severe hip shot and Beeson had a musket ball pass through both of his legs below the knee. He died the next day after I brought him to the hospital. Wescot lived for nearly a week after the fight then died from lockjaw.

I have always spoken of my determination to keep out of that "bull pen" of a public square as an illustration of "supreme cheek," and I think it was. I had no idea at first as to what I would do, but I had confidence in myself to believe that in some way or other I would succeed, and I did, and even to a greater extent than I had dreamed. It was "cheek," unadulterated, simon-pure, clear-quilled "cheek,"—that's all.

Following the battle of Richmond, Kentucky it is plain to see that the way for the Confederate army to march upon Cincinnati was widely open so far as any intervening Federal troops were concerned. It is always easier to see what should have been done after it is too late. It is easy to see now that instead of marching eastward from Richmond from six to ten miles to meet the on-coming Confederate army, which outnumbered the Federal forces five to one, General Manson should have fallen back to the

Kentucky River. The river should have been the Federal line of defense rather than moving the small force farther away from help of any kind in an offensive operation. General Smith in command of the Confederate rightwing of the army seemed to be intending to invade the North. He remained at Richmond several days and from there issued a flaming proclamation printed on large posters urging Kentuckians to join his forces and assist the South in gaining her independence. A good many soldiers enlisted with the Confederates.

Since I had been paroled to the town limits, I stayed with several others at a boarding house of a lady whose husband was a prisoner in Camp Chase at Columbus, Ohio. The woman treated us very kindly in the hope—a far-fetched one—we might sometime be able to do a favor for her husband. Captain Samuel Boughter of Company F was staying at the boarding house and consequently we were together much of our three days' stay at Richmond. For two or three months previous to this time there had been considerable friction between the officers and soldiers of two or three Indiana regiments and General Nelson. The men had written to Governor Morton upon the subject. General Nelson was a graduate of the Naval Academy of Annapolis and had served on board of some of Uncle Sam's war vessels in the "ante-bellum" days when flogging in the navy was a common punishment. Hence Nelson was a domineering, overbearing, and a most brutal officer in the army, but he was a loyal Kentuckian, as brave as a lion. The government at Washington was cultivating the Union sentiment in Kentucky and his competency and qualifications secured him a General's commission, but he was hardly the man to command freeborn Americans in a personal way.

The days of remaining in Richmond as a prisoner were growing wearisome. I made frequent visits to the hospital and to Colonel Link, who lay mortally wounded in a farmhouse just out of town. General Smith's Confederate recruiting officers were stirring up Southern patriotism creating a growing hatred of Federal officers. Consequently, a number of us got together, after the regular parole had been furnished to one and all, and decided to set forward on our journey to Cincinnati. The railroad between Lexington and Cincinnati was so badly injured in many places that no trains were possible. The long journey had to be made on foot, and accordingly, a number of us had provided a one-horse buggy with its owner as driver, to take the seriously wounded General Manson out of the country.

Shortly before dark we left Richmond, almost sure that to remain another day might get us into trouble with the "fire-eating" rebel element. We determined not to use the route that was taken by the great body of prisoners after they were paroled. We took a different route because we felt certain that the passage of so many men would leave the country bare of food, and the people living along the route would be agitated.

Winchester was the first county seat lying due north, and we had been informed that the road to travel there was a good one. It was far more pleasant in those hot days to march at night and rest in the daytime. After the decision to go straight north had been reached, the whole party set forth. We came to a bridge across a steam that was of considerable size and around the end of the bridge we could see eight or ten men on horseback. The growing ill will of the people at Richmond had put us on our guard, and we approached this body of men quite carefully. We were unarmed, though for myself I had put two fairly good-sized stones in each of my pockets. However, we went forward just as if no suspicions were entertained by any one of us, but just as was anticipated, the party was inclined to be insolent. One of the men asked us whether we had been paroled or not, and in response to the reply he ripped out an oath that "the North could never subdue the South, and so far as he was concerned his sympathy was entirely with the South and against the "invaders". Another one of the men used the expression, "If I ever fight it will be on the sunny side".

We managed to move past our unwelcome interlopers and thought it best to push forward as fast as possible in order to get as far away from the battlefield as could be done by an all-night march. Our speed was regulated by General Manson's buggy, and long about sunrise we entered the town of Winchester some twenty-five miles from Richmond. We stopped at a hotel with the inevitable saloon next door to the office. The saloon contained about a dozen men ranging from perhaps twenty-five to forty years of age and all of them in a rather happy mood. They could see that we were Federal soldiers from our dress and every one of them was anxious for news of the battle. They knew a battle had been fought, but as there was no telegraphic communication with Richmond the particulars they possessed had been filtered through to them by word of mouth. And they were sufficiently intelligent enough to know that much of it was unreliable.

When I left Richmond, I had only a dollar and a quarter, while Major Kempton, my special comrade, had forty-five cents! The party treated us very genteelly and was all in a joke-cracking, happy humor. One of them stepped up to me and remarked, "Stranger, if you will step up to that gentleman and call him General Humphreys, I'll pay for the drink and for a breakfast for yourself and friend." "I have no objection," said I, thinking of my own depleted finances. I asked him which gentleman and when he pointed him out for the second time I stepped up to him and said, "Why, General Humphreys, how d'ye do?" The entire crowd broke out in a loud roar of laughter. I was astonished and somewhat abashed for I expected nothing else than for the man I had called General Humphreys to resent my freedom of speech. I never learned the point to the jest, but there was something hidden behind it all, I felt sure. At any rate I had won two very excellent breakfasts of fried chicken, corn fritters and coffee by complying with the request.

We remained at Winchester during most of the day intending to do our traveling in the cool of the coming night. I discovered that there was considerable Union sentiment in that part of Kentucky, for many citizens approached me in a quiet way, with no eavesdropper near, and expressed their real sentiments. Of course the noisy, hurrah-sort-of-fellows were loud in their professions of loyalty to the outraged South. The party consisting of eight persons left Winchester about five o'clock in the evening of the day we had arrived.

The wound of General Manson was becoming more and more painful, and riding in a buggy was not at all helpful to its healing. His condition gave the rest of us considerable uneasiness. We pledged ourselves not to desert the old gentleman, and if we were compelled to leave him on the way, we would make arrangements to contribute to his comfort, so far as it was in our power to do. It was a flesh wound and not at all dangerous if he could have the proper care. It had become very painful and seemed to be growing worse from the jolting of the vehicle. We discussed the matter and determined that if his wounds grew no better we would arrange to leave him at Paris, the next town of any size on our route to Cincinnati.

The road to Paris was fairly good and we trudged along at a pretty lively rate through nearly all of the night. General Manson declared that he would be compelled to stop at Paris to wait the healing of his wound. We arrived at Paris early on the following morning, and stopped at the principal hotel of the town. Colonel Reuben Keis secured a room for General Manson, as well as a surgeon to dress his wound and to care for him during the time he would have to remain there. It had been determined to leave him for he was by this time utterly unfit to travel further. During the day following our arrival we stayed close to the hotel in order not to bring about an unnecessary brawl, for the town's people were highly elated over the victory the Confederate troops had won and were viciously in favor of secession. There had been streams of prisoners arriving at Paris for some time and the people of the town were inclined to be quite insolent in the presence of Federal officers.

I inadvertently asked the clerk of the hotel where the nearest point was to cross the Ohio River. He replied that Maysville was the nearest. Maysville was twenty-five or thirty miles nearer to Paris than Covington, the Kentucky town immediately opposite Cincinnati. It was sixty miles above Cincinnati where all paroled prisoners were headed. I also discovered by consulting with other citizens and guests of the hotel that an excellent pike road led from Paris straight to Maysville. Major Kempton and myself resolved to cut loose from the party and go to Maysville, realizing that there would be no difficulty in securing a boat to Cincinnati. This determination was reached for the same reasons we had chosen to take the route by way of Winchester rather than straight to Lexington, that being the scarcity of food supplies and the tendency to rouse the people along the route.

After Major Kempton and myself came to the conclusion to take the Maysville route, we suggested the plan to the rest of the party. All of them were disinclined to take a road that was thirty miles nearer to the river but sixty miles further from the destination of all of us. So the two of us alone decided for the proposed route. We made all the necessary inquiries, and late in the afternoon when the sun was about an hour high, we determined to set out on the trip. You will recall that I had only a dollar and a quarter when I left Richmond, and in order to avoid any trouble I had informed the landlord of the state of my finances on first arriving at his hotel. "All right," he said, "You need take no trouble on that account." I told him I would send him his bill on reaching Cincinnati.

Just as we were about leaving the hotel, the Major and myself, aware of the fact that the night's march was before us, concluded to fortify the inner-man with a sip of Bourbon whiskey, that being the region in which it had its home. I did not know, however, that the Major had already indulged to some extent before this last invitation to imbibe. He was at such times a pretty loud talker and did not care much what he said. On entering the saloon I at once discovered that it was pretty full of rough-looking characters, and as we stepped up to the bar I could see that all eyes were upon us. The Major in a boasting way declared that "We would whip the hell out of 'em yet." Perceiving that we were surrounded by ruff looking men and that one or two of them were rolling up their sleeves, I whispered to Kempton to keep still, and look around him. He was a very high tempered man, quick to resent anything of an insolent nature, but fortunately, he understood the situation at a glance. I took him by the arm and led him out into the hotel office. If he had imbibed one more drink, nothing I could have done would have quieted him for he would have insulted the biggest ruffian in the crowd.

The clerk at the hotel came to the door and pointed out the spot where we would leave the main street of the town, turn the corner and be on the very fine turnpike that led to Maysville, eighty miles distant. The last remark he made to us as he bade us good-bye was that he hoped to see both of us return again under happier and more auspicious circumstance. "By the way," he said, "a woman lives in the house on the opposite corner where you turn whose husband is in the Union army under Colonel Metcalfe." We thanked him and judged by his remarks that he was a Union man.

The sun was just half an hour high as we started from the hotel. We soon reached the corner where the Union soldier's wife lived. Seeing a pump in the yard and in order to get to speak to at least one Union woman, we made the excuse that we had stopped to get a drink of water. "Ain't you Union soldiers?" she asked. We replied in the affirmative and she soon confirmed the story of the hotel clerk by announcing the fact that her husband was in Colonel Metcalfe's cavalry. We told her we were paroled prisoners and had concluded to go to Maysville rather than to Covington, the way most of the soldiers who had been in the battle had gone. "Well," she said, "You will find the Maysville pike a good road."

There was a flouring mill right opposite the woman's house. She incidentally made the remark that the man who owned the one-horse wagon that was at the mill door, lived about six miles out on the Maysville road and perhaps we could ride with him as far as he went. Thinking the suggestion a good one, we went over and climbed into the seat. Pretty soon a tottering old man came out of the mill with a fair-sized bagfull of flour on his shoulder. Perhaps no man was ever more greatly surprised than the old gentleman was on seeing two Federal officers occupying the principal seat in his vehicle. "What you fellows doin' in there?" he asked. I at once assumed the speakership of the occasion and told him we were going to ride out with him as far as he went. "No you ain't," he replied, "and I want you to git righ out." "Jump in old man," I replied, "we are in a hurry to get out of town." "Hev you fellows been licked at Richmond?" he asked. "No," said I, "We licked Kirby Smith and all his army three times in one day, but we are tired and want to go home." "Well, you can't ride in my wagon, anyhow!" "Now, look here, old man," said I, "if you are going along with us, dump in your sack and jump in or we'll drive off without you." Very reluctantly the old man dumped his sack into the forepart of the small wagon in such a way that he could sit upon it as the driver, and thus we started.

He was decidedly anxious to talk with us about the battle of which he had heard some bits of truth and much fiction. He was in sympathy with the South through and through and wanted to discuss the question from his standpoint. I told him that discussion came too late just now. The war was on, and it would be ended only when one side or the other "threw up the sponge." "What d'ye mean by that?" he asked, the pugilistic quotation being new to him.

We finally got the old man into a more amiable frame of mind by jesting with him and telling him a story or two, so the by the time we reached his place, he was quite kindly disposed. He told us that about four miles further was a woman whose husband was in this damn abolition war and had gone out to fight with "You Northerners" under Colonel Metcalfe in a cavalry regiment and that she might keep us the night. We bade the old man good night and I hallowed back at him that as soon as we got rested up in Indiana, we were coming back to lick 'em again.

The facts are that while at the mill, I was awfully tempted to drive off with the horse and vehicle to make an all night run to the limit of the horse's endurance, but on examining the animal I discovered him to be an old, lazy, overfed piece of horseflesh. I saw that we could not get far before the horse would break down. It was very probable that General Kirby Smith's cavalry was not very far behind us and it would be a difficult matter to explain should we be caught running away with a horse and wagon.

We reached the house of the man who had enlisted in Metcalfe's Union cavalry regiment about nine-thirty at night. We told the lady who we were. She at once had some of her help set to work to provide us with supper and we spent a couple of hours very pleasantly with her. She was an intelligent lady, thoroughly enlisted in the Union cause and the lady-head of a very delightful country home. In a private talk with Major Kempton we decided to go on our way even though the lady insisted on our remaining all night. We concluded that the Confederate forces would follow up their victory by pressing on towards Cincinnati and it might be to her discredit with the Confederate authorities if they knew that she had harbored Federal officers.

At about eleven o'clock p.m. we set forward on our way to Maysville. At three o'clock in the morning we lay down side by side in a fence corner and slept from sheer weariness until awakened by the fierce rays of an early September sun. We awoke when the day was just beginning to lighten. We saw a village or town a mile or so ahead of us and we determined to push on to it and rest there during the hot hours of the day. The town we came to was Boonesborough—the original spot where Daniel Boone first settled when he emigrated from North Carolina into the "dark and bloody ground," later known as Kentucky. We stopped at the hotel and I told the proprietor about our financial condition right at the start. "All right," said he, "you can have whatever you want while you stay with me under such circumstances." We were sent to a room and rested until late in the afternoon when we arose to a piece of good luck. The leading man of the place owned about twenty head of very fine blooded horses, and his greatest fear was that the Confederate army would make its appearance and confiscate all of his fine animal for their cavalry and artillery. He was on nettles to get them to Maysville. The Major and I seized the opportunity to help the man and to aid ourselves in our progress to Maysville. We each rode an animal and led four, two on each side, and arrived safely at Maysville the next morning.

On arriving at the city, we went to the crack hotel in the place and once more I told the financial situation of both of us. "All Right," said the proprietor, "you are welcome to whatever you want." I asked him about how soon we could get a boat for Cincinnati. "Why," he replied, "the Forest Rose is due here right now." Just at that moment we heard a loud and hoarse whistle up the stream. We enjoyed a first rate supper then boarded the Forest Rose. The fare to Cincinnati was two dollars each. I told the captain the situation. "D'ye think I'd charge men in your situation anything after what you have passed through?" he asked. So we arrived in Cincinnati with the identical money in our pockets as when we left Richmond.

We hadn't gone a square in Cincinnati before both of us were arrested by the provost guard, as the city was under martial law. Sixty thousand men from all over the State with their squirrel rifles and old-fashioned powder horns and shot pouches had come from every county of the Buckeye State to defend the city. Every man in the town was in the trenches on the Kentucky side engaged in building fortifications. Every man on the street was liable to military duty, we, among the rest were forced to give an account of ourselves. General Lew Wallace was in command of the city and its defenses with his headquarters at the Burnett House. We were taken to him by the guard and were immediately released and given a pass with the freedom of the town. Here Major Kempton and I borrowed fifteen dollars each and forwarded the amount due to each of the hotels that we owed. We had arrived in Cincinnati several days ahead of those who came directly to Covington by tramping over the ties of the railroad.

I was ordered by General Wallace to remain at Cincinnati, take charge of all the paroled prisoners from Indiana and take them back to Indianapolis once they had arrived at Cincinnati. It was four days before the last of our State's soldiers reached Cincinnati following the battle of Richmond, Kentucky. Those men had a tremendous amount of pluck and endurance, for they used the railroad as a highway for pedestrians and pushed a railcar loaded with thirty sick comrades all the way from Lexington to Covington, the city immediately opposite Cincinnati, a distance of one hundred thirty miles. They would not desert their sick comrades even though some of the men pushing the heavy car were in an almost starved condition and completely worn out. After being placed in command of those belonging to Indiana to take home, I took charge of the detachments as fast as they arrived. Sometimes I would receive a squad of a half dozen and later maybe fifteen or twenty. These had to be gathered in an assigned point where rations could be issued and the men cared for. After the war was over the Twelfth Indiana returned home from Washington on the same Forest Rose with the same captain in command. He very pleasantly remembered our former ride with him from Maysville to Cincinnati.

Martial law was in effect and every able-bodied citizen of Cincinnati was taken to Covington and set to work in the trenches building small-extemporized forts for the artillery. Many of the citizens, in consequence of the danger threatened by the advance of the Confederates went into this work willingly. Some of them even entered the work anxiously because they feared the enemy might capture the city. Those who went unwillingly were forced to do the same work. Military law is rigid and readily enforced by men with bayonets ready and willing to obey.

It must be remembered that the Confederate army under General Kirby Smith, then presumably marching on Cincinnati, was quite large in and of itself. At the same time General Don Carlos Buell, in command of the Union forces was falling back on Louisville, while General Braxton Bragg, was following him on parallel lines. General Buell reached Louisville about the time of the disaster at Richmond and prepared to defend that city. About two hundred of the Twelfth succeeded in making their escape from the Richmond battlefield and arrived at Lexington in time to join General Charles Cruft, who had been ordered to retreat from Lexington to Louisville.

The whole country was wildly excited when I left Cincinnati with a very large trainload of paroled prisoners. It was soon discovered that the militia had been called out at almost every station to guard the railroads in order to prevent the tracks being torn up by raids of rebel cavalry. Amongst the paroled prisoners to arrive at Cincinnati was Marsh H. Parks, of Warsaw, Indiana at the time a sergeant in F Company, who was sometime after promoted to adjutant of the Twelfth. I attached him and one or two others to myself while I was engaged in meeting and receiving the returning soldiers. It was a very difficult and tedious work to receive the homecoming members of the regiment. The command was so new that neither officers nor men knew one another and they arrived at all hours during the day and well into the night. To aid me in this matter, I sent six or eight men out on the railroad coming into Covington to gather up the members of my own regiment. These aids could only do so by asking everybody to what regiment they belonged. I can truthfully say that those four days were wearisome ones to me, and after I had gotten all of the men on board the train, ready to start for Indianapolis, I was almost broken down through sheer weariness and for want of sleep. Martial law was so rigid and so well enforced that one could not procure a glass of lemonade, could not even get shaved, or buy a cigar save in the office of hotels where boys were placed behind the stands. Every citizen of both cities was aiding in constructing earthwork defenses to prepare for whatever might come.

The paroled men were loaded in boxcars for the journey to Indianapolis. I had learned that a passenger train would leave Cincinnati a couple of hours after the paroled prisoners' train. I was so tired out that I at once determine to proceed with the train assigned me to conduct the men home and then stop off at Lawrenceburg and await the passenger train. I would take the passenger train to Indianapolis and should arrive an hour before the slow-going soldiers' train. I told Parks what I intended to do and directed him to remain with me. Unfortunately when we reached Lawrenceburg the train did not stop at the downtown depot but came to a halt nearly a half mile from the principal part of town. The conductor pointed out to us the proper direction to walk, and told us to follow back on the railroad for a certain distance and then turn right.

The night was exceedingly dark, although there were a few lamps at long distances apart that gave just about sufficient light to make the road more difficult than it would have been if it had been without any lamps. We were getting along the best we could, taking an occasional stumble, when all at once the cry of "Halt!" rang out right in front of us. We obeyed the order at once and could readily perceive that the sentinel was a greenhorn at the business, for instead of directing one of us to come forward and give the countersign, he was at a loss what to do. I told him I would come to him and explain who and what we were. I approached him and informed him that we were paroled prisoners bound for Indianapolis. This was satisfactory to him and he told us where we could find a hotel. When we bade him goodnight he pulled out a flask of whisky and wanted both of us to drink with him. He belonged to the militia regiment of that section of the State, which had charge of guarding quite a length of railroad. It can readily be perceived that railroads would be as safe from a rebel raid without any guard as they would be with a guard such as he. It was always found unsafe for guards to be supplied with whisky.

On reaching the hotel, we found the office floor fairly covered with men lying flat upon it, some with blankets under them and some without. Among these we also found some Union soldiers who had been in the battle at Richmond. They had crossed the Ohio River below Cincinnati and had reached this place by trudging every mile of the way on foot. They had failed to go to Cincinnati and consequently knew nothing about the arrangement to carry them back to Indianapolis by rail. I told them of our own arrangement to take the passenger train and that I would make the effort to get them to Indianapolis. Parks and myself stayed at the hotel awaiting the train and learned that it had been delayed for some unknown reason. The hotel was so crowded that our attempt to get a couple hours of much needed rest was a flat failure.

In his wisdom, Governor Morton had very wisely organized the militia of all the border counties that were most interested in preventing raids across the river, but in time it included nearly all of the counties in that section. At times the organization proved quite effective, too, and especially it assisted in holding in check the home opposition to the war.

We finally were able to board our passenger train and arrived at Indianapolis about one o'clock, coming in only a few minutes ahead of the soldier's train. Parks and myself were there ready to receive the homecoming members of the regiment. I had telegraphed the authorities at Indianapolis that the troops would reach the capital early in the morning and consequently there were officers at the station to notify us what to do. The officers conducted the entire party out to Camp Morton, where quarters had been assigned. We were to go into camp and await the exchange of prisoners.

I learned at Indianapolis that nearly two hundred of the Twelfth Regiment had made their escape to Lexington. They did so singly and in squads of two to four, and in small detachments of ten or twelve. They had continued their flight all of the night of the day following the battle. When they reached the city they came under the command of Brigadier General Charles R. Cruft. General Cruft had received orders to fall back on Louisville and the men of my regiment were included in and added to the force already there. The appearance of General Kirby Smith's cavalry in the vicinity of Lexington so hastened General Cruft's departure that he issued an order to destroy all of the army supplies that were gathered there. This included a great many army wagons, rations, clothing and supplies of all kinds required by an army.

In this great destruction, the stored trunks of many officers who were in the Richmond fight were also burned. Among these was my own trunk containing a full-dress uniform of the very finest of goods, and gold-plated buttons. I also had a brand new fatigue uniform that had never been worn. Worse of all was the loss of the very beautiful officer's sash. An estimate of the cash value of the trunk and contents made it over four hundred dollars.

I applied for a letter from Governor Morton for the transfer of the members of the Twelfth regiment who were at Louisville. I was well aware that this might be a difficult thing to do, for the men who escaped from the battlefield still owed their allegiance to the government and could be retained. I suggested to Governor Morton that in order to secure the transfer, a telegram from him to the Secretary of War would no doubt prove of great service, and so it did. Governor Morton was one of the governors upon whom the administration leaned very heavily, and always was sure of his support. So when I formally presented the request for the transfer of the men, the telegram had already been received from Washington by the officer in command at Louisville, instructing him to send the men of the Twelfth to Camp Morton and to provide for their transportation. After about two weeks, all of the members of the regiment, except the killed and wounded, were once more joined together.

From the time the regiment was once again together until an exchange was made early in November, company and battalion drills were performed as well as blank cartridge firing practices. The officers and men found these practices to be of great advantage to them during the future service the command was to render to the country. The regiment became very proficient in all the drills pertaining to the duties of a soldier. Blank cartridges were issued to us by the barrel. Although it required time and close practice, the entire command finally arrived at such a degree of proficiency that the whole regiment could and did respond to the order "to fire" as though it were but a single gun instead of eight hundred at once that had been exploded. Practice and drills were kept up for weeks and when the exchange of prisoners was arranged, it could be said without boasting that few regiments were more efficient in all of a soldier's duty. I received a letter from General William T. Sherman, written August 1863 at the cantonment known as "Camp Sherman" near Messenger's Ferry, over the Big Black River in Mississippi. After witnessing the regimental movements in battalion drill and on dress parade at the special invitation of General Hugh Ewing, Sherman wrote, " It is the best drilled volunteer regiment I have ever seen". He also complimented all of the regiment's officers and enlisted men very handsomely.

Time in Camp Morton passed slowly while we were on parole. Of course we were busy in learning the duties of soldiers. There was talk in the newspapers of a great "Castor-oil Expedition," that was to be undertaken shortly by the Western army. There was a great deal of guessing among the newspapers and the people as to what was meant by the "Castor-oil Expedition." At the time Vicksburg and Baton Rouge, both strong points on the Mississippi River, were held by the Confederacy. All at once some journalist pounced on the correct definition. Castor oil is known as an efficient physic and what could be clearer than a castor oil expedition meant that it was to "purge" the Mississippi or in other words, to clear the entire length of the river of every vestige of the Confederate army.

The best thing that could have happened to the Indiana Twelfth was the appointment of Rev. M. D. Gage, to the vacant chaplaincy of the regiment. Since the Twelfth regiment was quickly reorganized, hastily equipped, and rushed down as fast as cars could carry it to Richmond, Kentucky, where it met the disaster already described, no chaplain had been appointed. One morning while we were awaiting exchange, the appointment of Rev. Gage was announced in the papers. He was at the time a sergeant in the Eighty-ninth Indiana Infantry and by entering the service had already given proof of his loyalty to the cause and his willingness to personally help save the Union from destruction. To most of the officers and enlisted men he was a stranger at the time. I undertake to say, without any fear of truthful contradiction, that he was the best and most efficient man of his rank in all the Western army. That sounds like high praise, but every surviving member of the regiment will, I know, attest to its truthfulness, as would all those who have passed "over the river", were they still on this side of the dark waters to make themselves heard. I want to repeat that the luckiest thing that came to the Twelfth while waiting for our exchange was the appointing of Rev. M. D. Gage as chaplain and sending him to us in that capacity by Governor O. P. Morton.

In the days of the Civil War the duties of the chaplain were scantly defined, either in regulations or otherwise. I presume such a blunder has been amended in the army of today. The Chaplain roamed "at will," in most regiments. In the absence of prescribed duties, men like Rev. M.D. Gage found much to do and to do it well, too. He generally made his headquarters at the hospital, if we were in camp, where he could be of service to the sick, the wounded, the disabled, and minister to their wants. He took charge of the mails, sent letters back to "God's country," as the boys very generally designated their home, wrote the letters for those who could not do so, taught soldiers how to write, saw to sending soldiers' money home to their father, mother, or "dearer one still," and became the all-in-all of the soldiers of the regiment. At the close of the Atlanta campaign he carried a very large sum of money home well sewed up in a belt with every package marked properly so that when he reached the express office at Louisville, he could send them to the points directed by the owners. If I remember correctly, there was twenty-five thousand in the belt, a big inducement should anyone not be in possession of the strictest honesty.

There was one feature connected with our stay in Camp Morton that gave me considerable trouble and much uneasiness. In the haste of filling up all of the regiments that had been recruited during the summer and fall, many boys were enlisted who were under the age of eighteen. They had made the statement to the mustering officer that they were over that age. Upon the return of the Twelfth to Camp Morton from the disastrous field of Richmond, Kentucky, members of the party that opposed the war would hold out the inducement to these young men to free themselves from further service because they were underage. Two young men who had been paroled had succeeded in getting out of the army, an attorney having been furnished to attend to the legal features of the case at the expense of and in the employment of the "opposition to the war party."

I had all the captains of the companies furnish me a report of the number of men in each company that might be under the age of eighteen. I found it would decrease the aggregate number of men in the entire regiment nearly a full hundred. That same night, while I was in Indianapolis, I called the attention of Colonel Dick Ryan to this condition of my regiment, and I told him that agents were sowing discord among these young men. He was a good lawyer and either was at that time or shortly afterwards became the Lieutenant-Colonel of what was known as the Thirty-fifth Indiana Infantry or "The Irish Regiment." Colonel Ryan informed me that he would take the subject under consideration and I should hear from him the next day. At about ten o'clock the next morning, Colonel Ryan called at my headquarters and told me he had hit upon a plan that he was sure would work. He had already provided himself with the blank form of a letter he proposed to have me sign as commanding officer of the regiment to be sent by mail to the parents of every young man who attempted to try such a dodge to escape the service. In brief the letter was a threat to the parents to commence suit against such as undertook the "dodge" they were put up to by outsiders for obtaining money and property under false pretenses. The government, in 1862, paid a bonus of twenty-five dollars to each soldier as soon as he was mustered into the service, and he received a new suit of clothes valued at about twenty dollars. The young men acquired this property and money because they had falsely represented themselves as being over eighteen.

If my memory serves me correctly, there were only two more applications for release, and one of these had been made on the very day Colonel Ryan hit upon the plan to brake up the scheme. Copies of the letters referred to were sent to the boys' parents and a hurried reply came back that their son would and should remain in the service. The story and the words of the parents were purposely circulated all over the regiment. Throughout the camp not another attempt to get out of the service on such an excuse was tried. A trap was laid to catch the agents who were engaged in sowing the seeds of discontent into the regiment. Two of the agents were pointed out by one of the young men who had been tampered with, and they only escaped being ridden out of camp on a rail by the "skin of their teeth." They disturbed the command no more. I have often thought that the ruse originated by Colonel Ryan came just in time. And though perhaps not legal in form, there was justice behind it and it worked out admirably, which ended the uneasiness I had entertained for several weeks previous.

On the morning of the 17th day of November 1862, the daily newspapers of the country announced a general exchange of prisoners and everyone affected rejoiced. Now there was a chance to become part of the "caster-oil expedition." The excitement in the camp and all over Indianapolis was great. While there was no general order on the subject, the government of the prisoners in Camp Morton had been most liberal. The Twelfth had been hastened to the front by the invasion of General Kirby Smith, and in consequence many men left for the front with their families not well provided for. The authorities were quite liberal in giving the paroled soldiers short leaves of absence to revisit their homes so they could make preparations for longer absences. Therefore, when the announcement of a general exchange was made public, quite a large number of the members of the regiment were at their homes.

CHAPTER 6

Incident at Holly Springs

> The oppressed of the earth to that standard shall fly,
>   Wherever its folds shall be spread.
> And the exile shall feel 'tis his own native sky,
>   Where its stars shall wave o'er his head;
> And those stars shall increase till the fullness of time
>   Its millions of cycles have run—
> Till the world shall have welcomed their mission sublime,
>   And the nations of earth shall be one!
>   —George E. Cutter

The order to march so quickly followed the news of the exchange that something over a hundred enlisted men and eight or ten officers had not even time to get back to their command. I had been at my home and when I reached Indianapolis, I found that I was twenty-four hours behind time. All of the officers and men, who found themselves in a similar predicament, were gathered together to take a train over the same route the regiment had. We hoped to overtake the main train by the time it reached Cairo, Illinois, or at any rate before the regiment took the boat from there to Memphis.

The train we had taken to Cairo went no farther than Mattoon, Illinois, so the party had a lengthy wait at Mattoon for a train from Chicago. The place was already becoming known as hostile to the government and it was unfortunate that a big anti-war meeting was to be held that day. I say unfortunate for the reason that Captain Conner and myself, along with two or three others missed the train, which the others took to their destination. The landlord with whom we stopped was a prominent Union man, decidedly outspoken and very free in his comments about those who were acting treacherously to their country. He was telling Captain Conner and myself that threats had been made to attack his hotel on that day and he urged us so strongly to assist him that the train we should have taken slipped away without our knowledge. While Captain Conner and myself were chagrined over the fact that we had missed the train, the landlord was overjoyed. His place had been attacked once before and he was glad for the additional help in his defense during the time we were waiting for our train.

The landlord had made provision against being attacked again by procuring quite a large number of condemned muskets from Springfield. He insisted on Captain Conner and myself taking charge of the men he would, could, and did muster for the purpose. He could place about twenty men at twenty different windows, which would make a stout defense of his house. Fortunately while there was considerable derisive hooting at the old man by the wagonloads of men as they went by on their way to the anti-war meeting, no attack was made. The old gentleman afterwards wrote me that he was real sorry that the anti-war men had got word of the preparations he had made for the defense of his hotel. He closed his note by saying that because he was so well prepared to receive them, he regretted that they found out, for if there had been an attack "those with whole bodies would not have been that way afterward." We left the old Union man's place about six hours later than the remainder of the party, but caught up with them awaiting the arrival of a steamboat to carry us to Memphis. . I still remember a number of the officers who accompanied the belated party: Captain Rooker, of Company E, Lieutenant Lenfestey, of C, Captain John B. Conner, who was the founder and publisher of the Indiana Farmer at Indianapolis.

Cairo was a most important town for it is at the confluence of the Ohio and the Mississippi Rivers. As the business part of the town lies from ten to fifteen feet below the level of both of these rivers, substantial levies are required to keep the whole town from being flooded. For a time during the war, the Confederates were arranging to capture the town for the sake of the supplies that were gathered there. Clear through the war it maintained its importance and the town improved to such an extent that at the close of the war it was a thriving city of several thousand people.

We finally got away from Cairo with the hope of rejoining the regiment at Memphis. The trip took us past Columbus, Kentucky, a point that the Confederates had strongly fortified at the beginning of the war. We also passed another strongly fortified place on the east shore of the Mississippi River, Fort Pillow. We reached Memphis in due time only to ascertain that the command which we were so anxious to join had already left with about thirty thousand men under General William T. Sherman. The army was to act as General Grant's right wing in the advance Grant was already making direct from Holly Springs where a large amount of supplies and ammunition were collected. The intention was to close in on Vicksburg from the east and attack that strongly fortified point from the rear. General Washburn, who was in command of Memphis and Fort Pickering, could not be induced to permit our party to take up the line of march followed by the main body that had left two days before our arrival. He declared we could not get a half dozen miles out of the city ere we would be surrounded and perhaps captured by guerrillas. It was out of his power to give us an escort, as his forces had been stripped of all its cavalry.

General Chalmers was the head of a body of troops, which northern soldiers always designated as guerrillas because they generally operated independently of the main body of their forces. After the passage of

Sherman's troops through the territory covered by General Chalmer's Confederates, they had become more and more vigilant. They had captured many soldiers, who, like ourselves, were making an effort to catch up with the main body under Sherman. General Washburn declared that if he permitted us to follow up the rear of General Sherman we would again be captured to "a dead certainty." He also told us that the only thing for us to do was to take a return steamboat back to Columbus, where we could take the cars from there to Holly Springs and from thence join our respective regiments. It must be remembered that many officers and soldiers at Memphis belonged to other regiments and were in the same dilemma as we were. Since the boat and railroad lines were operated by the government, General Washburn furnished us with transportation back to Columbus on a boat and also provided transportation over the railroad.

The city of Memphis stands on a high bluff overlooking the Mississippi River. When Memphis was captured by the Union forces some of its citizens won the ill-will of our soldiers engaged in the fight by shooting soldiers who were endeavoring to swim ashore from a wrecked gunboat. Several men were shot through the head as they tried to reach to the shores from the burning wreck. As a consequence, for a time, the officers had to keep a constant lookout to prevent some of our men from retaliating.

After two days, a steamboat arrived and took us to Columbus, Kentucky where we obtained a train going in the proper direction. Guard troops were scattered all along the railroad line and the greatest of vigilance was required to keep the rails intact as squads of rebel cavalry were constantly trying to destroy culverts and bridges. When we reached Holly Springs, I learned that the Twelfth was at a place called Wyatt Bridge, which was an important crossing of the Tallahatchie River. The paroled members of the Twelfth had to walk about fifteen miles to join the regiment. The bridge at Wyatt was built by General Sherman's Engineer Corps. Most of the troops under his command crossed the Tallahatchie while my regiment had been left there to guard the bridge. The rest of the troops under Sherman proceeded southward and joined General Grant's forces near Oxford, Mississippi.

I received orders to abandon Wyatt and march to the point where the railroad leading from Holly Springs to Oxford crossed the Tallahatchie. Large amounts of supplies and ammunition were stored at Holly Springs and I had orders to draw rations from Holly Springs, which was located twenty miles north of the bridge I was guarding. We had arrived at the bridge without any supplies whatsoever and it became necessary to procure rations at once. Quartermaster McClellan was sent to Holly Springs as soon as we arrived at the railway bridge for rations. In the meantime, the Twelfth was subsisting on what the men could find in the vicinity of the camp.

The quartermaster returned from Holly Springs with word from Colonel Marsh, who was Colonel of the Eighth Wisconsin, the old "Eagle" regiment, that he would issue no rations to my command having had no orders to that effect from any superior officer. Of course, the Twelfth was considerably "worked-up" over the failure to procure supplies. I wrote a note to Colonel Marsh explaining the situation and sent the quartermaster a second time to Holly Springs with a copy of my order to draw supplies from there. The regiment was short and getting shorter of rations. Some of the foragers had come in with several hogs they had found in the Tallahatchie "bottoms" and also a couple of wild deer had been killed and brought in, but the supply of everything else had been used up. Things were getting desperate and I concluded to accompany Quartermaster McClellan on his third trip, fully aware of the fact that there was more power in a shoulder strap with an eagle in the center than there was one with a single bar at the end.

I reasoned with Colonel Marsh, explaining that my men were about at the starvation level and that it was folly for him to stand on the military quibble that he "had no orders to issue rations to my command." I showed him my own order to procure rations through him and finally he turned to his adjutant general and told him to issue five days' supplies for the Twelfth Indiana Infantry. So the quartermaster and myself went to the supply depot and procured wagons to haul the rations to the railroad station. After several hours of vigorous labor we had five cars filled and were ready to start for the bridge at seven o'clock the following morning. By the time this was done it was quite late in the afternoon and we began to look around for a place to get supper and to stay the night.

We were directed to a boarding house kept by a Methodist exhorter with whom quite a number of officers and sutlers had found superior quarters. Both of us were tired and worn out by the worry we had exercised in procuring the rations and seeing to the loading of the cars; consequently we went to bed early. We were aroused by the vicious snapping of small arms right in the streets near our boarding house. We both rushed to the front door to take a look at what was going on and found it was the first onset of Van Dorn's raid. The town was full of Confederate cavalrymen, who had charged on the gallop right into the town.

Right here occurred one of the saddest incidents I saw during the entire war. Quartermaster McClellan and myself had stepped out on the portico, so common to the residences in the South, to obtain a better view of what was going on, when bright little girl, with curly hair and handsome as a picture, pushed her beautiful face right between us, and she, too, gazed up the street. As she peeped uptown, she received a bullet almost squarely in the forehead. I felt her little hand clutch my coat and only when she pulled on it so heavily, did I know that she had been hit by the messenger intended, no doubt, for McClellan or myself. She was dead when I carried her to a lounge in the front room, and I shall never forget the scene when the mother and father knew that their little one was a victim of Van Dorn's raid. The picture of that scene in all its horrors comes before me even now at times, after the lapse of forty years.

It was afterward known that Colonel Marsh, as commander of the post, had received a telegram from General Grant at eight o'clock the night before warning him that he might expect a raid on Holly Springs. Van Dorn, with a large mounted force, had been reported by scouts as planning to make a dash on the railroads and supplies to the rear of Grant. Colonel Marsh was advised to keep a vigilant lookout for Van Dorn, as he was sure to strike at a point where there were so much munitions stored. Had the quartermaster and myself only known of that dispatch we would have escaped the great disaster. All that Colonel Marsh did to keep a vigilant outlook was to order two companies of cavalry under saddle by four o'clock the next morning to scout all the roads leading into Holly Springs. These two companies, being awake and their horses under saddle, were all that escaped from the town. Everyone else was taken prisoner.

When it is known that there were over a thousand bales of cotton in the public square or near it; that Colonel Marsh had information concerning the raid not less than seven hours before it occurred; that there were fifteen hundred infantry at hand, it was astounding that he made no preparation to meet the enemy. The four street corners could have been most effectually barricaded with cotton bales; the infantry could have assembled there and a defense of the place could easily have been made. The place certainly could have been held until General Grant sent relief. The effect of the whole thing was to compel General Grant to fall back upon Holly Springs from Oxford on his way to the rear of Vicksburg, causing him to abandon his whole plan of campaign by that route.

I saw Grant himself when late in the evening he arrived at Holly Springs. Although I had only seen him two or three times before, it did not take a physiognomist to tell by looking at his face that somebody's head was going to be cut off in a military sense. That evening the word went round among the soldiers and the people on the streets that Colonel Marsh was under arrest. I afterward heard that he was dismissed from the service, but events were occurring so rapidly that I never learned what really did become of him.

The rebel forces nearly all day long occupied the place. The town was set on fire several times and the ammunition that was stored in the brick buildings discharged itself until well into the evening. The destruction of private property as well as that of the government must have been way up in the thousands. Many of the sutlers whose goods were in Holly Springs lost everything. In addition to their goods, the Confederate private soldiers "made no bones" about robbing any one of the sutlers they came across. I remember seeing a Mr. Lash, then a resident of Goshen, Indiana, being compelled to shell out his money at the point of the bayonet. It was a large sum, over five thousand dollars that was taken from him.

During the day a Confederate officer with ample assistance was engaged in paroling the Federal troops. I remember that all at once something occurred that stampeded their party and caused almost a panic among the Confederate soldiers still occupying the town—the vanguard of Grant's troops was coming to the relief of the garrison. As the Federals marched into the place from the South, the Confederate raiders went flying out the North and East as fast as their horses could carry them.

The raid on Holly Springs was a great disaster, not so much in the loss sustained, but in the destruction of Grant's supplies causing an entire change in the apparently feasible campaign of attacking Vicksburg from the rear. The capture of myself and the quartermaster was only another of the many thousand of little things that can measure large results. The stubbornness of Colonel Marsh in refusing to honor my requisition for rations twice in succession had made it necessary for me to go along with the quartermaster to present the facts to Colonel Marsh, which lead to my capture. I had no business in Holly Springs; in fact, being in charge of a very important bridge over which all of General Grant's supplies must be taken in the campaign required me to be exceedingly attentive, vigilant and watchful. Of course, my place was with the troops guarding the crossing of the Tallahatchie River. For five days the regiment had not drawn a single ration from the government and had consumed everything within a safe distance of the camp, so that there was nothing left for me to do but go in person and obtain supplies if at all in my power.

It was these days of quibbling that had made me a prisoner for the third time. I would not have been within twenty miles of Holly Springs at the time of Van Dorn's raid if it had not been for Colonel Marsh refusing to comply with my order to issue rations to my regiment. On the other hand, had he let his officers know at eight o'clock the night before that he had received the dispatch announcing the raid, Quartermaster McClellan and myself and a number of others, who, like ourselves, were only temporarily in Holly Springs, all of us could have escaped. So here I was a prisoner for the third time. In all my life, looking back to that incident, I can truthfully aver that I was stricken with the worst case of blues that I have ever experienced. It seemed to me as though I were "hoodooed." I had met the enemy in the field three times and on each occasion I had been captured. I brooded over the subject to such an extent that I had fully determined to resign the position I held just as soon as I could reach a point where my papers could be forwarded.

The next day I was again called upon to perform a most disagreeable duty. When I left the railroad bridge over the Tallahatchie, of course the regiment would be left under the command of Lieutenant Colonel Kempton with whom I had made the journey from Richmond, Kentucky to

Cincinnati. The day following the parole Lieutenant Colonel Kempton found me on the dilapidated streets of the town. He had come from the bridge on horseback, leaving the regiment under the command of Major James H. Goodnow. From his story I learned that some of the flankers of General Van Dorn's raid had made their appearance in the vicinity of the bridge that the Twelfth was guarding. According to Kempton's account, immediately following this driving off of Van Doran's troopers, charges were preferred against him and forwarded to General Grant's headquarters signed by all the officers, except for Company G, Kempton's home company. Kempton's business with me was to have the charges suppressed as soon as they reached their destination. It was a sort of duty that above all others I disliked to undertake under the circumstances. I was also well aware that it was no time to ask favors of the command officer of an army that had been compelled to retreat owing to the neglect of officers to care for his rear, which had disastrous results. Under the circumstances, as well as to my own depressed feelings caused by being again captured through the quibbles of the same officer who would not issue rations to my regiment, I declared I could not comply with Kempton's request. With tears in his eyes he urged me to do him the favor and he pleaded so persistently, stating that it meant dismissal from the service if he was tried for the charges preferred that I at last acceded to the request so piteously made.

I went to Grant's headquarters for a personal interview. An orderly conducted me to the General's room and I broached the subject as soon as I could. It was the first time I had ever spoken to the General in command of all the forces in that region, and I readily admit that I was considerably frustrated not only at being in his presence, but on account of Kempton's charge of "disobedience of orders." I told him the situation of my own capture, and at his own interrogations and cross questionings related the incidents of Van Dorn's raid to the extent that it came under my own observation. When I told him about the charges preferred against Kempton, he listened sharply. I was convinced, as I had told Colonel Kempton, it was the wrong time to plead for an officer under charges of "disobedience of orders" and a breach of discipline. When I got through Grant said, "Very well, Colonel Williams, you can inform Lieutenant Colonel Kempton that when the charges reach headquarters, they will take the usual regular course." That of course meant a court-martial. I could not tell Grant what had had occurred while I was absent from the regiment but I informed him that Colonel Kempton was in town and hoped that I could receive a promise that the charges could be held until a fuller investigation of the case. I added on my own account that I had also hoped that Colonel Kempton could be left in command of the regiment since I had been paroled the day before. I informed General Grant that the major who would succeed the command if Kempton was held under arrest had no experience in military matters while Colonel Kempton and myself had had over a year's service in the Army of the Potomac.

"What's that?" Grant said. "Did you say he had a year's experience during the present war?" "Yes, sir," I replied, "and while the present major is an excellent man, he has only seen about three months of service." "Well," he replied, "you can go back and tell Colonel Kempton that the charges will be held here at these headquarters, but also inform him that I shall expect of him during your absence the strictest obedience to orders, and a divorce between all his soldiers and an article that is ruining many excellent officers, as you can perceive by looking at the dilapidation visible in this once handsome town." Grant took that sly way to have me warn Kempton against indulging in "the article (alcohol), as well as to hint that Colonel Marsh was guilty of the same thing. That, at least, was the interpretation I placed on his remarks.

When I rode back to where I had left Colonel Kempton—I had used his horse to ride to Grant's quarters—and informed him of the success of my mission, he was overjoyed. He was so elated that I at once suspected he intended to revenge himself on every one of the officers who had signed the charges against him. On the strength of the suspicion, I exacted a sacred promise from him to do nothing of the kind during my absence, and he solemnly declared nothing of that sort should occur. He was very grateful to me, in words, at any rate, at the time, but I left with a well-defined suspicion that some of the officers who had signed the charges would be made to feel the effects in the course of time. I believe his gratitude to me was genuine for I was informed on my return to the regiment after about three months' absence that every charge and specification made against him could have been proven by many witnesses, then nothing could have saved his being dismissed from the service.

The next day all the paroled prisoners were assembled in the public square of the town preparatory to marching to Memphis, where they would find transportation to the North to await another exchange of prisoners. A full division of Grant's troops under the command of Brigadier General Quimby was to accompany the paroled men and officers to Fort Pickering. The arrival of the large body of troops at the Fort created a sort of disorder and a couple of days were consumed in arranging men and officers' quarters. The second day was just drawing to a close and I had procured stationery for the purpose of writing my resignation, when an orderly rode up to the front of the quarters occupied by myself and asked if I was Colonel Reub Williams. Receiving an answer in the affirmative, he handed me an army regulation envelope. I tore off the receipt on the cover and handed it to him. He bid me good evening and departed. On perusing the enclosed I found it to be an order signed by General Ashboth, the commander of Fort Pickering, putting me in charge of nine steamboats on which I was to take the paroled prisoners consisting of about eighteen hundred men and officers to Benton Barracks, located at St. Louis, Missouri. Right then and there I had to settle the question whether I would send in my resignation or obey the order to take a fleet of steamboats to St. Louis.

I was never more surprised during the war than in receiving this order, and right then I decided to defer the sending forward of my resignation until after I had complied with the order to take command of the fleet of steamboats. Had I known in advance of the great responsibilities I had assumed, I would have declined and allowed someone else to take the duty, if at all possible. This did not enter my head at the time for it was the duty of officers or soldiers to obey and strictly obey any and all orders they may receive.

The period was the gloomiest that the North knew during the entire war. There had been many mishaps during the few months preceding and there was a wide spirit of opposition not only among the people at home but also among the soldiery in the field to the arming of the Negro and permitting him, as President Lincoln wisely said, to fight for his own freedom. Looking back after forty years the great wisdom of President Lincoln in this matter can readily be perceived. It should be remembered that about as fast as "Abraham journeyed southward," great bodies of colored people came within the lines of the Federal army, and after doing so it became necessary to feed and clothe them whether they rendered a quid pro quo or not. That wise man at the head of the nation proposed to arm them and let them perform military duty by guarding the forts and fortified points, as well as to make pioneer corps out of them to build corduroys, bridges, etc.

The proposition however created no little dissatisfaction at first. Nine companies of an Illinois regiment grew so angry over the arming of the Negro that they went over to the enemy, bag and baggage, ammunition and property of every kind. Only Company K remained faithful to their colors and their oaths. But in a short time the good sense of the American soldier sanctioned the measure. And, especially after some of the colored troops, led by white officers, acquitted themselves so creditably in battle, support grew for the colored troops. The storming of Fort Wagner in Charleston harbor, at Milliken's Bend, where they helped to add to the glory of July 4, 1863, by soundly whipping the Confederate army of eight thousand men under General Marmaduke, and won a great victory to add to Gettysburg and Vicksburg, added to their acceptance.

I began my preparation for the fleet of nine steamers, big and little, which was required to return the paroled prisoners of Holly Springs to their respective rendezvous in the North. These consisted of about eighteen hundred men, but there were fully that many more of a miscellaneous sort composed of discharged and furloughed soldiers, officers going home on leave, others on orders transferring them to other portions of the army. It had been estimated by those who knew the length of time it would require to go from Memphis to St. Louis that it would take seven days at the most, and so supplies were drawn for that many days. Besides the rations, a large amount of forage was required for there were fully a hundred head of horses scattered all over the fleet belonging to officers that had to be cared for.

When I went on board of the particular boat that was to be my headquarters during the journey, I honestly believe that every man, who was not opposed in his heart to drinking, had already imbibed a sufficient amount of intoxicants. This state either compelled him to show up his more brutal instincts or to excite his risibilities to a degree that made him obnoxious in his familiarity and to excite mirth in his comrades. I at once ordered the captain of the boat to close his saloon. Since similar conditions prevailed on all the other boats, I got a couple of rowers and a small boat to take me to every vessel comprising the fleet and delivered the same order to each captain.

There was no armed force on any of the nine boats to assist in enforcing orders. I was totally alone for there was not a soul on board with whom I had any acquaintance. Even the officers, especially those, who had been paroled, did not render a particle of assistance in keeping and preserving order. In fact, for thirty-six hours, if the majority of officers did anything, it was to promote the disorder. Of course, I could only be on board one of the boats at a time, but I had also taken the precaution to appoint one officer to take charge of the men on each particular boat. I cautioned the officer to do the very best he could and to surround himself with a number of other officers to assist so far as moral suasion could do in preserving order. This was a very essential matter for on the Missouri side of the river, there were numerous bands of guerrillas that were stationed at points where the channel of the river compelled all boats to come near the river bank on that side, thus making it an easy matter to pick off men with individual shots, or to fire a sweeping volley.

For the first thirty-six or forty-eight hours pandemonium reigned. Discipline counted for nothing. A dozen different men at various times threatened to throw me overboard, and it sometimes looked as if they intended to do so. On the third day a number of officers, perceiving the difficulties under which I labored, one by one, came to my assistance and rendered whatever aid they could under the demoralized condition that prevailed. The fourth day, the disorderly ones themselves began to feel ashamed of the course they had pursued, as well as from the fact that the supply of whisky had given out, and a better order prevailed from that time forward. But the first three days was an ordeal for me through which I would not willingly pass again for much money.

The water in the Missouri was low and on two occasions two of the larger boats grounded and stuck so fast that it was impossible to pull them off the bar with another vessel using a towline. Both of them were relieved from this position by bringing up other boats to their sides and having all of the men transfer themselves temporarily to these. Thus lightened and with the assistance of the towline they were pulled off the bar. The fleet had just gotten into line in mid-stream when we discovered a body of cavalry hastening to the point where the boats had been stuck. This incident, I am confident, very much helped to restore at least a portion of the discipline without which a body of men becomes a mob. The enlisted men on board began to get it through their heads that it was better to obey orders and they saw that without authority there was great danger that the voyage might end in disaster.

It was during the "lightening" of the two boats that I took occasion to visit all of the officers I had appointed at the start to see how they were getting along in the management of unarmed and unruly men. After receiving the respective reports of the eight officers, I was satisfied that we had fared just as well on board of the headquarters boat, for every one of the eight declared that they would not go through another scene of the kind again. One officer declared that he had been twice seized to be thrown overboard and would have been, had it not been for a sergeant and two men coming to his assistance.

The day following the "lightening" of the stranded boat, a big company of guerrillas had gathered at a point where it was absolutely necessary for all of the boats to come near the Missouri bank. The sharp eyes of the pilot on the lead boat discovered the guerrillas in time to warn the men standing around on deck to seek cover. I have already referred to Company K, of the One Hundred and Ninth Illinois, as remaining true to its colors when the other nine deserted and went over to the enemy in a body. This company happened to be on the third boat in the line. As the vessel came up to run the gauntlet, its captain, having had time to discover the guerrillas and to see that something "was in the wind," had ordered his men to the upper deck and placed them behind all sorts of barricades. They delivered a volley into the midst of the rebels as their boat passed. As I was on the lead boat, which had already passed the danger point, I could discern it was effective so far as wounded men were concerned, for I could see three or four struggling on the ground evidently severely wounded. Since it was very close range, it is very likely that several were killed outright. On every boat there were men and officers who had their revolvers with them, so that as each boat passed the spot, they took from a safe cover as many shots as their revolvers held. Only one man was injured and his wound was caused from a splinter being knocked into his face by the bullet from a guerrilla carbine striking the woodwork of the boat.

It had been estimated that the trip would require seven days but, owing to the many impediments cause by low water, the seven days were up when we reached Cairo, which was slightly more than half way. All our rations and forage were consumed with a big distance yet to go. There was nothing to do except stop in Cairo and draw supplies sufficient for the remainder of the trip. By taking to a small boat, I communicated with the captain of every one of the steamers as they came past my rowboat that was held in the stream by competent rowers. I had determined to take no risks by landing and giving the men a chance to go ashore and once more "bowl up" at the hundreds of saloons near the wharf. Therefore, I had cautioned the captains and directed them to anchor in mid-stream, as well as to collect the small boats on the forward deck so that the boats could be guarded to prevent the men from using them to go ashore. This done, I landed, taking along with me three officers as assistants, and went to the headquarters. I made the situation known to the Brigadier General in command at Cairo, and unlike Colonel Marsh at Holly Springs, he did everything he could to assist me even though he had no orders to do so. It took about three hours to get the supplies required on board the steamboats, as they had to be drayed for nearly two miles.

I returned to the boats with the supplies only to find the men once again in an intoxicated state. I was angry as well as nonplussed as to the way in which the whisky had been obtained. I had noticed that the wharf was almost covered with barrels of whisky when I firs landed at Cairo, but it was late in December, ice was floating both in the Ohio and the Mississippi Rivers, surely no one had ventured ashore from boats anchored out in midstream! Yet that was precisely what had been done. The men had procured the whisky by swimming to the wharf and then floated several barrels to one of the boats in midstream where it was distributed in canteens, coffee pots, tin cups, etc. to all who desired any of the mischief-maker.

The surprise to me was very great. I had left peace and order on board and returned a little over three hours later to a rabble of intoxicated men. Many of them were already verging on the fighting stage, while others had passed it and had fallen to the floor so far gone that they neither knew or cared whether they were alive or not. It was there and then that I learned that when men were determined to possess themselves of whisky they could and would do it. The barrels were found and their contents, what was left, were poured into the Ohio River.

Within an hour after we had returned to the boat, we got things straightened up and the captain of the lead boat signaled the other eight to hoist anchor. We arrived in St. Louis three days later. We marched from the wharf out to Benton Barracks, where excellent quarters were assigned to the officers and men. I can truthfully say that I never felt more relieved in my life than when I procured a receipt giving the number of men that had been safely transferred from Memphis to Benton Barracks. During the twelve days trip, I had not slept a full hour at any one time, and had never felt safe for a single moment.

The next day after I turned over the paroled soldiers to the officers designated to receive them, I discovered an order at the headquarters of Benton Barracks—a standing order of the government of the camp and the disposition of those who arrive at the barracks, paroled, as my command had been—directing all officers not assigned to such duty as their parole permitted from Ohio or from Indiana, should report to Camp Chase, Ohio. I at once applied for transportation via Indianapolis to Columbus. When I reached Indianapolis, I stopped and with Governor Morton's assistance, procured at leave of absence allowing me to return to my home. I would await exchange there and in the meantime keep in touch with the commanding officer at Camp Chase through correspondence, so that I could at once be notified when an exchange of prisoners was made.

It had already been decided that an officer under parole, having only agreed not to take up arms against the Confederate State or to give information to the enemies of those States, could without violating the agreement put in his time in recruiting. On reaching home I received an order to that effect, and succeeded in enlisting many stalwart young men during my tedious stay at home. The whole number recruited was over fifty and during the entire war, I, at all times, had recruiting parties at home sending new men to take the place of those who were killed or had died from disease or discharged for disability. This is the reason why the muster-out roll at the close of the war, showed that the regiment had contained over fourteen hundred men.

The time during which I was waiting for an exchange was gloomy enough, and the disloyalty to the cause of the Union at home was not only discouraging, but also disheartening. There were many, many men here in this county openly and avowedly favoring the South. They were sometimes bold enough to avow their sentiment, though usually—except the outspoken ones—tried to deceive those whose heart were in the Union cause. I have fully a dozen letters in my possession now, written by fathers to their sons who were soldiers in my regiment, urging them to desert and come home, insuring that they would be protected in so doing by those who were opposed to "this damn abolition war." One young man—an excellent young fellow, but easily influenced by his father—decided to obey that father rather than the oath he had taken to aid in upholding his government and to assist in preventing the Union from being disserved. He was afterwards recaptured and on trial was sentenced to confinement in the Alton, Illinois penitentiary. I tried very hard to secure his release from the prison, on the promise that he would return to his command and faithfully fulfill the duties of a soldier, which he had sworn he would do, but he died before the effort made to secure his release was accomplished.

The boy, being an honest and upright young man, felt the disgrace to such an extent and grieved over his position so greatly that when he was taken ill, he grew rapidly worse and died in disgrace. I have often wondered what must have been the thoughts of the father who had induced a young, confiding son to commit so grave a crime, when the country was struggling for its very existence as a Nation.

CHAPTER 7

Playing Jokes on Grant and Sherman

How dear to our hearts are the days when we soldiered.
As fond recollections present them to view.
The long line of earth-works, the deep tangled thickets
And every rough spot that our army life knew;
The long parks of cannon with harness and saddles.
The picket-roped horses oft trying to roll.
The cook-house, the guard tent, the muskets stacked nigh it.
And the old coffee kettle that hung on a pole,
The sheet-iron kettle, the smutty old kettle,
The old coffee kettle that hung on a pole.
—War-Time Lyrics

The glad news, in the close of April 1863, came to all of us that an exchange had been effected for a large number of officers and enlisted men. I had been kept in touch with the regiment every few days by receiving letters from many of the men and officers belonging to the Twelfth, so that I was kept fairly well informed of what was going on within the command. I knew of its marches, its camps, and everything pertaining to what I have often designated as "a family." Of course I proposed to at once rejoin the regiment. It was stationed at a stockade that the regiment had named "Fort Loomis" after the brigade commander. The stockade was near Collierville, about thirty miles east of Memphis on the Charleston and Memphis railroad. It was at the same point where a few months later General Sherman and a portion of his staff came very near being captured, and would have had it not been for the valor of the Sixty-sixth Indiana Infantry assisted by a detachment of the Thirteenth Regulars. These two commands held the rebels off until reinforcements could be hastened to them from a point about six miles west of Collierville. It was a close call for the General, and I heard him say afterwards that it was the narrowest escape he had during the entire struggle unless it might have been from musket balls, the nearness of which he could only estimate by their singing.

I left Indianapolis the latter part of April 1863 headed for Memphis, Tennessee. The trip from Cairo to Memphis was quite tedious and, as luck would have it, a number of us took passage over a slow boat, although a very large one, the Maria Demming, a triple-decker. There were parties of guerrillas on the Missouri side of the Mississippi and we had to keep a sharp lookout when the current required us to closely hug the shore on that side of the river or to take on fuel. The fuel was stacked up in cordwood lengths and there would always be a man at the shore to ascertain whether the boat was in need of wood. Very generally the lookout at these wooding places was a Negro, but there would always be a white man present with whom to bargain for the wood. The wood was always green in consequence of the great demand by the government as whole fleets of steamboats were continually passing up and down stream. It is a wonder that we got along as fast as we did with the kind of combustible material with which to make steam.

I think we were six days in making the trip to Cairo. The party, which was to stop at Memphis along with myself, put up at the Gayoso House, an old but very popular hotel in ante-bellum days. Those of us, who were to go east on the Memphis and Charleston railroad, ascertained that we could not get away to our respective camps until the next day. We therefore put in the afternoon in strolling about the place revisiting and feeding the many squirrels in the small park in almost the center of the town. In the evening we attended the theater, where a celebrated star, Julia Daly, appeared in the leading role.

The next day, I left for "Fort Loomis," where my regiment was located. It did not take long to make the thirty-mile trip. I shall never forget the hearty and enthusiastic reception given me by the men on my return to them. Major Goodnow had the regiment drawn up in line and as I came into the stockade, I was almost deafened with the cheers that were given to me. The men had not seen me since the morning I had left at the Tallahatchie Railroad Bridge to seek rations for them at Holly Springs.

It will be remembered that I had suspected that Lieutenant Colonel Kempton, would on his return to the regiment "make it hot" for those who had signed the charges, and so he did. According to their story, he persecuted and belittled them in every possible way that would annoy them. They were so indignant at the way he had treated them during my absence, that a copy of the charges were dug up, recopied and filed at my headquarters the next morning. I tried to induce the officers not to do so, but they had been so humiliated while I was gone by the Lieutenant Colonel, that the presentation of the charges was insisted upon, and of course, I could not prevent the course pursued. Kempton was arrested, the charges forwarded, and the Lieutenant Colonel after a time was allowed to resign under charges "for the good of the service." I sympathized with Kempton greatly. He was a good officer and a bright man, but in reaching out for revenge in defiance of my suggestions to him, he over-reached himself, and was compelled to resign in partial disgrace. He died before the war was over, and as the charges could have been proven by many witnesses, perhaps it was better the way it turned out than to have been peremptorily dismissed from the army.

Previous to coming to camp at Fort Loomis, the regiment had been located at Grand Junction, one of the most unhealthy and disastrous stations the command occupied during the war. There was the prevalence of sickness among the men and a large number died during their stay. They had been removed from Grand Junction to Fort Loomis only a few weeks before my arrival. The change from a low, flat, wet camp to one so much its superior had produced a most revivifying effect upon the men. The gloom had hung over them like a pall, brought on by the loss of so many of their comrades, and the serious illness of so many more, so when I rejoined them they were just recovering their spirits and thoroughly enjoying camp life.

In the daily life of the regiment that I commanded, it was well understood that when on duty the very strictest discipline was to be maintained. And when the men were "off duty" a freedom from irksome restraints was carried to the limit. The regiment would go through prescribed drills every day that the weather permitted. This feature was greatly neglected by most of the other regiments, but as a consequence of keeping them up the Twelfth became the best drilled, disciplined and uniformed regiment the Fifteenth Corps contained.

"Fort Loomis," as it was nicknamed, was a stockade that was used in the war of 1812. During its occupancy it was the headquarters of the regiment, at which there was usually about six companies. The other four were scattered a few miles east and west of the stockade, each a mile or two apart. Among the general orders was one that forbade the passage of citizens through the camps on the line of the railroad. The order required all persons of this character to be brought to headquarters for examination. If the commanding officer discovered no reason why they should be detained, the individual could be given a pass.

The need for these strict orders can be well illustrated by the following incident that occurred soon after I had rejoined my command. It was a bright morning in the latter part of May that I discerned from my tent an old-fashioned barouche—a vehicle quite common among the wealthier people of the South previous to the war—in charge of a soldier approaching the camp. The barouche was drawn by two horses and even at some distance I could perceive that it contained an old man in the front seat who was acting as driver and an elderly woman and a younger woman in the seat behind. The guard halted the carriage in front of my tent and reported that his party desired to pass through the camp. As the old gentleman—he was probably very near seventy years of age and quite feeble—climbed out of the barouche, I could easily perceive that he was frustrated and nervous. I invited him into the tent. He came in quite slowly, and it was easy to see that he was considerably agitated. I thought this came from being stopped so frequently on his way out from Memphis, for if the different headquarters between Fort Loomis and Memphis had obeyed their orders he had been stopped at least three times before reaching my camp. He said to me that himself and the two women desired to go to Grenada, Mississippi, and when I asked him if he had procured permission to do so, or had a pass from headquarter to Memphis, to allow him to make the trip, he became more and more shaky.

"Let me see you privately," the old man said. I then directed the Sergeant Major, who was present, as was the guard to step outside. The old man very deliberately pulled a large pocketbook from his breast pocket. He very deliberately opened it and offered me a fifty-dollar greenback to permit him and the women to go on and also for me to give him a pass that would free his party from being similarly stopped as he had been. Immediately I placed the old gentleman under arrest and told him that both himself and the women would have to be sent straight back to Memphis under charges of attempted bribery. Both the old gentleman and the old lady came very near fainting, but the daughter undertook to plead with me to permit them to go on and join their relatives at their old home at Grenada. Of course, I refused. I told all three of them to be ready to take the train back to Memphis in about an hour and a half. "The team and barouche," I told him, "would follow the next day on the cars." The two old people came very near collapsing, and the incident goes very far to show how an officer in the position that I was in, is compelled to harden his heart when stern duty requires it. For aside from the bribe offered and the pleading and tears of the women, I deeply sympathized with them in the terrible position they found themselves.

After they had left camp under guard of an officer and two men, a close search of their carriage disclosed that the rear seat had been loosened and a small box placed beneath it then nailed shut again. This box was chock full of quinine and morphine bottles. There were over a hundred bottles of these articles of war contraband. Quinine and morphine rose to a fabulous price during the war in the Confederate States and could be procured by that side only with gold. The next day the barouche, horses, quinine and morphine were all sent to Memphis, accompanied by a full statement of the case. All of the party was confined in "Irving Block"—the place used by the United States government for a prison. The troops left Fort Loomis soon after this and I never heard what became of the case. The three were probably kept in durance for awhile and then released. I always wondered how the party reached Fort Loomis, if the heads of the three posts between mine and Memphis obeyed their orders. The question, of course, arose— did they accept a bribe?

Directly after this incident and quite suddenly, so far as the troops were concerned, an order was received from General William Sooy Smith to assemble the division for the purpose of going to Vicksburg to reinforce General Grant. The whole Confederate army of that part of the Confederacy, under the command of General Pemberton was cooped up by

Grant in Vicksburg. The town and its garrison was closely besieged, but as General Joseph E. Johnston, of the Confederate army, was approaching Grant's rear from Jackson, Mississippi, with a body of twenty-five thousand men, it was necessary that re-enforcements be sent to prevent a disaster. Therefore, nearly all of the troops in Southern Tennessee and Northern Mississippi were assembled at Memphis as quickly as it could be done. The brigade to whom the Twelfth was attached consisted of three additional regiments, the Twenty-sixth and the Ninetieth Illinois and the One Hundredth Indiana, all of them Infantry service.

This brigade assembled at Collierville, Tennessee, and there awaited the message that transportation had been provided. Consequently, on June 6th, word came that the necessary number of steamboats had assembled at Memphis. The troops intended for the expedition arrived in that city in time to take the steamers on the 9th of June 1863. Those who saw that flotilla of fourteen fine steamboats, either from the shore, or from one of the boats will never forget it. It was the regiment's usual good luck, with a little engineering on my own part, to secure passage on the "Belle Memphis," at the time one of the handsomest steamers on the Mississippi. We left the boat at the mouth of the Yazoo, just above Vicksburg in just as fine order as when the regiment first set foot upon its decks. A detail had been made a few hours previous to landing to "police" the boat from the pilothouse on the top down to the place on the lower deck occupied by the stevedores. The men were greatly complimented by both captain and crew of the boat, declaring that it was the only instance of the kind they had known since the war commenced.

Grant's lines touched the river both above and below Vicksburg, thus cooping up the thirty-three thousand confederates into the town as closely and as safely as though they were in an unbreakable jail. The reinforcements that arrived were intended to prevent General Joe E. Johnston from doing any damage to Grant's rear. These forces were landed a short distance up the Yazoo River and occupied both Snyder's and Haine's Bluffs. They were near where General Sherman had met with a severe rebuff at Chickasaw Bayou a few months previous. I remember the evening the troops disembarked the orders were given not to permit the enlisted men to bathe in the waters of the Yazoo. The Yazoo was a sluggish, malarious region and bathing in its waters was considered dangerous. In fact, the meaning of the term "Yazoo River" in the Indian language is "River of Death." In addition to being a health measure the order contained a warning that it was dangerous to enter the stream on account of the alligators that occupied the stream in large numbers. However, anyone who has been a soldier knows that there never was an order issued that there was not some soldier who would violate it, and such was the case in this instance.

I had the order read to the regiment at the first dress parade held after disembarking, and I presume that the heads of all the regiments did the same. About eight o'clock the next morning, I learned that a soldier from some Illinois regiment had not only disobeyed the order, but paid for his disobedience by the loss of a leg. In spite of the order, he and a few of his comrades had ventured into the stream and he barely swam a rod ere he felt one of his legs grabbed by an alligator. The amphibian was frightened away by his comrades, but the soldier's limb was so badly mutilated and injured that it had to be amputated. The poor young fellow found that to him the river was what its name signifies—river of death—for he died afterwards in a hospital.

The Brigade to which the Twelfth belonged remained in this vicinity for a few days and then was removed to a point called Oakridge. Lieutenant Colonel Heath, of the One Hundredth Indiana, then in command of the regiment during the Colonel's absence, and myself established our headquarters in a building that stood just off a public road, but surrounded by trees and a dense undergrowth, which was built for a Masonic Lodge. This was one of a number of such lodges I saw while in the South. They were all built high from the ground. This one especially stood upon posts about eight feet high so as to prevent anyone from prying upon whatever might be in progress inside. With the exception of a plantation home about a half-mile away, no other occupied house was near the lodge.

Colonel Heath was from Elkhart, Indiana and was always full of fun and ready for a tussle of any kind. I remember the first night that we occupied the building it was so warm and the mosquitoes so numerous that shortly after we lay down to sleep we got up and began walking around in our nightclothes and finally got into a wrestle. We approached one of the windows and by some hook or crook, but wholly by accident, I threw the Colonel out of the window. As it was an eight-foot fall, I lost no time in getting to his assistance. He was not injured further than that his limbs were fearfully scratched with briers, a bunch of which had prevented his fall from breaking his limbs. After we had lighted a couple candles so that we could see how bad his injuries were, we found his limbs streaming with blood from brier scratches but no further damage was done. But the Colonel never heard the last of the incident until he retired from the service, caused by a wound received at Missionary Ridge.

Our troops were quite idle, no doubt awaiting the course that the Confederate General Joe E. Johnston would pursue. It was well known that he was moving up from directly east of Vicksburg with the avowed purpose of attacking Grant in the rear. During those days of tedious waiting, Grant's army had received another reinforcement consisting of the Ninth, known as "Burnside's corps," the latter officer then being in command at Knoxville, Tennessee. The Ninth was then commanded by

General Park who was an excellent, competent officer. His coming put it in the power of Grant to turn on General Johnston and drive him east ward across the State of Mississippi or defeat him in the field, if he could be caught.

The days preceding the fall of Vicksburg were tedious to the troops and officers as well. The army was lying in loose order, not having gone into regular camps since the orders to march against Johnston were expected at any time. It was during this time of idleness that a soldier found an iron key at an abandoned and dilapidated old blacksmith shop. It was about the most awkward and ill-shaped specimen of handiwork one sees in a lifetime. It weighed considerably over a pound and was made by a Negro slave who had turned his hand to blacksmithing on a plantation. It was evidently intended for a big door key and was out of shape in every conceivable way.

The newspapers had been having much to say of the "Key to Vicksburg." One of the papers would have it that such a point was "the key" to the situation, while that of some other journal was just as emphatic in asserting that some other point was "the key". In fact, Northern newspapers had something to say about "the key to Vicksburg" almost every day. Major Baldwin, of the Twelfth, a well-informed and intelligent officer, was as thoroughgoing a wag as the regiment contained. Most regiments had many of these witty fellows who were found to be so valuable as the war progressed, in keeping up the spirits of a regiment or company. He was shown the homemade key by myself, and at once he conceived the idea of sending it to General Grant. Consequently he had it neatly made up in a package, using an official envelope and directed it to the "Commander-in-Chief of the Union Forces Surrounding Vicksburg." He had pasted a label on its long and wide stem, bearing the legend, "The Key to Vicksburg." The package went up through the regular channels, via brigade, division, and corps headquarters, and thus to its destination.

From an officer belonging to General Grant's headquarters, I afterward learned that Grant received it with a broad and appreciative grin when he perused the sentence pasted on the handle of the key. The entire staff enjoyed the joke to a great degree. The correspondents about headquarters thereafter were unmercifully twitted over the "Key to Vicksburg." Some of them, it was known to the staff officers, had used the expression several times in their respective journals. These were plagued to such an extent that one of them became quite restive under the constant "nagging" and complained to General Grant about it. The General only laughed at the jest.

This, however, was not the first jest of a similar nature that was played upon our commanding officers, for only about a week previously a soldier found an old shoe, such as were worn by the negro slaves in the Gulf States. These shoes were manufactured on a large scale at Boston, and were purchased at wholesale by planters of Mississippi preceding the war.

They were of very coarse leather, of a tan color, and the sole was of wood, sometimes oak and sometimes hickory. They were manufactured with the idea that they would be strong enough to last for years. I saw a number of that particular kind of shoe while in the vicinity of Vicksburg. This particular shoe was fourteen and a half inches in length and broad in proportion. In fact, it was its immense size that induced the soldier to bring it to my headquarters as a curiosity. And so it was, indeed, for when set upon the ground it took on the appearance of a canoe, with a "raise" in the stern.

When the Major saw it, he at once proposed to me to play a joke on General Sherman, and I entered into the spirit of the jest. He had it put into a package similar to that of the key already mentioned—this was the first joke of the kind we perpetrated. Right across the wooden bottom of the seven-inch-wide shoe the Major had pasted a label bearing the inscription, "The identical shoe worn by the foot that kicked Sherman off this bluff." As we were occupying, at the time, a bluff near Chickasaw Bayou where Sherman had met a severe repulse from the rebels a couple of months previously, the point to the joke can be readily seen. I was just a little suspicious that General Sherman might be a little touchy on the point, but I finally permitted it to go. A few days thereafter, when meeting one of Sherman's staff officers, I asked him how the General took the big-shoe joke. "Oh," said the officer, "the General laughed a little over it, but the staff fairly yelled with delight when they saw that Noah's ark of a shoe, and the duty it had been made to perform. "But," he said, "if I were you and Major Baldwin, I would never perpetrate a similar joke on the old gentleman," and we didn't.

Late in the afternoon of the third day of July the division received marching orders and it was to be an all night march. The skies were threatening and the indications pointed to a heavy rain, but a soldier never consults the weather, he only takes the kind that is sent. The rear of Vicksburg was made up of a succession of ridges with deep depressions between them to such an extent that it reminded me of an old-fashioned washboard. In forcing the Confederate army into Vicksburg, this sort of ground was very favorable to General Pemberton, as all of these ridges had to be taken one after the other. In some instances the tops of the ridges were tunneled, forming a covered way for teams to take ammunition to the besiegers and thus avoid the artillerists. On our side the artillerists grew to be very expert shots and I remember of hearing some of our soldiers grumbling at a gunner for putting a shot right through the face of the town clock that occupied a tall tower within the city of Vicksburg. They were particularly lamenting the fact for the reason that the infantry soldiers had become accustomed to change guard by the time kept by this clock.

Soon after the troops began their march, the storm that had been threatening burst upon the columns. I can truthfully say that neither before nor since have I ever witnessed a more fearful storm than the one that prevailed that night. There had been a drought preceding this storm, and the roads were dry and hard, so that at first the men trudged along in the rain in fairly good humor, as the night was hot and the falling rain was rather cooling. But as the storm continued it became frightful. The road led through a timbered region and after the first deluge of rain, a fearful wind followed. Trees were crashing and falling in every direction. The lightning was vivid and incessant. At times the lightening seemed to crackle along the ground right under the feet of the men. An occasional frightened horse, having run away from or thrown its rider, ran wildly through the troops. It its mad fright it would dash at headlong speed right into the moving ranks.

The deluge of rain was so great that all at once the head of the column came to a halt, and the entire body stood still. The ripping of timber and the fierce flashes of lightning seemed scarcely to have a moment's intermission between them. It was while the pealing and reverberations of this wild storm were at its height that some soldier, way up the head of the column, started up at he top of his voice that old army song of "John Brown's body lies moldering in the grave." It was caught up all along the line and within a few minutes it was taken up by five thousand voices. I can say that song was never before rendered with such an accompaniment of thunder, lightning, tempest and the crashing of falling trees as it was on the night of the third of July, 1863 in the rear of Vicksburg. The storm lasted for something over an hour, then weather cleared away and the moon showed its welcome face once more. The army took up its line of march, really refreshed by the drenching it had received.

The sick and disabled men of the various regiments had been left, when the march began, at the hospital that had been established on top of one of the numerous ridges already referred to, in a beautiful pine grove. The next morning we learned that it had suffered terribly from the effects of the storm. A pine tree had been blown over by the wind and fell across several of the tents killing several men outright and wounding some twenty-five others. Among the killed was Major Parrott, of Lagrange Indiana, a member of the One Hundredth Indiana, and a prominent citizen of that city. He was a noble, patriotic gentleman. I had made his acquaintance only since my return to the regiment, but had formed a warm attachment for him. He had hobbled out to the front of his tent to bid me good-bye as my regiment passed the hospital. I was greatly affected on hearing of his death so soon afterward. Such, however, was the life of a soldier! There is safety nowhere in wartimes, and thousands of men met their death by accident, instead of being killed in the forefront of battle.

The Ninetieth Illinois regiment of the same brigade to which the Twelfth belonged was composed wholly of Irishmen from the Colonel down to the smallest drummer-boy. Even their Chaplain was a priest from the "Old Sod." There had been a serious friction of some months' duration between Colonel Tim O'Meara and Captain Pat Flynn. The latter had just received a commission as Major of the regiment from Governor Yates. Colonel O'Meara was determined that Flynn should not be mustered into that position, and he could prevent it by withholding his signature to the papers required by the mustering officer. Of course, Flynn grew sulky and had refused to accompany the expedition we were then making unless it could be in the rank to which he had been promoted. The appointment being but recently received, the men in the regiment had not generally heard of it. Following the storm, I was riding at the rear of the Ninetieth regiment when one of the men said to a comrade.

"Jamie, did you know we hev a new Major?"

"I do not," said Jamie. "Who is the lucky man?"

"Pat Flynn," was the response.

"I don't know of a man that deserves the promotion more," said Jamie, "he minds his place so well in the rear!"

When the reader bears in mind that the proper place of the Major is in the rear of his regiment, and Pat Flynn was then thirty miles behind, the ready wit of Jamie can easily be perceived. Pat Flynn received his promotion, however, for Colonel O'Meara was killed at Missionary Ridge in the following November, thus removing all oppositions.

It was improbable that the Confederate army was fully aware of the reinforcement that had been hastened to Grant. The arrival of the Ninth corps enabled the Union commander to turn the tables on the Confederate forces, and to at once place them on the defensive. One of the reasons why the troops under General Sherman made the all-night march, was, if possible, to strike the confederate forces at the crossing of Big Black River. And this they did even before the Confederates had crossed that stream in any force. At the river, however, we met the enemy for the first time, and immediate preparations were made to cross the stream. This was along in the evening of July 4th, and a detachment from each regiment, my own included, effected a lodgment on the East Side. The men forded the stream by carrying their muskets high above their heads. They were in sufficient force to hold their position during the night, and the next morning the entire division crossed over and began the pursuit of the Confederates. The Union advance guard kept the Confederate rear guard on the go almost without cessation, although occasionally they would make a stand only to find themselves in danger of being flanked, which compelled them to continue to retreat or be in great danger of being captured. The main body of Johnston's army, I imagine, never ceased their rearward march until it reached the city of Jackson, the capital of the State of Mississippi, about thirty miles east of Vicksburg.

On the evening of the fifth, General Sherman had closed up to the suburbs of the city and with the exception of the East Side, soon afterward had his own army fairly well entrenched on the first line. In making such a movement the commanding officer of a regiment or a brigade is often sorely troubled in securing supplies. It is not to be expected that the servants in charge of the rations either could or should keep right up with a command that was in constant touch with the enemy. Such was my position the night the Federal forces closed in about Jackson. My regiment was on the front line, and the pursuit of the enemy had been so continuous all day that myself and those belonging to my headquarters had not a bite to eat. The order reached us just as the shades of night were falling that no fires should be built. That meant no coffee, the soldier's main dependence. Even at that early period of the war, and before it was over I came to the conclusion that coffee was the most sustaining article of all the rations issued by the government. When worn out with an all day march and constant skirmishing, more than all else, a tin of good, strong coffee did more to enliven a collapsed soldier. It put him in a condition to resume his march or to sustain more of his laborious work than all else he consumed, even though his haversack might be crammed with bacon, hardtack, beans, rice, and all that a full ration comprises.

None of the members of the headquarters mess had come to the officers, and as a consequence myself and all those about me, who usually partook of their rations at regimental headquarters, were in possession of not a bite to eat. It was a hungry crowd that at about ten o'clock that night, proposed to procure some rest, and rolled themselves in their blankets, immediately in the rear of the first line of infantry. Just as I was about to lie down, Henry Flowers, who enlisted at Etna Green, Indiana, came up from the rear and asked me if we had partaken of anything to eat. He had seen our headquarter servants about two miles in the rear and suspected that we had not eaten. On hearing that we had been dinner-less, he said he believed he could obtain some green corn and a tin full of coffee. He left and was gone for a full half-hour, but on his return he carried with him nearly a half-bushel of husked roasting ears and a camp kettle was swinging over his shoulders. To prepare the corn a fire was absolutely necessary, as we neither could nor dared to eat it raw. I told him about the order that no fire should be kindled, but he got around that by rigging three or four rubber blankets on stakes on the enemy's side and behind these he built a fire and boiled the corn, having first shaved the grain from the cob. When well cooked, he added a couple pounds of lard he had captured during the day and mixed it with the corn. On ascertaining that there was no salt for this mix, I went to one of the soldiers lying in the front line and he very willingly divided his supply with me.

This incident is related only to show those who have come upon the stage since the war the difficulty that even officers had to undergo in emergencies, for it must be remembered that at no time during the war were rations issued to commissioned officers. They being compelled under the law to buy their supplies from the commissaries, and under such circumstances as have been described, it was not probable that there was a commissary within ten miles from where we could buy rations.

The next morning the fight was on in earnest. The enemy was driven wholly into the town, and so closely were the Confederates enclosed that they ran the lines of some of their breastworks, on the north side at least, right under some of the houses in the suburbs. I heard quite a number of citizens berating the Confederate officers for building their works so close to the center of town that every shot or shell from the Yankee guns could not fail to do much damage.

In those days it was the custom for each division to furnish a detail for either pickets or skirmishers, and place the whole line crossing its front, usually three brigades, all under charge of a single officer, a Major or a Lieutenant Colonel. Major Baldwin, of the Twelfth, was detailed for this work and as he had just been appointed a Major, he was in his glory. In closing, the Twelfth was on the first line and met with considerable opposition, losing several men due to wounds, but none killed outright. The picket or skirmish line is generally placed as far in front of the leading line of troops as is convenient and safe. In this instance it was nearly a fourth of a mile in advance of the main body.

I remember on one occasion that I heard the sputter of musketry straight in front but on the right flank of the Twelfth. Baldwin had been giving close attention to his skirmish line, but I feared that he might be at the other end of the lines and therefore I galloped out to the front to see if anything was wrong. I found the Major taking a rest on a mattress that some of the men had requisitioned from some of the better class residents near by. It was placed under a "lean to" made of boards the upper ends of which rested on a pole propped up against two trees. Baldwin was nearly asleep. I aroused him and told him about the increased firing from the enemy over on the right and it seemed to me that they were preparing to "rush" some point over there. He had been on duty for a considerable time and turned over preparatory to taking another nap. I insisted that he should get up and go see if there were any suspicious movements on the part of the enemy. Very reluctantly he did so. He had just gotten on his horse to accompany me over to the right, when a shell thrown from a fort of the rebels crashed right through the boards of his "lean-to", struck the mattress upon which he had been lying, ripping it all to pieces. There can not be a shadow of doubt but for my coming, and insisting that he should get up and go along with me, that he would have been torn into shreds. Such instances as this are called "providential escapes," but they occurred many times during the war and whatever they may be designated, they were certainly strange and bordered on the miraculous, most assuredly. The bursting of the shell covered us with leaves and twigs from the trees and splinters from the boards. We hastened our departure to the threatened part in time to prevent that portion of the skirmish line from falling back under the pressure the enemy was making. And by rushing up a company to the support of our line, the advance was at once checked.

The brigade that the Twelfth was attached to lay in the trenches for five days. It rained every day and the men became so covered and plastered with the red mud that it was relieved and permitted to go to the rear to rest and clean up. It was during this period of idleness that Major Baldwin and myself thought we discovered signs of withdrawal on the part of the enemy. We were firm in this belief and the day after the regiment was withdrawn from the front line, we concluded to see for ourselves whether our suspicions were well-founded or not. When night came we crawled up to the fort that defended the main road leading out of the town to the north which contained six guns. The closer we got the more we were convinced the Confederates meant to withdraw from their lines and most likely leave Jackson to itself. We were so close upon the sides off the north face that we could hear every word that was uttered and became convinced that the enemy was engaged in wrapping the wheels of their artillery with gunny sacks to prevent them from being heard by the Yankees while being withdrawn. As soon as we could crawl back, we mounted our horses and hastened to inform those in higher command of the facts.

General William Sooy Smith felt disposed to sneer at the probability that the rebels would give up such an important position without a fight. The Major and myself felt somewhat chagrined over our treatment by a superior officer as to the value of our information that we had taken such great risk to obtain. We sent a written note to General Park, the officer in command of all the troops next to General Sherman, whose headquarters were too far away for us to attempt to interview. We went back to our quarters determined to be up at three o'clock in the morning ready to accompany the troops as they passed into a deserted town.

Sure enough, when we reached the lines, the discovery was just being made that the enemy had evacuated the city during the night—a fact that we two had know as early as nine o'clock on the evening previous. Of course, neither of us had any command, and in fact, no special business there save the personal one of being present when the troops found out what we had known for hours. Major Baldwin and I thought it a great loss that our information was cast aside by General Smith for we saw a great advantage to attacking a retreating army. General Park told me afterward that had he earlier notice of the valuable information we had procured he certainly would have arranged for an attack all along his front at daybreak.

The next time I saw General Sherman was at Black River. I related to him the incident and the information we had placed in General William Sooy Smith's hands as early as ten o'clock on the night previous to the evacuation. This was the first he had heard that positive information of the proposed retreat was known in our lines. His comments were anything but complementary to General Smith, who, he said, regardless of his own opinion about the withdrawal of the enemy should have hastened to inform his (Sherman's) headquarters with the valuable information. He expressed great regret that General Smith had been so dilatory in a matter of such great importance.

On entering Jackson, we were compelled to cross over the Confederate earthworks and, by hunting smooth places to cross, the incline of the works being in our favor, we soon got our animals through. After crossing the line and proceeding to the main street of the city, it was just breaking light. We discovered that we two men were the only mounted ones in sight. The Ninety-ninth Indiana Infantry stood at the head of the street and were soon afterward joined by their officers who had found considerable difficulty in getting their animals over the works. Temporarily the Major and myself attached ourselves to this regiment for we knew most of its officers very well. A detachment of advance guards was sent forward by the Colonel of the regiment to which we intended to belong for a short time. Just as the colors of the regiment "broke out," the sun began to peep above the eastern horizon. The regiment took up its march southward on one of the principal streets of the city. The enemy could be heard apparently about a mile distant, but no rebel soldiers were in sight. We continued with the Ninety-ninth until we reached the State House, where we left the troops that were under orders. We proceeded to do as we pleased, being visitors in the city of Jackson and entirely free from military orders and discipline, for the moment at least.

Major Baldwin was a daredevil sort of fellow, well informed, and held a hatred for the rebels that was most intense. He was perfectly fearless of consequences in anything he might undertake. He disappeared around a street corner where he was absent for a short time. When he came back he had with him two demi-johns of wine, one in each hand. He requested me to watch these demi-johns, as he had to get a string so that he could tie them together and swing them over that pummel of his saddle. He was gone but a brief time and returned with a heavy silk cord as big in diameter as a man's finger. He had found the cord in the parlor of a mansion, back from the streets, which had been used, before the Major cut it loose, for holding back the heavy lace curtains at one of the windows. He also cut about a yard square right out of a piece of velvet carpet in the same room to use for a saddle cover. He used it for that purpose as long as he was a member of the Twelfth.

Major Baldwin and I roamed around the central part of the city. We visited the State House, talked with those citizens who were willing to converse with "a damn Yankee," and tried to procure something to eat. But food was a scarce article in any of the towns in the South after it had been besieged. We got some delicious corn bread that only the "darkey mammies," even to this day, know best how to make.

Baldwin was recently commissioned a Major and on the morning we entered the town he was riding a mule. He expected to be mustered into his rank within a few days and was looking for equipment for the horse he would be procuring. He visited the saddle and harness shops in the town and he secured a number of articles that he "needed in his business" as Major of the Twelfth Indiana Infantry. At one shop he had procured a military bridle and a saddlecloth, halters, spurs, etc., and both of us when we got ready to go found ourselves—our horses rather—loaded down with plunder. Four more demijohns of wine had been added to Baldwin's string of two, making six in all.

The Major on going into a Catholic church, found a box of altar candles and had them, box and all, strapped on his mule, using the halter and its strap to tie it on. These candles were eighteen or twenty inches in length and thick in proportion. I insisted on not taking them at all, but he insisted that when night came he was going to illuminate the camp of the Twelfth regiment in honor of the great victory. So, when we were loading up it was found that he could not carry the six demijohns of wine and the box of candles, and therefore, requested me to carry the wine on my horse. I declined at first, insisting that he should leave the box of candles and then he would have plenty of room. I finally agreed, however, and the demijohns were transferred to my animal. We got on our animals, and were compelled to ask the assistance of some of the Federal soldiers near us, for the animals were so piled up with plunder that we could just poke our heads through its top.

I remember the town clock indicated eight-thirty a.m. when we started back to camp, so that we had been in town nearly five hours. It was about three miles from the center of the town where we loaded our traps back to camp. We had already gone two or three squares when, on looking up the street we discovered General Park and all his staff, consisting of sixty to seventy-five mounted officers and orderlies coming our way. Here was a pretty fix for a Colonel and a Major in the United States army to be in on meeting the officer second in command of the Union forces! I hastily looked on both sides of the street for an alley through which we could escape meeting the General, but there was none. There was nothing to do but face the dilemma as best we could.

I have said before that Major Baldwin was a great wag and therefore, I commanded him to ride right past and say nothing. But to my utter astonishment, just as we approached the head of the cavalcade and General Parks was eyeing us both, the Major sung out at the top of his voice: "General, you'd better hurry up, or you won't get a damn thing!" I was looking at the General in the face at the time and not ten feet distant from him, I perceived just the faintest tinge of a smile steal over his face, and knew it was all right. Instead of being reprimanded or even arrested,

Baldwin's ready wit had made it impossible to do either. In an instant the whole staff broke out with a loud laugh that clinched the whole matter.

It was easier for a mounted man to go into the town over the breastworks than it was to come out. The reason for this lay in the fact that there was a slant on the outside that permitted the horse or mule to climb up to the top and thus over. Coming out, however, the earthworks were generally perpendicular, and it was very difficult to get any animal to leap up to the top. When the troops came in they dug down a portion of the breastworks in many places in order to get the horses of the officers over in going into the town. In a number of instances the breastworks of the Confederated ran right under the houses. It was under such a house that I got an opportunity to pay off Major Baldwin for some of his personal jokes on me. He was riding ahead on his mule and had found a place under a small frame house where the breastworks had been made steeply slanting, where he thought we could get out. He tried it, but his mule refused to go up the slant.

"Here," Major said, "Colonel, take this whip and give the mule a cut, and I guess he will climb out."

I did so, and the very first lick I gave the animal he kicked up behind and bumped Baldwin's head against the sleepers of the floor above.

"Hold on," he cried, "that won't do." But remembering his pranks, I kept on touching up the mule, while Baldwin's head played a steady tattoo against the beams and floor. I laughed until I was as weak as water. We called a soldier who was not far away to help us get the mule over the works by leading him, and when the soldier got hold of the halter, I gave the mule another harder cut. Like a flash, the mule bolted over the works, Baldwin having all he could do to keep on his back.

When we got back to camp, we had our cook fix us up a fine breakfast. Afterward both of us went to our tents for rest, for we had been up nearly all the night and were considerably wearied over the night and the next morning's work. Major Baldwin and I had found over three hundred napkins in one of the stores and when the regiment was dismissed at dress parade Major Baldwin distributed them to the soldiers as far as they would go. The next day it was reported all over the division that Governor Morton was furnishing the Indiana troops with napkins!

As soon as it became dark we illuminated the camp. Carpenters had bored holes in the trees and fitted in a piece of wood with a hole at its outer end to hold the candle. The illumination of the Twelfth over the victory was an immense success. We had singing, speeches, and other accompaniments from the sixteen piece military band of the Twelfth. It was the only band of the kind in the corps at the time, except the Thirteenth regular regiment. Many men from other commands came to the celebration.

Playing Jokes on Grant and Sherman

After the Confederates' main column withdrew from Jackson, Mississippi, it was pressed for some distance into the piney woods by General Sherman's cavalry. Sherman prepared at once to return to Vicksburg, his own corps, the Fifteenth, going into camp on the west side of the Big Black River at a point about twenty-five miles east of Vicksburg. Here my own regiment—in fact the entire brigade—had a delightful camp. We were bivouacked in a fine grove that included many palmetto trees, and all of the regiments of this brigade, wherever the ground permitted, laid out their camps on the plan laid down in the tactics.

In returning from Jackson, Mississippi, the rear guard was followed by a detachment, perhaps a full brigade, of rebel cavalry and occasional skirmishes took place. At a village about midway between Jackson and the Big Black, our brigade went into line behind some trees and permitted the following Confederates to come up quite close, then opened up with a few volleys. The "Johnnies" were surprised, for they had no idea of the situation. Their loss was severe while ours was trifling. This surprise acted as a deterrent, for the next day the Confederates were very cautious and followed our rear guard at a respectful distance. The pursuit was discontinued altogether after the Big Black was reached and crossed at Messenger's Ferry.

I always think of the cantonment at Messenger's Ferry, named "Camp Sherman," as a pleasant period of soldier life. The camp my own regiment occupied was a very agreeable one. I was able to secure many comforts for the members of the command, and I remember one thing that came to many of the members of the regiment as a godsend. I happened to be up at Sherman's headquarters, when a wagon train of supplies arrived. In "nosing" around I found that there were five barrels of soured cabbage on one of them, along with other goods. Being well acquainted with the commissary and especially friendly with him, I asked him if I couldn't secure a couple of barrels of that soured cabbage.

"Certainly," he replied, "all you will have to do is to sign a requisition and receipt for it, and send one of your wagons after it."

Aware of the fact that the demand for such an article would be very great because the dry army rations with its salt meat lead men to crave something sour, I hastened back to my camp to get a wagon to convey the cabbage to my headquarters. The distance to the camp was over a mile and as I rode back I could see that two barrels would scarcely go around the regiment, so I accompanied the wagon and teamster that was sent after the two barrels of kraut. I induced the commissary to make it two more barrels explaining that it would be better to let one regiment have enough to go around than to send the five barrels out in a way that no one would get more than a spoonful!

"That's so," the commissary agreed, "and while you are at it you might as well take the whole five barrels."

"All right," said I, "there is plenty of room in the wagon for the five and that will give each man a pint apiece, according to my reckoning—only a mere bite each for a hearty soldier!"

I refer to this incident to show that I always tried to be mindful of the men under my immediate command, and at all times to secure for them whatever was possible. The cabbage referred to was covered with as sour vinegar as I ever tasted and was cut in cubes instead of being sliced, suggesting the old-fashioned way of cutting kraut with a sharpened spade. Never did the men appreciate anything more keenly than that issue of sour kraut.

Although we were in Messenger's Ferry in the hot season of the year, July and August, my regiment was more healthful than most of the others in the same division. I account for this partly in this way. A general order existed that each regiment should engage in battalion drill two hours in the forenoon and two in the afternoon—the hour set for nine a.m. and two p.m. The order was a standing one and issued from division headquarters. I remember that many regiments would go out at the designated time, loll around for awhile in the hot sun and return to quarters to repeat the same process in the afternoon. I reasoned that about all that was required was to give the men proper exercise, therefore I had company drill in quarters for a half hour in the early morning, breakfast at seven o'clock, then about an hour of battalion drill and nothing more till dress parade in the evening. I soon discovered that this pleased the enlisted men. They were taking a deep interest in the fact that other regiments were complimenting them for their soldierly and orderly appearance. When it was discovered that sickness was much more prevalent in other regiments than it was in the Twelfth, I was satisfied much of it came from drilling at more appropriate hours as much as possible in that hot climate.

While the Fifteenth Corps lay at Camp Sherman for over two months with the Twelfth Indiana Infantry drilling every day that it did not rain, stirring events were occurring up in Tennessee. General Braxton Bragg in command of the Confederate forces had given up Chattanooga, which was occupied by the troops of General Rosecrans. But in doing so he had spread his supporting columns to such distances that they were not well in hand. General Bragg quickly discovering this concentrated his army so as to bring on the battle of Chickamauga—a struggle that was by some called a drawn battle—but was a defeat for the Federal forces. General Rosecrans' army was cooped up in Chattanooga on very short supplies and its immediate effect was so far-reaching that it broke up the fine and pleasant camp of the Fifteenth corps. The Fifteenth was at once designated for service in Tennessee and was ordered to Vicksburg to take boats for Memphis. We broke camp at Messenger's Ferry on September 28th.

CHAPTER 8

Battle at Lookout Mountain

Thirteen dollars a month for standing as targets
    For heaps of cold lead and old iron and steel,
But Sherman says we are better for what we endured then,
    And we can't make a point of the General's deal.
We ate "salt horse" and hard-tack in all kinds of weather,
    Some rations we drew and some others stole;
But still, my old chums, we will always remember
    The old coffee kettle that hung on the pole.
                                 —War-Time Lyrics

    We were six or eight days in making the trip to Memphis, for it must be remembered that the slowest boat regulates the speed of an expedition, and there was the difficulty of procuring fuel to make steam for the boats. The wagons, already heavily laden, had to be unloaded to be used in collecting and conveying wood still uncut from the forest. The wood was green and it was a problem knowing whether the burning of it made "sweat" or "steam."

    On reaching Memphis it was soon discovered that the First division of the Fifteenth corps was to move eastward. After the surrender of Vicksburg and the capture of Jackson, and while the troops were in camp, ten percent of the enlisted men of the army had been given a furlough for thirty days and the officers a leave of absence for twenty days. These "furloughs" and "leaves" were expiring just about the time the division reached Memphis, and a good many of those who had enjoyed the liberality of the government rejoined their respective commands.

    The route of the march was along the Memphis and Charleston railroad. The division to which the Twelfth belonged marched on foot while the remainder of the corps was transferred to Corinth by rail. I had taken advantage of the offer to permit officers and men to return to their homes, and I arrived at Memphis from the North a couple of days after the Twelfth had left. I took a car and rejoined the regiment in Mississippi at a small village called Burnsville. The order came to resume the march to Iuka and Corinth in Mississippi. The region had been fought over in the preceding year and the Confederates under General Albert S. Johnson and General Beauregard had their headquarters at Corinth previous to the battle of Shiloh. After their defeat, the Confederate army fell back to Corinth.

    The Union forces always called that battle by the name of "Pittsburgh Landing" and the Confederates official cognomen became "Shiloh", for the reason that a church of that name occupied a central point in the battlefield. The Federals called it "Pittsburgh Landing" for the reason that all steamboats stopped there because it was the nearest point to the battlefield on the Tennessee River. By common consent the battle name given to it by the rebels has become general.

Aware of the importance of checking the eastward march of General Sherman's forces, as a supposed reinforcement to General Rosecrans' army then cooped up in Chattanooga, the Confederates had assembled a large force in his front. Skirmishes and small contests were of frequent occurrence. This was the case until Corinth was reached. During this time, however, General Sherman had also assembled quite a number of steamboats at Pittsburgh Landing and played quite a trick on the Confederates by suddenly withdrawing all of his forces, except the cavalry, from the rebel front. The infantry had quickly marched to boats and transferred to the east bank of the Tennessee. The cavalry afterward withdrew, and as the Confederates had no means of crossing the stream, the march of Sherman to reinforce the Army of the Cumberland was wholly unimpeded. The object was to reinforce General Rosecrans' army as speedily as possible. Rosecrans had been removed and General Grant was placed in command of the army of the Cumberland and the army of the Tennessee.

The move on the part of General Sherman, while a surprise to the Confederates, was a godsend to our troops, for it enabled the Fifteenth corps to pass through a fine region of Tennessee with plenty of forage. The days were warm, not uncomfortably so, while the nights were cool. The army previous to crossing the Tennessee had been in the habit of putting up their tents every night, but after crossing the river this practice was almost wholly abandoned. The reason was that the regimental wagons were seldom up in time and it was quite a task to pitch tents every night. Consequently the troops got into the habit of lying down in their blankets, leaving the wagons unloaded. The nights were frosty, but as we were well supplied with blankets, I never slept more soundly nor more thoroughly enjoyed the army rations than I did on that rapid march to Chattanooga. We had broiled or fried beefsteak every morning and a plentiful supply of coffee. It was the most pleasant and healthful long march I made in my four years of soldier life.

As a consequence the corps to which we belonged arrived at Stevenson, Alabama on the fourteenth of November in prime condition, except a good many of the marching men may have been footsore and shoeless, for the roads were extremely hard on shoes. We proceeded to Bridgeport the next day. Bridgeport was the base of supplies for the army at Chattanooga, and as the Confederates held the point of Lookout Mountain between Bridgeport and Chattanooga, all supplies had to be taken by wagons on the north side of the Tennessee River through the

Seguatchee Valley to Chattanooga. The distance traversed was forty miles, but it was sixty by this route, and over the very worst of roads. The fall rains had set in and the mud was so deep that the axles of the wagons dragged along the tops of the roads almost the entire way of the sixty miles.

There was a partial refitting of the troops of Sherman's command at Bridgeport, some necessary articles of apparel, such as blouses and stockings being furnished. The troops there received orders to move toward Chattanooga, the corps taking the best road leading in that direction and not the one used by the supply train. From the close of the battle of Chickamauga up to the arrival of reinforcements from the army of the Potomac under General Joe Hooker, and those of General Sherman, the army of the Cumberland, had been on unusually short rations. As far as the live stock, horses and mules, not a bale of hay or sack of oats had reached our army in and around Chattanooga from that date. For a time no attempt was made to feed the animals and it must be remembered that the men and officers alike suffered from the lack of rations. There were occasions when food was so scarce that the corn on hand intended for the animals was used for the men. The animals had to live on what they themselves could pick up. Mules actually ate up portions of soldiers' blankets, gnawed and chewed their own harness, and many a wagon tongue was so weakened by their gnawing that new ones had to be provided. Quite a number of the quartermasters of the army of the Cumberland had green trees cut and hauled into camp for the mules to browse upon.

Ever since the civil war, I have had the highest regard for the mule, and I have sometimes said that had the army been compelled to use horses alone, the war would have lasted a year longer. The mules that lived on blankets, harnesses, wagon tongues and basewood during the close of autumn and the beginning of 1864, were still in the army at the date of the Grand Review. Few soldiers would not take off his hat in salute to an old, faithful, genuine, army mule!

The rebels occupied the "nose of Lookout Mountain" right over and high above Chattanooga, and had placed a couple of pieces of artillery on the mountain. When the first shots were fired from these pieces, the muzzles of the guns being necessarily greatly depressed, the guns kicked themselves loose from their trunions. Afterward these guns were hung in chains so that the recoil was overcome. The Confederates annoyed our troops in the valley below, but did little or no particular damage.

I remember an incident that occurred following the battle of Missionary Ridge and the march of the Fifteenth Corps to the relief of General Burnside, who was cooped up in Knoxville by General Longstreet, that can be better told here, as it relates to the short rations in vogue inside of Chattanooga. Immediately following the battle of Missionary Ridge, and while the division to which my regiment belonged was pursuing General Bragg's broken and flying troops, an order came when we were near Ringgold, Georgia, directing General Sherman to at once turn about and go to General Burnside's relief at Knoxville. The order was at once, but grumblingly, obeyed. The division returned to the vicinity where they had first met the enemy in the battle of Missionary Ridge, and where they had left their knapsacks previous to going into the fight. Here they expected to get their blankets, but the knapsacks had been removed, probably upon some officer's order. As it was in the closing days of November, the march to Knoxville was made without the knapsacks.

We were absent twenty-one days, and the entire expedition had to subsist wholly on the country in a region that had already been devastated by both armies. Consequently the Fifteenth Corps was a hungry body of men and the march was exceedingly hard on the officers, who had to purchase their supplies at all times. I was exceedingly hungry and worn out. I had felicitated myself all the last day of the march that I would proceed at once to Chattanooga, after I had gotten the men encamped, to get a good square meal with my old friend, Captain Andrew S. Milice, then Captain of A company, Seventy-fourth Infantry. I had not seen the Captain for a couple of years, as we had been serving in distant divisions of the army, he in the department of the Cumberland and myself in the Army of the Tennessee. After I had arranged everything so I could be absent for a few hours, I mounted my horse and proceeded to the town of Chattanooga, a distance of six miles down the river. On arriving at the Captain's tent it was almost dark, but I at once told him what I had come for and "that I had not had my hunger appeased for a single moment in twenty-one days!"

I could see, for it was not yet dark, that the Captain blushed a little after I told him that I was "hungry as a she-wolf" and had come to him for a square meal.

"Why, yes," said the Captain, hesitatingly, "of course!"

To tell the truth, however, he did not seem to be as enthusiastic as his words seemed to indicate, but I heard him give directions to his colored man to make a fire and put on a pot full of water. That sounded well to a hungry man, but the Captain still seemed backward for old friends who had known each other since boyhood days. I couldn't get the Captain to talk freely, much as I tried, but finally supper was announced as being "spread" under a fly outside of the tent and we both went out. The "spread" show a half-dozen hard-tack and a pot full of the black tea. I could easily perceive that the Captain was chagrined over the meager "lay-out". He then informed me that although it had been over three weeks since communications with the North had been opened, yet there had not been more than a fourth ration issued to each man on any day. The officers had all they could do to procure enough to keep them going; scarcely any of them had had a full meal since the battle of Chickamauga.

Many times since the war I have jested with Captain Milice about my riding six miles to get a hard-tack supper with black tea! The people at home have never fully known the suffering the men endured at Chattanooga previous to and for days following the battle of Missionary Ridge. I have related this anecdote out of its regular order for the reason that it tells how scarce supplies were.

About the middle of November 1863, the troops under General Sherman left Bridgeport and marched up the Tennessee River with Chattanooga as the objective point. We reached a place called Shell Mound, from which point we left the river, and marched up a deep cleft in Sand Mountain, known as Nickajack Cove. Shell Mound, a station on the railroad, no doubt received its name from the wonderful and vast accumulations of shells that were unearthed in the construction of the Nashville and Chattanooga railroad.

The road up the Nickajack Cove was a winding one up Sand Mountain, near the top of which was located "Castle Rock Coal Mines." The road had been dug and blasted from the mountain's face, and was just wide enough for team and wagon to move forward. There was an ever-present danger on the side down which the deep ravine descended almost perpendicularly. Night overtook the troops in the ascent of Sand Mountain and when darkness came it was too dangerous for the teams to proceed. The drivers were ordered to lock the wheels of their wagons and await daylight, as two wagons had already plunged down the declivity.

During the Creek Indian war, General Jackson led his Tennesseeans up this same road, and this was perhaps the first time that troops of any kind had either climbed or descended by that winding and dangerous road since the days of "old Hickory." On reaching the summit of Sand Mountain, I found a gray-headed and gray-bearded coal miner, an Englishman from Cornwall, standing near the main entrance to the mine. He had been working in the mines before the war came and these were the first "Yankee" troops the old gentleman had ever seen. He was quite reticent at first, but by speaking to him politely and gentlemanly, he soon thawed out. I spent a half-hour with him very pleasantly, even if he did throw about his "h's" and "o's" so promiscuously that they were half the time in the wrong place, and half the time the wrong ones were used. He was evidently of a religious turn of mind and believed the South had espoused the wrong side of the question, as slavery was so utterly wrong.

While I was talking to the coal miner, the cook of my headquarters' mess came up with his coffee pot and whatever else he could carry in his haversack. He had been looking for me, as he knew that I had not had breakfast. He spread out his poncho on the ground on which he placed some coffee, bacon, and a dish of fresh beef's liver and the usual hard-tack. When all was ready, I invited the old Englishman to take breakfast with me. He politely declined, but I could see the aroma of the coffee was having an effect on him. Therefore I insisted he join me. After he had taken his first sip of the coffee, he informed me that it was first he had tasted since New Years Day 1862. "Of course," he said, "the people have substituted for coffee but it never came close to the genuine thing." He was so pleased with his breakfast that I whispered to the cook to roll up about a quarter of a pound in a paper and when I left I gave it to him telling him that maybe his "old woman would like a taste." It is not often that one hears an expression of such genuine gratitude over a trifle, as came from that old Englishman in Northern Alabama.

After reaching the summit of Sand Mountain all the troops had been gathered up, for they had been widely scattered in gaining the summit, the order reached us to march. We passed across the wide, level reach on the top of Sand Mountain, arriving at its brow overlooking Lookout Valley. A splendid panoramic view of the handsome little town of Trenton lay peacefully and seemingly undisturbed in the valley below. We were the rear brigade of the division that day and remained there for some time.

Orders came for our brigade to debouch into the valley, and this was quietly done. The two brigades that proceeded ours, marched some distance up Lookout Valley, the first one, I think, about fifteen miles, the next one about half that distance, and our own only a mile or two outside of Trenton. The whole movement was a ruse intended to deceive the enemy who occupied and used all of Lookout Mountain that lay between us and Chattanooga. Every brigade and regiment was ordered to cover as much space as possible, even to the extent of dividing the colors and the music so as to make each regiment appear as two to the watchful Confederate eyes. At night, each regiment built double the amount of fires that were needed in order to create the idea in the minds of the Confederates that a large force was marching southward with the intention of ascending Lookout at a point where the mountain was much lower and more accessible.

The Confederates were watching from a distance of four or five miles and it could be seen that the strategy was working, for detachments of Confederate cavalry, evidently acting as observation corps were frequently spotted. I also had it from several prisoners who were captured at Missionary Ridge a few days later, who asserted that they had been members of regiments who were engaged in watching the movements of the Yankees in Lookout Valley for two days. I took these prisoners with me after their capture at Missionary Ridge clear to Knoxville and then returned to my troops. During the trip they became much attached to the men under whose charge they were, and on returning to Chattanooga fully one-half the number, which was seventy, were anxious to enlist in my regiment. But I could not procure an order permitting it, as the consent of the War Department would have to be secured before it could be done. These prisoners were mostly North Carolinians and were taken along because I could find no one to take charge of them after receiving the orders to make a forced march to Knoxville, following the battle of Missionary Ridge.

After making the spread of force in Lookout Valley, General Hugh Ewing, our division commander, received an order to break camp and pass with rapidity to the mouth of Lookout Valley. Just before reaching it, the division was halted and a hundred rounds of ammunition was issued to each man—forty in the cartridge box and sixty for the pockets of each soldier. That made every enlisted man understand that a battle was near, for it was a sign that could not be mistaken.

The issue having been made, the march proceeded and continued until the Fifteenth corps was opposite the mouth of Chickamauga creek about six miles above Chattanooga. In getting to this position the Fifteenth Corps had crossed the Tennessee at Brown's ferry, all save General Osterhaus' division. The Confederates were very actively employed above the ferry in chopping down trees and felling them in the river for the purpose of destroying or at least injuring our pontoon bridges. This they were quite successful in doing. The first two divisions had succeeded in crossing when a large tree came down the already swollen stream and broke the bridge in twain despite the efforts of the pontooniers to prevent any such disaster. It was for this reason that General Jeff C. Davis' division of the Fourteenth Corps was assigned to General Sherman's command. Davis' division was a large one and it too went to cross the Tennessee, at the mouth of Chickamauga creek, while General Osterhaus' troops were left with Hooker's forces to climb and capture Lookout Mountain the next day.

Previous to all these movements so briefly described, General Grant had his pioneer and pontoon corps busily engaged in building boats two miles above the mouth of Chickamauga Creek. Here they took up a mile square of ground, within which no citizen was admitted, nor soldier either, without written authority. The strictest secrecy was adhered to. A large number of boats were constructed here and done so slyly that there were but few of our own army that knew anything about what was going on.

The night before General Sherman crossed the Tennessee all of these boats were occupied with the maximum amount of soldiers. The boats were to float down the Tennessee, gathering in all the Confederate posts above the mouth of the stream as silently as possible, not a shot to be fired without orders, and only then, if absolutely necessary. This movement was most successfully accomplished, and it is a wonder that something did not happen to put the Confederates on their guard. However, the night was dark, which was greatly in favor of the boat party and the river was high so the boats required no rowing, only a helmsman. The location of all the picket posts of the rebels were known beforehand and every one of them, except the last one, was captured without firing a gun. At this one, located near the mouth of Chickamauga creek, a rebel soldier heard a noise in the water and perceiving a dark object on the stream, fired at it without dreaming that it was an enemy boat. The party landed there, capturing all but two soldiers of the picket post. Those two succeeded in getting away and presumably carried their information to their own headquarters.

The pontooniers at once threw up a slight defense, and the steamer Dunbar, which was operated by the Confederates, and had been captured two days before, was used to conveyed a couple of companies of Federal troops across the river. Two more companies were hurried over by the Dunbar, and in the meantime work on a pontoon bridge was going forward at a rapid pace. My own regiment was among the first to cross the river.

All the troops that had been transferred to the opposite or south side of the river had built a strong fortification and a battery was soon in position, thus rendering an attack from the Confederates a very dangerous thing to engage in. I remember meeting Colonel Ed Wood, the head of the Forty-eighth Indiana, whose regiment lay near the north end of the pontoon bridge. His men had been at work all night and were then engaged in eating their breakfast. The Colonel had a "fly" erected and was resting under it as a cover. When he saw me at the head of the Twelfth, he ran out, took me by the hand and begged me to get off my horse and have a cup of coffee, adding, "Colonel Reub, you're going to catch hell over there!"

The contest that was to end in the capture of Lookout Mountain began at the very base of that grand projection of nature by the skirmishers of both armies. It was not many minutes after it began until the combatants were entirely obscured by the smoke of their own guns. The soldiers who were spectators watched the ever-rising line of battle as the Confederates retreated up the rocky sides of Old Lookout followed by the continually pursuing line of the Federals.

Away up the sides of the mountain was a plateau of more level ground, perhaps large enough for a couple of regiments to stand upon. No smoke had ascended to cover the plateau and it lay in the bright sunlight. All at once the ranks in gray retreated across this bit of level ground and in a few moments "Old Glory" burst out on the plateau in all its splendor of colors so dear to the heart of every patriot. The lines that were broken by the steepness of the rough ground and the breath-consuming climb of the "boys in blue" all at once straightened out on their regimental flags. The incident became historic, and the name "The Battle Above the Clouds" took its place in army literature. All below was still enshrouded in the smoke of the struggle. What a cheer rent the air from the soldiers lying in the trenches below as they saw the colors of each regiment burst out on that bit of breathing ground! The cheer was taken up and ran along the line from Hooker's daring men to the extreme right of Grant's line, to those of Sherman seven miles distant on the left. So peculiar was the lay of the ground that by the use of an officer's field glass "Old Glory" could easily be seen as it rose "above the clouds" in that memorable picture made by the troops on their way to the top of Lookout Mountain.

During the progress of the battle for the possession of Lookout Mountain, General Sherman had gathered all of his division commanders at his headquarters, including each brigadier commander. I was the senior, and consequently the ranking officer in the command, next to Colonel John Mason Loomis. Loomis therefore invited me to accompany him to Sherman's headquarters, for he knew that he might be disabled in the coming fight and the brigade would fall under my command. He had also placed the right wing of the brigade in my charge for the approaching contest on the morrow. General Sherman took the party to the most salient points on the north bank of the Tennessee River and pointed out the position of the enemy from maps that had been previously secured through the secret service corps of the War Department by spies.

I have often thought that the carefulness of "Old Billy", as his boys delighted to call General Sherman, was of great advantage to the Federal commanding officers. For each brigade commander was given a brief, hastily sketched fragment of paper representing the immediate front of each brigade, and the position to be occupied as far ascertained to be used as a partial guide. Just as soon as a sufficient force had crossed the pontoon on the Tennessee, each division was pushed out into the wooded ground that lay in the immediate front. As each division formed on the right or left of the first one, taking position, orders were given for the men to breakfast, and then the captains of companies had them replenish the supply of "hard-tack" and bacon in their haversacks. The supply of cartridges was also seen to. Each box was required to have the regulation forty in number and sixty rounds stowed away in the pockets, and sometimes in the lining of the men's coats. This was necessary for it was not known how many of the enemy might be met or when a commissary or ammunition wagon would be seen again.

Along in the afternoon the bugles of the various divisions, brigades and regiments following one another, sounded the advance. The troops in two solid lines with elbows touching moved forward at "quick step". A cloud of skirmishers was a good distance in the advance. It was only a few minutes for our skirmishers to meet a similar body of Confederates placed there to impede the Yankees' advance.

As the main body of the Federal line pressed forward, it produced a like effect on our skirmishers, who covered the ground so rapidly that the roar of musketry became almost continuous. It sounded to those in the rear very like "the double drag," one of the earliest feats of drum-stick skill, taught to a snare drummer at the beginning of the war. It was plain to be seen, even to the veterans in the ranks, let alone an officer, that the enemy did not intend to make a real stand until their troops had reached the summit of the most eastern point of Missionary Ridge. Consequently the enemy was pushed hard and while the main body made several stands, yet the eastern-most hill was captured just before dark. While at no time could this first attack on the enemy be called a battle yet there were several killed and wounded on the Federal side as well as many Confederates. The dead and wounded of the contest along with a couple hundred prisoners fell into our hands.

Perhaps half a mile to the west toward Chattanooga loomed a larger and higher hill than the one we had captured. We bivouacked on the first hill leaving the second one for the next day. We cared for ourselves the best we could during that weary night. All through the lengthening hours, we could hear the noise of the rebel troops at work in building fortifications, the cries of the teamsters, and the rumble of twenty-pounder Parrotts being placed in the embrasures hastily prepared for them.

At about three a.m., I received an order to have the men breakfasted and ready to march at four-thirty. Every man in that corps knew that an order like that meant "business" and it was obeyed with alacrity. Almost every man had destroyed the letters he had received and had preserved in his knapsack letters he had written to father, mother, sisters or brothers, or to "a dearer one still," bearing in mind as he did that it might be the last one he ever penned. Few men desire to leave a previous correspondence in their knapsacks or anywhere on their person on the eve of going into battle, and very often I have seen soldiers destroying letters as they watched the signs that indicated a coming battle. The evening before our advance on the enemy, I saw our faithful, patriotic Chaplain, M.D. Gage, carrying over his shoulder a weighty haversack containing letters written after we crossed the Tennessee River.

At a very early hour the brigade was formed and marched down the declivities of the hill captured on the evening proceeding. On reaching the level ground, the brigade was marched westward in the direction of Chattanooga, staying well concealed in a skirt of timber. On reaching a point directly in front of the railroad tunnel, the command was moved forward almost to the edge of the timber, and in front of which the ground was wholly open. The tunnel ran through a depression that existed between the hill we had already captured and the one that it was yet to take, if possible. Over and behind the big hill we had just vacated lay another division of General Sherman's corps.

My orders were most positive not to go any farther in the open ground and to "lie down!" Of all the orders I ever received during the war that was the most irksome, difficult and dangerous to perform. As the brigade emerged from the timber solid shot and shell were poured into it from the summit of the hill that during the night was transformed from a smooth-topped hill into a formidable fort with twenty-two pieces of artillery. Fortunately for the men of the Twelfth and One Hundredth Indiana regiments and the Twenty-sixth and Ninetieth Illinois regiments that they were so close under the guns that their muzzles could not be depressed sufficiently to make them effective. Consequently the shot and shell screamed and shrieked over the heads of the men. But for this, there would have been few, indeed, left to tell the story. Nevertheless, the shot and shell crashing and tearing into the trees cut off large limbs that fell upon the men wounding, bruising and maiming many before they left the shelter of the timber. A solid shot struck a large tree that stood close to where Adjutant Jared D. Bond of the Twelfth and myself were sitting on our horses. A large piece of the tree struck the Adjutant on the side of the head, knocking him senseless from his horse. Captain Frank Aveline, of Fort Wayne, one of the brightest boys of his age in the army, while holding his sword above his head, urging his men to preserve their alignment, had the blade almost bent double by a solid shot. The next moment a musket ball struck him squarely in the center of the head, killing the handsome young man of twenty, the youngest commanding officer in the corps of his rank.

I was almost frantic over the order compelling me to hold the men "at a lie-down" in a place so greatly exposed. I sent orderly after orderly asking permission to get up close to the hillside, to charge to the top of the ridge, to do anything, in fact, rather than lie under that withering fire and the big shells from Parrott guns. Back came the order each time to "tell Williams to hold his ground until further orders."

For over four hours the men lay in the open, the target for that rain of solid shot, shells and musketry, to which we could not effectively reply in kind. I have talked to many men since the war who were in that engagement and who were eye-witnesses to as brave a feat as men are ever called upon to sustain in war time. Never was a heart more severely wrung with anguish than mine was to see that slaughter of brave men in the field of battle. I finally received orders to fall back to the timber from whence the first advance had been made, and did so, the presumption being that we had acted as a target and a menace for the enemy long enough. About half an hour before receiving the order, I heard the first volley of musketry from a point much nearer to Chattanooga than where Sherman's field of operations lay. This later grew into a steady roar. The crashes of musketry came from Bragg's Confederates firing at the Federal lines engaged in scaling the heights of Missionary Ridge, further down the line toward Grant's right.

During every moment of the four hours that my regiment and the Hundredth Indiana Infantry lay under that rain of shot, shell and musketry, reinforcements were sent to the besieged hill in our front by Bragg, without a break and always on the double-quick. To the right of where we lay "in the open" was a depression in the highway that ran along the summit of the Ridge. This road was plainly visible to us from where we lay and was, during all the time we were in the field, filled with Confederate troops hastening to reinforce the second hill. Bragg needed to reinforce his right because the railroad leading to Atlanta was his only connection with the South and it was a very necessary means for supplying his army. Another point that no doubt led Bragg to hold on to this hill with a tenacity that induced him to deplete his left of soldiers was not ascertained until the next morning. At an early hour the orderly sergeant of I Company discovered that a soldier by the name of McClure who was on the skirmish line was unaccounted for. A search had been made for him by his comrades to no purpose. He could not be found among the wounded or dead, and as no prisoners had been taken, his absence created an uneasy feeling all through the regiment. So, early the following morning I undertook to search for him myself. I had all the horses belonging to an infantry regiment mounted for a search party. He was not found and nothing has ever been heard from him since.

It was during my search for young McClure that I discovered additional reasons for Bragg to reinforce his right flank. Behind the second hill immense quantities of supplies were stored. The corn was piled up in sacks as high as could be reached above an army wagon. There was ammunition and quartermasters' stores there by the acre. It was from this point that the Confederate army occupying the whole length of Missionary Ridge clear around to Lookout Mountain was supplied. A railroad track had been laid the whole length of the Ridge and rations and other stores carried to them by an engine and a couple of freight cars. The tracks were laid entirely on top of the ground with no grading, except to bridge some otherwise impassable points. All this great quantity of supplies and ammunition were threatened by General Sherman's attack. And though the Federal army was not aware of this large quantity of supplies, Bragg was, and it was to aid in saving them that he massed so many men in front of General Sherman's troops.

The men put in a dreary night following Missionary Ridge. The loss of the regiment had been very heavy. Several were killed on the skirmish dash across the open ground before they reached the "railroad fill" which gave them excellent shelter. The rebel skirmishers had come down the hill as far as the opposite side of the "fill". It is a positive fact that the Federals laid their guns on the rail of the road on the one side, while the Confederates did the same on the opposite rail, neither one feeling safe in making himself a target by looking over to see what his opponent was about.

The brigade suffered greatly in the loss of officers. Colonel John Loomis and myself being about the only two field officers that remained unscathed when the fight was over. Colonel Timothy O'Mara of the Ninetieth Illinois was killed outright, his Lieutenant-Colonel Owen Stuart, of Chicago, an exceedingly portly man, received a ball that passed clear through him. The ball did not even puncture an intestine, and within two months he was back with his regiment and came into full command of the regiment as a result of the death of his Colonel. The Adjutant of the same regiment was very badly wounded when a piece of a shell struck him a side blow, tearing away his sword-belt and lacerating his entire left side from the hip up to the middle of his ribs. Lieutenant Colonel Heath, of the One Hundredth Indiana, was struck by the ricochet of a shell and so severely hurt that he never returned to his regiment.

Following the struggle both men and officers were worn out. I had a fly stretched over my headquarters to keep off the November dew. I took a former Mississippi slave into my service as hostler when I passed through Corinth. He went by the name of "Big Ben", and he became one of the most faithful of servants. Whenever I was absent the big fellow—he was over six feet in height—would cry like a baby. "Ben" came home with me at the close of the war and I secured work for him at Indianapolis for three dollars a day. Within five years, Ben had gotten married and had a home of his own in a suburb of Indianapolis.

About as soon as the fly was stretched, "Big Ben" made his appearance with a frying pan on his back, two crackers rattling around in a very big haversack, and a pound of bacon without a streak of lean to be seen in it. He said: "I done know'd yo' want somethin' to eat as the last yo' had was at fo' in the mawning, en I's ben huntin' fo' yo' fo' two houhs." The bacon was fried, the crackers munched, and I was grateful to "Big Ben" for even such a "stay" to the gnawing in my stomach.

During the night I had received orders to have the regiment ready to start in pursuit of Bragg's army by five o'clock and that the commissary sergeants should have rations for the men provided before that hour. We were camped in what might be called the "Bottoms of the Tennessee," and at daybreak we discovered that the fog was so dense that one could not make out the figures of another person at six feet away. After breakfast the regiment had to get into line preparatory to the march by feeling and hearing their way. An orderly offered to conduct us "out of the fog!" We started and had proceed about a half mile when all at once the head of the regiment stepped out of the fog into bright sunshine. The fog seemed to have been cut off with a knife. One could stand with half his body in the sun and the other completely hidden in the fog.

It was here that the Twelfth regiment received a high compliment for their conduct in the battle of the day before. An Iowa battery had been camped on the sunny side of the fog-line and a sergeant, when he discovered it was the Twelfth coming through the fog, called to the men of the battery: "Here comes the head of the brigade that lay in that hell-fire storm of shot and shell nearly all day yesterday. Boys, form up here in line and let's give the Twelfth three cheers!" Quite a number of the Iowans marched along with the regiment for some distance and I could hear them saying that in lying there under those guns so long was the bravest act they had seen during the war.

The line of pursuit was up Chickamauga Creek and the men tripped along at a quick pace for they knew they were following a defeated, completely routed enemy. The road was in the bottom of the creek and along each side were farms. We had gone about a mile when one of the men, who had been scouting ahead on his own account, reported that there were fifty or sixty rebels at the farm house just ahead. Halting the regiment I directed every mounted man to come to the front. I placed Major Baldwin in command of the regiment and dashed up to the farmhouse with eight mounted men.

The Confederates had left their rifles stacked in the dooryard, so my men were able to move in before the rebels had a chance to reach their guns. The Confederates surrendered at the word of command, and not a shot was fired on either side or was anybody even accidentally hurt. It was a bloodless victory and shows how badly dispirited were Bragg's troops over their defeat for, before that fight, no eight men could have so easily captured sixty-five rebels. Among the prisoners was a fourteen piece Louisiana regiment brass band.

Prisoners were not what we wanted as we marched southward from Chattanooga, for they had to be guarded, which meant all-night duty as well as all day. However, after my men had divided some of their rations with them, and given them coffee at the first halt, these men at war with one another the day before, now fraternized in a way that was pleasant to see. It was not long until the troops marching on the road occupied by us made the discovery that other Federal troops were joining in the pursuit on other roads. After marching probably ten miles we could hear an occasional shot from some battery way over to our right. The effect of this was to accelerate the pace of the men. Soldiers are very curious and the men on the march were very anxious to ascertain what sort of men were behind the occasional gun we heard. Later the troops met several ambulances with wounded men in them. It was discovered that Bragg's rear guard was disposed to show fight and afterwards we found out that the Confederates had taken a very strong position at Ringgold, where they had massed two or three batteries. The pursuing Federals had pushed up on them without sufficient caution and had gotten badly hurt for their negligence. The Seventh Ohio Infantry came out of that partial surprise with no officer for duty, as every one of them was killed or wounded.

Just as we received the news of the Ringgold affair an orderly came from General Hugh Ewing, our division commander, directing him to halt his command and to give the soldiers a rest and food. We had been pursuing Bragg's army for nearly twenty miles and we were now to retrace our steps. General Sherman's corps was ordered to move back to the pontoon bridge across the Tennessee at the mouth of Chickamauga Creek and there, after supplying his soldiers with rations and ammunition, to proceed with all haste to the relief of General Burnside's army. Burnside's troops were cooped up in Knoxville and were hemmed in on all sides by General Longstreet's Confederate corps.

It must be remembered that Sherman's corps had marched all the way from Memphis to Chattanooga, and as a result, nearly one half of the men were without shoes. They had reached their destination in time to participate in the battle of Missionary Ridge on General Grant's left, and consequently were surprised that Sherman's corps had been selected to still continue their march for a distance of about one hundred and forty miles further. The tired men of Sherman's corps reasoned among themselves that the troops of the Cumberland confined at Chattanooga would have been glad for the opportunity to go to Knoxville in the place of Sherman's men.

The subject was considerably discussed among both officers and enlisted men. I frequently overheard the troops talking over the question for days afterwards. However, it is no part of a soldier's duty to discuss the "whys or wherefores" of an order. It was his duty to obey, no matter whether a blunder or mistake had been committed or not, hence, after the march towards Knoxville began the men were as cheerful as ever. One and all entered into the spirit of the duty to which the corps had been assigned. Worn out with travel and almost barefoot, as many of them were, I can look back and remember the cheerfulness of the men. Each day the corps marched on, ever increasing the number of miles per day they traveled, for there was the haunting fear that they might arrive too late to deliver Burnside's troops.

The men knew that Confederate General Longstreet wold be informed of Sherman's approach and would make a determined effort to capture the half-starved defenders within the fortifications. In fact, he did make several attempts, but fortunately in each instance he was repulsed with heavy loss. Union soldiers stretched telegraph wire from stump to stump over the intermediate ground from whence an assault from the besiegers could come. This was done at about knee high and, as it could not be seen in the onrush of a charge, it tripped the enemy so that two or three volleys were thrown into them before they knew what caused the disaster. Many men fell to rise no more at this sort of a barricade.

Before starting on the Knoxville trip, I had made the effort to turn the sixty-five prisoners over to the provost guard. I went to General Blair's headquarters, taking the prisoners along with me. General Blair at once refused to have anything to do with them, and the talk over what should be done with them grew warm. I asserted that I would not permit my men to "foot it" all day on a forced march and then stand guard over prisoners at night, when they could just as easily be turned over to the proper officers and conveyed to Chattanooga, only six miles distant. I grew so insistent over this point that he threatened to put me under arrest and he was in no pleasant mood when I left him—nor I either, for that matter. I took my prisoners back to my headquarters. The next morning at an early hour, as we were about to set out on the march to Knoxville, I called up all the prisoners and told them what I intended to do. I was not going to put a guard over them at all, but they should march along with the men of the regiment and to forage for themselves just the same as my own men. I exacted a promise from each one that he would not endeavor to make his escape or leave the regiment without my permission. All of those sixty-five prisoners kept their promise to the letter, and each one of them marched right along with the men of the regiment to the vicinity of Knoxville, and returned with us to Chattanooga with not a man missing. I noticed that the first day or two they were reluctant about foraging and declined at first to enter a farmhouse, cabin or smoke house. By the third day, as hunger began to assert itself, they grew bolder and finally would go right in along with my own men.

These men were turned over to other officers after our return to Chattanooga. Fully one-half of them, after being with the Twelfth for twenty-one days, offered to enlist in my regiment. There was no authority to do this short of the Secretary of War, so it was not done, and I was always sorry that it wasn't. The majority of them were from Western North Carolina and some of them claimed they were forced into the Confederate army. The morning they were entrained for Federal prison at Camp Chase, Ohio, I was at the depot and every one of the sixty-five shook hands with me before starting, some of them with tears in their eyes, and once more they begged me to secure permission to join my regiment.

The trip to Knoxville was a severe one, a journey that tested the pluck and endurance of all the men. The orders assigning the Fifteenth corps to the duty of relieving General Burnside required that the march should be a rapid one, as the conditions were such that Burnside's force, which had been short on rations for weeks, might be compelled to surrender before Sherman's relieving expedition should get there. The troops were stripped of every impediment that might cause delay. Not even a tent was allowed to either officers or men.

The road to Knoxville was along the Tennessee River most of the way. The Tennessee valley was most beautiful with well-fenced farms. While there was no special objection to slavery, that form of labor was almost unknown in East Tennessee. The farms were almost totally cultivated by whites. Here and there an old and faithful slave could be found at some of the wealthier homes. This was very noticeable to the men who had done duty down in Mississippi and in West Tennessee where the colored men held in bondage greatly outnumbered the whites.

After a few days the haversacks of the men were becoming empty. Forage parties were organized and sent out to gather up whatever would answer for food. After the troops reached Greenville, the place where ex-president Andrew Johnson lived and where his little square sign, "A. Johnson, Tailor", was still nailed up over the door of a house on one of the principal streets, the supply of food grew very scarce. The situation looked very gloomy, for from then on we never passed anyone who was not hungry. The need, however, to reach and attack Longstreet's troops was so great a necessity that the men bore their hunger cheerfully and willingly made big marches each day.

Without shoes the men's feet were bruised and cut as they tramped over the rough ground. It was after Greenville that I found the men had discovered a substitute for a worn-out pair of shoes. I saw many soldiers who had cut a piece out of the hide of a freshly killed beef sufficiently large for each foot, put his foot in the center of each and draw up the sides all around his ankles and tied it with a string. It was left on the foot and soon became dried and hard, but it fit the foot so well that no corns worried him at all! It was a wonderfully effective substitute, and many soldiers wore them all the way back to Chattanooga, where they were supplied with new shoes.

Sherman's small army was now approaching Knoxville. Orders came to close up the ranks of each regiment, to gather in all the loiterers, and keep in ranks. Directly a halt came, and I discovered that General Sherman and his staff were only a short distance to the front, so I rode over to catch some of the news. It was while I was there that an officer followed by a couple of orderlies came flying across an open field. I could guess by the large envelope he carried that he bore important news. He delivered the written message to General Sherman, who soon announced that General Burnside's missive was to the effect that during the night General Longstreet had raised the siege and was twenty miles out on his retreat into Virginia! General Burnside very eloquently thanked General Sherman for coming to his assistance, stating the arrival of his corps that threatened an attack upon Longstreet's rear, compelled the Confederates to get out of range as quickly as possible.

Knoxville was so badly stripped of supplies that it was out of the question to permit a large body of men to enter a town filled already with starving troops and citizens. We were ordered to go into camp right then and there. The rest came as a godsend to me because a few days before I had sprained my ankle and the injury was so painful that nothing could have been better than the complete rest obtained by two days in camp.

The two days rest did the soldier a vast amount of good although food was dreadfully scarce. I am sure that articles were used for food that under more favorable conditions, had commissaries attempted to issue such truck, would have cause a mutiny in the camp. Let me relate an instance. Small gristmills were quite numerous on the streams in the region as the waterpower was used to operate the mills. There were places that averaged a water mill every mile or so. Some of these mills ground corn only, but here and there were very old mills that were erected by the first settlers. In these old mills flour dust had settled upon all the joists and crosspieces and beams to a depth of an inch and sometimes more. I have known soldiers to gather this unpalatable dust, the accumulation of years, take it into camp where they mixed this "gray-headed" dust with water, made a kind of dough of it, baked it on a board before their camp fire, and ate that sort of truck. I tasted a morsel of the mixture and told the soldier who gave it to me that there would be more real nourishment if he would lie down on his back and let the moonshine in his mouth for a few minutes. Such was the "stuff" out of which bread was made during the march to Knoxville.

It was necessary to go over new ground on the return march to Chattanooga so that foraging could be done in a region that had been less raided by both armies. After marching some distance the head of the column stopped in front of a big double-hewed log house. An old and stoop-shouldered man, who was overjoyed to see us, hobbled out to the gate to chat with the men who were defending the Union. He claimed to be ninety-five years old and called his son over who was seventy-five. Both of these men were firm in the conviction that the Union was to be preserved, as it was plain to see that God was on the Union side. I humored the two old men considerably while I talked to them and made them extremely happy when I presented them with a pound of coffee, the one plentiful ration the army had on that trip. When I left both these old men never ceased for a moment in grateful thanks for the coffee. Their farm had been frequently raided and every particle of food that could be taken had been carried away, yet they made no complaint. The coffee seemed to make everything right.

The return march was made in no special haste and the corps was at least three days more on the way back than going. The country, even in December, was beautiful. The weather was quite cold, making the march severe on the barefoot soldiers, yet the troops were in a merry mood. A quantity of supplies was sent to Charleston and it was there that a full ration of hard tack was issued to the men. It was the first they had received in twenty-one days. For myself, I never took kindly to hard bread, better known by the expressive term, "hard tack." It was to me a tasteless food, difficult to masticate, but I presume an excellent substitute for the real "staff of life" in nutritious qualities. This hard tack tasted better to me than it ever had before and from that time on I had a certain respect for it.

The army stopped at Charleston for a day or two. The next stop was on the identical ground where the preliminary arrangements and the formation of the troops were made at the opening of the battle of Missionary Ridge. While the ground looked familiar, the return to the same ground where the brigade had suffered so greatly in killed and wounded called up sad memories of lost comrades. I remember a number of the dead had remained unburied. Most of these had been found in a short, deep ravine on the southern slope of the second hill. The remains of these men were gathered up and buried in a row with headboards made from pieces of cracker boxes. Their names were written as plainly as possible with a lead pencil. Thank God, the remains of these men who had laid down their lives to preserve an imperiled nation, were afterwards either taken to their homes in the North or gathered up and placed in the large and beautiful national cemetery located not far from where they fell.

We remained here only a few days resting up, adding avoirdupois, and refitting every soldier with new shoes who needed them. In the Twelfth regiment there were only sixteen pairs of shoes that were still useful. The new shoes were of a new form that had just come out which was considered a great improvement upon those issued to the entire army for the first two years of the war.

All through the war both men and officers were ever ready for a march, a skirmish, or even a great battle, and my observation was that the most wearisome days they put in were those in camp. It was for this reason that the Twelfth always introduced pastimes, games and novelties of various kinds and kept themselves busy instead of lying in their tents brooding and complaining. Consequently there was great rejoicing in camp when a the order was received directing General Sherman's command to proceed to Northern Alabama, making Huntsville the headquarters, with the brigades and divisions to be stationed among the various important villages along the Memphis & Charleston railroad from Stevenson to Huntsville. It fell to the lot of the brigade of which the Twelfth was a member, to be located at Scottsboro, a small village somewhat strategically important. It was here that the troops put in the winter of 1863-1864.

Card 1:

W | 12 | Ind.

Reub. Williams

Rank Col..... 12 Reg't Indiana Infantry.

Age 30 years

Appears on

Field and Staff Muster-out Roll

of the organization named above. Roll dated
Washington, D.C., June 8, 1865.
Muster-out to date June 8, 1865.
Last paid to Dec. 31, 1864

Clothing account:
Last settled ...., 186 ; drawn since $..........100
Due soldier $............100; due U. S. $..........100
Am't for cloth'g in kind or money adv'd $..........100

Due U. S. for arms, equipments, &c., $..........100
Bounty paid $............100; due $..........100
Valuation of horse, $..............100
Valuation of horse equipments, $..........100
Remarks: Promoted to Lt. Col.
from Capt. Co. "J." 17 Aug.
1862. Promoted to Colonel
vice Link Deck 17 Nov.
1862. Received notification
of appointment as (over).

Book mark: ....

(840) M. Michael Copyist.

Card 2:

W | 12 | Ind.

Reuben Williams

Rank Col..... 12 Reg't Indiana Infantry.

Appears on

Field and Staff Muster Roll

for Jan & Feb., 1863
Present or absent ....
Stoppage, $..........100 for ....

Due Gov't, $..........100 for ....

Valuation of horse, $..........100
Valuation of horse equipments, $..........100
Remarks: Paroled at Holly Springs, Miss.
Dec. 20, 1862.

Book mark: ....

(857) M. Michael Copyist.

CHAPTER 9

Winter Camp at Scottsboro, Alabama

Great God of Nations, thy goodness has crowned us.
A land and a people peculiar to thee:
Let thy wisdom and power, still mantled around us,
Preserve what that goodness has taught to be free.
—George W. Young

The winter of 1863-64 the command of which the Twelfth was a part, was stationed at Scottsboro, Alabama. There were a number of empty houses in the little old village so many wives and daughters of the officers came down to be with their husbands and fathers, and stayed in these very excellent winter quarters. The soldiers of my regiment had built the handsomest camp that any of us saw during our absence from Indiana.

The regiment was given a piece of ground, sloping up the south side of a mountain and covered with stone from the size of a baseball up to one about the size of a watermelon. The lay of the ground could not have been better for an ideal camp except for the stones. Every man in the Twelfth went to work and after hauling away the stone with the regimental wagons, the ground was cleared and the men then proceeded to build a camp. The stones that were removed filled sixteen hundred wagons and were hauled to a spot a quarter mile away and dumped into a ravine. All the members of the regiment entered into the spirit of camp construction with so much vigor that every one of them took pride in the building and ornamentation of a place they were to occupy as winter quarters. The grounds were laid off with tape lines precisely as laid down in the plat given in the tactics. The regiment had the "wedge" or "A" shaped tents, which were the showiest of all the tents when they were set up correctly.

The grounds on which the rows of tents were located had a considerable slope and therefore gave an excellent chance for drainage. A covered ditch was dug from the head of the company down the slope. At the upper end an empty barrel with both heads knocked out was set in the ground and into this everything that accumulated in company quarters was cast and was carried away by water and the deepness of the descent.

At the head of the company the men built an arch composed of evergreens. The center of each arch depicted the letters of the company constructed out of telegraph wire covered with evergreens. In front of the tent of the Colonel the men built a similar arch with a tall pole through the center where the garrison flag was raised. The numeral "12" was supported from the center of this arch. In front of the headquarters the boys constructed a sanded floor about twelve feet in width and this was covered with evergreen boughs the entire length, about a hundred feet. The boughs were laid on cross-pieces supported by posts and latticed in by splitting long lath from the dead cedar trees found on the side of the mountain. Every morning the whole camp was "policed" and the "company street" swept with hand made brooms.

In addition to the beautiful camp, the men erected a round-log guard house, a commissary and quartermaster's stores. And the greatest of all, they built a large, round-log chapel in which the chaplain held religious services at regular periods, and prayer meetings every Thursday night. These meeting were well attended. The Rev. M. D. Gage, as chaplain, possessed the unbounded love and esteem of every member of the regiment whether religiously inclined or not.

This camp attracted the attention of many visitors, and even soldiers of other regiments came from six or eight miles distant to see it. Theodore R. Davis, the artist correspondent of Harper's Weekly was sent from Huntsville to sketch a picture of the camp for publication in that illustrated journal and it appeared about a month later.

The winter was an important period in the history of the Fifteenth corps in several ways. The special one being a change in its commander. The creation of the Military Division of the Mississippi, and placing General Sherman in command of it, Grant being made a Lieutenant-General and placed in command of all the Federal armies, made it necessary to give the corps a new commander. A rumor prevailed that General Frank P. Blair was to succeed General Sherman. This created an ill feeling among the officers of the corps that a body of them committed a breach of military etiquette that might have gotten them into difficulty. Some of the leaders so resented the placing of General Blair in command of the Fifteenth that they induced quite a large number of officers of various ranks to go to General Sherman's headquarters to protest against the Blair appointment. Sherman gave them a pretty severe "rap over the knuckles" for assuming to dictate who should be the leaders of the armies. General Sherman then informed them that General John A. Logan had been selected for the position. I had gone along with the officers, and I knew that few of the men had given any thought to the breach of military discipline that they were committing. But it turned out all right and the corps were overjoyed that it was "Black Jack Logan" who was to be at the head of the Fifteenth Corps.

During the winter the army put in at Scottsboro the social features of the town "took on airs". Tuesdays and Fridays were the days that both whites and Negroes were to draw rations from our commissary. It wasn't long until the soldier boys were well acquainted with the people within a fifteen-mile radius of Scottsboro. As there were no enemy near us the wives and daughters of the Federal officers came down from the North in large numbers to visit. At one time it was estimated that there were about eighty of the female sex in the Scottsboro camp. With all these ladies gathered there, it is no wonder that some one proposed having a big ball. The town possessed a good-sized plain-framed building used as the town hall. In this building was a large long room especially suited for a waltz, cotillion or a gallop. Then it came about that the writer was named as "chief cook and bottle washer" for the coming ball. Invitations were sent out to all the young ladies whose names were on the commissary's list for drawing rations, kindly requesting them to join in the dance at the date fixed.

I was fully aware that some sort of means would have to be provided for the ladies to reach Scottsboro, as few of them had horses or vehicles. Many of them lived fifteen miles distant and they would have to be sent for. Henry Flowers, a soldier from Etna Green, Indiana, was sent for and I put him in charge of six ambulances. He with a driver for each one was to go out in the country and bring in every girl and married woman who wished to attend the ball at Scottsboro. Along toward evening on the day fixed for the dance these ambulances began to arrive in the village "loaded to the guards." Here was a dilemma! What was a man going to do with all these women? They had to be cared for, and I solved it in this way. I secured a large hospital tent, a brand new one, and had it set up near my headquarters. And from the same obliging quartermaster I secured a whole bale of blankets—a couple hundred probably. As fast as the women arrived they were turned into the big tent. I also sent out and borrowed all the looking glasses, big and little, in the possession of the officers and pinned them up at various points inside the tent. It was understood by all the ladies from the North, and insisted upon, that the visitors should be handsomely treated in every way, and should be taken to the quarters of the officers engaged in getting up the dance for at least one meal. Since the Southern ladies had no way to procure the fashionable hoop skirt, they made their own wide spreading skirt using grapevines for the hoops! The dance was a great success and was talked of for a long time after.

General Grant's promotion to Lieutenant General of the army was an office created for him by Congress. The lifting of General Grant from a Major General into the new office was followed by the creation of "the Military Division of the Mississippi," which placed all of the Western troops under the command of General William T. Sherman. Grant by his new rank became the supreme commander of all the army no matter where stationed. The law creating a Lieutenant General was a long step and a most important one in hurrying along the close of the war. Previous to the making of Grant a Lieutenant General, there was no higher officer than that of Major General, and of these there were many. The question of rank was fixed by the date of commission only, and this led to bickering, faultfinding, jealousies and a general lack of unity among the leaders in the field. General Halleck, representing the War Department in Washington, seemed to have an ill-will against General Grant both before and after his very successful operations leading up to the capture of both Forts Henry and Donelson. This ill will seemed to follow the General up to and even after the battle of Shiloh. In the Army of the Potomac, the faultfinding and bickering were greater than it was in the West and led to placing the army in that section under many different Major Generals. The moment that Congress created the position of Lieutenant General and Grant received his commission, the question of rank was definitely settled from that time forward.

An almost brotherly feeling existed between General Grant and General Sherman. The latter gave to his chief that unbounded loyalty and capable assistance without which not even a Grant could have succeeded. Sherman extended to his new superior officer in rank and command, warm, hearty, and efficient support. I firmly believe that more than any other officer the war produced, Sherman possessed the love and high esteem of the men he commanded. It was a common saying among the troops that they always felt safe and ready to obey any order they might receive from Sherman. It was even said that the "his army was willing to assault hell itself, if Sherman was in command". Looking back, the making of Grant a Lieutenant General of the army carried with it more elements of success than almost anything else could have. Not a single serious reverse occurred from the hour that he assumed the supreme command of all the forces of the United States until Lee surrendered at Appomattox.

Every day in camp the regiment went through battalion drill and became almost a machine that could be doubled up on itself and in an instant spread out in line of battle. The movements were done at the double-quick constantly changing to the four points of the compass, firing and reloading. They performed as many as eight different and distinct battalion movements, including forming and reducing square, before coming to a halt. Drill was witnessed whenever it was performed by hundreds of spectators. The band had a stand built in the edge of timber and furnished "double-quick" music for every movement made. Since there was a lack of special duties for the Chaplain, I thought of the plan of closing the dress parade with a short prayer following the manual of arms usual at a parade and the "beating off" of the band along the front of the regiment. During the prayer, the men stood at "parade rest", each soldier slightly tipping his cap. This was the first time where a prayer on dress parade was seen and heard, to my knowledge, during the entire war. The Twelfth was the only regiment to utilize its chaplain in that way.

We had amusements of many kinds while in camp. I remember one morning a snow-balling in which the men drew off and took sides, and although we were so far down South that one would hardly suppose it possible to have a game of that kind, yet such was the case. The snow was in splendid condition to make snowballs. The game came very nearly seriously, and would have done so had I not been watching it very carefully. As the game progressed the men grew warm in the work. It became a charge from one side only to be driven back again by the other, and I could see that the hotheaded on each side were rapidly losing their tempers and presently instead of snow balls it was stones that were used as missiles. After a few us had been hurt on both sides, there was a rush of the contestants for their guns, and for a moment, I had all I could do to bring order out of the chaos that followed the stone throwing. Discipline, however prevailed and obedience to orders soon restored the men to their everyday selves.

During the winter of 1863-1864 the troops stationed at Scottsboro became quite intimate with all the people in the country for several miles around, and on Sundays quite a number of citizens made it a point to visit the camps of the various regiments. I know of one, at least, who went back there after the war, and married the girl he courted during our stay.

Another thing occurred that winter that was of great importance to the troops. Those who had enlisted in 1861, by order of the War Department were granted a furlough of thirty days and hundred dollars to every man whose term of enlistment was not far from completion, if he would re-enlist for a second term of "three years or during the war." I made a strong effort, backed by General Logan, to have the order include the Twelfth, as there were about one hundred and fifty of its members who had been in the service since the very beginning of the war. They had served the first year in the original regiment and on its reorganization once more entered the service. The wording of the order, however, was against us. The rule that was adopted only permitted those to re-enlist, beginning with the date of the muster-in of the regiment as a body. This cut the Twelfth out and although there were men in its ranks who had served longer than whole regiments of soldiers to whom the order applied. All these facts were succinctly made out and sent to the Secretary of War, asking that the regiment be included in the order for re-enlistment. But the decision was against the proposition. The regiment remained at Scottsboro while quite a number of regiments from the same division and even the same brigade got the opportunity to go home on a junketing tour with transportation furnished home and back and a four hundred premium for doing so. The plan, however, was a good one for it enabled the army to maintain its efficiency by the return of those seasoned veterans.

Those pleasant days flitted away rapidly with only an episode or two worth recording, one of them being an expedition made up from various regiment of the corps to make a reconnaissance in the direction of Dalton, Georgia, where the principal headquarters of the Confederate army was located. This expedition was to see what the Confederates were doing. Dalton lay some distance south of the old battleground of Chickamauga, and the rebels there were no doubt doing about the same as the Federals were, that is making every possible preparation for the campaign that would come in the Spring. During the raid on Dalton, the troops had several skirmishes, and one of them almost large enough to be called a battle. The Federals orders were not to precipitate an engagement but only obtain information as to what the rebels were doing, and I to ascertain if any large body of their troops had been withdrawn from the Chattanooga front or not. Discovering that they were still there in force, the expedition returned.

It was during this winter that General Sherman went down to Vicksburg and organized a large body of troops. The intention was to make a raid upon Meridian, an important point on the railroad that ran from New Orleans to Richmond, Virginia. In order to prevent the massing of too heavy a force in front of Sherman after the Union troops returned from Dalton, another expedition was organized to assist Sherman. A force of five thousand men was sent across the Tennessee and further South into the State of Alabama. Colonel John Mason Loomis had gone to his home in Chicago, which left myself in command of the brigade. The expedition was made of details of regiments from the different brigades and divisions that were encamped all along the line of the railroad from Stevenson to Huntsville. The troops assembled at Larkin's Ferry, where a pontoon bridge was thrown across the Tennessee River.

The passage of the men over the river placed the Federals in a region that had neither been fought over, raided, nor had it been foraged for supplies by either army. As a consequence, the men lived like "fighting cocks" as soon as their feet pressed the soil of this plentiful region. My whole command on the first evening after crossing the pontoon where we went into camp awaiting the arrival of the entire force intended for the raid, had a plentiful supply of fresh beef. The commissary had forgotten, or else someone else had failed to place on the wagons, a supply of salt. Salt was selling inside the Confederacy at five dollars a pound and none was to be had. There was considerable grumbling among the troops over its absence. But the next morning, a Yankee soldier had discovered a spring that gushed from the base of a very high hill in the vicinity, the water of which was strongly impregnated with salt. Extending his discovery he ascertained that a quantity of pure salt could be found in the immediate vicinity. It had been formed into crystals much resembling round, rusted stone. When these "stones" were broken it was found to be pure salt, created by the evaporation of the water. This "Yankee" had discovered an article almost as valuable as gold to the people of the region, which never was found by those who had lived there for a hundred years.

The next day the troops took up their march southward. The road lead up a ravine and widened out until finally the level country was reached. The head of the column had not proceeded far until it met a detachment of Confederate cavalry. A skirmish at once took place. One feature of the expedition was to make it appear as large as possible to the eyes of the enemy. In order to make a display of the force; the regiments marched with a quarter of a mile of space between them so that the citizens that we passed would magnify the force into an army when they gave the information to the rebels. The Confederates were never in sufficient force to compel the expedition to do more than halt for a short time. The Federals marched down into Alabama as far as Lebanon. Probably a thousand mounted men confronted the march at times but they were always routed. The object of the raid was to favor General Sherman's operations. We learned afterward that the raid was quite successful, for a considerable force of Confederates was detached from the troops defending Meridian, and sent to see what the raid in Northern Alabama really meant.

During the absence of the troops who had re-enlisted and had gone home on their thirty days' furlough, the picket duty was considerably heavier than it was previously. There were no armed bodies of Confederates on the North side of the river during the winter of 1863-1864, but it was well known that communication was kept up with the soldiers of the Confederacy by their families. As a consequence a close watch was kept along the river by detachments of mounted men. Very often these troops found canoes and skiffs landed on the northern bank, having evidently been used by citizens or soldiers in the Confederate ranks to revisit their families on our side of the Tennessee. The orders were to destroy all these boats and that a stricter watch should be kept as these visiting soldiers were no doubt acting as spies as well as visitors to their homes. Of necessity these visits had to be made in the night. It always struck me that little if any information of any particular value would be gleaned in a nighttime visit by the enemy. However, the orders were quite strict on the subject. I received an order to gather up all horses possible and make up a detachment for the purpose of making a thorough examination of the country that lay between the Memphis & Charleston railroad and the Tennessee River.

The One Hundredth was located at Bellefont. In obedience to my instructions, and in order to secure as many mounted men as possible, I had started to Bellefont with all the horses and riding mules that my own and the Ninetieth Illinois regiment could furnish. At Bellefont I was able to add thirty-two more men, which made a force of seventy-five. This was not a large force but sufficient for the purpose intended. The country was thinly settled and in many places layers of rock cropped out of the ground.

We moved at a rapid gait and these rocks were worn as smooth as a floor by wind and water, making horseback riding often difficult and dangerous to infantry soldiers, unaccustomed to riding.

Colonel Johnson accompanied the detachment from his regiment, and although it was really unnecessary for either him or myself to go along with the raid, both of us went along for the novelty of the affair and to relieve some of the monotony of camp life. The horses and mules used on such occasion were unacquainted with any drill, which would not have been the case had the command been composed of cavalry. It was not long after the troops left Bellefont until we were informed that the advance guard was nearing a river. I ordered the men to be quiet, to move forward at a walk and to keep themselves and their horses hidden. There was a bend in the stream and from which an extended view could be had both up and down the Tennessee. Near the stream the command was halted and a couple of soldiers were sent forward alone to ascertain if there were any boats or canoes in sight or any men crossing the stream from either side. They had scarcely gotten into position until one of them crawled back to the head of the column with the information that two boats, one a canoe and the other a skiff had just landed on the north side of the stream. As near as they could make out a couple of horses were on the bank near by. Colonel Johnson asked for the privilege of taking charge of a detail to secure the horses before the strangers themselves could reach them. Accordingly he took about six men and quietly went to gather the horses. The main body moved close to the river and as the two men discovered the larger party, they at once rushed for the horses, reaching them about the same time as Colonel Johnson did. The two men were taken prisoner without a shot being fired.

The two boats had been pulled partly out of the water and our men destroyed them by lifting large stones as high as they could and dropping the stones on the bottoms of each. The skiff was easily broken, but the canoe withstood several attempts before the bottom fell out. The two prisoners claimed they were citizens living on the south bank of the Tennessee and had only crossed over to get some food and medicines for the relief of a sick family. Their story was probably true, but as my orders were strict, they were sent back to Bellefont for further examination. The order to destroy all means of communication used in crossing the river was general, and the boats would have been broken up whether anyone had been found near them or not.

The expedition proceeded on its way and about an hour later the advance guard discovered two mounted men to whom they gave chase. One soldier waited for the main column catch up. As soon as the information was given, the whole number of troops was ordered to move forward at a gallop and join in the chase. As long as the fleeing individuals remained in the undergrowth they were comparatively free from discovery.

Colonel Johnson has scouted all around his camp when first located at Bellefont and informed me that in the direction the men were fleeing they would soon be in open ground. Sure enough, the detachment soon emerged in an area almost free from undergrowth. The advance guard reported the men in sight, riding as fast as their horses could carry them. The order was given to chase them at full speed. It was quite a helter-skelter pursuit. Some of the horses would stumble and throw the men mounted on them over their heads. Some of the men were so unaccustomed to riding on horseback that their pantaloons were pushed up to their hips. The sight of them would have made such superb cavalry officers as a Sheridan or a Custer grit their teeth at such untidy appearance on the back of a horse.

The main body rushed upon on area that was smooth wet rock. When my horse first struck the slippery rock going at a fast gallop, he slid on all four feet for a distance of thirty feet. This fact was established on the return of the troops as on of the soldiers measured the ground by the scratching of the horse's almost brand new shoes on the solid rock. It was here that more than a dozen men, unaccustomed to horseback riding, met their "Waterloo". Those who remained mounted on faster animals continued the pursuit. After a long chase, both were captured and sent under guard to Huntsville. What became of them I do not know. They were probably kept in the guardrooms for some time and then dismissed. I knew of a number of those similarly captured who were not tried as spies but let go after a short time. Few Federal officers or the men composing the troops in the field can be accused of cruelty towards their captured enemies. On the contrary, I have often seen the men of my own command share the last scrap of rations they possessed with newly captured prisoners.

During those days of waiting for the return of spring there were many ways for putting in the time. I often made visits to General Logan's headquarters at Huntsville. During one visit to Huntsville made by Major Baldwin and myself, we witnessed a horrible accident. Baldwin and I had gone to the depot after a day and night's visit, where we had gone to hear the celebrated actress, Julia Daily. The depot was situated well out on the north side of town. We were waiting for the train to depart for our camp at 9 o'clock in the morning. As we reached the depot, we noticed a full battery of artillery going out to some open fields at the north of town for a drill. Both of us knew the officers of the battery quite well, and two of them rode over to us to shake hands. It was at this moment that the wheels of the leading caisson of the battery struck the rails of the road and in an instant there was a flash of vivid light, a deafening boom, and a body-shaking jar. Then we heard the screams of dying horses and groans from wounded men. The havoc was fearful. Both the men who were sitting on the seat of the caisson had been blown into fragments. The span of horses next to the wheels had been almost wiped out of all semblance of what they were before the explosion. The rumps of both the horses in the lead had been blown away. Up in a nearby tree was the main trunk of a man with mangled fragments clinging to the limbs of the tree. It was a fearful sight brought about by the careless packing of the shells in the caisson. There were four men and four horses killed outright. Several horses were so severely wounded that they had to be killed. Seven men were badly wounded. It is certain that if the two officers had not come over to speak to Major Baldwin and myself, they would have been killed or wounded also, for the place of one of them on such a march is at the side of the caisson that exploded, and the other would not have been far distant.

On another occasion Major Baldwin and myself got a seven days' pass to Nashville, which was a great congregating place for officers and men on their way either to their regiments or their home. We dined at a first-class restaurant. A soldier longs for fresh vegetables that are missing from army rations. It was February when we visited Nashville and it was too soon for early vegetables, except onions and radishes procured from hothouses in the North. Our bill for a single meal of onions and radishes was $4. When we found that a single piece of rye bread was twenty cents, we could see that four dollars' worth of radishes and onions was not out of proportion.

During the winter of 1863-1864 important changes were made. One was the assignment of Brigadier-General Hugh Ewing—a brother-in-law of General Sherman—to Louisville, Kentucky. Brigadier General William Harrow was then placed in command of the First division of the Fifteenth corps. The officers and men of the division very much regretted the change. They had formed an attachment for General Ewing, who had been in command of them from before the capture of Vicksburg. Soldiers form an attachment for their superior officers largely in proportion to the way they look after the interests of the men they command. General Ewing did everything he could in his power to look after the commissary and quartermaster department of his division—departments that are very essential to the enlisted men.

General William Harrow was an Indiana soldier, having first entered the service in the Fourteenth Indiana Infantry, but all of his service up to his arrival at Scottsboro was with the Army of the Potomac. The latter was against him for it must be admitted that Western officers and soldiers held a sort of prejudice against the eastern army. The New England states possessed such excellent militia laws previous to the war that when Lincoln issued his first call for seventy-five thousand men; the Eighth Massachusetts was on its way to Washington the same day.

In order to suppress this prejudice as much as possible, I determined to give General Harrow a reception on his arrival at Scottsboro. Colonel John Loomis had gone home with his regiment after it had almost unanimously re-enlisted for a second three years' term, leaving me his position in his absence. Colonel Loomis had left his brigade quarters with all the tents standing and I had transferred my quarters from those of the Twelfth to the brigade. We prepared to welcome our new division commander in a handsome way. His coming had been announced, and in order to provide for him, a fine new officer's tent was pitched. A lounge secured by some of the men in a raid was provided for him. A table had been set under the fly of a hospital tent and an addition of handsome canned goods was added to the regular soldier's rations. The "staff of life" was a splendid light bread, baked in an outdoor oven, instead of the usual hard tack. It was a fine dinner to which General Harrow was conducted on his arrival at Scottsboro.

I gave a reception to General Harrow partly because he was from Indiana but more to break down the prejudiced feeling entertained by any man from the eastern army. The course he pursued failed to win either the officers or the men to him. He pretended to be a strict disciplinarian, to which very few had any objections, for most men had by this time been in the service a sufficient length of time to know that discipline and a strict obedience to orders is essential in a good army. General Harrow was far from possessing the necessary qualifications to induce men to obey him. One of the first things he introduced was the punishment of the men for slight infractions by compelling them to sit astride a pole fitted up for the purpose at his headquarters. On occasion I have seen as many as three straddling the pole at about six feet from the ground, their feet tied together on the underside and a guard with a loaded musket with fixed bayonet, marching back and forth underneath. On discovering this mode of punishment for the first time, I was sorry I had gone to the trouble to give him a reception on his arrival. He was probably sixty years of age, and while he may have possessed military knowledge, he never gave evidence of its possession during the Atlanta campaign the following summer.

Quartermasters, commissaries and ordnance officers were exceedingly busy as stores and munitions of war were constantly arriving in preparation for the coming campaign that was to be on a grand scale. That winter the entire army exchanged whatever musket they had for the improved new Springfield, up to that time the finest gun on the face of the earth. The "man behind the gun" was proud of the new firearm and took better care of it then he did his old one. There had been an effort made to provide this division with the new Spencer, a gun that fired seven shots in about the time that a man with a muzzleloader would fire two. But for some reason none but the Forty-sixth Ohio secured this special arm previous to the opening of the Atlanta campaign.

In a short time the absent regiments were back in their old places. Colonel John Loomis returned with his regiment, the Twenty-sixth Illinois. Loomis must have been sixty years old during the war and his hair and beard were white as snow. I always liked the old man even if he did possess the faculty of compelling his colonels to get up in the night to read some frivolous order which might just as well been delivered after breakfast the next morning. He was a truly patriotic old man and possessed many good qualities.

The old gentleman had been hankering after an appointment as Brigadier-General ever since he first assumed command of the troops in the capacity as a Colonel. There was considerable rivalry between him and Colonel Charles Walcott, of the Forty-sixth Ohio for the position. Both men were aware that it was unlikely there would be more than one appointment from the same division. Not long after the return of the veterans, I was surprised to receive an order directing me to take command of the First brigade, First division, Fifteenth corps. Colonel John Loomis had resigned. That evening at his headquarters I urged him to remain in the army at least through the coming campaign. He informed me that his business at home would not permit it. When the war broke out, he had dropped everything and entered the service. His business losses due to his absence had been very great. The troops were drawn up in a line to bid him good-bye. The scene was quite affecting. He had been with the brigade for over a year and in the service almost three. The tears ran down the cheeks of the kind-hearted and thoroughly loyal old man as he shook hands with his fellow officers and bade them good-bye.

As the spring of 1864 approached signs were plentiful that there would be "something doing" during the coming summer. In the West the forces that would be active in the coming events were the Army of the Cumberland, under the trusted leader, Major-General Thomas; the Army of Tennessee, under Major-General McPherson; and a portion of the Army of the Ohio, under Major-General Schofield. These troops were distributed all the way from Vicksburg to Chattanooga, at which point a force numbering close to one hundred thousand men assembled in the early days of May 1864. While these preparations were going forward in the West, Lieutenant-General Grant was engaged in mustering his forces for offensive operations against General Lee, with Richmond, the capital of the Confederacy, as the objective point.

CHAPTER 10

Fighting Against General Joe Johnston

O, the trees were in bloom, and the tailing arbutus
Wove a carpet of beauty o'er highland and dell,
When we stood by our guns at the dawn of the morning,
As down the long line rang the words: "All is well."
And our hearts they were light, for we heard in our fancy
The Sabbath bells chiming o'er hill top and lea;
And our homes they seemed nearer as we listened that morning,
When Sherman rode forth on his "March to the Sea!"
—War-Time Lyric

The concentration of General Sherman's forces was effected by the close of the first week in May. We took up a march from Scottsboro to Chattanooga passing over nearly the same route for the fourth time. The route was still lined with the carcasses of mules that had died during the winter. It was said that in a single mile not a step could be taken by man or beast without stepping on the fragments of some sort of dead animal. The road was entirely cut out of the solid rock and not sufficiently wide at any point to permit the passing of teams. It was the custom to ring a bell that the passage was clear for a train of wagons. I saw disabled mules cut loose from their harness on one occasion, and still alive, pushed off the bluff down into the Tennessee River, there to suffer and struggle for awhile from the injuries before rendering up their last breath.

On arriving at Chattanooga, the greatest activity prevailed. All surplus baggage was ordered to be stored, and there were several restrictions on tents and wagons. Officers were limited to the barest necessities and the enlisted men were held down strictly to what the soldiers very appropriately designated "dog" or "pup tents". A full camp of tents was never more beheld. While in camp, I had the opportunity to revisit the scenes of the struggle of Missionary Ridge and took along with me Lieutenant Larry McCarty, an aide-de-camp of my own staff, of the "Ninetieth Ireland" as the Ninetieth Illinois was called by the boys. We climbed the Ridge not far from where General Bragg, of the Confederacy, had his headquarters. On reaching the elevation and casting my eye back toward Chattanooga and the lower land lying below the ridge clear out to Tunnel Hill, it became a bewildering wonderment why Bragg did not hold harder to a line and position of such great natural strength. I believe that the General became panic stricken himself on that fatal day for the Confederacy.

If I remember correctly, it was the seventh day of May 1864, that the right wing of the army, to which the brigade I commanded belonged, set forth from Chattanooga on a march that has since become known in history and song as "The Atlanta Campaign." My brigade had been together for more than a year and consequently each of the four regiments composing it had become attached to one another. This brotherly feeling was noticed in many brigades and was partly due to the fact that each regiment had passed through the fires of battle together. There was not only an attachment existing, but also a perfect dependence, each regiment feeling that it could rely upon either of the other three in all emergencies. The First brigade, First division, was composed of the Twelfth (my own), the One Hundredth Indiana, the Twenty-sixth Illinois and the Ninetieth Illinois.

It may be well at this point, to mention briefly the general formation of General Sherman's army, as it set forth on the memorable campaign. General Thomas occupied the center; General McPherson the right; and General Schofield the left. General Hooker held the right center. Several divisions of some of these corps had been left in the rear, mainly to guard the railroads and supply depots. General Sherman's Army was supplied by only one line of road running from Chattanooga back to Louisville, Kentucky. This was a long line that had to be protected from Confederate cavalry raids, guerrilla bands, and even hostile citizens who were capable of, and could do, much damage by burning bridges or blowing up tunnels. Sherman's greatest fear was that supplies of all kinds, but especially ammunition, might be cut off by some disaster. A two days' battle would consume all the ammunition on hand, and leave him powerless for a third day's struggle and this fear kept him uneasy at all times.

General John Logan had taken command of the Fifteenth corps and was long entrusted to General Sherman as "Black Jack". He came to us having already won a splendid reputation under Grant. He had been with Grant from Belmont to Forts Henry and Donelson. He was at Shiloh, and in all the operations about Corinth and in the siege of Vicksburg. He possessed a striking figure as an officer and instantly won his way into the hearts of the officers and men composing the corps. He was esteemed and beloved by every man in the Western army and idolized by his own corps.

It was well known that the Confederate army was in heavy force at Dalton. Forts had been built on that ground, as well as entrenchment's at all essential points. Throughout the entire Atlanta campaign the Federals had to force the fighting. The Confederates acted on the defense, and were always behind cover, so that Sherman's army was compelled to drive the enemy from behind breastworks, while his own troops were always exposed in "the open." Besides the infantry, there were three divisions of cavalry under Kirkpatrick, Stoneman, and Gerard.

The first day's march after leaving Chattanooga brought us to Crawfish Springs near the Chickamauga battlefield. We crossed over a portion of the battlefield. Although this was May, and that battle was fought the previous September, some of the soldiers of the Twenty-sixth Illinois found seven skeletons in a small but deep ravine. They reported the incident to my headquarters. I directed that a detail from that regiment should be made and the remains buried as decently as circumstances would permit. I rode over to the spot to see how they would manage the interment. From the scraps of uniforms and the buttons picked up, as well as the cartridge belts that were still buckled around two of them, it was plain to see that they were Federal soldiers. A deep grave was dug and all the remains were deposited in the same receptacle. Boards were found to cover them and the dirt replaced. A cracker box was procured whereon was written in fairly legible lettering the words. "Seven unknown dead, killed on Chickamauga battlefield." It was the best that could be done under the circumstances and I have often wondered since if those remains had been gathered up and taken to the near-by government cemetery that was established after the war for a more appropriate disposal.

General McPherson had the command of the right wing of the advancing army, which consisted of Logan's Fifteenth corps and two divisions of the Sixteenth corps under the command of Major-General Dodge

The third division of Logan's command had been retained at Huntsville, Alabama, to protect the railroad from that point eastward to Stevenson. The march resumed and we crossed the Little Chickamauga River at Glass Mills. Soon afterward the troops entered the Cane Creek valley. No Federal force had ever passed through that region which was a very fertile region free from the destruction of the war. At Shipps's Gap, our forces passed into what was known as Armuchy Valley and camped at a small village called Villanow. I was eating breakfast when a staff officer rode up and delivered me a written order stating that I would be assigned one company of cavalry and a section of artillery (two guns), after which I was to proceed to the mouth of Snake Creek Gap. There I would meet a similar body of troops under the command of Colonel Weaver. The officer having the oldest commission as to date was to take command of both brigades and be exceedingly vigilant, for the post was one of danger and the command was liable to be attacked at almost any moment.

Upon arriving at the mouth of Snake Creek Gap, I found Colonel Weaver of an Iowa regiment, whose term of service would be over in a few weeks. Colonel Weaver's commission was found to be the oldest by three or four days and he consequently assumed command of both brigades. The artillery was placed in the best possible position to defend the north mouth of the gap against any emergency, with the cavalry placed at some distance away on each flank. The troops were then given a rest while waiting the anticipated coming of the enemy. We had arrived at the gap about noon and after supper I thought it would be the proper etiquette for me to call on my superior officer at his headquarters. I took along my adjutant general Captain George Nelson, of Fort Wayne. We found Colonel Weaver considerably excited over the responsibility of the position in which he found himself. He talked a good deal about the expiration of the term of service of his regiment, which was not far away. He remarked that he thought it was hardly proper to a regiment whose time was so nearly out for such an important and dangerous duty. I disagreed with him in a pleasant manner, and I told him in all probability the nearness of the end of the enlistment of his regiment was not thought of either by his superior officers, and perhaps not even known. "Surely," said I, "the inducements would be very great to fight to the last drop of the hat!" He did not take my talk with any special favor and Captain Nelson afterwards said that he seemed to think I was poking fun at him, but I wasn't.

After conversing with Colonel Weaver for a couple of hours over the prospects of the campaign, Captain Nelson and myself were returning to our own quarters, when an officer rode up to Weaver's tent. He had some difficulty in dismounting and I scanned him more closely and discovered that he had been drinking to such a degree that it was plainly perceptible. We had been back at our own quarters perhaps an hour and I had retired to my cot under the fly, when an orderly rode up with the request that I should come to Colonel Weaver's headquarters. I at once arose and upon reaching Colonel Weaver's tent discovered him under a strain of excitement. He at once informed me that the officer who had arrived as we were leaving his headquarters had told him that if he remained in his present position until daylight his whole force would be either slaughtered or captured. I could not believe the story and told Colonel Weaver that I had noticed the officer's condition when he arrived and that I did not believe he was responsible for what he said. "Oh, yes," remarked Colonel Weaver, "he tells me he came directly from the direction of Dalton over the top of the mountain, and he could see the Confederates marching in heavy column for the mouth of the gap." I tried to reason with the Colonel that such a story could not be true, but he more I argued with him the more confident he appeared to grow in the belief that we were to be attacked.

I left for my own headquarters, but first found the officer who had brought the news to Colonel Weaver. The officer was just recovering from a "spree" that had placed him in a state of delirium. I "pumped" him awhile in the tent and was convinced that the whole story was a hoax. About one o'clock in the night I received an order from Colonel Weaver directing me to have all of the teams belonging to the Fifteenth corps turned around and to be prepared to take the road in the direction of Chattanooga. I went straight to Colonel Weaver's headquarters. "Why," I asked him, "have you received any other order than the one brought by the drunken officer we have both seen?" He replied in the negative. "Don't you know," I continued, "that to put all the teams into a retrograde movement, could only mean that a disastrous battle had taken place somewhere at the front. That could not be the case or we would have heard the guns, and it would not be a drunken officer bearing the news of such a disaster, but it would come from our commanding officers, and in writing, too?" Weaver asked me again to turn the teams of the Fifteenth corps around to prepare to march to the rear. I refused. Weaver remarked that he wold turn about those that belonged to the Sixteenth Corps. I again told him I refused to obey such an order unless it came from General Logan or General Harrow.

At about five o'clock in the morning following this night of excitement, I received an order from General Logan to move forward, right through Snake Creek Gap with all the troops and transportation belonging to the corps. We had an early breakfast and were ready to move right off. Colonel Weaver had already turned a good many of his teams with their heads to the rear, and I afterward learned that he consumed all of the next day in getting them headed south again.

In passing through the gap I met General Kilpatrick, the cavalry leader, in an ambulance, quite seriously wounded, being taken to a hospital in the rear. I rode up to the ambulance and asked him if he was badly hurt. He was wounded in the shoulder and replied that he did not think it was serious, but that it would so cripple him in his active duties that he thought it best to go at once to the hospital at Chattanooga to have it heal as speedily as possible. He returned to his command shortly before Atlanta fell.

A few minutes later I met General Logan and told him what had occurred. I remember I asked the question: "Suppose I had received a peremptory order from Colonel Weaver to turn the teams around, but feeling and almost knowing the he was committing a very grave blunder, what would have been the consequences?" In a jesting way Logan remarked: "Colonel Williams, you could easily and successfully have been court-martialed for possessing so little sense as to do such a thing when you knew that no disaster had come to our arms!" Nevertheless, the question was not fairly answered, for Weaver was my superior officer and entitled to my obedience, and I was always glad that it was a "request" instead of an "order" to place the transportation of two entire corps directly opposite to the course they were to take.

The south end of the gap opened out into a comparatively level region and that evening the troops were deluged with a down-pour of rain that set all the small streams and gutters into an uproar. I had been ordered as my command debouched from Snake Creek Gap to move into the more level country and was given directions by a staff officer from General Logan headquarters the direction in which the troops were to face. It was getting late when the soldiers began their move to the point designated for the bivouac for the night. While they were engaged in stacking arms, along came a woman, wild with fright, screaming at the top of her voice, leading a small boy, with two larger ones following. Upon seeing the troops in her front yard, she thought there was an impending battle and was endeavoring to seek a place of safety. I stopped her and endeavored to soothe her the best I could. It took some time to convince her that there was not going to be a battle in her front yard and probably not near her home either. I asked her where she lived and she pointed to quite a large old-fashioned hewed-log house. I decided that it would be better for me to make my headquarters in her house through the night, as all the camp equipment we had was wringing wet. She was elated with the idea and had probably heard that it was generally safer around the headquarters of an officer than anywhere. The aroma of coffee could already be detected on the air since some of the troops had been long enough on the ground to prepare their suppers. She no doubt suspected that wherever there was an officer's quarters there would be coffee, a beverage that she had long been without. I asked her to show us the way to her home and myself and staff took up our quarters for the night with the first native Georgia woman we had seen.

The cook at my headquarters, a Frenchman who had learned his trade in Paris, was a splendid cook, an artist really, "Theodore," as we called him, was able to fix up really palatable dishes out of he most meager supplies. He spread before us a delicious meal of broiled ham, coffee with condensed milk, and a variety of canned fruits. The only thing the meal lacked was bread. We had the inevitable "square cracker" with a piece of mica in the center, hard tack.

After the men folks were served I told the woman that she could reset the table and she and her children should sit down to their own supper. She had recovered from the nervousness occasioned when she saw the troops and thought a battle would soon start. It was well understood that when not on active duty my headquarters was generally a sociable and often merry place. It became so on this night as I had surrounded myself with a very genial and companionable set of young men for staff duty. After the woman and her children had concluded their supper and the lady had cleared away the dishes and set the table out of the way, the whole party was ready for any sort of merriment. The children, along with their mother had gone to bed in the second story. After prying around for a time, Captain Hazzard had come across four suits of Confederate uniforms, which he found in a room leading off from the dining room. He suddenly made his appearance clad in Confederate gray. His appearance was so changed that on first sight he was taken for a Confederate soldier until he broke out in his natural tone of voice.

The discovery of the uniforms of the enemy, suggested further search and two more uniforms and three muskets were found which had been concealed in a closet. How to account for them in this house was discussed pro and con. The probabilities are that General Kilpatrick, whose troops were the first to push through the gap, may have charged in so rapidly that the Confederates stopped in with the woman, who had already informed us that her husband was in the army under General Johnston. They had hidden their guns and by assuming citizen's garb, had passed themselves off as residents of the neighborhood. Others thought that they may have been a scouting party, but as the guns were the regulation old-time Springfield musket, "caliber 69," this idea did not receive any more advocates than the one who suggested the idea. However, the finding of he uniforms and muskets led to other things, and the big lower floor of the house was converted into a scene of merry-making. Larry McCarty of the "Ninetieth Ireland," being a splendid singer, lead off with a patriotic song. Captain Ed Webster recited Patrick Henry's forensic effort in the Virginia House of Burgesses, just preceding the Revolutionary war. The hours flew away with first a recitation, then a song, until it was after midnight when it was thought best to take some rest in order to fit the party for the duties that the morrow might bring.

It was about one o'clock, while Larry McCarty, who had a great number of songs at his command, was in the midst of a rollicking Irish ditty, that a heavy knock came at the front door. An orderly opened it and an officer on Logan's staff came in, and inquired for Colonel Williams. Several Confederate uniforms had been put on by those most prominent in giving the impromptu entertainment of the evening, of which I was one. I was standing next to the officer requiring after me but I was not recognized in my "new clothes". I asked him what was wanted, and as soon as he heard my voice he burst out in a loud guffaw from which he could scarcely recover. He was finally able to deliver his message, which was that my brigade should be prepared to move promptly at three o'clock and a staff officer from General Logan's headquarters would show the way.

As soon as the staff officers could shed the paraphernalia they had assumed for the occasion, each one was sent to the commanding officer of each regiment of the brigade with the order to have the men ready to mover promptly at three o'clock. The whole night had been wet and disagreeable. Promptly at the hour of three in the morning, myself and those whose places were about me were ready to move. None of the party had more than an hour's sleep and even that no doubt much interrupted. The noise and confusion cause by the getting ready to leave the house had aroused the woman and she had arisen and come down stairs to see us off. This reminded me that I ought to at least leave her enough supplies for the needs of herself and children for a day or two. I directed the driver of the ambulance that carried the headquarters' rations, to leave the woman a ham and a couple of pieces of side meat, with a plentiful supply of hard-tack (I was always willing to give away hard-tack), with a pound or so of coffee and a "quarter of tea." The woman was deeply grateful for the gift. Early on in the war I had seen how devastating it was to the country to have an army march through it. The destitution that followed the march of a large body of troops appealed to my humanity so strongly that I very often left supplies to needy ones.

The passage of the Union troops through Snake Creek Gap had the desired effect for as soon as Resaca was threatened by the Federal troops the Confederate General Joe Johnston ascertained that he must give up his strongly fortified position at Dalton. Johnston could not allow a large force to get between his army and Atlanta, the principal point he was defending. A strong fight was put up by both the center and the left of the Federal army. The tenacity with which General Sherman showed in holding on to "Rocky-face Ridge" and "Buzzard's Roost" and other points to the left of General McPherson's Army, which was passing through Snake Creek Gap almost unimpeded, goes to show that General Johnston gave up Dalton just as soon as he safely could.

As soon as Johnston yielded Dalton, it was very plain that he would concentrate his retreating troops at Resaca. When I met General Kilpatrick at the southern mouth of Snake Creek Gap, he declared to me that if he had a brigade of infantry support when he came out upon the more level ground surrounding the village of Resaca, he could have easily captured the town. This would have cut Johnston's army off from Atlanta and placed the railroad in the hands of the Union forces.

At three o'clock the men had had breakfast and were ready to march. The campaign was just opening, but the mood among the men was that we would in a short time be knocking at the gates of Atlanta. Few dreamed that it would be into the fourth month ere the contest would be closed with victory. Under the leadership of the staff officer that had been assigned to us by General Logan, I found the First, Second, and Fourth divisions of the Fifteenth corps lying along the Rome road. The brigade which I commanded was placed on the extreme left of General Harrow's division and my own regiment, the Twelfth formed on the left of the brigade. I was ordered to join to General Osterhaus' division. I was also directed to throw out a heavy line of skirmishers to join those already in position. My brigade was the last to arrive since it had to come the greatest distance. Taking along an orderly, I rode out into the woods to see that the skirmish line was well placed and I was greatly surprised to find it so near the main body of troops. I decided that the skirmish line was not sufficiently distant and I rode on outside of the line in the direction of the enemy. I had gone but a short distance when I passed a large oak tree with two Confederate skirmishers behind it. I didn't discover them until I was close enough to one of them to have grabbed his gun with my hands. I could see that when he saw me he was excited and had a case of "buck fever" and nothing but the latter saved my life on that occasion. He banged away with his musket, bringing down a shower of small limbs and leaves all about my head. But before he could recover, I had turned my horse and given him the spur. My orderly followed me and both of us got back to the main body, where I told the officer in command that so far as I could see the skirmish line was sufficiently distant for comfort!

Around three o'clock in the afternoon the order was given to move forward. Soon the troops penetrated the woods that lay in their immediate front, easily driving the Confederate skirmishers before us. The lines came to open fields and the enemy opened on the Union troops with artillery, doing some slight damage. The skirmish line was pushed across the open fields and up the ascent beyond, the main body followed and the enemy hurried away with his artillery, giving up the outer line of defense to close in upon the town of Resaca. After a short halt at the point where the Confederate artillery had been stationed, the bugles again sounded the advance. Soon after the troops began this last movement the rebels opened up with a murderous and vigorous fire from a battery posed on a hillside beyond an open field. The brigade was halted in a clump of timber, but my own regiment, under the command of Lieutenant Colonel Goodnow, advanced into the open ground, where it suffered considerably. I ordered it to retire a few rods in order to secure the cover of the timber. Again the line was moved forward over the open field to another strip of woods in which the troops could secure the aid that timber always furnishes. It is always difficult to keep a long line in close order, and in moving through the timber, a gap had grown of considerable dimensions in the main line caused by the unevenness of the ground and the undergrowth in the woods. There was great danger, I thought from this gap. I rode over to General Harrow and informed him of the gap that seemed to me to be growing constantly wider. The conversation ended by his peremptorily directing me to move right straight ahead, even pointing to a knoll that he directed me to move to with the right of my brigade. The fulfilling of such an order could not have any other effect than to widen the opening, unless the other troops were directed to close upon mine. However, orders must be obeyed and I pushed forward as directed. On reaching the knoll, I discovered that the troops were right in front of a six gun battery of the enemy, stationed behind strong fortifications.

Here was a dilemma for which I was not responsible, but the enemy, on discovering us, opened up with every one of the six guns. Fortunately, however, they fired over the troops. I directed the men to lie down and there they remained until they ran out of ammunition. At about one o'clock that night other troops had been brought up and closed the gap of which I had informed General Harrow. At the same time, the brigade being out of ammunition, was relieved by another one of the same division. As the troops were withdrawn, I met General Harrow and I frankly told him that the loss would not have been so heavy had he corrected the constantly growing gap of which I had informed him. He got quite angry, and so did I. My brigade had lost heavily and I told him that he was responsible for a large portion of the dead that lay out there in the front. This angered him and he threatened to put me under arrest, and so we parted there in the dark on the battleground, with bullets still raining around us like hail.

General Harrow's treatment worried me greatly. The loss in the brigade I commanded was the heaviest of any of the three belonging to the First division and this was my first battle as a brigade commander. I did not sleep well that night, and at daylight I mounted my horse and rode over to General Logan's headquarters and told him everything that had occurred between myself and General Harrow, including his threat to place me under arrest. Logan's reply and instructions were for me to "go back to my command and conduct myself as if nothing had occurred," that he was "after General Harrow's scalp and he thought he would get it before the campaign was over".

I might as well add right here that Harrow was maneuvered out of his position after Atlanta fell by breaking up his division and creating a new one for General John M. Corse, the hero of Altoona Pass. So far as I know General Harrow never again commanded troops in the field, after the disposition was made. He was killed in a railroad accident in the southern part of Indiana directly after the war ended.

The loss of the brigade was very severe, owing to the fact that the enemy could and did enfilade the advancing line on both flanks because of the opening gap. My own regiment being on the left flank of the advancing troops suffered to a greater extent than the other three. Major Baldwin had his horse shot under him just as the troops came under the fire of the first entrenchments. Captain Thomas Peoples a good officer and an upright patriotic citizen who had been married but a short time before his enlistment, was killed.

Captain Peoples conceived the idea while we were at our winter camp that he would be shot in the next battle in which he might take part. This presentiment held him in complete thrall and he adhered to it at all times. Myself and his brother officers did everything in their power to disabuse his mind of the delusion, but he persistently held fast to the belief. At first his brother officers made sport of the idea but seeing that this did no good, they proceeded to present all kinds of arguments to induce him to yield the presentiment. Nothing could alter his belief. I met him a few days before the battle of Resaca and asked him if he still entertained the presentiment. "Yes, Colonel," he replied, "I feel that I am to be killed in the first fight that takes place, and if anything, I am more firm in the conviction than ever before." He did not seem to be in the least dejected, and so far as those near could observe, he was just as lively and apparently happy as ever.

Just before the brigade encountered the terrible fore of the enemy he said to Sergeant B. F. Perce of his own company: "I shall be killed in this battle, but I am ready." As Captain Peoples and the sergeant lay down near each other, and while in the act of raising his head to look about him, a ball from an enemy's musket struck him squarely in the center of the forehead.

After darkness had set in his body was carried to the rear by Sergeant Perce and others, where the blood was washed away and he was prepared for burial. At midnight, what remained of a noble, patriotic, earnest man was committed to the earth. Chaplain Gage officiated in prayer and a touching reference was made of the young wife in her far away Indiana home. Presentiments of the kind were quite numerous during the war days. His death caused a deep depression in the ranks of the members of the regiment for the Captain was a man very highly respected by the men and officers of the Twelfth.

General Sherman spent the day after the first contest of the two armies at Resaca in bringing up General Hooker's corps that had been fighting the enemy at Rocky Face and Buzzard's Roost. General Johnson's division of the Fourteenth corps was held in check for a short time by the concentration of a very heavy force of Confederates in his front. Hooker's advance with the Twentieth corps came up in the nick of time enabling the Federals to not only drive back the enemy, but to recover the lost ground and to bring on a severe engagement in which each side lost quite heavily.

In the evening General Morgan L. Smith's division of Logan's corps charged a strong position of the enemy in his front and drove the Confederates from their hastily prepared works. The Confederates, smarting under their loss, made a heroic effort to recover the lost ground. In so doing Rebels suffered severely, but to no purpose. My brigade was ordered up to the support of General Smith's division in their efforts to repulse the enemy. But my regiment's services were not needed as Smith's division had reversed the works they had taken from the enemy and was well prepared to hold what their gallantry had won.

On the left, the troops under "Fighting Joe Hooker" resumed the battle early the next morning. The Sixteenth Corps under General Dodge was ordered across the Oustenalia to threaten the Confederate commander's communications. At the same time General Schofield's forces moved around our left flank in the hope of getting to the rear of the Confederates. To checkmate these movements General Joe Johnston, on the night of the 15th of May, withdrew a portion of his army while a savage front attack was being made by his center. About midnight he moved his lines forward as if intending to bring on a general battle by assaulting the Federal works. A fearful cannonading began at once, accompanied by the steady roar of musketry. For more than an hour this continued, accompanied by the yelling and cheering of the troops on both sides. The roar of the artillery and loud rumble of the bigger guns was heard continually. When the morning dawned, it was discovered that General Johnston had withdrawn his entire force, giving up Resaca to the Federals. The skirmishers of the Twenty-sixth Illinois, of my brigade, were the first in the town, and assisted in the capture of two fleeing guns from a belated battery.

General Johnston may be credited with success, for he got his army out of the rapidly enveloping folds that within another twenty-four hours would have captured him. Soon after the taking of Resaca came the order for a vigorous pursuit of the enemy. It wasn't long until each regiment, brigade and division was assembled on the road, each in its proper place, and the march began. The hospital corps was left behind to care for the wounded and to bury the dead. Often the soldiers did not know which of their comrades were killed or wounded until "roll call" made those absences known.

The right wing of Sherman's army was quickly put in motion, crossing the river at the ferry below the town and camping that night on the Rome road. The center, under General Joe Hooker, followed up directly in the rear of the Confederate line of retreat, which was along the railroad toward Atlanta. A strong division of Confederate cavalry formed the left of General Johnston's retreating army. This force was kept in sight by the Fifteenth corps all day. The Confederate commander of the cavalry endeavoring to stem or stay the progress of the pursuing forces at every favorable point, which caused occasional halts on the part of the infantry.

The next day our part of the army reached Adairsville. Here a junction was made with the Fourth corps under command of Major General Howard, whose advance had quite a heavy skirmish at this point in the early morning. When we left Adairsville the Fifteenth corps diverged from General Johnston's main line of retreat. After passing through a few mile of extremely rugged and barren country, the corps emerged though a gap in the hills into a highly cultivated and beautiful scope of country. It was a large plantation owned by an Englishman, at least he claimed English citizenship. The English colors floated from the top of his princely home. It was indeed an elegant place, as there were gardens of flowers and refreshing fountains adorning the land. The placing of the English flag over the palatial residence was, I thought, a mistake. Of course, it was intended to save the property, but no doubt it offended the Southern soldier and gained no sentiment from the Northern side. There was an antagonistic feeling against England on the Union side caused by the fear that England, would in time, espouse the Confederate cause. The Federal soldiers did not destroy the property in any way, but it was a chickenless, geeseless, turkeyless, and pigless plantation that the Federal army left behind when it resumed its march.

The next point the army reached on its onward march to Atlanta was Kingston. As usual, a lively skirmish took place there before the Confederates yielded the town. Our side suffered slight losses while the enemy left behind eighty killed and wounded. The arrival of our forces at Kingston was at almost the same time that General Jeff C. Davis with his division occupied Rome, one of the most important towns in that section of Georgia. The Federal army was now about two-thirds of the way to Atlanta. The journey was slow in progress. General Sherman, in order to make sure of his supplies, and especially of his ammunition, had his Engineer and Pioneer corps engaged in reconstructing the railroad as fast as possible. He would have the troops lie in camp for two, three and even four days waiting for the railroad builders to catch up. Other parts of the army over on our left were frequently engaged with the enemy. General Thomas, along with the center, had advanced his troops to the Etowah River, while General Hooker's command lay to the left of Thomas and somewhat to the rear.

After the railway repair was completed, the pursuit of the continually falling back army was resumed. The enemy had taken up a strong position just south of the little village of Dallas. At Pumpkin Vine Creek it had been determined to "park all the teams belonging to the Department of the Tennessee", which included those of the Fifteenth, Sixteenth, and Seventeenth. The wagons of these three corps closed up in compact form covered a square mile of ground. I know this to be a fact because it fell to the lot of my brigade to be placed in charge of all these wagons that were heavily loaded with supplies. If drawn out on the road in close marching order the wagons would have made a four-mule team procession eleven miles long. The skirmishers with the advance guard were easily heard as the army closed up on the Confederates four miles distant from the "parked teams".

I was greatly affected by the responsibility of guarding and preventing the hundreds upon hundreds of teams from falling into the hands of the enemy. It was a very large area of ground to protect with the four somewhat depleted regiments that were under my orders. Fortunately a four-gun Iowa battery was assigned to my command and it arrived soon after I took charge of the important duty. After distributing the force at my command, so that in my judgment it could best subserve the very responsible duty in hand; I placed the four guns in commanding positions in accordance with the views of the Captain in command of the battery. I had my own "fly" pitched and, weary and almost worn out, I had my cook prepare supper. I had scarcely sat down to eat the rather plain supper that "Theodore" had provided when a staff officer rode up with a pencil-written message from General Logan informing me that a heavy force of cavalry had been detailed by General Johnston to make a raid around the right and rear of our army. The message directed me to be exceedingly vigilant and watchful. This was in the evening and I reasoned that no attack on the trains would be made that night, but rather at daylight. I set myself and staff to work to have the small command prepare for an attack at any moment. We went to each regimental commander and I impressed upon all four of them the necessity of watchfulness of the most vigorous character. About midnight another staff officer reached my headquarters urging me to do what I had already done and to have the brigade mustered at daylight to stand under arms for a time at least, as every indication pointed to an attack upon the large "park" of supplies.

A Company of cavalry had reached me at about four o'clock in the morning and was lying low. At dawn I directed the officer in command of the mounted troops to scout for a couple of miles around the large camp to see if there were any signs of the enemy. They were out a couple of hours and reported nothing dangerous in sight. There were several staff officers and orderlies who kept me in "hot water" with their reports of a brigade of Texan cavalry having been sent to destroy the supplies. Aware of the fact that my force was entirely too small to guard a mile square park of teams, I gathered my own staff and went through the trains compelling every loiterer to assemble on a greensward near by. I routed out from among the wagons very nearly six hundred soldiers who had no business with the teams. This straggling and loitering had begun as soon as the army started on the march from Chattanooga. Some of the men had sore feet, still others were chaffed by the shoulder strap of the cartridge box. Some had one thing for an excuse and some another, but the majority of them were the usual "play-offs", who had found the wagons to be an easier way to get along than up at the front with their braver comrades.

I not only added a small regiment to my all too meager force, but by sending a detail through the teams I procured a sufficient number of guns and equipment to arm them as well and to furnish them with ammunition. I detailed a Captain from the Twenty-sixth Illinois to command them and furnished him with several Lieutenants to assist. This squad of men, made up as it was from almost every regiment of the three corps represented was placed at an important gap in the line.

All that day the scare was kept up by the frequent arrival of staff officers and orderlies bearing dispatches of various kinds to me. Most of the dispatches urged the utmost vigilance. I believe that the fear of losing such a large quantity of supplies was as much feared up at the headquarters that out-ranked mine as there was with the men that were guarding them. However, quiet prevailed all through that day and the next night. I was only too glad to receive a message from General Harrow to move up to the front with my brigade starting at daylight. A brigade of infantry belonging to another corps had been directed to relieve me in the duty of guarding the trains.

At daybreak a staff officer was sent to conduct the brigade to the front where it was to go into the battle line. The bugles sounded the advance just as the sun arose and the band of the Twelfth Indiana struck up a lively quickstep as myself and staff took our places at the head of the command.

The march had proceeded for about a mile over a wagon track road with dense underbrush close up to it. The underbrush was as high as an average man's head and very heavy. I was slightly in advance of the entire staff, a military rule under such circumstances, when right at a slight turn in the road ahead of me a man stepped out of the brush. He was clad from head to foot in Confederate gray. I gave my horse the spur and at once drew my Colt's revolver from its holster and had it at his head before he was scarcely aware of my presence. To this day I am glad that I did not pull the trigger. Had I done so one of the best of General Logan's scouts and spies would have paid the penalty of what is called "the fortunes of war". He looked up in my face with a sort of half smile and remarked: "Colonel Williams, don't you know me?" In a moment I discovered that he was a man with whom I was well acquainted for we had conversed many times at General Logan's headquarters. He walked along beside my horse for a short distance so as not to delay the march and told me he was starting out on a very dangerous, yet very necessary duty. He was ordered to go around the left flank of General Joe Johnston's army and gather up all the news possible concerning the enemy. His main objective was to ascertain if the Confederates had any reserves behind their line.

The spy wore a blonde, curly wig and he looked older than I had known him. I asked him what course he would pursue in case he was arrested. He said, "In all such cases circumstances must govern my course of action." He was going to represent himself as a soldier of General Lee's army, home on a furlough, in case of detention. He showed me a furlough actually signed at the Confederate War Department at Richmond by a prominent Confederate, General Robert E. Lee. The furlough had gone up through the regular channels and had been approved by all the headquarters through which it passed. He was classed as being in an Alabama regiment and had passes, forged of course, from Confederate officers. I was surprised to see how well he was prepared to represent himself as a Confederate soldier. I bade him good-bye when he informed me that he had gone far enough and would now make it to the Confederate lines some four miles to the south.

I don't know why I did not pull the trigger when I put my revolver to his head for I was thoroughly convinced that he was a Confederate soldier. Perhaps it was an innate feeling on my part against shooting a man apparently defenseless as he was. Whatever it was, I have always been glad that for some cause unknown to me, my hand was stayed at the precise moment to save the man's life.

The brigade soon came to the little village of Dallas and from there proceeded to the rear line of troops just over a mile distant. We arrived in mid morning and were placed in a pleasant grove, sheltered to some extent from the enemy's guns should they open up. About noon I received orders to place my brigade on the extreme right of those already in line and continue the line of fortifications across my own front. I learned that there had been a disposition on the part of the enemy to find the exact point where the Union line ceased.

After my brigade had taken its place and was busily engaged in erecting its entrenchments, I decided to examine the immediate region surrounding my own right and see for myself the lay of the land. I took a portion of my staff and rode out into the heavy pine forest where we came upon a thin line of cavalry videttes. They informed me that they belonged to General Wilder's brigade, whose headquarters I would find about a half mile farther to the West. Keeping inside the line of mounted pickets, I went to see General Wilder. I found him surrounded by his four regiments of mounted infantry in an open glade among the pines. He and his troops were taking a needed rest. I told him that the Confederates were attempting to ascertain the precise right of the Union forces. I suggested to Wilder that the gap between my brigade, which was at the extreme right of all the infantry troops of Sherman's army, and his own, was thinly covered with pickets. He informed me that he would move up closer and place a heavier line of pickets between the two brigades, which he did within a couple of hours.

The next morning the enemy's pickets were unusually quiet. I gave permission for a certain number of men from each company in camp to go to a small brook in the rear of the line o wash their clothes and to take a personal bath. The men were only too glad to receive such an order, for all of them were extremely dirty with the red clay of Georgia. This permission depleted the number of men immediately behind the works very sensibly. These men were absent during a thrilling moment, for soon after they had gone to the brook, a wicked fire from the enemy's artillery broke upon the line. Fortunately the shells passed well over the men in the trenches. My own headquarters were near the brook, and I at once ordered the men who were bathing to return to the works with all possible haste. These words were no sooner out of my mouth than there came "the rebel yell". Nothing else that could have happened could have inspired the men to get back to the works more speedily than that rebel yell. The long line of rapidly advancing gray emerged into an open space keeping up the continuous "yell". Instant word was sent to each regiment to reserve their fire, which was obeyed, but when it did open upon the gray-clad line, the attackers melted before the seething fire of the Union forces. Men were never made who could withstand such a fire delivered at close range. Scarcely a shot from the Union lines failed in its mission. There were a few Confederates who reached the entrenchments untouched. Quite a number of these were jerked over the Federal works, choosing to surrender rather than attempt a retreat though the line of fire.

It was a bravely executed charge and but for that "rebel yell," I have sometimes thought, the enemy might have succeeded in overrunning my works. The men washing their clothes and bathing dropped whatever it was they were doing and ran for the works as if the fate of the entire army depended on his individual presence at the works. Some of them reached the trenches with nothing on but their shirts, but they knew where their muskets stood in the works with the cartridge box hung by its strap at the end of the ramrod. All of them got there in time to deliver the first volley.

I stood near Hank Flowers of Etna Green, Indiana, who called my attention to an advancing Confederate soldier of immense size and who carried a knapsack that seemed to fit him in size for it was nearly as large as a small bed tick. "Colonel," said Flowers, "I am going to pick that man off at the first shot for making an animal of himself in carrying such a load!" Sure enough, when the smoke cleared away after that fearful volley, not a bullet of which went wild, I saw that powerful man stretched on the ground, his big knapsack near him and himself in the last throes of dissolution. Flowers did not have an atom of grudge in his make-up and I mention such an incident as this to show the perfect coolness of the men while engaged in battle.

Back in the heavy timber the confederate officers made an attempt to rally their men for another attempt, but they did not succeed. The second brigade on my immediate left met the onset the same way. It was estimated after the fight was over that the Confederates lost twenty-five hundred men in killed and wounded while our own loss was remarkably small in number. The charge and its repulse were hardly over when Generals Osterhaus and Harrow, both division commanders, rode down the line complimenting the troops for their work. A short time later "Black Jack" Logan with his staff also rode past the line of men who cheered him as the Fifteenth corps did few officers.

The men of the second brigade fought like demons. That brigade occupied an angle in the works immediately on the left of my own. My remembrance of the fight is that a heavier force of Confederates was massed in front of the Second than before my own. I judge so, partially because the enemy held on a longer time there than they did in front of my four regiments. A second line of the enemy pushed forward as a support to the main first line, but both lines were met by the withering fire poured upon them by the Second brigade. The Forty-sixth Ohio, commanded by Colonel Wolcott, was armed with the Spencer repeating musket and this was the first that regiment had an opportunity to use this rapid firing musket. As a result, the killed and wounded in front of the Forty-sixth was fearful to contemplate. The ground was strewn with dead bodies in front of both my own and Col. Wolcott's brigades. The dead was lying so thick at some points that they lay on top and across one another. The Confederate line on the left of my command made their attack with the greatest possible bravery. The First Iowa battery belonging to General Harrow's division had been pushed forward to the skirmish line previous to the Confederate charge. There was insufficient support of infantry and it was in possession of the enemy for a short time. It was retaken in a fierce counter-charge by the Federal troops. It was on that day that I learned the value of the several weeks' practice the Twelfth had in blank cartridge firing back in Camp Morton. There is no doubt whatever that the practice was of immense value to our side on that day. Cooler men never stood up before an enemy. The Captain of each company had his men fire by volleys, and not a shot was wasted so far as I could observe. I was then and there convinced of the value of well-drilled troops.

Farther east than Dallas the corps under Generals Hooker and Thomas were continually engaged with the enemy to a greater or lesser extent. In advancing his lines General Hooker had a severe contest with the enemy that was afterwards known as New Hope Church where he lost very heavily, as the enemy did. The Federals did nothing more than hold their position, but afterwards General Hooker compelled the Confederate commander to fall back.

In our own front the pickets were quite active both day and night. The enemy made only minor attacks upon the Union line by occasional "rushes" of the skirmish line to be met with the usual check when they approached the Federal main line. One or two slight charges, involving a couple of regiments of the enemy were made, but as they were met with the usual withering fire from the Union line, they fell back to the trenches. The enemy generally sought his own main line in a hurry for the orders were to pursue them closely as soon as they began to retire.

It was when the Union forced occupied these lines that I had another tilt with General Harrow, my division commander. In looking back to the scene now, I am convinced that he held a grudge against me ever since I had the verbal "set-to" with him at midnight following the battle of Resaca. He sent an orderly with a message requesting me to come to headquarters for instructions. I did so and he informed me that I was to double the strength of the present skirmish line of the whole brigade and be ready at three o'clock the next morning to advance the lines. Of course, I presumed that it was to be a general advance of the whole line, but nothing was said upon the subject.

Promptly at the hour mentioned in his order the skirmish line of my brigade, already doubled in strength, moved forward. The men very soon came in contact with the enemy's picket line. The Union line, now the strongest since it had been doubled, was able to drive the enemy before it. It was pushed so hard that the enemy almost began to fall back on the run. It was now nearly daylight and I looked back to see if the main line was following, in order to take advantage of the ground we had already recovered, which was nearly a mile. I was surprised that I could not see any movement of any kind in our own trenches. My own skirmish line had no trouble in driving back the "Johnnies", but as I had received no further instructions than those to start at three o'clock and push the enemy to the rear, I confess that I was surprised that there was no attempt to hold the ground taken. I kept on moving up and I am sure I could easily have captured the slight works that were discovered about a quarter mile ahead of me.

As the troops neared the works, now plainly visible in the increasing light, the contest grew much warmer. All at once a volley was fired apparently right out of the ground from a reserve picket post that had been dug to a depth that just permitted the men's head to reach above the level. Two or three were killed and several wounded from this volley. At this moment I received a written order to fall back to the main line. I was just lining up the men for a "rush" when this order reached me. I am positive now, as I was then, that but for that order I could have carried the entrenched line of the enemy, for it could easily be seen that there were but few men behind the breastworks. But orders are orders, so I slowly gathered up the skirmish line preparatory to obeying the order. When the skirmish line was concentrated, it was found that the loss in killed and wounded was greater than any one would have guessed. Seven were killed and twenty-three wounded.

When I thought of this loss of life and the additional wounded for a freak expedition, I confess I was angry. Think of it! Seven men killed and twenty-three wounded on a three o'clock in the morning expedition amounting to nothing of value as a military movement. Consequently when I met General Harrow back at the mail line, I was still more angered, when he remarked, "Colonel Williams, I am sorry that you made that advance at all!"

"What?" I said, "Sorry that I made it! Why, you ordered me in writing to make it and for the life of me I cannot see what it was made for unless it was to add a few more dead to the number and to fill up the hospitals with additional wounded!"

I was angered and felt amazed when he seemingly undertook to make it appear that it was a scheme of my own! The facts are that General Harrow, after the expedition started at three o'clock that morning concluded to disown the order for the advance, as General Logan reprimanded him for taking the authority upon himself to send out an expedition that might interfere with the plans of General Sherman. It was plain to see that an important movement of some kind was going forward on the Confederate side even then. It was fortunate for me that I had retained my written order. From that time forward there was a coolness between myself and General Harrow since he had been ready to permit a subordinate officer to bear the blame when he was really responsible.

General Sherman, after General Hooker's engagement at New Hope church, decided to develop his own left flank and the Fifteenth and Sixteenth corps were directed to hold themselves in readiness to relieve

General Hooker's troops in the center. This would permit Hooker to move over to Sherman's left, and if possible, to envelope the Confederate commander's extreme right. At ten o'clock on one of the last days in May, the extreme right of General Logan's corps (my brigade) was directed to withdraw from the fortified position to be immediately followed by Wolcott's Second brigade. Scarcely had my own troops gotten out of the trenches and marched maybe a quarter of a mile, when an order came to make all haste to get back into the entrenchments we had just left. The enemy had penetrated our design, either by information obtained from some citizen, or from the movement of Sherman's troops elsewhere. The enemy had already opened with artillery, which was followed directly with the vindictive, scornful, "rebel yell," giving the well-known sign of a coming charge.

The brigade returned to the trenches at the "double-quick" and the "about face" movement. Fortunately the Union troops succeeded in reoccupying the works before the Confederates reached them. The enemy, finding our troops still in their old position, returned to their own lines. The bark of the skirmish line and the roar of the artillery continued all through that night.

The wounded were conveyed in ambulances to the rear of the line that the Fifteenth corps was to occupy after relieving General Hooker, preparatory to making a second withdrawal from the enemy's front. The withdrawal of a line of troops from the front of a vigorous and active enemy is a very ticklish thing sometimes. And there is nothing a soldier dreads more than to receive a volley in the back. Withdrawing troops are always caught in the open, and while they may be the bravest of men, a continuous fire from the rear very generally has the effect to accelerate their speed. It is also usual in such movements to leave behind a heavy skirmish line to occupy the works intended to be vacated as long as possible, in order to convey the idea to the enemy that the lines were as well-manned as usual. This course always has the effect to make the attacking force move forward carefully and slowly. The withdrawal of my own brigade from the front of the enemy was one of the most unpleasant and trying duties I ever had to perform. I had to withdraw three times during the campaign, and in every case it was to take up a new position in the line at some other point. In this case the skirmishers held the line so closely and kept up the firing so vigorously that the enemy was deceived for a long time. The main body was fully three miles on their way to the new position before the enemy discovered that they had been held back by a strong skirmish line only. Consequently all danger from a rear attack had passed. Very soon afterward the division to which my brigade belonged reached its destination and went into the position assigned them on the extreme front.

General Hooker's forces had been on their way to our left and the enemy's right for some time. It was during the night of June fourth that General Joe E. Johnston abandoned his position and fell back towards Marietta. Thus another "Sabbath day's journey" had been made towards Atlanta, the destination of both Federal and Confederate commanders-in-chief. The retreat of the Confederate forces permitted a brief rest on the part of General Sherman's army. This short cessation of hostilities became necessary due to the condition of our communications. Cars were running from Chattanooga to Etowah River; the railroad bridge over that stream was still in an incomplete condition. A large body of soldiers, including a regiment of engineers, was busy building a new bridge.

In retiring his lines the Confederate commander yielded to us Altoona Pass. The arrangement was to have the railroad completed to Acworth with all possible speed. It was at Acworth that General Sherman assembled the principal part of his army, using his immense wagon trains to forward supplies over the still unfinished section of railroad. It was here that General Blair joined General Sherman with the portion of the Seventeenth corps that had been left behind at the opening of the Atlanta campaign. This additional force was just about sufficient to make up the losses of the army incurred from Dalton and Resaca. These troops were warmly welcomed by their comrades, whom they had fought with at Vicksburg in General Grant's operations around that stronghold.

The troops' rest that I mentioned did not last long, although it was badly needed by those who had been on duty both night and day. Their weariness was caused by the inability to keep clean by bathing, for the red clay stuck to the men's clothes with a tenacity of modern mucilage and caused constant discomfort. How the troops welcomed a camp near a river or even a small running stream, for it gave them the chance of limbering up their pantaloons, shirts and socks so as to make them somewhat more pliable than had been the case for more than a month.

W | 12 | Ind.

Reub Williams

Rank Col., 12 Reg't Indiana Infantry.

Appears on

Field and Staff Muster Roll

for Sept - Oct, 186 3.

Present or absent ___ Present

Stoppage, $ ___ 100 for ___

Due Gov't, $ ___ 100 for ___

Valuation of horse, $ ___ 100

Valuation of horse equipments, $ ___ 100

Remarks: Rec'd leave of absence 20 days Sept 17" 1863.

W | 12 | Ind

Reub Williams

Col. 12 Ind Infy

Return

of the 1st Brigade, 4th Division, 15th Army Corps,

for the month of Jany, 1864.

dated Scottsboro, Ala

Jany 31, 1864

shows the following with regard to the officer named above:

Post or station Scottsboro, Ala

Remarks: Comdg 1" Brig 4 Div

15 A.C.

Reub Williams

Rank Col., 12 Reg't Indiana Infantry.

Appears on

Field and Staff Muster Roll

for Jan & Feb, 186 4.

Present or absent ___ Absent

Stoppage, $ ___ 100 for ___

Due Gov't, $ ___ 100 for ___

Valuation of horse, $ ___ 100

Valuation of horse equipments, $ ___ 100

Remarks: Comdg 1" Brig 4" Division 15" A.C. by order Col. Comis

---

W | 12 | Ind

Reub Williams

Col. 12 Ind Infy

Return

of the 1st Brigade, 4th Division, 15th Army Corps,

for the month of Feby, 1864.

dated Scottsboro, Ala

Feby 29, 1864

shows the following with regard to the officer named above:

Post or station Scottsboro, Ala

Remarks: Comdg 1" Brig 4 Div

15 A.C.

CHAPTER 11

Battle for Kennesaw Mountain

A sudden shock which shook the earth, 'mid vapor dense and dun,
Proclaimed along the echoing hills, the conflict had begun:
While shot and shell athwart the stream with fiendish fury sped,
To strew among the living lines the dying and the dead.
                —Unknown

It was mid June when Sherman once more put his army in motion. It was known that the enemy was located on both sides of the railroad at Big Shanty. Here General Joe Johnston, with additions to his forces, held on for three or four days. General Sherman, by extending his lines on both flanks, enveloped the enemy to such an extent that they were forced out of their entrenchment. The Confederates were compelled to retire to their defenses at Kennesaw Mountain. Kennesaw Mountain was deemed by the enemy to be impregnable. The Kennesaw line was the last one available to the Confederate commander north of the Chattahoochie River. A strong feeling prevailed in our own army that serious and severe fighting was before us.

Kennesaw Mountain is situated in a comparatively level country, rises directly from the plain and is quite free from forest growth. Right out of this level plain it rises to quite a height, and is about a mile and a half in length. The north and west sides are exceedingly abrupt, making those sides difficult to climb. The mountain lay directly across the path of the Northern army. Very wisely, General Johnston had incorporated Kennesaw into his line, and by placing a battery on its summit and covering each flank of the battery with a strong skirmish line, the mountain could be held with comparatively few men. On each flank of the mountain, but particularly the western end, the Confederate line stretched all the way to Pine and Lost Mountains, two detached mountains.

From the summit of Kennesaw Mountain was a fairly plain view of Atlanta and, of course, of the movement of the Federal line. I remember in approaching the mountain a couple of days before General Sherman occupied the final line that was held until Johnston retired across the Chattahoochie River about a mile to the left of Kennesaw, there was a large grove of trees occupied by the enemy. I have, since the war, thought that whatever Confederate troops occupied this piece of timber must have done so through a mistake, a misunderstanding of orders, or a blunder of some kind, for these troops were so far away from the main line that they had no hope to escape. My brigade and a portion of the Second were ordered to "gather them in," if it were possible. Two guns from an Iowa battery were sent for with orders to report to myself. The infantry had been drawn up behind a rise of ground that hid them from the view of the enemy, so that in rushing them forward a few feet their muzzles would have nothing intervening between the men and the guns and the enemy in the timber. All of the Infantry was drawn up in the same manner and was ordered to lie down to await the bugle sounding the charge, then make all possible speed to get to the enemy and capture all that were in the woods.

The intervening ground could not be examined without giving information to the enemy and hence it was a great surprise to one and all in that mad charge to find between them and the timber was an exceedingly crooked and very deep, sluggish stream. The line was broken as it struck this stream, but holding their muskets high above their heads the men splashed through. Some men climbed out over the very steep banks and then helped others until all had crossed the stream.

There had been an order issued to do away with all horses so that the enemy could be more easily surprised, but I had held onto mine and was the only officer present on horseback. I looked at the stream and concluded that my horse could jump it. I rode back about forty feet and sent him at the stream at full tilt. His hind feet stumbled in the sod as they landed on the opposite shore, but he soon scrambled up and I took command of the remainder of the charge. The result was the capture of over six hundred of the enemy, all of whom were marched back into our lines with their own color flying as well as our own. Queerly enough three or four guns on the eastern summit of Kennesaw opened up on the retiring troops, who were in open view. The guns were more than a mile distant and the only damage they did was to kill two Confederates and wound several others.

The troops under my command received a very complimentary note from General Logan commending them for their bravery and the splendid results following the affair. The incident concerning the big jump of my horse was commented on for a day or two, and in order to settle the question, a squad of enlisted men went over to the stream to measure the distance. It was found to be twenty-three feet from the starting point to the place where his hind feet broke the sod on the opposite side. The jump was not great for distance, but here were but few horses that would have leaped a stream like that under the conditions. "Old Tom" went out and came back with the regiment and lived till he was thirty-one years of age. During his entire career he was the pet of the regiment and his name has been mentioned at every reunion the Twelfth has held since the war.

The approach upon Kennesaw Mountain, after the Confederate commander gave up his position at Big Shanty, was carefully conducted.

In following an enemy, this is a very essential point, for the retiring troops can and often do arrange for an ambuscade that unless due caution is observed, may inflict a heavy loss on the pursuing forces. The Federal army had learned much during this campaign, and it was very seldom that, any great loss occurred from this source. There were some quite lively skirmishes with General Joe Johnston's rear guard, at time almost amounting to a small battle.

The Kennesaw line seemed to be an easy one to hold from its natural position. When fortifications were laid out, planned and efficiently constructed by competent officers, it is not much wonder that the line that Sherman's army was approaching was deemed almost impregnable by both armies. The new position taken up by the Confederates was developed slowly but surely. There were some vicious fighting between the skirmish line of both armies, and it was about the middle of June that John N. Runyan, a first Lieutenant in the Seventy-fourth Indiana Infantry and resident of Warsaw, lost his leg. He was in command of a skirmish line of his regiment and while forcing the Confederates out of the very strong position that had been taken up, a shot from a Confederate sharpshooter struck him in the leg just below the thigh. The wound was so severe that amputation was at once necessary. Many men were killed and wounded by sharpshooters.

The main line of Sherman's army was finally formed. My brigade lay right under Kennesaw, not far from its center. The mountain lay east and west right across the path of the Federal army. The main line of my brigade was perhaps a hundred feet up the side of the mountain, on a sort of natural shelf, sufficiently level for the troops to occupy. The skirmish line in front was, perhaps, half way up the mountain, and it was a rugged climb to reach it. On Sherman's right, his line extended far to the west and clear past the length of Kennesaw Mountain. I had heard that the line extended for a distance of twenty-two miles. Of course, there were open spaces in this line of advancing army, but he introduction of the telegraph into the army movements had come into play successfully and efficiently. Each division was supplied with a telegraph outfit carried in its own wagon and consisting of instruments and a plentiful supply of wire with poles something similar to the "jacob-staff" carried by surveyors. When the division went into line the telegraph corps would wire the distance behind each division by stringing the wire on these "jacob-staffs". The divisions along the entire twenty-two miles were connected telegraphically in less than an hour. The war for the Union was the first time the telegraph was utilized in this very effective way. It is easy to see how many orderlies and overworked horses were saved from the oft-times hazardous duty of carrying written orders over such a long line.

Not far from where my brigade was stretched out along the side of the mountain two batteries were "parked". Although their officers were aware that but little execution was probable, the men were permitted to indulge in firing three or four shells from each battery at the Confederate artillery situated upon the summit of Kennesaw. Often when there was not much going on, save the never-ceasing picket firing, I rode over to the battery, having been given a tip from one of the officers that they were going to practice for a short time. I was sure to be there unless something more important was going forward. They would hand me a first-class field glass so that I could watch the shots and their effect. The gun's muzzle had to be greatly elevated for such a shot, but our battery got so it could make the "Johnnies" seek safety. The distance was estimated at somewhat over a mile and I am sure that at times their shots were effective, for on several occasions I saw Confederate soldiers hastening to a point as if they were giving relief to a killed or wounded man. My own troops lay almost directly under this Confederate battery, and consequently I took considerable interest in it, for if the time should come when a general advance was ordered, this battery would fall to the lot of my troops to capture.

The army had occupied the line already alluded to for several days when I received word from General Logan that my brigade would be selected to form a force composed of one brigade from each division of the Fifteenth Corps to assault the enemy's works. I felt flattered at being selected for a duty so important, but Colonel Charles Wolcott, in command of the Second brigade of General Harrow's division, claimed the honor of being selected since he outranked me by commission date. Colonel Wolcott was a very brave and competent officer, and previous to the war had taken a course in a military school in Kentucky. He insisted on his brigade being taken instead of mine. I always thought he desired to have the eagle in his shoulder strap replaced by the star of a full-blown brigadier general much more than I did. It was finally decided that Wolcott's Second Brigade should be selected. And after the whole affair was over I never regretted that mine was not chosen, because the slaughter was great—terrible in fact.

In developing the right of the Federal line, the army had closed in on Kennesaw and the adjacent region, especially on the west. The Fifteenth Corps was removed to become a support force to General Sherman, who had decided to assault the enemy entrenchments. This assault was made on the 27th of June. The Confederates held a strong position, but it seemed that General Sherman had grown weary of the reputation that he had won as "the great flanker". He intended, by this assault, to show to the world, but especially the "copper-head" press of the North that had been twitting him over the fact that thus far in the campaign there had been little real fighting and that Sherman's only success lay in his ability to "out-flank his enemy", that he could meet the enemy head on. This was not the first time during the war that the opposition press of the North had done an unwise thing. The First Battle of Bull Run was forced upon General McDowell before he was ready by Greeley's Tribune making its incessant howl of "on to Richmond". Perhaps General Sherman should not have permitted himself to listen to anything of this sort. The press in the earlier stages of the war had criticized Sherman frequently and severely, and I know of my own knowledge that he had no special love for the newspapers. They had persisted in calling him "Crazy Bill" when, directly after the First Bull Run, he had declared that it would take a hundred thousand men to overrun Kentucky. The New York Tribune and many other papers had jeered at him for placing the number so high. After the war, when any and everybody could see that his estimate was not out of the way, and after he had shown his soldierly qualities in the command of large bodies of men, many of the leading newspapers apologized for their earlier remarks and were loud in their praises of the man, who next to Grant, did more to suppress the rebellion than any other officer of high rank in the Union Army.

Full preparations were made for the assault. The ground in front was as closely examined and scanned as much as it was possible. The place selected to deliver the blow was formidable, as was that of any portion of the enemy's line. But if carried here it would secure the utmost advantage to the Union lines. The brave men that were to grapple with the enemy were formed under the cover of the pine forest and the undergrowth, one line behind the other, until the number on the ground was deemed sufficient. When the bugle sounded the charge the command, "Forward!" rang out from dozens of officers and the murderous conflict was on.

Right up into the face of the enemy these gallant men pushed forward without a waver in their ranks, preserving their formations splendidly in the face of the multiplied obstructions. Although these brave heroes of Fort Donelson, Shiloh and Vicksburg were falling in scores, never was there a greater exhibition of true bravery than that of the men who made the assault of Kennesaw Mountain. The Confederates were behind impervious entrenchments while the attacking troops were "in the open", and it was only murder to hold them there or to send other troops to their support. The order was given to retire to the original line from where this gallant band of devoted men had started. Awful shot and shell covered all of the ground over which they had to retire. The losses in going up and returning were great—over three thousand killed or wounded. Among those who were killed were Generals Harker and McCook. McCook was a Brigadier General and one of the family known before the war was over as "the Fighting McCooks". If I remember correctly there were five brothers in all, three bearing the single star, and one of them two stars, the remaining one carrying the eagle of the Colonel of his regiment.

No further battles took place of a general nature during the presence of the army in the front of Kennesaw, other than the usual picket firing which never ceased night or day. The Twentieth (Hooker's) and the Twenty-third corps continued the development of the right flank. The right flank proceeded to such an extent that the Confederate commander became alarmed for the safety of his communications with Atlanta, as our lines extended a long distance to his left and were closing in on his rear. General Johnston was compelled to continually reform his lines until at last his line of defense took on the shape of a horseshoe. Our right was growing closer and closer to the railroad, until at last he decided not to hold Kennesaw any longer, no doubt being fearful that his army might be caught by General Sherman at the crossing of the Chattahoochie. Therefore, on the night of the third day of July the Confederate commander gave up the formidable line of Kennesaw Mountain.

Kennesaw Mountain certainly was the strongest line the enemy had occupied since the opening struggles of the campaign at Resaca, Buzzard Roost and Tunnel Hill. To be maneuvered out of a position the enemy had deemed impregnable was most mortifying to General Johnston, as well as disheartening to his soldiers. Even the great majority of the Federal army was surprised at his yielding the position with only the one vigorous onset, and there was a growing feeling among the Confederates that General Johnston should be superseded. This feeling did not exhibit itself among the troops General Johnston commanded in the slightest degree, but was hatched and encouraged by Confederate officers belonging to the other commands. Each position the Confederate army gave up accentuated this feeling, and it is said to have been entertained and encouraged by Jeff Davis himself. When the Confederate forces fell back across the Chattahoochie River, General Johnston was removed from his command and General Hood named as his successor. After the war I met Johnston several times in Washington and formed a high estimate of the man, or, rather, my former high estimate of General Johnston was sustained based on this closer personal acquaintance.

There was one thing for which a high-up officer never, even during the war or since, received due credit and that was the constant strain that a commanding officer in the field was subjected to at all times. Even the enlisted man under his command seldom thought of it, or if he did, he never talked about it to his comrades, yet this strain was an ever-present feeling on the part of the officer whose word of command sent men into battle to perish by the score. The responsibility that the commander carried was his and his alone, as there was no one to share it with him, or take his portion of the blame should any be attached to the movement or the loss it might occasion. There were times when an officer was compelled to issue the order to some dear friend, some old-time friend, whom he sent forward to grapple with the enemy in a death struggle from which it was a mere hope that he might return alive.

Under such circumstances it is easy to see that such a responsibility would and in thousand of cases did, rack the nerves of the bravest among the superior officers. I am reminded that during the Atlanta campaign, General Logan sent for me not less than three different times in the nighttime. Once an orderly rode a distance of four miles to informed me that General Logan desired my presence at his headquarters and that he would conduct me to the place where it was located. There was no braver officer in the army than General John A. Logan, and there were few handsomer men when he was mounted on his charger. There are few men who served under his command after he became the head of the Fifteenth corps, who even dreamed that during the war there were periods when the great responsibility and constant worry brought on an inability to sleep. It was on such occasions that he sent for me and very likely for others to come to his tent and aid in soothing him to slumber.

Even during the war I was a great reader, and the orderlies at my headquarters had standing directions to bring in books when such were found in their "pilgrimages" about the country. I remember very distinctly that four of William Gilmore Simms' Revolutionary stories were captured and brought to me by my orderlies. I discovered that reading aloud to General Logan had a very soothing effect upon him, so the second time I took one of the Revolutionary stories referred to along with me, and after reading I generally had the satisfaction to see that this method proved efficacious. He would drop off into a peaceful slumber out of which he would come refreshed and cheerful. His over-strained nerves were relaxed, and in short, he was a fully restored man.

The troops, who saw him flying at the tip-top speed of the noble animal he rode on the 22nd of July, 1864, the day that the gallant McPherson laid down his life for the great cause, the day the Confederate General Hood was driven back into his breastworks and was consequently the turning point in the campaign denoting the fall of Atlanta, would scarcely believe that so brave a man had trouble shedding the worries of battle and could not sleep at night. It was these visits to General Logan that taught me that commanding officers worried greatly over the loss of life among their own troops, which affected them seriously and above all else prevented them from sleeping.

It was during the night of the third of July 1864 that Sergeant Horace Franklin of Company K, Twelfth Indiana, who was in command of a portion of the skirmish line about half way up the north face of Kennesaw, came to my headquarters. He told me that he believed something unusual was going on within the Confederate lines on the summit of the mountain. I have already stated that my brigade lay right under one of the batteries on top of Kennesaw, and the Sergeant seemed to think that the enemy was preparing to evacuate. He had crawled up close to the battery and said that all the conversation among the men was conducted in a very low tone, entirely different from their former loud talk. I went back with him and together we climbed up as near the guns as was prudent. I, too, came back with the idea that something unusual was really taking place. I could scarcely believe that the few hints and signs we could gather meant the abandonment of such a strong natural position. When I left the Sergeant I told him that at three o'clock in the morning I would strengthen the skirmish line with two hundred more men.

The men were ordered to proceed to develop what was taking place at the fort and vicinity, but by no means to force more than a skirmish fight, and obtain all information possible. This order was carried out and at precisely three o'clock the Federal skirmish line moved forward toward the summit of Kennesaw. The astonishment of most of the troops engaged, except Sergeant Franklin, was considerable when the men found the going up much easier than they expected. There was an occasional shot fired at them, but as soon as it began to dawn upon the minds of the main body of the skirmish line that the fort was practically abandoned, it was impossible to hold them back. The men made a rush for the summit, and it was this rush that enabled them to capture considerable over a hundred Confederates that had been left in the fort proper to keep up appearances and deceive the "Yankees" into the belief that the works were still manned. The rush came with such vigor out of the darkness preceding the dawn that many of the rebels fell into our hands, never dreaming that a force of over two hundred Federals were in their immediate neighborhood. Of course the men ran all over the fort, and at about sunrise I arrived on the ground and took command of the troops on top of the mountain. Word had been sent me as soon as the fort was in our possession. It was a big climb to the summit, so after sending word to division and corps headquarters by a mounted orderly, I at once began the ascent of Kennesaw. After reaching the men in the fort, I could readily perceive that the main army down below was receiving the news that the Federals were on top of the mountain. The rising of the sun a few moments afterwards disclosed "Old Glory" waving in the breeze and the troops below were hailing the flag with wild cheers.

A capture was made near the fort that I have never been able to solve, that was the discovery of over two hundred muskets lying near but outside the fort that had been occupied by the battery. A few of these were stacked in military order, and all of them might have been, but had gotten knocked over on the ground. It looked as if half a regiment of infantry had run away and left them. Myself and the officers about me could not account for such a large number of muskets being left by the enemy. The rifles were a godsend to the officers of my own and one or two other regiments. It is the duty of the Captain of a company to charge the price of the gun to the soldier who carries it, but who has lost or mislaid it. The cost is charged up on the payroll and the amount taken out of the pay due the soldier on the next payday. Very few officers liked to make this charge against their men. If I remember correctly, there were eleven men in my own regiment who had lost their guns. The Captains had carried the matter along for several months, but on the capture of these guns, which were Springfields, I turned over to the Captains a sufficient number to straighten their accounts against the soldiers who had lost theirs. This they did by turning them over to the ordnance officer of the corps and obtaining his receipt for them. This receipt would square the Captains' account at the ordnance office at Washington City. In that way the soldiers were saved the price of a gun being deducted from their pay. This done, all of the remainder of the muskets were also turned over as captured property.

After looking over the ground, and picking up a few things that were counted a curiosity, I directed the force to descend to the position they formerly occupied. When they arrived there they at once proceeded to get their breakfasts, but before it was over I received marching orders and directions to move out around the eastern end of the mountain in pursuit of the enemy. This was on the morning of the third of July, and the whole Federal army was once more in motion. The Fifteenth corps was directed to proceed to Roswell, a town situated twenty-five or thirty miles above the railroad bridge that crosses the Chattahoochie, a few miles north of Atlanta. The march took us through the quaint old town of Marietta, where the One Hundredth Indiana Infantry of my own brigade was detailed to guard and hold. This regiment remained there until the fall of Atlanta. I felt its loss deeply, because it left me with only three regiments.

CHAPTER 12

Moving Toward Atlanta

Our standards gay—War's bright heraldic page—
　　Our uniforms with gold and silver dressed,
Now rent and torn in battle's furious rage,
　　Blood-stained and marred with dust each glittering crest.
The light young hearts that made a jest of life,
　　And laughed at death, when we broke camp at dawn—
Changed are their merry songs for shouts of strife,
　　As hushed where Valor mourns a comrade gone.
　　　　　　　　　　　　　　—Robert J. Burdette

　　The third of July, as I remember it, was the hottest day the Northern army had thus far experienced. The corps was directed to hurry its movements, as there was an important bridge across the Chattahoochie at Roswell that was to be saved from destruction. The troops suffered tremendously on the march due to the extreme heat.
　　Roswell was a small village and the Chattahoochie at this point gave the town an excellent source of waterpower. The Confederates were operating a large cotton mill at this place engaged in the manufacture of all kinds of cotton goods for the Confederate army. It employed a large number of women. Here was a dilemma or rather a situation with which the Federal army had never before been compelled to grapple with. Here was a factory employing a thousand people in all—men, women and children—which the operations of both armies had rendered helpless. Enemies as they were, it would not do to let these operatives starve, and among the first thing done was to issue rations to every resident of the little village. The dilemma was soon disposed of by General Sherman who issued an order directing the officer placed in charge of the little town to take a census of the women. These women were to be given their choice to retire within the Confederate lines or to go north where the experienced women and children would be given employment in the cotton factories up there. I heard afterwards that over three hundred decided on accepting the latter proposition, and some of them were taken to Lowell, Massachusetts and other cotton manufacturing points. It was a wise proposition. There is one thing that can be said of the Union army and the officers that commanded it, and that is, they always took care of the people, even though enemies, so far as food was concerned.
　　I have already spoken of the long bridge that crossed the river at Roswell, which was most desirous to save from destruction if at all

possible. The advance guard that had been hurried forward in order to do this did save a large portion of it. The Confederates had attempted to destroy it by tearing away sections of the framework. They had first tried to destroy it by the use of fire, but this proved a failure without combustible material. The bridge was a long one but the two or three sections that had been torn out were soon replaced by the engineer corps. The army was only delayed for a couple of days as a result of the broken bridge. As soon as it was made passable all of the Fifteenth corps crossed over and immediately threw up entrenchments on the opposite side.

During the movements just described of the Fifteenth and Seventeenth corps, the center of the army under Generals Thomas and Hooker moved directly to the Chattahoochie railway. It was plain to see that the Confederate General Johnston intended to retire within the defenses of Atlanta. The Sixteenth and Twenty-third corps had succeeded in crossing the Chattahoochie and the Fourth, Fourteenth and Twentieth were also maneuvering to get on the south bank of that stream. The Fifteenth and Seventeenth had crossed the river at Roswell, thus very seriously threatening the right flank of the Confederate army. The crossing of the Chattahoochie River was one of Sherman's most skillful acts during the war. It was a brilliant piece of military maneuvering. Just think of it! With the entire Confederate army confronting him, he crossed a wide stream without the loss of a single man.

On the 17th of July 1864, the Fifteenth corps received orders to close up on the east around Atlanta. It should be remembered that the Fifteenth and Seventeenth corps formed the extreme left flank of General Sherman's army during the advance upon Atlanta, following the successful crossing of the Chattahoochie River by his entire army. Decatur is a village that lay on the line of railroad that ran to Charleston, South Carolina and connected with other lines leading up to Richmond, Virginia. In occupying the village of Decatur, the railroad connection with the latter places was severed. After the Federal line closed in about Atlanta, the Confederate forces possessed only one line of railroad, that leading to the south via Griffin to Milledgeville, Georgia.

It was during the march of these two corps in taking up their position near Atlanta, that the battle of Peach Tree Creek was fought. It was also during this period that General Hood superseded the Confederate General Joseph E. Johnston. While on the march the sound of that fierce struggle could be distinctly heard. Immediately on taking command General Hood inaugurated an entirely different policy from what had been pursued by General Johnston. General Hood had won the reputation of a "fighter," and he doubtless deserved the name. The battle of Peach Tree Creek was Hood's first demonstration after he had succeeded to the command. He evidently intended to win and really seemed to think that he would do so. On the Union side it was principally fought by Thomas' Fourteenth corps

Moving Toward Atlanta

and Hooker's Twentieth. After the battle began it raged with ferocity seldom equaled during the war. The weight of the attack fell upon General Joe Hooker's corps. General Jeff C. Davis' division of the Fourteenth corps, composed largely of Indiana troops was hotly engaged and maintained its reputation won on so many previous bloody fields. Time and time again General Hood tried to penetrate the Federal lines, meeting with a severe repulse after each effort, bravely though made. Both sides in this battle fought like demons. As a consequence, both sides suffered heavily. Hood threw his troops on exposed points with the reckless bravery for which he had become noted, only to be driven back with equal valor and with heavy loss.

While these events were taking place, the forces that had crossed the Chattahoochie were, in obedience to orders, engaged in closing in on the east-northeast side of Atlanta. The Army of the Tennessee formed the extreme left of the Federal army. The Sixteenth corps was held in reserve at Decatur and the Seventeenth became the left of Sherman's line. The Fifteenth was next on the Seventeenth's right and the Twenty-third corps was on the right of the Fifteenth. All the troops on the 20th of July, except the reserve at Decatur, moved forward and took up their position in line about three miles east of Atlanta, forming an irregular arched gateway of a circle about the doomed city. The Fifteenth corps covered the railroad.

Such was the position and situation when the Federal lines began to press the defender of the city that General Hood had undertaken to hold in spite of Sherman. I remember very distinctly that, along late in the afternoon after the troops had taken up position in front of the partially well-manned line of earthworks, I, along with two orderlies, was looking for a place to pitch my own headquarters tent. In doing so we ascended a rise of ground in a forest thickly set with large pine trees. The ground for some distance sloped away towards Atlanta and was heavily covered with dense undergrowth. I had about decided on the spot for my headquarters when all at once a bullet whistled by me just as I was dismounting from my horse. I was surprised because I could see in every direction except into the thick undergrowth. The singing of another bullet quite near me induced me to remount my horse and make an investigation. By this time all the staff and orderlies had assembled, and I told them about the whistling bullets and directed that they should accompany me in ascertaining where the missiles came from.

The party rode in the direction of the undergrowth, the officers with their revolvers ready and the orderlies with loaded carbines. We proceeded in a body and as soon as we reached the edge of the underbrush an orderly saw the hat of one of the Confederates over the top of a fallen tree. He went to where he could see the full length of the fallen tree, then came back to me and told me he thought there was a dozen or more Confederates behind the log. I directed those present to form a line and we would make a dash upon them. Evidently these rebels had not discovered our party until they heard the noise occasioned by the horses feet. We were upon them in less time than it takes to tell of the incident. One or two men fired at random, but hurt no one, and finding themselves surrounded, they surrendered at discretion. There were eight of them in the party and none escaped. On the way back to the place I had selected for my headquarters, one of the men told me that the horses of the scouting party were hidden in a ravine to the west and north of where they were captured. I made a detail of a dozen men with directions to see if the horses could be captured. They took the man whom had given the information along with them as a guide and returned with eight rather underfed and small horses.

On that evening the army that had crossed the Chattahoochie River at Roswell went into line in front of the entrenchments occupied by the Confederates. In closing up the lines there was considerable vicious skirmishing at times and many men were killed or wounded during the approach. Colonel Greathouse of the Fortieth Illinois regiment led his troops down a descent of about a half-mile. There they met with such heavy opposition that Greathouse moved his entire regiment up to the skirmish line as a support and became involved in a struggle that cost our side dearly. Colonel Greathouse was killed as well as many others.

The Federal line was drawn up quite close to the Confederate entrenchments during the night. It was late in the afternoon of the day following the death of Colonel Greathouse that General McPherson and General Logan with all their staff, rode up to my headquarters on a sort of reconnoitering expedition. The coming together of these two general officers with their respective staffs made quite a body of mounted men. My headquarters were slightly behind the summit of the rise of ground, which was covered with pine forest, and General McPherson expressed the desire to go to a point where he could make a closer and better observation of the Confederate position. I remember hearing General Logan objecting to the head of the army of the Tennessee the general would be unnecessarily exposing himself to the bullets of the enemy. He felt there was too much at stake to risk the life of the officer second in command of the entire army. General McPherson, however, persisted, and accompanied by General Logan and their mounted men in all making over a hundred, started out. The party had gone something over half way down the descending slope, when the watchful officer of some battery discovered the body of mounted men through the trees. All at once a volley from a six-gun battery sent its shell apparently right into the midst and over the General and his attendants. Over a dozen were wounded and a couple killed by the first discharge. At the second volley a young man acting as purveyor for General Logan's headquarters, riding just at my side was struck by a fragment of shell. His right arm was literally torn from his body and he fell to the ground.

It did not take long for those who remained mounted to get out from under the range of those vicious guns. I remember hearing General Logan once more impressing on General McPherson the folly of exposing his person to such an extent, stating that whatever information was required concerning the Confederate position could be furnished to him from other sources without risking the life of the commanding officer, and that an accident to him might disarrange the movements of the entire left wing of the army. The incident caused many comments among the "rank and file" of the army as soon as it became known. This was the situation of affairs in the immediate vicinity in which the writer was a spectator.

All night, over to the right, the great Federal anaconda was slowly but steadily drawing closer about the beleaguered town. The Twenty-third corps, the Fourth, the Fourteenth and the Twentieth, were all engaged in going into position on the north of Atlanta, each corps joining as rapidly and as closely as possible. Some of the movements had to be made in the nighttime, but when fully completed, a continuous line ran from the southeast of the town around to the west and turning southwest. It is always a big undertaking to close up an army in the act of commencing a siege because the enemy is always just as active as its opponent is. In many cases the ground coveted by the besieging force has to be fought for, while in others, it is given up, being defended by only a line of skirmishers. All of the creeping up has to be carefully and watchfully done. It must be borne in mind that even when no special contest is under way, men are being killed and wounded every hour in the twenty-four. Many losses came from the "wear and tear" of the opposing armies being in close proximity while nothing more than picket firing was in progress. No mention was made of this loss in the general summing up, save by company and regimental reports.

On the eastside of Atlanta the picket firing during the night of the 21st of July had been extremely lively. A half-dozen times during the night I visited the skirmish line to see that the men were awake and attending to their duties, for there was nothing I feared more than a surprise. I am aware of the fact that I have on many occasions when near the enemy, walked the whole length of my own picket line, when scarcely a man composing it ever knew that I had visited it at all. I have always owned up to the fact that I did this through fear, rather than bravery. I feared that the enemy might find a weak spot caused by some of the men going to sleep or at least becoming so drowsy and weary that they could be overcome. As I could not sleep when the enemy was near, I put in my time very often in visiting the picket line.

There were no indications of an impending battle when the troops of the Northern army lay themselves down to rest. The men slept rolled in their blanket using the canopy of heaven for a covering for even the "dog tent" had been dispensed with. Every one knew that the skirmish fire was at times quite rapid and heavy, but few were aware that we were on the eve of a great battle.

Before it was light on the morning of July 22, 1864, it was discovered that the Confederate line in the immediate front of the Fifteenth corps facing from Atlanta directly on the east, had been evacuated during the night. This withdrawal of the enemy's forces in our front had been effected during the heavy picket firing that continued all through the night. I rode forward with an orderly to what was the Confederate entrenchments the night before, and found the entire line on both sides of the railroad that lead east out of Atlanta wholly evacuated. With all possible haste I dispatched staff officers, one to General Logan and one to General Harrow with the information. In a very short time I received orders to move forward and occupy the late Confederate works by "reversing" them. Within a very brief time, we had converted the rebel entrenchments into a very excellent protection facing inward toward Atlanta. The troops that moved forward to this new line, consisting of most all of the Fifteenth corps, were considerably surprised at this movement of the enemy.

While my three regiments were engaged in turning the breastworks, I determined to inspect the region lying between the new line and the city of Atlanta. I took an orderly and rode out in the direction of the town. There was a wooded slope between the works and the suburbs of the town with the trees standing in rather "open order" making it easier to see an enemy and prevent surprise and capture. I rode a full mile toward Atlanta and on one occasion Orderly Ruff—that was his name—suggested there was considerable danger in getting so far away from supporting troops. I had ridden clear past a match factory located near the railroad in the suburbs of town.

The withdrawal of Hood's troops must have been en masse, for in that morning's ride neither the orderly nor myself met or even saw an enemy. We rode leisurely back to our own line. Shortly after reaching my own command, very heavy artillery and musketry firing began away off on the left and rear. This heavy firing was so steady that it was easy to know that our troops to the rear and south were engaged with a large force of the enemy. Very soon after this heavy firing started a staff officer rode up to me and in a low tone of voice announced that General McPherson was mortally wounded. It was requested that the information be kept from the main body of troops as long as possible. Of course, I was greatly shocked. I had been personally acquainted with him during the operations around Vicksburg and he was one of the most genial, pleasant, agreeable and sociable among all the higher officers I had ever met. The officer who had conveyed this disastrous news had scarcely left when another staff officer from Logan's headquarters rode up with an order for me to send a full regiment over to the left and the staff officer would conduct it to the position. I very reluctantly sent the Twenty-sixth Illinois for I was left with only two regiments to fill the space of over a quarter of a mile of earthworks.

This was the situation that called for reinforcement from the right. The Sixteenth corps was held in reserve at Decatur when it was ascertained that the Confederate forces had withdrawn from the front of the Federal army facing the town from the east. General McPherson at once decided to place that corps on the extreme left of the entire Federal line because General Hood had moved his troops at night around to the Federal left. The Sixteenth corps was swinging around along the road when, all at once, Hood's veterans assailed them. They soon got into fighting trim, and it was while placing the troops in position that General McPherson received his death wound and died shortly afterward. From this first attack until about one in the afternoon the fighting was fierce.

It was a battle as had never occurred before or afterwards, for during the day, whole brigades and divisions fought from one side of the earthworks for a time, only to leap over them to repel an attack from the other side. It began to look as if our army was getting the worst of the struggle. The heavy fighting had drifted towards the left of the position held by my troops. All at once from the left of my line I could see about a quarter of a mile away what I took to be about two brigades of Confederates getting ready to charge our works. The "Johnnies" came with a rush, charged right up to the line and, as a portion of the enemy overlapped the defenders, about seventy-five or a hundred broke over our line. After the rebels got inside the Federal entrenchments they didn't seem to know what to do. I detached two companies of the Ninetieth Illinois and pushed them down upon this body of men that had broken through. I rode down to them and commanded them to throw down their arms and surrender. As there seemed to be no one in command of them, they decided to obey the order and surrendered at discretion.

With the exception of this incident, my reduced brigade remained idle during a great deal of the fighting that had been going on. Shortly after making the capture of the rebels, a corporal came in from my own front with the announcement that the enemy was bringing troops and forming them into line on the ground that myself and an orderly had ridden over that morning. I at once sent a staff officer to find General Harrow and give him the information I had just received. The corporal had scarcely left me on his return to his picket line when another soldier arrived bringing the news that more troops were assembling in my front in a double line. I sent additional staff officers to find General Harrow and later sent still another one, but all returned without success. Two more staff officers were sent to hunt for the general. The last word I received was that the Confederates had formed five lines deep and were evidently about ready to move upon the Federal line at my position.

The railroad, to which I have alluded several times, passed right through the Federal works in a deep cut. On my side of the railroad was Captain DeGrass' battery of twenty-pounder Parrots. They occupied the summit of the ground that made the deep cut of railroad necessary. Between the battery and my own right was a regiment belonging to General Morgan L. Smith's division; the remainder of which was all on the opposite side of the railroad from my troops. I had taken the precaution to send word to Captain DeGrass and the commanding officer of the infantry, an Ohio regiment, that they might expect a charge from the enemy. The Confederate force had the advantage of being in timber until they neared the works where the ground was clear for perhaps a couple of hundred feet. The Confederates came with a rush, but were completely checked at the edge of the woods. I had sent my horses during the day to the rear, where they were hidden behind an old tannery. I was on foot and near the center of the two regiments during the charge. I had never seen the enemy before more completely repulsed. Not a man reached the works during this assault. The enemy was literally mowed down as with a scythe in front of both these regiments.

Right here I must relate an incident that came under my own eye. While my regiment lay at Scottsboro, Alabama during the previous winter, I had enlisted several young men whose home was in that State. One of them had been fairly well off before the war—or rather his father was. There were five slaves belonging to the estate and all of them had run away except for a boy of twelve or thirteen. The young master of this boy did not know what to do with him. He was a very bright colored boy, but full of fun. It was easy to see that he was a favorite of his young master. I told the soldier to keep the slave in the regiment and make him useful, if none of the superior officers made any objection and I was sure they wouldn't unless someone complained to them.

When the Atlanta campaign opened, I frequently saw the little colored imp getting wood and water for his young master when in camp and often carrying his knapsack or gun when on the march. The owner of the boy was only a few feet from me when the assault alluded to above came, and I glanced at the young Alabamian and saw a black hand handing him a cartridge. The boy was sitting on the ground biting cartridges and handing them to his master just as fast as he could fire them. The soldier was enabled to shoot at a much more rapid rate by this assistance of the little Negro boy. It was not often that a Southern-born man fought on the Union side during the "War for the Union" with his own slave to assist him. The young man came home with us to Indianapolis after the war where he was paid off, and when I bade him good-bye, the boy was still with him.

The enemy had been so handsomely repulsed in my own front that myself and men were rejoicing greatly. We never dreamed that the rest of the line over on our right at the deep cut had not fared so well. None of the troops or myself even thought of disaster. The boys were already making jests out of the various matters witnessed by them during the fight and repulse, when all at once came a volley from perhaps a thousand men fired straight into the backs of both of my regiments, at fairly close range. The Confederates had captured two of DeGrass' guns and a large body of the enemy had surged right through the deep railroad cut. They then had turned their muskets upon my two regiments. There was only one thing to do and that was to form a line at right angles facing them, but the enemy certainly outnumbered my force more than three to one and was constantly increasing. My force was compelled to yield ground. I ordered the Ninetieth Illinois to quickly form behind the big tan-yard building already referred to, and as soon as they did, I would have my own regiment, the Twelfth, join their line.

This was done, but I lost many men from that unfortunate fire, all the more grievous because we had so splendidly repulsed the direct assault made upon us. To make matters worse, a Federal battery well over to our right and of course on the opposite side of the railroad, seeing the rebels running through the railroad cut, opened up, no doubt killing and wounding many of them. My own troops, being hidden by the great number of Confederates between my troops and the battery, were also in the path of every shot and shell. The shelling of our own troops aided the enemy considerably, but it was one of those accidents that sometimes occur in the excitement, the thunder, the roar and the crash of battle, and which at times is difficult to avoid.

Assistance finally came from General Harrow, and with a rush the Confederates were forced back over the lines they had left. The chase was kept up until the enemy re-entered the town out of which they had come in the morning. The fight for the recovery of the works was over before dark and that big day's work formed the groundwork for the cyclorama of "The Battle of Atlanta," which some years ago was placed on exhibition at Indianapolis. It was a very correct picture of the battle, a picture that never failed to thrill the spectator, especially if he had been a participant in the great struggle of the 22nd of July 1864.

My two regiments suffered severely on that day, nearly all the loss occurring by the Confederates breaking through the lines at the railroad cut after they had been repulsed. Henry Weaver, a Lieutenant in I Company, his home was around Oswego, Indiana and Lawrence Parks of F Company of Warsaw, were both lost on that day. Weaver was mortally wounded and died sometime the next day. Parks died that night from the effects of five wounds received at different times and was buried by torchlight.

What a scene that was following the nearly all-day battle of July 22, 1864! All the troops engaged in that wild struggle who had come out of it with their lives and free from wounds, were wearied almost to the limit of endurance. Many of them had gone "on the double-quick" to the more dangerous points where, after assisting in repelling the onslaught, had immediately been called to other endangered place. The men were so wearied that they were ready to sink to rest wherever they were when the announcement came that the battle was over. Both armies were so completely tired out that it was scarcely necessary to place pickets between the contending forces. This was done, of course, but neither side was in a condition to threaten the other.

Late in the afternoon of that day, the Twenty-sixth Illinois regiment of my brigade returned worn and weary. The members of all three of the regiments were directed to seek the best position possible around the old frame tannery to which I have frequently refered. The building was quite a large one, and I had directed that a burial party should go out and bring in all the dead Confederates they could find for burial that were close to the tannery. The seriously wounded of the enemy had previously been gathered up and brought in over the works. I ordered a detail to tear away all the boards from the tannery to procure material for those who could not walk to lie upon. I presume that the tearing down of the old tannery caused the different opinions among the party that was responsible for the most excellent and life-like picture of "The Battle of Atlanta", that was placed on exhibition at Indianapolis.

I was well acquainted with Theodore R. Davis who had much to do with the designing of that picture all through its construction. Preceding and during the Atlanta campaign, Mr. Davis was the regular artist correspondent of Harper's Weekly, and nearly all of his articles were illustrated by himself. After it was decided to locate the cyclorama of "The Battle of Atlanta" at Indianapolis, a company was formed to provide for the expense of the project and to secure a special building for it. This was done and a corps of artists were gotten together under charge of Mr. Davis. A number of surveyors went to Atlanta for the purpose of getting material of every kind so as to have the great picture historically correct. I received a letter from Mr. Davis, as did many other officers connected with that portion of the struggle, asking what was the color of the horse I rode, the kind of equipment, and other information I could give them in order to have the forthcoming picture as absolutely correct in all its detail. In giving him the information, I alluded to the big tannery that stood very near the line of works occupied by my brigade and directly in its rear. I was surprised at receiving within a few days a second letter from Mr. Davis making the statement that quite a number of officers who had command of troops on that identical ground declared that no such building existed on the day of the great fight. Of course, I was astonished. Mr. Davis declared that for himself he could not say if there was such a building there or not on July 22, 1864, but fully a half dozen officers, some of them commanding regiments on that day, were firm in their assertion that no such building existed there at that time.

Knowing so well as I did that such a building did exist and it was a conspicuous figure in the landscape, I wrote Mr. Davis repeating the statement that a big tannery building was there on that day. It took a full month of correspondence before the question was finally settled that the building did exist and formed quite a feature in the great picture. But for Mr. Davis' letter to me asking for information the "The Battle of Atlanta" cyclorama would have been incorrect in one of its salient features.

The horrors that followed Hood's defeat on the 22nd of July 1864 were unimaginable to those who have not been in battle. Over a hundred and fifty wounded men had been brought inside of our entrenchments. A corps of half a dozen surgeons and hospital stewards labored all night through with men wounded in every conceivable way. Some had an arm hinging by only a shred, others had broken legs, and others had musket shots straight through their bodies. In fact, there were no two whose injuries resembled each other. Worn out as I was, it was after midnight before I could close my eyes in sleep. The cries and groans of the severely wounded and the dying kept me awake until, so wearied, I fell asleep in spite of the horrors of a night I have remembered ever since. The scene "after the battle" is one that will haunt the spectator for as long as he lives, for surely it haunts me to this day.

Following the battle of the 22nd of July there came days of more leisure (that is not a good word for there was seldom leisure for either side, when two such armies as that of Hood's and Sherman's were close together). The "wear and tear" of two such bodies of men in close proximity could only result in the loss of many lives even though no battle was in progress. Both sides were keenly active; each watching the other like two gladiators pitted one against the other as was so often the case in the Coliseum at Rome. The skirmish line was always active and many lives were lost and many wounds have been carried ever since the day described as "The Battle of Atlanta".

General Sherman had directed that defensive works be build by the Twenty-third corps, through which he intended to withdraw all the forces from the eastern portion of Atlanta. The withdrawn corps he intended to use to extend his lines on the extreme right of the line of his whole army as it was then confronting Atlanta. The withdrawal of the Federal lines from the left commenced at a very early hour on the 27th and continued until all the troops of the extreme left were inside the fortified line the Twenty-third corps had provided for their safety during that ticklish movement. On the evening of the 26th of July an order came to the Fifteenth corps to be ready to march at daylight of the morning of the 27th, and it fell to the lot of my brigade to bring up the rear. Soldiers always seem to be ready to undertake any new move, no matter how dangerous the undertaking might be, and I was not surprised to learn that, after partaking of an early breakfast, the men were ready to march.

General Morgan L. Smith came into the command of the Fifteenth, following the assumption of the command of the Army of the Tennessee by General Logan, occasioned by the death of General McPherson. When this movement began, it was very quickly plain that the command of a corps was too big a thing for General Smith. It was not long after the withdrawal began until the new General had the Fifteenth corps into the only trouble it had ever known. As soon as the Confederate discovered that the Federal line was falling back, they pushed out a strong body of men in pursuit. General Smith rode up to me considerably frustrated. He directed me to place a regiment behind an already fortified position in order to hold the advancing enemy in check. As my own regiment was the nearest I directed it to take up the position selected by General Smith.

I continued the march with the other two regiments of my brigade. We had proceeded about a mile and a half, when I caught up with General Smith and his staff. I asked him if he had ordered the regiment forward that he had directed to be left to stay the onward march of the Confederates. "Why, no," he said. "Haven't they been ordered to rejoin the forces yet?" "Not that I know of," said I. I dashed back to bring up my own regiment, if they were not already captured by the orders of our new commander. Racing my horse at full speed, I soon covered that mile and a half and with all haste withdrew the Twelfth from a position in which they would have been surrounded, most probably, within the next twenty minutes. Taking my place at their head, it was not long until they rejoined the corps. If I had not asked General Smith if the regiment had been ordered forward the pursuing Confederates might have captured every one of them.

All of the 27th was taken up in the move to the extreme right of the Federal line, the troops making this march camping that night in a sort of haphazard way. It was well after dark before my own command had secured suitable grounds to lie down upon. It had been a wearisome march often delayed by some check at the front of the troops. Frequent stopping is almost as wearisome and far more annoying to marching troops than if the movement was a steady one with no hindrances whatever. The standing around with a knapsack on one's shoulders, momentarily expecting to hear the order to move is very annoying and tiresome.

At an early hour on the 28th, the troops breakfasted and were ordered to form in a line of battle ready to meet the enemy at any moment. The line moved forward in that way, no matter what might be the obstruction. I remember that I received orders to place two regiments in front, in line of battle, with the third on the right flank moving forward in what was known in the army as "four ranks", the latter regiment so placed that it could be ordered forward at a moment's notice to reinforce the two in battlefront, if its services should be required, but its main duty was to guard the flank.

We had moved forward in this order for more than a mile when an order came to halt. The order was obeyed with the two regiments preserving their battle front, while the other that was marching at right angles with the other two, either stood still or lay down just as they were. All at once we could hear the vicious "spitting" of skirmish firing out at the front. It was neither active nor prolonged at first, but as there was a slight eminence a few rods in front of the lines, I directed that the two regiments should more forward to its top. There was a fenced field down the opposite slope right in front of this position, and I directed that the soldiers should remove all the rails and place them right in front of their line. While this was in progress I rode over to the left to see the position of the brigade that joined mine there. I found Colonel Oliver of the Fifteenth Michigan at breakfast. While talking to him I heard a fusillade among the skirmishers over in front of my own command. Colonel Oliver made the remark that "It was nothing," and suggested to me to "jump off my horse and take a cup of coffee with him." I was about to comply when the skirmishers broke out again and I flew back to my command and reached the rear of my two regiments in line behind the rails. I found them engaged in repelling the first assault of a battle since known by the appellation of "Ezra Church", fought on the 28th day of July 1864.

From that time forward during all that day there was sufficient work to keep my men employed without a moment's intermission. The Confederates made seven distinct charges on the Federal line, which was repulsed each time. In some of the charges they came very close up to the line of rails. After each assault the men took their bayonets to dig the ground and their tin plates and hands to scoop up the dirt over the rails and improved their works. The battle of Ezra church was certainly one of the most satisfactory to the men engaged in it and to myself. It seemed that General Hood had divined the movement General Sherman was making, or else he had absolute information, which could easily be the case, for every man, woman, and child was ready to give full information of the movements of the "Yankee" troops and did so all through the war. In any event General Hood, knowing that his left flank would be in danger and that the only railroad leading out of Atlanta, had been destroyed for a distance of thirty miles, resolved to attack the Federal forces while they were making the move. This is why he massed a large force on his own left and made the repeated charges on the 28th.

The Hood assaults were repulsed with terrible slaughter. Sometimes the assailants came three and four lines deep; and the withering fire of the defenders would so decimate the first and second lines that the third and fourth knew that they were moving to certain death and would retire. The onsets and repulses lasted all day long. The last one late in the evening was so feeble. I thought it was only made to recover a portion of the ground, which was covered with their dead, in order to secure the bodies of some of them for a more decent burial than could be given in the field. This fiercely contested battle was fought all day long without a shot from artillery and only infantry participating.

Very soon after the forming of the line in the early morning, General Logan and a portion of his staff rode along the line and remarked: "Colonel Williams, you have a very important position here on the extreme right of the army, and you must hold it at every hazard. Other brigades will be sent up as rapidly as possible and will be added on to your right in order to extend the flank to the north." I replied by telling him that "I would hold the position till the last man was killed or disabled." But a few moments elapsed after he had given me this verbal order, until the enemy made its first assault, which was so gallantly repulsed.

What worried me the most was ammunition. The troops had marched forward to the position they occupied through a forest, without roads, and not a man in the command had any idea where the ordnance wagons were located. Being a purely infantry fight, the troops were using up ammunition at a rate that alarmed me and I did not know where to send for more. Fortunately just about the time the last half dozen boxes of ammunition was carried up to the battle line, an ordnance train belonging to the Sixteenth Corps passed along about a half-mile to the rear. I was at once informed of the passage of the train consisting of ten or twelve wagonloads. The staff officer I had sent with a request for two wagon loads returned announcing that the officer in charge refused to issue to any other than troops of his own corps. It did not take me long to stop that train and alter the officer's protest. I took two wagonloads up to the rear of the brigade and had them unloaded in a close patch of shrubbery. I saw there was not time to "mince matters", and if the ammunition could not be had in a kindly way, there was the plan of force. And I would not miss such an opportunity to supply my troops with an article so badly needed. The Twenty-sixth Illinois fired seventy thousand rounds that day and the other three regiments fired like amounts. One very large and rugged man engaged in carrying boxes of cartridges up to the line was overcome with fatigue and heat and dropped dead on his way to the line with a box of ammunition on his shoulder. A box of cartridges weighed an even hundred pounds and there were a thousand rounds in a box.

In one of the charges that was made, the enemy came clear up to the line before they were completely repulsed. A Lieutenant Colonel belonging to a Tennessee regiment came so close to the improvised works, that Captain Sam Boughter from Warsaw, Indiana, grabbed him by the collar and pulled him inside our lines. The Captain took into his possession the three gold stars, one each side of the Confederate's collar, six in all. That Confederate Lieutenant Colonel was the sulkiest prisoner that I had ever seen and for more than half an hour he showered the most vindictive curses upon us one and all.

General Jeff C. Davis' division of the Fourteenth corps had been ordered in the early morning to march to a point a few miles to the right of the forces to be engaged on that day. After going that distance he was to move down on the flank of Hood's attacking force. It was afterwards ascertained that General Davis' division took the wrong road at a point where several roads diverged, and did not get into the position assigned him until about the time the Confederates made their last feeble attempt on our lines. It is easy to see what the result would have been had Davis' splendid division swept down on the flank of Hood's forces as they were making one of their four-line deep charges! Blunders cannot be avoided even in military matters. The mistake was easy to make for the march was in heavy pine timber with only wagon tracks for a road. Had the blunder not occurred, it is plain that all that portion of Hood's army would either have been put to a full rout or have become prisoners.

After the battle opened and we had repulsed the second charge of the enemy, Wolcott's Second brigade of the same division to which myself and troops belonged was put in position on my right, which up to that time was the extreme right of the entire Federal line. It was to the right of Wolcott's brigade where there was a small mounted force. When the third charge was made it overlapped Wolcott's brigade and came in such headlong force that these mounted men and one regiment of infantry gave ground. At this critical moment General Logan, with Major Hotelling, a staff officer, were riding by. The General at once discovered the signs of stampede and with the Major at his horse's heels threw himself in front of the over hundred men who were rapidly becoming panic stricken. With a few very strong and emphatic expletives, and by slapping one or two soldiers over the back with the flat of this sword, he closed the already widening gap in the line within a few moments.

During the battle of Ezra Church the fourteenth corps lay about two miles to the left of the troops engaged. Belonging to this corps was the Seventy-fourth Indiana Infantry. Lieutenant colonel Myron Baker was in command. Colonel C. W. Chapman of Warsaw, Indiana was its Colonel and Dr. J. K. Leedy also of Warsaw was its surgeon. I met Dr. Leedy while I was on the march to go into the position held on the 28th. We had not seen each other for a long time, but had been personal friends for many years. I was surprised on the morning following the battle to find him at my headquarters at a very early hour. He said that he was aware that we had been in a big battle at our end of the line and he could not rest until he came over to see if I, and many others he knew in my regiment, had escaped. He was wonderfully glad to see me and I suggested that after breakfast we take a ride over the battlefield of the day before. Being a physician he was most willing to comply. We went a short distance and were among the wounded and the dead. Teams were engaged in gathering the wounded and carrying them to the already improvised hospital. A corps of colored pioneers was engaged in burying the dead. This was done by digging a long trench and piling the dead into the ditch until the dead were considerably above ground. The Doctor counted two hundred and two in a single trench, and as the weather was exceedingly sultry, the stench was almost insupportable. The white soldiers could not bear up under the conditions so the colored pioneer corps was detailed to do the work. Some idea of the destruction of life can be gleaned by the statement that in front of my two regiments there were eight hundred dead gathered for burial. The usual estimate for battles similar to the one of the 28th of July is five wounded to one killed. This would give four thousand wounded and eight hundred killed before two regimental fronts in the repeated charges at Ezra Church. Our loss was small owing to the Union troops being behind breast works.

There was another thing Dr. Leedy called my attention to and that was the great proportion of blondes among the killed, compared with the brunettes. It was a fact that there were about four sandy-complexed men among the killed to one with black hair. It was a South Carolina regiment in front of my troops. The doctor accounted for the disparity by saying that the sandy-headed man went farther towards the enemy with his sanguine temperament, than the dark-haired brunette with his more phlegmatic nature. The reader can judge for himself, but it is a fact that the red and light-haired man very greatly outnumbered all others.

Following the removal of the three corps from Sherman's left to the right came the withdrawal of the Twenty-third and a portion of the Fourteenth corps, both of which took up positions on the right of the ground covered by the battle of Ezra Church. For several days the troops occupied the grounds of the battle, however, the line was moved forward in order to escape the foul odors that pervaded for more than a mile in each direction. The stench was more than a man with even the strongest constitution could stand.

Lucius Barber, a sergeant in K Company of the Twelfth, had written to his sister at Ft. Wayne, Indiana to send his company a barrel of onions. His sister took up a subscription in the city and sixteen barrels of onions came to my address. It made me wonder if some one back at the North had taken me to be a sutler and had consigned to me a quantity of onions to dispose of on a percentage. Sergeant Barber soon explained the matter. Nothing could have been sent to the men by their friends at home that would have pleased them more than these onions. Men who never ate onions before took to them "like a duck to water". The fumes of cooked and raw onions so permeated the atmosphere that men came from other regiments to buy the vegetable.

The sixteen barrels of onions were judiciously distributed. The hospital received a generous share. I can only repeat that Miss Barber more highly pleased the boys in the field by her generous gift of onions than even that great institution, the sanitary commission, ever did to the thousands of men that were supplied with the delicacies so liberally and generously sent. The gift and thoughtfulness of Miss Barber was so fully appreciated by the recipients that I thought it my duty to indite a letter of thanks to the young lady. I had the letter copied by Marsh Parks of Warsaw, so that it looked like steel engraving. The letter so pleased Miss Barber's father that he had it framed and hung it on the wall of his home in Ft. Wayne as a memento of the war.

Another incident came under my eye while the troops occupied this ground. The battle was fought over a field that contained a monument raised by a father to the memory of his son, who had been killed in the first battle of Bull Run. The monument was bespattered by the marks of bullets from both sides. Neither the father nor any of his relatives or friends could have dreamed when that monument was erected that within three years a battle would be fought on that spot in rural Georgia. Incidents like these show how wide was the field of battle over which the war for the Union extended. The distance from where the young man fell and where his monument was erected did not cover half the extent of the field of operations during the greatest war of modern times.

While there was not a moment during the war that the Union side lost faith in the final outcome, yet a feeling of gloom pervaded a large portion of the people of the North at this period, although it never showed itself in the army. "Copperhead" orators and newspapers made the most of the delay in the capture of Atlanta after Sherman's army had reached its outworks. The Democratic national convention held in Chicago in 1864, pronounced the "War for the Union a failure," in resolutions passed by that body at just about the time that Atlanta was ready to surrender. The gloom was confined north of the Ohio River and was greatly fostered by the members of "The Knights of the Golden Circle", a treasonable organization that in the closing months of 1864 exposed and made its traitorous objects and aims public. This organization protracted the war and furnished information to the enemy. Every member of the "Inner Circle", after taking the oath was in every sense of the word a traitor to his government. This will be fully detailed in its proper place in these memories of war times.

General Sherman, among the higher commanders of the Federal army, was in all probability the least affected by adverse circumstances and never permitted it to swerve him from whatever course he had marked out. There never was any special cordiality existing between the General and the large number of correspondents the leading newspapers kept in the field. He summarily dismissed B. F. Taylor, the war correspondent of the Chicago Journal. Mr. Taylor had joined General Sherman's headquarters at Huntsville and expected to act as a correspondent throughout the Atlanta campaign. In one of his first letters to his paper Mr. Taylor made the remark that "General Sherman's army now rested with its right at Huntsville and its left at Knoxville, Tennessee." General Sherman considered such a publication as "giving information to the enemy" and said there were plenty of opponents of the war ready, anxious and very willing to furnish the Confederates with all possible information concerning the movements of the army that he didn't need more.

A great loss was sustained by not having Mr. Taylor's brilliant and facile pen to describe the skirmishes, battles, marches, etc. pertaining to the Atlanta campaign. The publication of that, to Mr. Taylor, very innocent remark as to the location of Sherman's forces and perhaps the too hasty decision of the General, lost to the north a brilliant account of the campaign. After the war I talked with Mr. Taylor concerning the affair. He told me that he greatly grieved over the fact that this order forbade him to accompany the western army.

It was following the battle of Ezra Church that General Sherman organized a cavalry expedition to move around Atlanta, and if possible, to destroy General Hood's only remaining railroad connection with the South or anywhere else. One of the cavalry command was placed under General Stoneman, and if I remember correctly, the other was commanded by General Garrard or General Kirkpatrick. The idea was for these officers to join their forces after getting south of Atlanta forming a large force. The two forces failed to make connections and the consequence was that neither one was of sufficient strength to boldly carry out the original plan. General Stoneman did advance as far as Macon, Georgia, where he found a much superior force of the enemy and had to retire. In falling back, he and quite a large part of his command were captured. Those who escaped were so badly scattered that they were incapacitated from making a successful raid. For two weeks, perhaps more, the men who escaped capture came back to the main army in squads of four or five, two or three, and sometimes singly. They were worn out for want of food and ragged from constant night travel.

It was during the period of this cavalry raid that was probably the most trying to the enlisted men of the Atlanta campaign. The enemy in front of the position my men occupied were very strongly fortified and the lines were so close together that the pickets had to be changed after dark to keep from being seen and picked off. I presume that the enemy was forced to employ the same tactics. No special engagement occurred here for some time, yet, the daily loss of men killed and wounded by the picket-firing was growing in number to such an extent that it acted on the nerves of many of the men who lay behind the works. It was unsafe even to look over the top of the entrenchments, as some one of the enemy was sure to take a shot above it. The men would have preferred to have formed up for a charge than to lay in the trenches with the ever-growing loss of life. It was here that the enemy had a strong picket-post by a peach tree. It became known in our lines as "the peach tree post". I remember that General Harrow along with Colonel Wolcott visited one afternoon and, in walking along the lines, I called the General's attention to this post and told him that for the past four days we had an average of two per day killed or wounded from that post alone. "Why don't you destroy it?" he replied. "I don't like to take the responsibility of sending that sufficient number of men required to certain death in order to accomplish it," I replied. "Call for volunteers and let them try it," said the General. After Harrow and Wolcott had departed, in thinking it over, I concluded that perhaps it would be best. I sent for Sergeant Jack Mankin, one of the bravest, safest, and most reliable among the non-commissioned officers in the regiment. I told him what the General had said and asked him if he would lead the party to capture the post. "If you will let me pick my own men, certainly," said Jack. Permission was given and late in the ensuing night, Sergeant Mankin reported with ten men ready and willing to make the dangerous attempt.

Silently as ghosts they climbed over our entrenchments, nearly opposite the Confederate post. They formed along the works and in a very low tone Jack gave the command and with a rush they were soon forking the enemy out of the grave-like protection the "rebs" occupied, and briskly brought them back to our lines. Twenty-two were captured, one of them a First Lieutenant. Alas, the capture cost us two men, William Shaffer, of Company G, and David Vanskike, of C Company. It was a heroic bit of work. The post was known to be a strong one and the ten men were fully aware of the great danger in undertaking its capture. The next day General Harrow sent a very complimentary letter to Sergeant Mankin and his men. The Confederates were never permitted to reoccupy that post again and an end came to the constant loss of life on our side from the "peach tree post".

After Atlanta had fallen, myself and Marsh Parks went over to "peach tree post". It is to be regretted that the tree was not cut down and taken north for some war-relic museum, for from halfway up the tree down to its very roots, it was filled with bullets from the side facing the Union troops. Bullets stuck out of it in every conceivable shape with others buried in the wood. If properly preserved, it would have made a decidedly interesting war relic.

Head Quarters 1st Brig. 4th Div. 15th A.C.
Camp Sherman Miss 8 Sept 1863.

Lt. Col. John A. Rawlins
 A. A. Genl.
  Dept of the Tenn.
    Sir

I would most respectfully request that a leave of absence be granted me for the space of twenty days.

I certify that a competent field officer will be left in charge of the Brigade.

I have the honor Colonel to be
Your Obedient Servt
Reub Williams
Col 12th Indiana Infantry
Comdg 1st Brig. 4th Div. 15 A.C.

CHAPTER 13

Atlanta Campaign

"Forward! The bugles call: ready am I:
For though my step had lost its springing gait,
I am more prompt to march: quick to obey;
Less apt to question or to hesitate—
Yet when some belted trooper gallops by,
I lift my eyes, warned by the swift hoof's tramp,
And hail him with the infantryman's cry—
"Ho, comrade, tell me, how far it is to camp!"
—Robert J. Burdette

The above lines taken from poem from the gifted pen of Robert J. Burdette, the poet-lecturer, exposes so well the difference between the old seasoned soldier and the new recruit, or an old regiment as compared with one fresh from home. The new men so unaccustomed to the duties of a soldier failed to take advantage of the situation and rest at each call of "halt", but would stand around with his heavy knapsack on his shoulders, instead of lying down for a brief moment. The "toughened" old veteran took every advantage to do as little as was actually necessary. He was "quick to obey" and less inclined to find fault or question whatever order he might receive. Many times I have known, when the bugle rang out the command to "halt" that within the lapse of sixty seconds the entire regiment, if it were an old one, would be lying down just outside the highway with their feet toward it. For even a rest of a few minutes brought relief, and the veteran made his knapsack carry him by becoming a support for a brief moment. The new regiment or a recently added batch of recruits would walk around bearing their full equipment—knapsack, haversack, gun and cartridge box—and consequently was more tired when the bugle sounded "the advance" than he was before the "halt."

The two armies facing each other to the northwest of Atlanta had their respective lines drawn exceedingly close together. The army itself was not aware of what was agitating the head of the commander-in-chief and it would be unwise for an army that such matters should be known to the masses. If everybody knew what was to be the next move it would be practically certain that the object in view would be defeated. During these weary, harassing days of watchfulness, sudden alarms and daily loss of lives, our commander was very quietly, but energetically, vigorously yet patiently, working out the plan that was to give the Union forces, Atlanta. The final result placed him way up toward the head of the list of great military geniuses. The plans for retiring the entire lines of the Federal forces were decided upon as early as about the middle of August. But for prudential reasons the movement had been postponed. While waiting a large portion of the army was not idle. A strong body of soldiers, with engineer and pioneer corps, were busily engaged in constructing heavy works back at the railroad crossing of Chattahoochie River, about five miles from the rear of the Federal lines. This was done so quietly that a large portion of Sherman's own army did not know it was in progress. If I remember correctly, it was on or about the 25th of August 1864 that the withdrawal movement began. My own command was in the front line of the trenches at the time. The Fourth corps moved out to the rear and right, having first detailed a very strong skirmish line to keep up a more than ordinarily vigorous fire to cover the movement for the enemy. The Twentieth corps fell back to and occupied that already prepared works for its reception at the railroad crossing of the river. These movements presented the appearance to General Hood in Atlanta that the Federal army was in full retreat.

On the next night, August 26th, the right wing also withdrew to a line of breastworks having previously been constructed. These troops marched in the direction of Sandtown, where there had been a bridge to cross the Chattahoochie. The feint of General Sherman was eminently successful in deceiving the Confederate General who construed the movement as a full retreat back to Chattanooga and the abandonment of the Atlanta campaign. So badly were the Confederate General and his officers deceived by the movements of Sherman that General Hood officially declared that General Sherman's army had retreated across the Chattahoochie River. The citizens of Atlanta held a jollification ball over the retreat of the "Yankees" the same night. A reconnaissance in the direction the Twentieth corps had taken only led the Confederates to confirm the first report that the Federal troops had been withdrawn. What an awakening was to come to General Hood, his whole army, and the citizens of Atlanta.

Nearly the whole of Sherman's army, except the Twentieth corps, was at that moment south of Atlanta engaged in tearing up the railroad to Macon. At Fairburn, a few miles southwest of Atlanta, the road had been thoroughly destroyed for a distance of twelve miles. The rails were placed in such a condition that they never could be used again. In the beginning of the war when the railroads were torn up, it was the usual practice to make log heaps of the ties. The ties were set on fire and then the rails were laid over the heated logs until they could be bent around a stump of a tree or anything else that came in handy. It had been ascertained through prisoners and spies that these rails were gathered up and taken to rolling mills in the South that could straighten them as fast as they could be hauled to the mill. In the beginning of 1864 an ingenious blacksmith in the Union army had invented clamps that put an effective stop to the straightening of railroads. It required two men and two clamps, one at each end of the rail, turning them in opposite directions, when at the hottest point the rail would have more of the appearance of an auger after it was manipulated by these clamps than anything else. There was no machinery within the Confederacy that could straighten a rail thus twisted.

It fell to my lot on the swing of the troops around to Jonesboro to report with the troops of my command to General Belknap who then commanded a brigade in the Seventeenth corps. Both brigades were to proceed to a deep cut in the railroad and to destroy all of the rails possible until further orders. General Belknap became Secretary of War under President Grant. His wife became involved in a suttlership scandal, which came with a crushing, bewildering force that compelled him to resign his position. He was a high-minded, patriotic man and would have scorned to stoop to a dishonorable act.

The two brigades tore up railroads all that night, and in some deep cuts shells were deposited under the dirt and debris, not so much for any destruction their explosion might cause, but to scare away the Negroes that would probably be employed to repair the road.

At daylight the following morning we were relived from this tiresome duty. I was placed in command of a train and ordered to conduct it to Jonesboro, where the troops that had marched all night were located. General Hood had discovered that instead of Chattanooga, Jonesboro was General Sherman's destination. Hood had blown up everything in and around Atlanta including a large number of loaded freight cars and had set out with whatever troops remained in Atlanta. General Hardee was in charge of the Confederate forces that were endeavoring to make a stand at Jonesboro. In connection with Hood's blowing up Confederate property at Atlanta, after he found that Sherman had so grossly and cruelly deceived a man with only one leg, he detonated everything. The shock was so great that the shaking of the ground awakened me. I was at the time very near to Jonesboro, so the distance from the explosion must have been close to eighteen miles.

On both sides of the road, as the train I was guarding slowly made its way, we found dead Confederate cavalrymen whose command had evidently made frequent stands against the Federal army. One man we found was just dying and another was so badly wounded that he could not stand up. I turned him over to the hospital department, which took him to Jonesboro in an ambulance. He was very grateful and so expressed himself to me many times. I called at the hospital to see him on two occasions, but what became of him I do not know.

I arrived with the train the night before the charge was made on the town of Jonesboro. The men were worn out from the long, slow motion required with such a train. The train of wagons when drawn upon the road in marching order covered a distance of nearly eight miles. Since my troops were "off duty", I determined to visit General Sherman's headquarters, which was situated on a high point to the north and slightly west of the town. The location gave a splendid view of the scene of operations and I was glad that I had gone to that point. I could easily see that General Sherman was wholly engrossed, and what was more, I could plainly see that he was greatly irritated as well. As near as I could gather, the cause was that he was impatiently waiting for the troops he had sent around Jonesboro to the left to get into position. Like the old war-horse he was he similarly was engaged in "chomping his bit". On the north side of the town all was ready for the charge, and I could look down upon the formation of the Fourteenth corps where it was waiting for the order to "rush" the enemy. I feel confident that General Sherman, tired of waiting to hear from the Fourth corps on the left, had resolved to make the charge anyhow and did so. To me, high above the charging men, it was a magnificent sight. While the line was somewhat crooked, it did not look that way to me. The whole line seemed to rush forward with the Union cheer rather than the rebel yell. It was not long until I could distinguish the gray fleeing before the on-rushing line of blue. It was in that charge that the boys of the Seventy-fourth Indiana Infantry from Kosciusko County, Warsaw, Indiana captured a full Confederate battery and received high compliments from the division commander. The leader of the charge on the battery received a congressional medal for bravery.

The enemy evacuated Jonesboro without receiving any orders to do so. The principal part of the Confederate army holding the place left for the south on the "double-quick". The result of the charge was the capture of the place, many of the enemy killed and wounded and something over twelve hundred prisoners. A large portion of the prisoners belonged to what was known as "Cleburn's division", under the command of General Pat Cleburn. General Cleburn was later killed at the battle of Franklin. The prisoners belonging to Cleburn's division at Jonesboro were the sauciest and most stubborn of any I had ever seen during all the war on either side. They were so extremely bitter in their denunciation of their capture that they came very near provoking a riot after they had surrendered. They had carried their curses to such an extreme that very fortunately for some of them, I had the opportunity to suppress a movement designed to stop their cursing.

A hundred of the enlisted men of the Federal guard had made up their minds they would stand the abuse from the prisoners no longer, and fully armed and without an officer among them, they proceeded to where the largest number of prisoners were held. They were determined to compel the rebels to cease their abuse or they would fire into the crowd. It was mere chance that I was riding towards my own men and, catching from their repeated threats what they were going to do, I finally succeeded in stopping them before they reached the prisoners. I told them what a disgrace it would be to have the news go out to the world that the Union army had sunk so far down in the scale of humanity as to murder unarmed prisoners. Some of the men at the head of the marching squad began to listen to me and the march was halted. The rest, coming up and hearing the remarks, they began to see they were engaged in a matter for which they might be ashamed of as well as severely punished. They hesitated and hesitation meant, of course, the relinquishment of the intended design. I have always been glad that I happened to be the instrument in frustrating an act that, no matter how grate the provocation, could never have been smoothed over.

Of course, the blowing up of a large amount of property in Atlanta by General Hood ended the campaign. The destruction of freight cars gathered there was a great loss to the Confederate cause. It was told that eight hundred freight cars were destroyed, many of them still loaded with supplies. Few historians that I have read make any mention of how serious a loss that many cars meant to the Confederacy. Few make any mention of the serious hardship to the Confederacy that was caused by the destruction of railroad connection in the Southern States. It was difficult for the people south and west of Virginia to reach Richmond at all because of the lack of railroad facilities. Nearly all the railroads in the "Gulf States" had been raided and some of them almost totally destroyed. The South had no means to replace the loss of locomotives or iron rails, as they could not be built, nor rolled at any point in the Confederacy. The destruction of railroads was a tremendous help to the North.

There was another disadvantage under which the South labored right from the beginning of the war, and that was its lack of newspapers. Soldiers of the Union army were greatly encouraged by the home and metropolitan newspapers of the North. By the close of the first year of the war, postal facilities in the army were superb. Newspapers and letters would reach soldiers in the field generally within three or four days. Before the war, there were distributing offices to which point all letters nearest it were sent and where the mails were sent on to their destination in sacks conveying only such mails as went in the same general direction. The postal service of the United States, as now conducted, is a marvel in speed, correctness in delivery, and perfect safety. Yet the plan now in use is a legacy of the war. I have been told by Confederate soldiers that after the first year of the war they received no more letters that came from States west of the Mississippi. Even before the fall of Vicksburg it was difficult to smuggle letters across the Mississippi intended for Lee's army. After the fall of Vicksburg, it became almost an impossibility for any member of the army around Richmond to receive a letter from persons living in any of the States west of the "Father of Waters".

The home paper was often a godsend to the soldier. It helped to stem the coming of that worst of all soldier's complaints—homesickness. Ask any doctor who served in regiments and hospitals, and he will tell you that many young soldiers, fresh from the farm of their parents, and perhaps never six miles distant from his birthplace, will tell you that many such young men died from the effect of homesickness outright, and in other cases it laid the foundation of diseases that ended in death. In the first company that left Warsaw for the war, there was a case of death from homesickness. Charles F. Davis, who lived a few miles southeast of town, was twenty-three and was engaged to be married. He was a large young man for his age. For the first five or six months he was unusually active and in good spirits. At about that time he became at first listless, then rather peevish, the doctor claiming that he could find nothing seriously the matter with him, except an intense longing to go home. At Warrenton Junction, in Virginia, he was sent to the regimental hospital, and as the time for which the regiment had enlisted was near its expiration, the doctor thought that the prospect of going home would revive him and that he would pull through. This was not to be the case. Homesickness had too strong a hold upon him, and he died in a hospital in Washington City the night before the regiment was mustered out. His father, Abram Davis, having been telegraphed for, was at his bedside when the messenger who carries a missive for us all delivered it. His remains were brought home with his mustered out company, and his was the first funeral services held in Warsaw with military honors after the war began. The entire company was present at his burial. His was not the only case of deadly homesickness, which came under my observation, by any means.

It is a wonder that publishers were able to do as well as they did in placing pictures in their newspapers. It must be remembered that photography during the war period was almost in its infancy and the "snapshot" was wholly unknown. The "half-tone" engraving was unknown and every picture the newspapers contained during the war were prepared for the press with the slow process of a pencil sketch and then the cut done on wood by the engraver. This required much labor and consequently much cost. Some of the pictures of skirmishes and battles were marvelously realistic when the facilities, or rather the lack of them, are borne in mind. The copies of papers received in a regiment were literally worn out in passing through the numerous hands that longed to read the news. However, it was the "home" paper that delighted the soldiers most. Many times I saw one man reading the news from "back in God's country" to almost his entire company, all of them eager listeners. To a very large extent the confederate soldier knew nothing of this sort of support to his "cause". The news from home was a great encouragement to the men to do their duty, sure of the fact that if they lived to return, a reception awaited them praising them for "duty well done".

The Confederates who had occupied Jonesboro retreated south along the railroad to the station of Lovejoy, where General Hardee had, with the troops under his command, determined to make a stand. This partial stand of the Confederate army was "not for long". General Sherman had decided to move his army back to Atlanta. I had been directed to proceed to Atlanta in advance of the main body, taking under my charge about two miles of loaded and empty wagons. I was directed to go into camp at East Point. Although it was called "East Point", it lay about four miles nearly west of the city. It had been an important telegraph station previous to the breaking up of General Hood's "Jollification Ball". I found excellent camping ground in the immediate vicinity. I made my headquarters near the former telegraph station, pitching the tents composing it on the grass-plat near by. At this period of the war all houses, stations, etc, used by soldiers were so numerously inhabited by "gray-backs" that tents were far preferable and I used them when at all possible. Speaking of tents, the usual square one issued to officers are about as comfortable a habitation as any one could wish for, and no matter how cold the weather they could be made a pleasant sleeping place as even the costliest of residences. If the tents were properly "banked up" on the outside, for the best of drainage possible, they could not be excelled.

I went to the telegraph station, and from examining the contents still found in the room, I concluded it must have done quite a large business during the days that General Hood was ascertaining the precise route on which General Sherman was retreating to Chattanooga! Scraps of paper covered the floor and on all sides there were signs of hasty flight. Left behind were a number of telegraph implements—an article that must have been of great value within the Confederacy. The clerk at my headquarters began picking up the copies of some of the dispatches sent to the commanding officer of the Confederate cavalry operating west of Atlanta. There were half a dozen dispatches sent to the officer, whose name was Lee. But whether it was General S.D. Lee, Fitzhugh Lee or some other one of that name, I am unable to say, for I have never learned who commanded the mounted forces of General Hood at that time.

I perused the dispatches and knew that, in time, they would become a valuable relic of the war days. I mailed them to my wife at Warsaw, directing her to take care of them. Unfortunately, she has never been able to find them since my return from the war, although they are about the house somewhere. Of course, there were no replies to these messages as they were copies of orders and directions sent to the officer commanding the mounted forces that were watching the Federals.

I read all of the dispatches and I am confident that I can give the gist of them from memory until the real copies are found. The first one was a warning to the officer in command of the mounted force, sent by General Hood, urging him to be vigilant and active, that his (Hood's) scouts reported a movement of Federal cavalry to the west of Atlanta. It was thought to be only a small force, acting as flankers of the main Federal army which appeared to be falling back. Another one sent, perhaps an hour later to the East Point operator was to the effect that the mounted force of the northern army seemed to be larger that the Confederate scouts had first reported. It again urged the confederate commander to be exceedingly active in obtaining news and to use haste in dispatching whatever he obtained. Then came another lapse and still another message for the cavalry officer, briefly stating that there were indications that a body of infantry accompanied the Federal cavalry and, if possible, to obtain information as to how large a force it was.

Still another delay and then an additional message, that the news from his mounted scouts led to the belief on Hood's part, that a large body of the Union army was moving to the west and south of Atlanta. The officer was to ascertain without fail something reliable as to its size and the course in which it was moving. The next, and it may have been his last message before the full force of the great calamity came to the Confederate army, closed with the advice to do the best he could under the circumstances. The indications were that the whole Federal army had passed around Atlanta and was at that moment engaged in destroying the railroad at Fairburn.

I have only given the substance of the dispatches that General Hood had forwarded to his cavalry officer. Hood's fright grew, as scout after scout came into Atlanta from the various mounted bodies, until at last he blew up all of the valuable Confederate stores, freight cars and much valuable property, and totally abandoned the city that had just held a "jollification" ball.

The fall of Atlanta occasioned an outburst of patriotic enthusiasm all over the North. It was a great victory from standpoint of military achievement. It fully showed that General William Tecumsch Sherman was one of the world's great soldiers. From the hour the campaign opened until its close the Federal army was compelled at all times to act on the aggressive. The Federal army was always compelled, whenever an assault was determined, to make it "in the open", while its enemy lay behind well-built works. This was so great an advantage, only those who have had an experience in the difficulties to be overcome, can fully appreciate it. There cannot be any doubt that General Sherman could have captured Atlanta by direct assault at the crucial moment, but like the wise General he was, he knew that such a course would cost many valuable lives, hence, he resorted to the maneuvers that so completely deceived General Hood. It is almost wonderfully laughable to perceive how General Hood was deceived by General Sherman's splendid moves on the chessboard of war. Hood seemed never to reason the case that, with such an army as General Sherman possessed, "retreat" was simply out of the question. He permitted himself to be fooled by following the Twentieth corps back to the Chattahoochie River. The manner in which he was enlightened that, instead of a retreat the Federal army was making an advance and had fully severed his only communications with the outside world, was shown in the dispatches from General Hood sent to East Point.

I have already stated that I had gone into a very pleasant camp at East Point. My troops were the first to arrive with the Twentieth corps, under General Slocum, arriving very soon afterward. General Slocum took possession of Atlanta and the following morning, accompanied by a portion of my staff, I visited the town and called on General Slocum. I informed him where I had been directed to go into camp. Up until that moment he did not know that any of the troops that had been at Jonesboro were so near him. Atlanta presented a most forlorn aspect. Everything was in a dilapidated, torn-up condition and the effects of the siege could be seen on every hand. In 1870 I visited Atlanta and rode all over the city and visited all of the battlefields in which myself and troops had participated. Northern money had been poured into the city. Atlanta was a thriving place. The five years since I had ridden down its streets had worked a transformation indeed.

Within a day or two all of General Sherman's forces, that had been operating at Jonesboro and Lovejoy, had assembled at Atlanta and gone into camp in such a position as to make its defense easy should occasion require it. There was a station a few miles south of Atlanta on the Macon railroad known as "Rough and Ready", an appellation that was conferred on General Taylor following the Mexican war. The Confederate forces established an outpost there. A detail of enlisted men from many Federal regiments went there under a flag of truce, while offices of Generals Sherman and Hood arranged an exchange of prisoners, such at least, as had not been taken to Andersonville or any other of the stations where prisoners were kept. The truce lasted several days. It was at this time that the division to which my brigade belonged was broken up, in reality to let General Harrow off from active service in the field. A new division was formed to which General Corse was placed in command and General Harrow never held a command after the fall of Atlanta.

It was soon after the capture of Atlanta that I applied for a leave of absence, a favor that I ever afterwards wished had been refused, for my going home at that time prevented me from making "The March to the Sea". It also compelled me to serve on that wearisome "Military Commission" that tried "the Indiana Conspirators". Lieutenant Colonel James A. Goodnow of the Twelfth Indiana Infantry had also secured a "leave of absence: and accompanied me back to Indiana long about the middle of September 1864. Major Ed D. Baldwin was placed in command of the regiment. If at the time I had had the least inkling that General Sherman had determined to make the trip that has since become historical the world over as "Sherman's March to the Sea", I would not have applied for a leave of absence. I would rather have been along with the men who made that astounding trip, a march totally at variance with all military tactics as every civilized nation up to that time had construed it, than have visited my home, pleasant though it was to do. "The March to the Sea" was successful, not so much in hurting the enemy by the destruction of railroads, bridges, etc, but by showing the world the hollowness of the Confederacy. There was only one real fight during the march and I was always proud that my own regiment took part in it. This battle is known in history as the battle of Griswoldville. It was fought by Colonel Wolcott's Second brigade of infantry and twelve thousand of the Georgia militia, which Governor Brown of Georgia had assembled to defend the State and, especially its capital.

I am compelled to rely upon Major Baldwin and the men belonging to the regiment for the details of the story of that fight. All of Sherman's army was moving in the direction of the seacoast. Governor Brown, was at that time was at "outs" with Jeff Davis, the president of the Confederacy. The Governor had made a demand for all Georgia troops in General Lee's command to be sent to the defense of their own State, but he was refused. He, therefore, had all the men and boys left in the city assembled as a militia. It was fully twelve thousand of this sort of troop that was to defend the capital from the oncoming Yankees. It was no part of Sherman's plan to stop and fight these raw levies and his army passed on in its march to the coast. Wolcott's Second brigade had been detailed to guard the rear of Sherman's army, and all at once found itself assailed by this entire body of militia. A brigade in the Fifteenth corps could not have numbered more than eighteen hundred, and a "hurry order" reached the rear of Sherman's marching column for reinforcements, and my regiment, the Twelfth Indiana Infantry, was selected to go to Wolcott's assistance. This required a retrograde movement of about four miles. The whole distance was made on the "double quick". On coming up with Wolcott's sorely pressed brigade, Major Baldwin halted the regiment, and after ascertaining where they were most needed, the regiment went forward by companies into line with orders for each company to fire as fast as they reached the front line. This led the confederate militia to believe that the woods were alive with "Yankees", and as each of the ten companies reached the line and discharged their muskets as fast as they could, the militia broke and fled. It is said they never stopped until they reached Macon, twelve miles distant.

I speak of this incident to show the value of drill and having a regiment under full and complete control in the hour of battle. Each company was magnified by the enemy into at least a regiment. The enemy at once took fright at the swarm of Yankees that were coming and ran away when it is a fact that not over four hundred of Federals were in the entire body that caused the Confederate stampede. Colonel Wolcott, after first thanking Major Baldwin and the Twelfth for coming to his relief, at once started to rejoin the rear of General Sherman's marching troops.

It was during General Sherman's occupation of Atlanta that the oft-perused correspondence between himself and General Hood took place. General Hood grew indignant over the order of General Sherman that all Atlanta citizens must leave the place, and sent him a very emphatic note condemning, in almost insolent language, the order for the citizens of Atlanta to vacate the town. It was in this correspondence between Hood and Sherman that Sherman used the expression that "war is hell, and you cannot refine it." I may not have in this sentence the precise words used by General Sherman, but the meaning is contained in the quotation. The point he made was that a military necessity compelled him not only to depopulate the town of its inhabitants, but that he was going to destroy a goodly portion of the city as a military necessity. He was only acting humanely in ordering the citizens to vacate a town that would be largely destroyed when he left. The discussion between the two commanding officers was very generally criticized all over the country. The "copperhead" press abused General Sherman almost like a robber and a pickpocket for adopting the course he pursued.

After the fall of Atlanta, many officers and enlisted men were given leaves of absence and furloughs. I was given a twenty day leave to revisit my home from which I had been absent from the previous November, and this was in the closing days of September. Lieutenant Colonel Goodnow of the Twelfth had resigned and went home on the same train. There were so many officers and men going home that it was difficult to catch a train, especially since so many cars were used for freight. There was seldom more than one passenger car to each train and many of them had none at all. We left Atlanta after it began to growing dark. The train's route would take us over the same region the Federal fought over and had gained. Lieutenant Colonel Goodnow and myself had secured a freight car and with our numerous blankets had formed quite a good bed on the floor by combining our blankets. The cars had passed Kennesaw Mountain and both of us occupied the floor on the west side of the train so that we could look upon the scenes of the operations up till third of July. We remained there some time and then lay down side by side on our blankets. There were other occupants of the car with who we were not yet acquainted. On top of the train was the Tenth Kentucky infantry, which had been ordered to some station north of Atlanta. As they were going only a short distance, the enlisted men occupied the top of the cars, filling them up the entire length of the train. These men were fully equipped and were being sent northward to perform guard duty.

It was nearly dark when the train passed Kennesaw, and soon afterwards night closed upon us, so that it was useless to try to scan the country. I soon fell asleep. The next thing I knew there was a sudden jar, and Colonel Goodnow and myself, blankets and all, were sliding towards the side door of the car. My first thought was that the cars had been thrown from the track by a Confederate raid, and my very next thought was of the regiment of troops on top of the cars. Of course, I had no authority over the regiment, but if my conclusion that the cars had been derailed by the enemy was correct, the emergency of the case led me to order the regiment down off the cars and to form in ranks along the west side of the train. By this time, either the engineer or the fireman came near the spot where I was standing, each of them carrying a torch, so that the men of the regiment could perceive that I was an officer. Every man in the regiment obeyed my command just as though it were my own regiment and in an exceedingly brief time they had formed their line, loaded their guns and I sent two companies to scout, one on each side of the road. Just as I had ordered the two companies to look for the enemy, if there was one, I saw a gray-headed man getting down the steps of the only passenger car the train contained. As he wore the eagles of a Colonel, I asked him if he was the commanding officer of the regiment. He replied that he was and I informed him what I had done. "All right," said the old gentleman, not at all offended that I had assumed command of his troops, but apparently glad of it for he thanked me very kindly for the course I had pursued.

The accident was plainly caused by the enemy. The track had been tampered with, but with the exception of two cars, which had been derailed, no special damage was done, the engine having passed over the obstruction without leaving the rails. The two cars, one of which I occupied, ran up the side of the bank in a way that tipped them sideways to about forty degrees. This was what created the sliding motion of Colonel Goodnow and my own bed and thus thoroughly awakened me. An examination of the surrounding showed horse tracks on both sides of the road, but the mischief was presumably done by a small party of Confederates, who, on seeing the troops so well prepared, doubtless slipped away in the darkness. That at least, was the idea of the Kentucky Colonel, whose place I had assumed for a few minutes for the reason, that I was at that time young and vigorous, had my clothes on, and fortunately the accident tipped me out of the car just at the right time to become the commanding officer of a Kentucky regiment as well as one from Indiana.

It must be understood that I proposed to confine these memories of war times to sights, scenes, tragedies, incidents and anecdotes that came under my own observation, including, of course, others of which I possessed sufficient knowledge to state them truthfully and correctly. For this reason I am compelled to be very brief in what I may say about the effort of the Confederate General Hood to force General Sherman to give up Atlanta by raiding his rear and cutting off his connection with the North. For almost a year previous to the fall of Atlanta, General Sherman had in mind the venturesome movement that finally came to be called "Sherman's March to the Sea". He had on more than one occasion broached the subject to General Grant, and he also communicated with President Lincoln on the feasibility of cutting the Confederacy in twain by such a movement. His superior officers, however, never gave their full consent until about the time that he had driven General Hood's army across the Tennessee River. Very suddenly then, after placing General George Thomas in command of all the forces at Chattanooga, and north of the Tennessee, to Nashville, General Sherman hastily returned with the force with which he had been pursuing Hood to Atlanta. At Atlanta active preparations began for the "march to the sea" by gathering the supplies that Sherman intended to take with him, consisting of a large supply of ammunition, coffee and hard-tack. Sherman expected to secure the meat that might be required from the country as he passed through it.

This all happened after I had left for my home, but I am informed from very credible sources that the army was weeded out to such an extent that the sixty thousand men who made that celebrated march were the elite of the army so far as health and physical endurance were concerned. Every man, who had an ailment of any kind, even though it may have been only an occasional headache, a sore toe, or whose shoes pinched his feet a little, was thrown out of each company. I have often heard men who were along with the troops that cut themselves off from communication with the North for over six weeks say that "Sherman's army would have stormed hell itself if Sherman was present to direct the attack, and was healthy enough to win at that!" His boys always had a great deal of confidence in Sherman.

General Thomas took up and fortified his position at Nashville during the closing months of 1864. The War Department at Washington became very impatient over the delay in General Thomas attacking General Hood's forces in his immediate front around that city. General Halleck, who during nearly all of he war occupied a position in Washington as a sort of confidential aid to the administration, was himself chafing against General Thomas. Halleck was disliked and often criticized by commanding officers in the field and was decidedly unpopular with the army in general. Halleck was determined that General Thomas should fight at once, or be displaced. An order was finally issued to relieve General Thomas, and General Logan was assigned to his command. This occurred after Sherman had cut loose from Atlanta and was deep in the pinewoods and swamps of Georgia. Halleck could not know, nor did he seem to care about the condition surrounding General Thomas at Nashville. He presumably was not aware, that in concentrating his scattered forces at Nashville preparatory to defending the place, that rains prevailed to such an extent that it was almost impossible to move artillery at all; that the elite of the Western army was absent with Sherman; that sleets were as common as the rains; that much of his artillery and cavalry were without horses; and the required time to prepare for an offensive movement against the

Confederate army. There was no more steady-going, reliable officer in all the Western army than General Thomas.

When I visited General Hooker at Cincinnati in order to obtain my release as a member of a second military commission, I discovered in looking over the register that General John A. Logan had taken a room. I sent up my card and received a very cordial invitation to visit him at his room. Like myself, General Logan had been anxiously awaiting the appearance of General Sherman and his army that was buried some where in Georgia. The General welcomed me warmly and, after inquiring about the Indiana Treason Trials, went on to say that at present he was ordered to one of the most unpleasant duties that had ever fallen to his lot since the war commenced. I inquired as to what that might be, and he informed me that he had been ordered to relieve General Thomas of his command at Nashville. "In my own mind I am confident," he said, "that General Thomas was and has been doing all in his power to get his army gathered in from all points of middle and southern Tennessee into a condition to meet the enemy. Thomas is a very safe and careful officer and is in a much better judge of the time to strike than General Halleck or anyone else as far away as Washington." General Logan was in deep earnest in all his talk and went on to say: "I have been very slow in filling this, as I think, unnecessary order. I stopped nearly two days at Pittsburgh and I have been here in Cincinnati since yesterday morning. I have delayed the trip in the hope that General Thomas would strike the enemy before I could reach Nashville and thus be relieved of this unpleasant duty, for," he said, "I want to rejoin my own men. I feel it would be wrong to relieve General Thomas at this moment."

Late that night, General Logan left Cincinnati very reluctantly for Louisville, Kentucky. Great must have been General Logan's joy on reaching Louisville the following morning to learn that General Thomas had "moved". The fleeing enemy was making all possible haste to place the Tennessee River between them and the pursuing Federals, with "Old Pap Thomas" at their head. Afterward, when I saw General Logan at his headquarters in the campaign that included the "Two Carolinas" in its operations, the subject came up. I asked how he received the news of the victory at Nashville. "It was the happiest news I ever received during the war, not only over the great victory, but it was such a great relief to me. I had delayed over four days on the road in hope that just such a thing might happen and I was overjoyed that morning." This incident shows the high honor inherent in General Logan in doing all in his power to prevent the humiliation of so grand a soldier as "Old Pap Thomas".

General Sherman introduced a new movement into the military tactics of the world by making such a long march in enemy country. In the North, and even in Europe, the leading newspapers predicted dire disaster to the army that was buried in the pinewoods of Georgia. Many soldiers of former wars declared that Sherman could never reach the coast, that his army would be headed off and annihilated. Great was the rejoicing when on Christmas morning near the end of 1864, General Sherman sent word to President Lincoln that "Savannah was ours," and begged to present him with a Christmas gift of twenty-five thousand bales of cotton. As this staple product was then selling at five hundred dollars per bale, it was no insignificant present.

Acknowledgment.

WARSAW, Ind., Sept. 22d, 1862.

ED. INDIANIAN:—

Allow me through the columns of your paper to present my thanks to Stephen B. Bond, of Ft. Wayne, for the present he made me last week of a splendid uniform, complete. During my short acquaintance with Mr. B. I have found him to be a true gentleman, a whole-souled, liberal man, and what is still better, in favor of prosecuting the war to a glorious conclusion. I am doubly grateful to him for this present, from the fact that I am not aware that I have done anything to merit so liberal a gift from his hands. Yours truly,

REUB. WILLIAMS,
Lt. Col. 12th Reg't Ind. Vols.

Now is the Time.

I am in want of a few more men to fill up my company, now encamped near Camp Morton, Indianapolis. The Regiment to which my company is attached, (the 12th) will in all probability, be the first in service of any other under the recent call for more men. It is to be armed with the Enfield Rifle with sabre bayonet, and uniformed in the best manner.

I shall leave this (Thursday) evening, with those already enlisted, but those who may desire to serve their country can leave their names either with Marsh. H. Parks or S. U. Birt, who will remain in this city until my return, which will be in a few days. The pay will be $13 per month, $42 per year for clothing, $100 bounty, and 160 acres of land. One month's pay and one-fourth the bounty, ($25) will be paid in advance.

The time for patriotic appeals to the people is past. What our country most needs now is MEN, and men too, who will FIGHT! Enlist at once, then, and let us crush this foul rebellion at once and forever!

CAPT. R. WILLIAMS.

CHAPTER 14

Indiana Conspirators' Trial

Then up with our flag—let it stream on the air;
  Though our fathers are cold in their graves.
They had hands that could strike, they had souls that could dare,
  And their sons were not born to be slaves.
Up, up with that banner! Where'er it may call,
  Our millions shall rally around,
And a nation of freemen that moment shall fall,
  When its stars shall be trailed on the ground.
                                —George E. Cutter

    I arrived home as quickly as I could on my twenty-day leave. I stopped for perhaps twenty-four hours at Indianapolis, mostly for business reasons as I was aware that a twenty-day's leave was only a short one. Hence, I hastened home as fast as possible. I arrived at Indianapolis during the midst of the excitement produced by the first arrests of the "Indiana Conspirators". A number of them had already been placed in confinement for joining and propagating the treasonable organization known as "The Knights of the Golden Circle". General Henry B. Carington was military commandant of the State of Indiana and had most skillfully and effectually, through the medium of fearless and intelligent detectives, unearthed the fact that all those belonging to this order and had taken the third degree, were actual, outright traitors to their country. It was determined to suppress this treasonable brotherhood in the interest of the Union Cause. General Carington was a peculiar man, possessed of undoubted ability. He was a most industrious and active officer in all that pertained to whatever position he occupied. He was an honest man as was shown in the fact that after eleven million dollars had passed through his hands during the period that he was stationed at Indianapolis in recruiting the army and supplying of volunteers and drafted men, every dime was faithfully accounted for to the last penny. Yet among the volunteer officers of the army then in the field, he was greatly disliked. I had become quite well acquainted with General Carington. He was a man who was very excitable at times, and on that account was illy qualified to command men in the field, yet I can say for him that he was one of the most faithful, correct and competent among the "office men" that were called into the field. After the war ended, I heard many officers who had spoken slightingly of General Carington warmly praise him for the efficient work done here at home, and for his honesty and competency in all cases.

It was General Carington and his corps of detective that unearthed and exposed the secret, disloyal, traitorous organization known as "The Knights of the Golden Circle". This organization permeated many of the states and in Illinois, Indiana and Ohio; each state could show a membership of over one hundred thousand. Many of these members were not fully aware of the traitorous attitude this treasonable association held towards the Federal government, nor could the generality of the membership know this until they had taken the third degree in which hostility to the administration was boldly announced. As all members of the order, when initiated into the Knights of the Golden Circle, took an oath coming from their superior officers, it is easy to see that this organization was intent on become a power for harm among the "copperhead wing" of the Democratic party. I am confident, but for the promptness of Governor O. P. Morton following the exposure of this secret organization and the arrest of some of the head officers by General Carington, there would have been war right here in Indiana. It must be borne in mind too, that the inner circle of this treasonable organization was fully armed with revolvers, and many lodges were supplied with guns, which were kept concealed.

The State of Indiana was in an uproar about the time of the homecoming of the officers and enlisted men that had participated in the Atlanta campaign. The excitement of the people was great and their opposition to the war party was extremely vindictive. It is a period in the affairs of this nation that I do not like to recall. A large number of Democrats remained true to the Union, and thousands upon thousands belonging to that party entered the service where they fought valiantly for the preservation of the Nation. The Democratic Party all through the war was under the control of men just as disloyal as was Jeff Davis, himself. These men were urged "not to leave their party to join in a damned abolition war," and every possible influence was used to keep them from fighting on the Union side.

I came home and remained here until my twenty-two days leave of absence expired, and then had it renewed for twenty days more, so that I could remain at home until after the election of 1864. There were many officers and enlisted men given furloughs to go home to vote, and this act on the part of the government angered the "copperheads" exceedingly. The party did not seem to recognize the fact that every resident of the State over the age of twenty-one had the legal right to vote at the polls in the township where he had his home. The Indiana Legislature, differing from many other loyal states, had refused to pass a law that was before the Legislature permitting the soldiers from Indiana to vote in the field. They could only vote by returning to their respective townships.

I remember the election of 1864, when O. P. Morton was the candidate for Governor and Abraham Lincoln for President of the United

States, that an even one hundred soldiers marched to the polls in Warsaw headed by Colonel J. B. Dodge and myself to deposit a ballot favoring the carrying on of the war until its enemies laid down their arms. The incident created intense indignation on the part of the "copperhead wing" of the party and their newspapers howled about the outrage for weeks after the election. It should be understood that the furloughed soldiers cast not a single illegal ballot, for each one had come home to exercise this undoubted legal right to vote.

My second leave of absence of twenty days expired and I went to Indianapolis on my way back to my regiment then at Atlanta. It came as a great surprise to me on arriving at Indianapolis to be detailed as a member of the "Military Commission" for the trial of what afterwards came to be known as "The Indiana Conspirators". The detail of course, could not be evaded, and it did cut me out of making "The March to the Sea" along with my regiment. Had I slipped through the capital of the State without stopping, I would have reached Atlanta in time to join the "great march".

The commission selected for the trial had to be officers above a certain rank. General Silas Colgrove was appointed President of the Commission. Colgrove was the individual whose troops found General Robert E. Lee's "order book" for the battle of Antietam. Colgrove at once ordered it placed in the hands of General McClellan, the commanding officer of the Federal Army. It is said that the trooper dispatched to find McClellan rode his first mount to death and was compelled to find himself another to complete the trip. Major Henry L. Burnett, of Cincinnati, Judge Advocate of the Department of the Ohio was chosen to conduct the trial in the same position as in a civil court. The prosecuting attorney and the remainder of the court were made up as follows: Colonel Wm. E. McLane, 43rd Indiana Infantry; Colonel Thomas J. Lucas, 16th Indiana Infantry; Colonel Charles D. Murray, 89 Indiana Infantry; Colonel Benjamin Spooner, 83rf Indiana Infantry; Colonel Richard P. DeHart, 128th Indiana Infantry; Colonel Ambrose A. Stevens, Veteran Reserve Corps; Colonel Ancil D. Wass, 60th Massachusetts Infantry; Colonel Thomas Bennett, 69th Indiana Infantry; Colonel Reub Williams, 12th Indiana Infantry; and Colonel Albert Heath, 100th Indiana Infantry. Ben Pitman, of Cincinnati, author of Pitman's system of phonetic reporting, was employed by the government to take down the proceeding in shorthand.

During the trial, every question and every reply was taken down verbatim and with the utmost accuracy. Consequently the book, "The Trials for Treason at Indianapolis. Disclosing the Plans for Establishing a Northwestern Confederacy" is an absolute and faithful presentation of the Commission proceedings. I make this statement so emphatic because the leaders of "The Knights of the Golden Circle" and their sympathizers sent the charge throughout the country that the trial was incorrectly reported and that the book was filled with falsehoods. On the contrary there never has been a case so voluminously reported and so free from errors or misstatements of any kind.

John C. Walker, of Laporte, Indiana was on the list furnished to General Carrington. He was a high-up officer in the order of "The Golden Circle", and anticipated that he would be arrested. Consequently he flew the state. The first man to be arrested was Harrison H. Dodd, of Indianapolis. When the commission began its session on the morning of October 7, 1864, Judge Advocate Major Burnett announced that the prisoner had escaped and asked for an adjournment for a few hours. It seems that Dodd had petitioned General Alvin P. Hovey to be allowed to occupy a room in the post office building rather than be confined in the military prison. He was given his parole of honor and Dodd's brother also pledged his word that his brother would not try to escape. No guards were placed on the outside of the building. Dodd was confined in a room on the third story of the post office building and about four o'clock in the morning he let down a string from a ball of twine he had been supplied by a visitor during the day. Accomplices below attached the twine to a heavy rope. Dodd pulled it up, tied it to his bedpost, and climbed to freedom. The escape of the prisoner on trial necessitated an adjournment of the court assembled. In making up the second commission, my name was forwarded to the Secretary of War and I was confronted with a dispatch detailing me as a member of the commission.

The people of Indiana were greatly excited. The situation had reached a condition that might at any moment kindle a flame of insurrection right here in Indiana. There were over a hundred thousand Indiana soldiers in the field, a condition in and of itself quite dangerous. The leaders of the movement favored an insurrection here at home as a means of assisting the South by attacking the rear of the Federal army and by compelling the Federal government to withdraw troops from "the front". The condition seemed so grave that General Alvin Hovey was placed in command of the district of Indiana. This gave General Carrington an opportunity to exhibit his qualities as a first-class detective.

The names of those placed on trial following Dodd's escape and the consequent break up of the court were: Willilam A. Bowles, at the time owner of the Indiana French Lick Springs; L. P. Milligan, a prominent attorney of Huntington, Indiana; Andrew J. Humphreys, a Democratic leader in Sullivan county; Horace Heffren, an attorney of Salem, Washington County; and Stephen Horsey, of Shoals, Indiana, who might be classed as "general utility" man for the "Knights of the Golden Circle". It was proven on trial that Steven Horsey had gathered up a number of muskets, rifles, revolvers, etc., and had stored them away in some secret place. He had a thousand pounds of powder stored for the use of the order.

While the trial of these men was going forward, the "march to the sea" was progressing. I remember how eagerly the members of the treason-trial court perused the morning papers when they gathered in the room set apart for the proceeding in the post office building. Those were exciting times. The arrest of these men for treason greatly dispirited those in opposition to the war. Many, who had belonged to the "Knight of the Golden Circle" in more subordinate capacities, became so alarmed over their leaders being arrested that they withdrew from their lodges. The trial drew its weary length along for ninety days. Sunday was the only day we were not in session. Large crowds of spectators attended the trial and the newspapers faithfully and clearly reported every word that was said in court each day. The perusal of the evidence created great excitement and indignation throughout the state and the country. The attendance finally became so great that it became impossible to admit so many people. It was decided to remove the court to a larger one in the Old State House.

Horance Heffren "turned State's evidence" and revealed under oath the whole murderous, treasonable plot of the organization. These men and many more were found guilty and all, save Andrew Humphreys, were given the death penalty. Mr. Humphreys was an officer of the order in Sullivan County. A body of men had assembled to stop the draft of four hundred men. Five of the government's enrolling officers had already been waylaid and killed in that section of the state. Mr. Humphreys advised the men not to violate the law in such a way and urged them to disband. His advice was heeded. When the commission gave its verdict, Andrew Humphreys was given a life sentence to prison, while all of the rest were give the extreme penalty—death by hanging.

To sum up the whole affair, the trial developed many crimes besides that of treason. All of the charges were sustained. It was fairly shown that there were a large number of Democrats here in Indiana and elsewhere who were engaged in plotting a "Northwestern Confederacy". It was also proven that the principal officers of "The Knights of the Golden Circle" were conspiring with officers and soldiers then in the service of the Confederacy. At one time there were seventeen Confederate officers, in disguise, stopping at the Bates House, in Indianapolis. These officers were to take command of the six thousand Confederate prisoners then confined in Camp Morton. The plan was to release the prisoners, attack the Indianapolis arsenal and there secure muskets to equip each prisoner. They would then march on Louisville and with the aid of Confederate soldiers in the field capture the city. There was also a plan to assassinate Governor Morton. There was not a dissenting voice in the commission as to the guilt of the men. The only difference of opinion was as to the form of punishment. The people of Indiana today were not generally aware of how near, how very near, the State came to having an insurrection in 1864.

I was overjoyed when the dreary trial was over. I now would have the opportunity to return to my regiment, or so I thought. I received an order detailing me, and all the remaining members of the commission just concluded to assemble in a similar court at Cincinnati to try a similar lot of conspirators who had attempted the relief of the Confederate prisoners held at Johnson's Island in Lake Erie. I almost resented the duty, for it prevented me from returning to my regiment. That day I went to Cincinnati to see General Joseph Hooker, who was in command of the department embracing Ohio and Indiana, in the hope of being relieved from the irksome duty of the coming court-martial. On making my statement to the General the next morning after my arrival, he complimented me considerably over my preference for active duty in the field, but also stated that as the detail was ordered by the Secretary of War, he would not dare to interfere.

I was greatly grieved over the matter. I could not start on my return to Indianapolis for several hours for want of a train so I hung about the General's office. I finally had the courage to ask him if he would telegraph the Secretary of War and ask that I might be relieved. The General got around this by saying that I might send a dispatch over my own signature, and he would "endorse it". This was done and within about an hour I was free from the objectionable detail. Having been on official duty I was entitled to transport back to my regiment. By this time General Sherman had captured Fort McAlister by Savannah. My transportation was made out by the staff-quartermaster for Savannah via New York City. At New York I was to procure the "Steamer Mellville" which leaving in four days.

I was greatly pleased over the result of my visit to Cincinnati, and hastened back to Indianapolis to make preparations to proceed to New York. Cincinnati was made out as my starting point so that I was compelled to return to that city in order to start over the railroads. I had to make three trips between Indianapolis and Cincinnati before I secured release from the commission and got started on my way.

At last I found myself in New York City for the first time. Edwin De Nyce was the regular paid correspondent of the New York Herald during the time the Fifteenth corps occupied the line of railroad between Stephenson and Huntsville. De Nyce made his headquarters with mine at Scottsboro, Alabama. He went with me through a portion of the Atlanta campaign, camping with me until he returned to New York. On the morning following my arrival, De Nyce was about the first man I met on stepping out into the street. He was then employed on the New York Telegram. The meeting was most cordial for we had always been friends from our first acquaintance in the field. It was not long until De Nyce ascertained my destination and about my transportation on the "Steamer Millville". When he heard I was to be on the Millville he said, "Here, you don't want to take that boat; she's old, unsafe, and in four days from now the Ajax, a brand-new boat that has just made a successful trial trip will leave for Savannah." I told him that I had already been on board the Mellville and had been assigned a cabin and had placed my baggage on board. "You can easily have your transportation changed from the Melville to the Ajax," he replied. "Both are in the government service, and it will make no difference to the owners of either, as they got their pay for the trip whether they carry anything or nothing." He insisted so strongly on the change that he finally went along with me to the Quartermaster General's office and helped in having the transportation changed to the Ajax.

Of course, De Nyce had no interest in the affair more than to have a visit with an old army friend, and neither of us could have known the wonderful results as I was personally concerned in that change of steamers. The Mellville started on time, as I would have done had I not seen De Nyce on the street. In a fearful storm that prevailed off Cape Hatteras, the Mellville went down, having on board over six hundred veteran troops on their way to rejoin their regiments. Only six or seven people were saved. The Ajax although it felt the same storm, got through to Savannah all right, but was eleven days and nights on the way.

The wreck and total loss of the Mellville created great excitement at my home. One of the clerks in General Hooker's office at Cincinnati was from a neighboring town of Plymouth. He had made out the papers for my transportation and was at Plymouth when the Mellville went down. He believed me to be one of the passengers on that ill-fated vessel and told his friends of the incident. The news was soon transmitted to Warsaw, setting my wife almost wild. She could not rest until she had interviewed the clerk of General Hooker's headquarters. Accompanied by her sister, she visited Plymouth, where she ascertained what the clerk knew. Of course, after landing at Savannah, and not knowing of the disaster, I was tardy in writing home. My regiment had been sent up to Beaufort, South Carolina and I thus put off writing until I arrived there, four or five days after reaching Savannah. The ever-present correspondent had written to his paper—there was no telegraphic communications at that time—stating that among the many officers "Colonel Reub Williams had joined his regiment having come on the steamer Ajax from New York." This was three weeks after I had left home, and of course, settled a question that I as yet knew nothing about. Peculiar things happen all about us in war times as well as during peace, with strange, unfathomable results. How many, many times I have thought how peculiar it was that the meeting of a friend in New York City, where I did not know a living soul, and taking his strongly insisted upon advice, probably saved my life.

I will return for a moment to my first voyage on salt water. The steamer Ajax was a brand new, large, powerful vessel. Besides myself and Thomas Hubler, then a small boy and a brother-in-law of mine, and without a shadow of a doubt, the youngest person mustered into service during the Civil War, he was not yet ten years old, there were perhaps twenty-five regular passengers. Quite a number of them were army officers, and others belonged to the Treasury Department who were going down to Savannah to make arrangements about opening the port of Savannah. In addition to this there was an even thousand of drafted men in charge of a company of "the Veteran Reserve corps" on board. These drafted men were fully equipped. Among the officers on board was General Webster, who for a long time had full charge of all the railroads that came into the possession of the Union forces as fast as they came inside of the Federal lines. There were two or three officers on his staff and their duty would be to open the damaged roads between places essential for use in the future movements of the Union army.

Following the opening of the Mississippi and other streams, the Secretary of War had issued a standing order which was printed on a large card in good-sized type to the effect that the ranking officer on board of any and every steam boat, ship, ferry boat, etc., should have charge of all men belonging to the army on board such a vessel. He was in no way to interfere with the Captain of the vessel and was only to preserve order and discipline among whatever troops might be on board. General Webster had his attention called to the card by the Captain of the Ajax and assumed command, which included the thousand drafted men on board. The vessel had passed out from Sandy Hook into the Atlantic. It was not long until the plunging vessel brought to all unaccustomed to it, the usual seasickness. General Webster was so seriously affected that he had to take to his cabin. Before doing so, he sent for me and, as I was next in rank, placed me in charge of the troops. I had felt a little shaky about the stomach for awhile, but I don't think it lasted over ten or fifteen minutes. General Webster was so sick he was confined to his cabin for five days, while many others recovered after a day or two. From what I saw, seasickness must be as hard to bear as any other disease known to mankind. There were men on that trip who would have preferred to die rather than go through another day of the terrible sickness, yet it is said that the disease has never been known to cause the death of any one. The Captain of the Veteran Reserve Company and nearly all of his men succumbed to seasickness early in the voyage and were not fit for duty.

On the morning of the third day, a well-informed and quite gentlemanly-appearing man among the drafted men came to me and complained that they had no means of making coffee. I went to the hold with him and there I saw such a sight that I would never like to have repeated. There the men lay, many of them vomiting continually, right over and on one another. It was a horrible sight and I resolved to relieve it at once. I ascertained from the man who came to see me that one of the cooks on board had been furnishing the drafted men with coffee, for which he charged twenty-five cents a tin cupful, made from the coffee the men had furnished to him. I resolved to put a stop to that sort of business, and assisted by the men who could get about, I had the cooks prepare a cauldron of coffee, and the well men delivered the coffee to the sick. A committee I had appointed ascertained about how much money the cook had taken from the men and he was forced to disgorge that whole amount. Then the cook was paid a reasonable amount for his trouble. The sum was quite large, and on arriving at Savannah, I turned it over to the head of the hospital, and took his receipt for it. From the time I adjusted the affairs of the drafted men, I could not pass the barracks they occupied without a squad of them getting together in gratitude and giving me three cheers. It was during the treason trials and on this trip that I learned that the drafted men were treated like animals. There is not a trainload of cattle passing through the country now that does not have better care than did the drafted men of 1864. Nothing could have been more horrible than the sight of that ship's hold on that trip.

After the "march to the sea" was made and was pronounced a success, the newspapers that predicted dire calamity for the movement saying it was "Crazy Bill's" freakish scheme, now declared it as " a mere picnic that anybody could have invented and carried out!" This shows the extreme the faultfinders of the war period went to in belittling the government. To tell the truth "the march to the sea" was far easier to make than any one supposed, but this was not known until after it was an accomplished fact. To many people in and out of he army, it looked like a foolhardy undertaking, a hazardous expedition, and to many military men, it seemed like sending an army to certain destruction. After it was over, the whole enterprise can be summed up in the statement that Sherman was right and all those who derided it and predicted disaster were wrong.

I remained at Savannah for several days waiting to get a boat to take me to Beaufort, North Carolina where my regiment had been sent. Since I had no duty to perform, I found time on several occasions to do some favors for the drafted men who had been placed in a Confederate barracks not far from the hotel where I was stopping. These men were kept as close as though they were prisoners of war. My heart went out to them and I succeeded in helping most of them to the different regiments to which they had been assigned. The old veteran who had been in the army since 1861-62 looked down on the draftee. They would criticize them for not volunteering early in the war instead of waiting until they were forced into the service. There were times when I had to interfere to prevent a knockdown. The more I mingled with those thousand men, the more sympathy I had for them. All of them had what they deemed a good excuse for not volunteering early in the war. Some of them were substitutes for others, who had been drafted, and received in many instances large sums from the person who hired them to take their place.

Savannah is an old town that had been blockaded almost since the war began, and looked rundown. It had the appearance of a half-dressed old maid, whose clothes had been out of fashion and repair for a half-century.

The war was responsible for this slovenly look. I roamed around the city at my leisure visiting many attractions. Before I left Indianapolis, James Ryan, whom I did not know, hunted me up at the Bates house and asked me if I would do him the favor of carrying a sum of money to a brother-in-law of his, who was no doubt in need of some other kind of money than Confederate currency. I told him if he was willing to trust me, a stranger to him, I would do my best to get the money to its destination. After I arrived at Savannah, one of the first things I did was to hunt up the gentleman whose street and number had been furnished by Mr. Ryan and delivered the message and the money. On opening the package I could see by his looks that its contents were a matter of deep interest to him. In jest asked him if it was all there. "Well," he replied, "my brother-in-law writes me that he was sending me four hundred fifty dollars and I find the enclosure precisely that amount. This money comes at a most opportune time for I have not a cent in the world except a few dollars in Confederate currency. My family and I have already missed two of our last meals because the Confederate money wouldn't buy anything whatever in Savannah." It was very plain that he spoke the truth, for while we were talking his wife, a Northern woman who had been "locked up" inside the Southern Confederacy for four years, came into the room, and when her husband showed her the letter her eyes filled with tears. The two were exceedingly grateful to me for delivering the letter, and very gracious, so gracious that I could hardly get away from them. There are occasionally pleasant episodes even in war-times.

While I was at Savannah every boat coming from the North was loaded with the men returning to their respective regiments and batteries who had been prevented by the strict medical examination from making "the march to the sea". There were constant reunions of tent-mates on their arrival.

After remaining at Savannah for five days, I with a number of other officers and soldiers, secured passage on a private boat and proceeded to Beaufort, North Carolina. I was disappointed to find the division to which my regiment belonged had been sent to "Gardiner's Cross Roads" in the direction of Charleston, South Carolina. Gardiner's Cross Roads was an important military post. It was on the direct road from Beaufort to Charleston. I could not go to Gardiner's Cross Roads for two days, so I put in the time wandering around the old town. The place was settled very early in the history of the "Two Carolinas". The houses were very old and the town had a peculiarly strange appearance to me. Many of the houses were built of a sort of cement made out of oyster shells. The taking possession of Savannah by Sherman's army gave the control of almost all the coast to Federal authority. Charleston and Wilmington, important ports, as well as some of minor importance, still remained in possession of the Confederacy, but even the Southern leaders knew it was only a question of time until control of these would be lost. Beaufort was an important shipping point and before the war much of the cotton was shipped abroad from there. The sea-island cotton grew on the islands just off the coast. Sea-island cotton is regarded as the finest grown anywhere in the world because of the length and fineness of its fiber.

On the evening of the second day while I was waiting for an opportunity to go to Gardiner's Cross Roads, I met Colonel William B. Wood on the street. After making an army acquaintance by introducing ourselves, I ascertained that he intended to start for Gardiner's Cross Roads on the following morning. I learned that my regiment composed a part of his command. When I told him I was the colonel of the Twelfth, he was overjoyed and at once provided me with a horse to make the trip with him on the following day. Early next morning Colonel Wood, with a portion of his staff and myself using a horse belonging to the Colonel, left Beaufort for our destination fifteen miles distant. The roads were execrable passing through a swampy region. Very slow progress was made, and we arrived about an hour before sunset. The men of my regiment, whom I had not seen since the previous September, gave me a very joyous reception. I found the men in rugged good health and dozens of them happy over the mail we brought from Beaufort. Some of this mail was in answer to letters sent home as soon as Savannah was captured.

Gardiner's Cross Roads was only what its name designated—a crossing of highways. The country was thinly settled with several arms of the sea extending inland. A bridge connected some of these arms of the sea. The troops, to which my regiment were attached, were acting more as a "corps of observation" than anything else. About five miles from the camp on the road to Charleston was another arm of the sea, crossed by a bridge. On the opposite side of this bridge was either a small Confederate fort or a stockade which was manned by Confederate soldiers. There was artillery in the fort or stockade. The bridge between the two forces was a half-mile in length and had been partly destroyed. There was no attempt made on the part of the Union forces to cross over and give battle to the enemy on the opposite side—indeed, the orders were not to bring on any engagement at that time.

I found the men of my regiment fully enjoying themselves on my arrival. The men found on the upper end of one of the bayous or arms oysters were plentiful. It was very seldom that the Federal army had been placed in a condition where it could regale itself with this well-known and delicious bivalve. After I arrived I directed that a detail accompanied by a wagon should be sent every day to gather in a wagonload of oysters. In anticipation of the return of the wagon loaded with oysters, the men in camp had built up lag heaps and had set fire to them so that there would be plenty of coals to cook the bivalve as soon as the fishing party returned. The oysters were eaten in every style: stewed, fried and raw. The most popular way was to pile a lot of the oysters in the shell in the crevices of the burning log-heaps and when it was thought that they were sufficiently cooked, they were pulled out of the fire. Many of the men like vinegar on them so when one of the wagons made a trip to Beaufort I had the driver bring out a barrel of vinegar. I remember it very well, for the barrel cost me twenty-two dollars, the same price I paid for a pair of Wellington boots that the driver also picked up for me. Prices were high at the close of the war. I distinctly remember that a Washington City tailor charged me one hundred ten dollars for a uniform coat to be worn at the Grand Review just as the war closed. Twenty-five dollars would have been a high price for the coat at the beginning of the war.

One day, General Sherman with a portion of his staff, came out to our camp. He arrived in the evening and he made his headquarters with Colonel William B. Wood. The next morning the General, having expressed his desire to take a view of the Confederate fort already alluded to and the bridge that led over to it, rode with a large party of mounted men made up of officers and orderlies, to the location. The General gave the position a close examination. He informed General Wood that he desired to convey the impression to the enemy that he was about to march his army to Charleston, and that he was going to use this road in the march. I could easily perceive by the order left with us that the General was perpetrating another ruse to mislead the enemy. Our orders were to move an augmented force out to the bridge, and to take with it a couple pieces of artillery. In a lower tone of voice, he suggested to General Wood that he lead the Confederates to believe that he was getting ready to move the main army in that direction. Additional regiments were sent to the bridge and after the artillery had fired several rounds apiece and had received about the same number of shots in return, a detachment of infantry was sent out on the Federal end of the bridge. They conducted their work in such a manner as to deceive the enemy without a shadow of a doubt. The plan pursued was for gangs of men to carry out planks on the bridge—and apparently laying them down on the structure. They were then passed down under it to other men and carried out to others and the same thing repeated. Thus the enemy could not help but believe that the Federals were engaged in reconstructing the damaged bridge. This ruse was kept up for two days, maybe more. The work was occasionally interspersed with an artillery duel, although the distance between the forces was too great to do much damage. The Confederate troops withdrew from the fort on the third day, although this may have been caused by the supposed surrender of Charleston.

After the withdrawal of the Confederates from the opposite end of the bridge, nothing unusual occurred in camp. The soldiers were "living like fighting cocks," for in addition to their receiving full rations they were filling up on oysters. A few days after the visit from General Sherman, an improvised scouting party, promiscuously mounted on horses and mules, ran into a detachment of Confederate cavalry, about five or six miles north of the encampment. The Confederates far outnumbered the small scouting party. Two soldiers were sent to camp for reinforcements. There was no regular cavalry with the troops, but every officer and enlisted man who could secure a horse or a mule armed himself and was on the way. The reinforcements arrived at the place where two dozen scouts were holding at bay fully two hundred and fifty well-mounted Confederates. The nearly fifty reinforcements turned the tide at once. Following a charge, the Confederates were put to flight. In the run many of the enemy were captured and brought back to camp. I entertained the notion at the time that the majority of them were glad they had fallen into our hands, for they knew they would have plenty to eat as long as they remained with "the Yankees".

During the stay of the Federals at Gardiner's Cross Roads, active preparations were going forward for the future movements of the army under Sherman. Most of the northern papers predicted a march upon Charleston. But at no time did General Sherman arrange for such a movement. The deception practiced at the bridge only shows that Sherman was very willing to have the Confederate leaders believe that such was his plan.

| W | 12 | Ind. |

Reuben Williams

Colonel Co. ...., 12 Reg't Indiana Infantry.

Appears on Returns as follows:

Dec 1862 to March 1863: Absent Paroled at Holly Springs Dec 20-62

Apr. 1863: Present Paroled at Holly Springs Miss. Dec 20/62

May to July 1863: Present

Aug. 1863: Present & absence not stated

Sept. 1863: absent on leave from Sept. 17 – 2-7 days

Oct. 1863: Present

Dec. 1863: Present

Jan. & Feb. 1864: Com'd'g 1 Brig 4 Div. 15 AC Jan. 16 – 64

Mch & Apr. 1864: Present

(over)

Book mark ....

G. M. Gen.
Copyist.

(6-46)

CHAPTER 15

Marching to Columbia, South Carolina

> The trumpet's piercing blast is still,
> The shackled slave is free;
> The Mississippi proudly rolls
> Unguarded to the sea.
> The snowy wings of peace are spread
> Where stood the embattled line;
> The tall Palmetto of the South
> Leans to the Northern Pine.
> —T. C. Harbaugh

Branchville, South Carolina was a small and unimportant place but a great railroad crossing. By taking that place and destroying the railroads Charleston would fall "like an over-ripe plum in his basket". It was with this end in view that General Sherman made all his calculations and dispositions of his troops. No one in the camp at Cross Roads knew anything of what was going on in the main army. And the troops did not know much about where the other forces lay that had made the "march to the sea". It took some time for General Sherman to re-equip his army after it reached Savannah. The distance from Savannah to the North is much greater by sea than many people are aware. Cape Hatteras is a dangerous point to mariners, being known as a graveyard of sunken vessels, and therefore it was, and still is, necessary to give it a wide berth. The Captain of the Ajax told me a wise ship's captain would sail fully two hundred miles east of the Cape, if he had a valuable cargo and vessel.

All of Sherman's supplies had to come by water, and it required a great amount of time to put his army in a condition to move northward to threaten General Lee's rear. All the time, from the fall of Savannah until the Union army started northward on its march through the Carolinas and Virginia, the officers and men who had been left behind previous to the celebrated march were rejoining their companies, batteries and regiments, by the hundreds. Every vessel sailing carried many of these men. The indications that the war was rapidly closing was so plain that men and officers absent from their commands feared that the end would come while they were away from their posts of duty.

It was at Beaufort that the Twelfth Indiana Infantry received two hundred and fifty drafted men. These men had been assigned to the regiment through the courtesy of General Harry B. Carrington. During the treason trial I formed an intimate acquaintance with General Carrington and as he held the disposition of the drafted men, he very readily conceded to my request to fill up the Twelfth with these men. They reached the regiment just before the march northward was commenced following the fall of Savannah. Nearly every one of these men was unfamiliar with the duties of a soldier, but in placing them among old veterans the most of them took up the new life quite rapidly.

It must be remembered that for the first few months of the war the Confederate army was in numbers fully the equal of that of the North. In fact, the South at the start was the better prepared than was the general government. It had one of their own at the head of both the war and the navy departments, who in anticipation of what was foreshadowed, had taken occasion to see that many thousands of muskets had been sent to various places in the South during nearly all of the Buchanan administration. He also arranged for the government's ships to be widely scattered when the first gun was fired. The North was very seriously obstructed at the beginning for the want of arms.

There were many different kinds of muskets issued to all of the men who enlisted for three months, and also to many who offered their services for "three years or during the war". The foreign made guns were very inferior. There was the Harper's Ferry musket, and the old-fashioned, big-bore Springfield rifle of our own manufacture; then came the "Belgian" with its beech-wood stock apparently weighing a pound or two more in wood than was necessary, and a very inferior gun in every way. These were followed by the Enfield, caliber 53, an English gun that was at least superior to the Belgian, and smaller shipments of other muskets and rifles. Previous to the opening of the Atlanta campaign, however, the entire army was equipped with the new Springfield, in all probability the best muzzle-loading gun ever placed in the hands of the soldiers of any nation up to that time.

I speak of this variety of guns and muskets in order to show the reader what confusion the different variety and the different sized calibers would make in the excitement and the destruction during the progress of a battle. At Shiloh it is stated that a regiment ran out of ammunition and an additional supply was rushed to them as fast as the teams could bring it. On arriving on the scene of battle, it was discovered that the ammunition was of the wrong caliber and hence as useless as none at all. Fortunately, the enemy did not know that the Federal brigade was out of ammunition, and hence did not take advantage of the situation. It is needless to say that the mistake was rectified as speedily as horses and men could do it.

Very early in the war the government prepared to make the arms of the infantry soldiers at least, uniform. The arsenal at Watervleit, Connecticut never stood idle for a single moment until there was a sufficient supply of the new pattern of the Springfield rifle in the hands of all its soldiers at the close of 1863 and the beginning of 1864. The people of Warsaw will remember that the black walnut stocks for these rifles were made in this place for over two years.

Since General Sherman had fully made up his mind to move inland rather than towards Charleston, the Twelfth was considerably "off the line of march" mapped out by the commander. The troops at Gardiner's Cross Roads knew nothing of the movement of other troops until they were under way. Very suddenly an order came to Gardiner's Cross Roads directing the commander of the troops to be ready to move by eight o'clock the next day. Early the following morning, every man was ready. I met General John Logan and a portion of his staff. All of his corps, the Fifteenth, was on the march. He had ridden over to Gardiner's Cross Roads to give directions to the course the troops were intended to take. They would be taking up the rear of the moving army, then already well on the way.

I had not seen General Logan since the previous September. He, too, had gone home after the fall of Atlanta and took an active part in the Presidential campaign in the closing weeks of 1864. It would have been a calamity for the country had General McClellan been elected on a platform of "peace at any price", which was the leading plank in the platform on which he made the race. General Vallandigham, the man who was banished during the war, was the author of this plank. The re-election of President Lincoln for a second term very greatly dispirited the people of the South. I have always thought the victory won that year at the polls was fully the equal in aiding to suppress the rebellion and bring the war to a close as any one of the great battles of the war. While Lincoln's election very greatly dispirited the Confederate soldiers, it also greatly "heartened" the soldiers fighting for the Union.

That morning General Logan was in the best of spirits. The majority of soldiers who made "the march to the sea" remember that it was only in South Carolina where a white flag was displayed to any extent by the people. It had, in fact, been an unusual sight anywhere in the region of country through which the Union army had traversed. Now, however, "a change came over the spirit of the dreams" of the people and the white flag was displayed from housetops and the gates leading up to the mansions of some of the planters. This subject came up in conversation with General Logan who took the ground that it was unwise for the people to display a white flag. He feared that, in hoisting the white flag, the people of the state would accentuate the soldier's view that, as she was the first State to begin the war, it would be unfair to those States that had borne the brunt of the conflict through which both armies had passed to let her escape comparatively unharmed. I have often thought of those comments made by General Logan that morning. Whether South Carolina suffered more in destruction of property, houses, barns, fences, etc., I do not know. But I do know from personal knowledge that the road passed by Logan's corps in South Carolina flew the white flag at almost every plantation. This was particularly noticeable because the troops had never seen the white flag displayed except as "a flag of truce", as a means of communication between the two armies.

Pocotallego was a town about a day's march from our starting point. It had been captured the previous day after a slight skirmish by a division of the Seventeenth Corps. On arriving there, we went into camp in the outskirts of the town. It was a county seat town and had almost literally been destroyed just previous to our arrival. As I rode through the streets, I noticed thousands of legal documents covered the streets. The thought came to my mind that there would be much litigation following the war, for the courthouses and public offices had been destroyed along with many records and legal documents. A passing soldier picked up what he called a "peculiar" looking document. He handed it me as I rode past him. I found it was a land grant from the Crown of England for a very large body of land in that section and was the original title to the land covered in the description. It was printed and written on parchment, and regarding it as a genuine curiosity, I enclosed it in a large envelope and sent it to Judge James Frazer of Warsaw as a curious legal document. During the war the judge was a collector of internal revenue for what was then the Tenth Congressional District of Indiana, and had his office in a small room on the second floor of the old county building in Warsaw. A few years after the war I visited the then vacated room that had been occupied by the judge, and found the old patent in a cigar box, almost destroyed by rats or mice. The judge had removed his office leaving the cigar box and the "grant" behind. He was greatly chagrined when I told him of the circumstance.

Charleston was still in possession of the Confederates at the time the march northwestward commenced, but General Sherman rightly concluded that after undergoing a siege of nearly four years without yielding, that it would finally succumb without firing a shot. The entire army proceeded northward, using at first, four main roads leading in the desired direction. The roads were not far apart, and by night one could almost tell the line passed over by all of the other corps by the reflection of the fires along the respective highways. As far as one could see bright fires were reflected upon the sky, indicating that a portion of General Sherman's army was camped there. One day's march was very like the preceding one, consisting of: skirmishes to prevent the enemy from destroying the long bridges; the capture of prisoners by the advance guard of each corps; the tearing down of houses in order to procure material to reconstruct a bridge; and the every day smell of burning pine and the clouds of dense smoke that sometimes enveloped the marching troops.

The march, after leaving Savannah was a very trying one. The weather was rainy which made the crossing of the numerous streams, creeks and even small rivulets sometimes very difficult. It seemed the only duty that the Confederate army in front of us performed was the destruction of the bridges in our front. The pioneer corps speedily reconstructed the bridges or built new ones. The bridge that crossed the Edisto River was two miles long and had to be reconstructed, which took a great deal of time. Frequently, on the opposite side of the river, the enemy would post itself and wait the on-coming troops with musketry fire until all of a sudden the Confederates doing this kind of work would have to fly, as crossings had been made by the Federal troops.

Each day's march was usually a duplicate of the preceding one for the entire trip. The weather had grown more comfortable. The heavy rains had ceased and there were no wading in streams for a few miles. The men's clothing became dry. I can truthfully say that the clothes worn by the officers and men for the first hundred and fifty miles were never fully dry for a single moment. I mean, of course, those soldiers who were at the head of the army. Those who came afterwards and found the roads all passably repaired with no streams to wade, possibly did get their clothes dry between heavy showers. The march was a hard one. The regimental wagons had been taken away. At the beginning of the war every company in a regiment was supplied with two wagons to carry tents and camp equipage, while the regimental headquarters were given three. These were afterwards reduced to one wagon to the company, and when the "march to the sea" was outfitted even this one wagon was forbidden and a single pack mule was issued to each company. From that time forward the army never fully recovered its supply of wagons. Lieutenant Colonel Baldwin, who commanded the Twelfth while I was on "The Treason Trials" informed me, after I relieved him from his command, that previous to leaving Atlanta on the great march, he had all he could do to procure an extra animal for the very fine band the Twelfth had maintained all through the war. He did finally get a regular "jack" instead of a mule. A large amount of fun was had over the "band's jack-ass".

The march through the Carolinas was made in the same fashion. Each company had a mule, which carried the few camp kettles, long-handled frying pans, extra tin cups, etc., and all property conceded to company ownership. I was always sorry that I did not bring the handsome, chunky little burro that was consigned to my own headquarters home with me. He was so low in stature that I could stand with one foot on the ground and throw the other over his body at the withers. He was as kind and as playful as a kitten, full of pranks, but always reliable. He would be turned loose when the march began in the morning, and without being given any attention whatever he would join the company of horses and riding mules that belonged to regimental headquarters. He never strayed away from the regiment for any distance. Nearly every soldier in the regiment played with this handsome and very intelligent little animal. "Big Ben," the colored man who cared for and fed him daily was a great favorite of the mule. He had given him hard tack, ending up with a lump of sugar so often that he had learned to rob Ben's haversack. A more intelligent burro I never saw than was "Abe," the "regimental pet."

Whenever my mind runs back to the tramp through the Carolinas, I think of the vast amount of suffering on the part of the citizens, and the immense destruction of property, and the starvation that must have ensued. The march covered a width of about forty miles and was no doubt done purposely to allow the Federal army to subsist on the country. It would have been impossible for General Sherman to supply his army in any other way than by subsisting on the country through which it passed. It would have been out of the question to carry supplies in wagons over roads that had to be corduroyed for hundreds of miles before the artillery could pass over them. Even had it been undertaken to use government supplies, the wagons could not carry supplies for more than three for four days and there would have been no way to replenish them. This explanation does not in any way lessen the sufferings and perhaps the starvation of the people along the routes of march. While the citizens of the country were with the army, they could easily procure enough food from the Union soldiers for present maintenance. But after the army had gone by, I have no doubt that actual starvation occurred in some instances. It is not over-stating the facts when I say that the country was stripped of everything that it possessed in the way of food for man and beast. I feel certain that some people must have literally starved before they could reach a region far enough away from the line of march to still possess something to sustain life. It should also be remembered that the Confederate troops, under General Wade Hampton and Joe Wheeler, engaged in the attempt to impede the progress of the Federal army, was also compelled to subsist on the country. It had the advantage of first reaching the region for supplies and perhaps, in some instances, destroyed whatever food supplies they could not use.

The Union army was followed by an immense number of colored people ranging all the way down to the infant at the breast. The children ranged from the toddlers all the way up, and men from twenty years of age to the old, decrepit, stooped, white-haired old man of eighty years or more. These followers of the army were of every shade of color. None of them knew where they were going or what would be done with them. It was stated that when the army reached Savannah that there were fully ten thousand colored people of all ages that followed the troops that made "the march to the sea". This statement may have been overstated, but there were certainly a large number.

One occasion I had to ride back along the line of march for some purpose and it was then that I beheld a portion of that great number of colored people following the route that the Fifteenth had taken that day. Not all were colored people though, for there were many whites among them as well. The whites were in every sort of vehicle imaginable. Sometimes the usable parts of two broken wagons were combined into one.

One-horse wagons had been put in repair, and with a few articles of household goods, from two to five children were loaded on the wagon, with their mother to preserve order and the man leading the horse or mule with a halter, the luxury of lines being discarded. Most of the followers were blacks. The children were begging their mothers for something to eat and hundreds of the little ones were crying from the hunger and the fatigue. It was a heart-touching sight, and I came as near as a soldier should to shedding tears myself over the want of want of food, the hunger of the little ones, and the utter helplessness of their elders. It was a sort of misery that touched me to the heart, and I at once remounted my horse and hastened to the head of the command, resolved to alleviate some of the suffering. It was growing toward sundown when the troops went into camp. I summoned Marsh Parks to my aid and directed the regimental ambulance to be unloaded. While this was being done, I went to the men of several companies and begged of them to divide whatever rations they might have to share with those following the army. Soon I had as much as the ambulance would carry and then Parks and myself were on our way to the rear on our errand of mercy.

I had especially solicited from the men a small installment of coffee from each in the belief that it would go as far as a great deal of food would to aid these starving people. We gave this to the women folks, charging them to make it go as far as possible. It was out of the power of any one to relieve all the hungry, but we made our supply of food go as far as possible. We tried to give food to mothers first whose children were actually suffering from lack of food. I often think of that night scene in South Carolina even yet, and the gratitude that came from these helpless people lying along each side of the road touches me to the heart even yet. Quite a number of the men and officers in regiment became enlisted in this charitable work. Every night when the army was on the march, many would go back, after the troops were encamped, to relieve as many as possible by dividing our own and by begging those who could not go along back with us, to contribute a portion of his rations to keep these people from dying.

The country through which we were wading and bridging in South Carolina was historical ground. It was the home of, and the scene of operations of General Francis Marion—"The Swamp Fox," of the Revolution. For two or three days my regiment camped near the battlefield of Camden. Rations had been exceedingly scarce and in the barren region immediately adjacent, forage could scarcely be found. A large portion of our army had passed over the same route and stripped the plantations of what little they possessed. Horses and mules were captured on sight and all the mounted men in Sherman's army were in that way kept supplied with new animals.

We moved to another historic place: Lynch's Creek. It was there that General Horry of Revolutionary times came near to losing his life. A herd of about two hundred cattle was with the Fifteenth, and as it was getting toward dark, it was too dangerous to cross the animals on the narrow bridge at night, so the regiment went into camp. My men were grumbling about the scarcity of food to more than an ordinary extent, and in my judgment, the nearness to them of this herd of beeves, in part accounted for their growling. I overheard their talk, but orders to the effect that not a single animal should be used were of the strictest kind, and punishment was threatened for even the slightest violation. After hearing their grumbling for awhile and knowing that the men were really hungry, the foragers having been unsuccessful for two days, I called Sergeant Franklin of Company K to my headquarters. During the conversation I informed him my orders that not a single animal should be butchered by the men, and if anything occurred I would probably get into a scrape. When I dismissed the Sergeant, I repeated that not a "single" animal should be killed, accenting the word "single" emphatically and frequently as he left me. The Sergeant took the hint and within a couple of hours three or four very large and fine steaks were received by my cook. After the Sergeant discovered the play upon the word "single" he hunted up the commissary sergeant of the regiment and in order to still obey the command the men killed "two" animals instead of a "single" one. They very quietly issued the two beeves to the hungry men of the regiment. Soldiers have a way of seemingly obeying orders even when they were in reality violating them and words sometimes have a double meaning to them.

The march through the Carolinas never brings up pleasant recollections, as do other campaigns and marches. General Wade Hampton was in full command of the enemy, which included in its make-up General Joe Wheeler's cavalry, who participated in the Spanish-American war. There were some infantry in General Hampton's command, but most of it consisted of mounted infantry and the regular Confederate cavalry. Sherman's army at this time was approaching Columbia, the capital of South Carolina. The country was low and flat. The river bottoms, and many of the creeks as well, were exceedingly wide. The continuous rains had made the currents of the streams swift. However, the army pushed ahead despite of all these drawbacks. The enemy did nothing more than to compel Sherman's troops to make new roads, and often to supply the streams with a better bridge than the one they had destroyed in order to impede the progress of the Federal army. Thus as the army neared Columbia it was presumed that the Confederates would make a stand to defend that city.

As a boy only eight years old, I had perused "Horry's Life of General Marion" so frequently that I knew its pages almost "by heart." As a consequence, I remembered much of the ground covered by the book referred to, and many of the scenes described by General Horry came fresh to my memory on visiting the region in person. Then, too, my grandfather, after serving his full time in "The Maryland Continental Line," as a body of the Revolutionary troops from that colony was designated, re-enlisted in the colonial service of South Carolina under General Francis Marion. He was along with "The Swamp Fox" on the occasion when General Marion surprised and captured over two hundred British and Tories and released nearly the same number of American prisoners.

As General Sherman's army was subsisting wholly on the country, the commissary train of wagons scarcely carried anything else than hard bread and an ample supply of coffee and sugar. In order to cover an ample region for foraging purposes Sherman spread the different corps of his army as widely apart as was possible. This was also necessary because the war was already in its fourth year and from the firing on Fort Sumter, the farmers and planters' crops yearly decreased in area for the reason that only the blacks were left to cultivate them. After the beginnings of the war the Confederate Congress passed what was known as "the tithing law". It provided that an eighth of all crops went to support the confederate army in the field. In the barns and out-houses planters and farmers had many sacks in bundles furnished by the Confederate government marked in plain letters "Tithing Sack", which were to be filled and sent to the Confederate commissary department at Richmond. I never knew the name or number of the crops of which the law demanded, but I saw sacks filled with wheat, corn and other farm products. What struck me as remarkable was that the Confederacy even demanded its share of peanuts. The peanut was even then a crop generally cultivated on a small scale, but since the war it has become a very important product.

I remember once entering a barn where my horses had been stabled during the night, and was astonished at seeing a couple of dozen large gunny bags of peanuts bearing the legal label, "Tithing Sack." That particular lot of sacks failed to reach Lee's army and was "gobbled up" by Sherman's omnipresent soldiers. I presume it matters but little at this late day whether the raiser of these peanuts got due credit for them or not. He should have done so, however, for he had shown his obedience to the law, rigid and hard on the agriculturist as it was, by setting aside the government sacks filled to the string with peanuts. He had done all in his power to comply with the law and to aid the Confederate commissary.

During all of the northward march of the Federal army, the Confederates could only guess what Sherman would do and were he would go next. General Hardee was in command of the city of Charleston and was still holding out against the Federal fleet. General Wade Hampton was at the head of the troops in General Sherman's front, and the ubiquitous General Joe S. Wheeler was engaged in flying hither and thither with his cavalry. The entire Confederate troops in that region were under the command of General Beauregard. Beauregard, it will be remembered, was the officer who was at the head of the confederate troops that fired on Fort Sumter. In his advance on Columbia, General Sherman had so covered the country that his opponents were kept guessing all the time as to the course he intended to pursue. In fact, Charleston was so seriously threatened that for a time the enemy concluded that town would be the objective point. Cooped up in Charleston, General Hardee was no doubt very anxious, for it was plain to see that with his communications entirely severed, he was in a dilemma of a very unpleasant nature. Hood's army had in effect been almost obliterated at the battle of Franklin and the subsequent defeat at Nashville, so no help could come to the Confederates from that direction. It was understood that the remnant of his army with which he had recrossed the Tennessee and afterwards placed under the command of General Dick Taylor, son of ex-President Zachary Taylor, had passed over the railroad at Branchville with a body of Hood's troops just before Sherman's army struck and destroyed all the railroads for many miles around. Such was the situation as General Sherman's army slowly but steadily crept up on South Carolina's capital.

On February fourteenth—St. Valentine's Day, though wholly unobserved except by the exchange of musketry firing on the skirmish line—the Fifteenth corps arrived at Sandy River, said to be fifteen miles from Columbia. It was about sundown and the troops were in camp when I heard a volley of musketry out in front and hastened out of my tent to direct assistance to the skirmish line. From every company of the regiment I could see the old veterans engaged in buckling on their cartridge boxes, and without a word of command from any officer were hastening out to the assistance of their comrades "on the double quick". I mounted my horse and followed. Very soon I heard the firing of the Union muskets. It seemed that two picket posts had been stationed quite close together. The officer who had stationed them there had only left them for a few moments when a detachment of about a hundred Confederate cavalry "rushed" these two posts. The enemy was leaving with the prisoners, when the veterans who had gone up to help so rapidly emptied several saddles, that the captors fled quickly and abandoned the prisoners. The pickets resumed their duties and were a little more prudent during the rest of the evening and the night.

As the division to which I was attached began to close up on Columbia, the Twelfth regiment was confronted with a Kentucky brigade. For nearly a full day the Twelfth, with Colonel Wood's entire brigade, was compelled to march in line of battle. This was a hard way to move. The ground marched over was covered with a pine forest most of the way, but the trees were scattered, and consequently there was no danger of a surprise since the enemy could be seen at all times. I remember that on one occasion a soldier of my regiment brought me a common envelope, which he had found sticking to a small tree at about the height of a man. It bore no address but on opening it, I discovered scrawled clear across a full page the words written with a lead pencil—"Beware the Kentucky Brigade". We had been pursuing the brigade from early morning until late in the afternoon when the note was handed to me, without being able to bring the Kentucky Brigade to a stand. The Federals had not as yet found anything to "beware of". A short time after receiving the words of caution the Kentuckians did make a stand at a stream called Congaree Creek. The stream, while not large, possessed extremely rugged and steep banks, mostly of a rock formation and hence fairly easily defended. The main line of the Federals immediately following the brigade came to a halt until the ground could be investigated. A regiment was sent up stream and another one down stream to investigate. It was not long until it was plain that the enemy in my own front showed signs of wavering. They had begun to fear that the two regiments, or at least one of them, might find a crossing. I saw that the members of the Kentucky brigade were becoming uneasy from this movement, and therefore, I obtained permission of Colonel Wood to push them at the bridge. At the bridge the enemy had two pieces of artillery. The battery fired two shots, one from each gun, but before they could reload, the company that had been directed to take the bridge, was over it. The battery retreated in order to save their pieces of artillery. The company had dashed across the bridge and saved it. As it was growing toward sundown, the corps went into camp with Congaree Creek in their possession.

After crossing the Congaree, the region was entirely free from trees and every other impediment that would tend to mar our movement. A brigade of Sherman's cavalry had arrived, and at the same time the enemy had sent out a large number of mounted men to reinforce the troops that had just been driven across Congaree Creek. These mounted men of both sides were in plain view of the troops that had crossed over the stream into a large open meadow. The enemy continued to advance towards the position of the infantry that had captured the bridge, which was now increased to three divisions of the Fifteenth corps. The divisions formed in the open space in "echelon", that is, one division behind the other, each division placed so that it could readily move forward and be formed on the one in advance, thus continuing and lengthening the line of battle on either desired flank. All this time the enemy seemed to be increasing in numbers, so it looked as if there was to be a fight worth seeing and all "in the open", too. It was a handsome sight to a soldier and well worth looking at.

Federal Cavalry had formed in position to flank the confederates the moment the infantry advanced to the attack. The Federal mounted men were secreted in the timber along the edge of the Congaree. The infantry moved forward by division to get within rifle range of the enemy, who seemed to be awaiting the attack. The sun was sinking to rest and its rays produced a beautiful effect as its declining rays burst on the bright muskets of the infantry. After the infantry had moved forward, perhaps a fourth of a mile, the Federal cavalry moved up and threatened what was the right flank of the enemy. On discovering this force of mounted men, the enemy waited no longer, but at once began to retire, slowly at first, but gathering momentum as the Federals came on. It soon became a trot, then a scramble, then perhaps a panic, for apparently they never stopped till they had crossed over and into the city of Columbia. The Fifteenth corps went into camp in that open meadow that night, but were annoyed all through the dark hours with a battery that continued to throw its shells into that wide open space, doing no special damage. During that steady shelling not a man, horse or mule was killed and only three of the soldiers were slightly wounded from the fragments of the exploding shells. I remember how exceedingly weary I was that night, for I scarcely lay down on my blankets ere I was sound asleep. The shells as they rolled past would arouse me at times, but want of sleep and rest would so overpower me that, before the screeching shells exploded, I would drop off to sleep again.

The enemy had crossed over to the Columbia side of the Congaree River and had destroyed the fine and costly bridge over that stream to prevent pursuit. They likewise destroyed the bridges over the Saluda and Broad Rivers, thus wholly giving up the region of country south and west of the city. Our pontoon train hastened to the point that had been selected for the crossing of the river so that the troops could capture the city. The pontoon train had to run the gauntlet of the battery that had played upon the troops all through the preceding night. The shells were poured into it as it passed in full sight of the gunners of the confederate battery. The train received no injury whatever. The teamsters put their teams on the run, and the train was only for a short time within reach of their guns while passing. A bridge of boats was thrown across the Saluda, the Broad and the Congaree Rivers.

The following morning the troops moved forward to the river, and two batteries were placed in position and opened on the city, producing great consternation among the citizens, but eliciting no reply. That evening, the Fifteenth corps leading the advance moved up to where the pontooniers had already succeeded in laying a bridge of boats across the Saluda. On the seventeenth of February, a detachment of skirmishers from the division to which the Twelfth belonged drove back a considerable number of mounted pickets and afterward were unopposed. Mayor Goodwin, accompanied by a number of prominent citizens, came out to meet the troops carrying a flag of truce and formally surrendered the city. This was in the forenoon, if I remember correctly. Colonel Stone's Iowa brigade moved forward as skirmishers with orders to cover all the streets with troops so as to prevent mob violence, and to uncover any ambuscades the enemy might be tempting to form. The remainder of the Fifteenth corps, with the Twelfth Indiana in the lead, with its splendid silver band playing "The Star Spangled Banner," and each regiment with its colors flying, made the triumphal entry into the city that had passed the first ordinance of secession taking South Carolina out of the Union.

After riding at the head of the column for about half a mile, I stopped to converse with General Charles R. Wood. When I turned to again ride in the front of my command, I discovered quite a number of citizens with new tin buckets and cups moving along with the head of the column and presumably giving the soldiers water. I dashed up to the front, and before I had quite reached the citizens the fumes of whisky fairly loaded the air. It did not take me long to stop that "unauthorized" issue of whisky, or to surprise a half dozen citizens who were scared "out of their boots." The issue of whisky ceased right there.

The Northern Indianian.

FLEMING T. LUSE . . . . EDITOR.

WARSAW . . . . . INDIANA.
THURSDAY, ... MAY 22d, 1862.

Interesting Ceremony.
From the Washington Republic.

At an early hour this morning, the Twelfth Indiana Regiment, which had enlisted for twelve months, and whose term has expired, marched to the mall in front of the White House, and were reviewed by the President previous to their return home. After marching into close column, they faced the steps where Mr. LINCOLN's tall form stood, amid a throng of officers, Congressmen and citizens. Colonel ——, the commander of the regiment, rode his horse to the front, and addressed the President as follows:—

"The Twelfth Indiana Regiment is about to return home, and it has come into the presence of the Commander-in-Chief of the Army and Navy to express their approval of the manner in which you have conducted the war for maintenance of the Government. They pray that Heaven's choicest blessing may rest upon your head, and assure you, upon their return home, of their continued support and devoted affection."

To this address the President replied, with much feeling as follows:—

"Soldiers of the Twelfth Indiana Regiment—It has not been customary heretofore, nor will it be hereafter, for me to say something to every regiment passing in review. It occurs too frequently for me to have speeches ready on all occasions. As you have paid such a mark of respect to the Chief Magistrate, it appears proper that I should say a word or two in reply.

"Your Colonel has thought fit, on his own account and in your name, to say that you are satisfied with the manner in which I have performed my part in the difficulties which have surrounded the nation. For your kind expression I am extremely grateful, but, on the other hand, I assure you that the nation is more indebted to you, and such as you, than to me. It is upon the brave hearts and strong arms of the people of the country that our reliance has been placed in support of free government and free institutions.

"For the part that you, and the brave army of which you are a part have, under Providence, performed in this great struggle, I tender more thanks—greatest thanks that can be possibly due—and especially to this regiment, which has been the subject of good report. The thanks of the nation will follow you, and may God's blessing rest upon you now and forever. I hope that upon your return to your homes you will find your friends and loved ones well and happy. I bid you farewell."

CHAPTER 16

Columbia Burns

The Union! The Union! The hope of the free!
Howesoe'er we may differ, in this we agree—
Our glorious banner no traitor shall mar,
By effacing a stripe, or destroying a star!
Disunion? No never! The Union forever!
And cursed be the hand that our country would sever.

It was a wild and windy day when we entered Columbia, as is seldom known. The wind came in ferocious gusts. There would be a space of calm then again a gale-force wind would break out, carrying away everything that was not fastened down. I am confident that a fire of some sort was in progress at or near the railroad depot as the columns marched down the street. The streets were comparatively free from people, although some people curiously watched from each side of the street, as the troops march by. The Fifteenth corps marched on clear through the city and took up its camp on the opposite side of the town in a very handsome location. Orders were strict that the troops should all remain in their respective camps. This was done because the enemy could command a very respectable army, and might make a dash on a corps or division that was somewhat isolated. The men also tended to keep close to camp because of the blustering, disagreeable weather, and the men were somewhat weary of the toilsome marches and were willing to enjoy a daytime rest.

Along in the evening just after the regiment had partaken of "hard tack" and coffee, I received an order to move my regiment down into the city to assist in quenching what was then thought to be rather an incipient fire. The order to move down was obeyed with the regiment's usual alacrity. Major Baldwin had been an old St. Louis and Fort Wayne fireman. I directed him to take charge of the men in this fight with that sort of an enemy. When the troops arrived in the city they found a large portion of the downtown portion ablaze. The city was provided with eleven old-fashioned hand-engines, and all of these were placed under Major Baldwin's direction and manned by the members of the Twelfth regiment. Never did men work more faithfully, and with the Major's experience I thought most successfully, too, for they succeeded in several instances, quenching the flames on the buildings at which they were at work. Their efforts to subdue the flames were fearfully handicapped by the exceedingly high wind. The wind carried pieces of burning boards and shingles and even small pieces of burning timbers that were fanned by the high winds, which started other buildings on fire. This occurred so frequently that the men of the Twelfth, towards midnight, were almost worn out with their ceaseless efforts.

The fire had steadily grown upon the men who were making such a heroic effort to stop the flames. Toward midnight the water in the cisterns gave out, and after that but little effort was made to struggle with the fire demon. Even before the water gave out, Major Baldwin informed me that several of the hoses of the working engines had holes cut in them, compelling the substitution of other lengths of hose if there was any to be had. The changing of the hoses required time that should have been given to the fire itself.

I directed the men, although they were almost worn out, to help the people in every possible way. This they did and continued all through that fearful night. I am going to give my own version of the way the Columbia fire was kept going after the flames burst forth, because the origin of the fire was much discussed following the end of the war. I have not a shadow of doubt that the fire originated from the burning cotton at the depot. Lighted tufts of the cotton were seen flying in the air as the Federal troops marched into the city. There was a large number of bales of cotton at the railroad depot that were near a supply of ammunition. These burning bales were scattered by the explosion of shells that caught fire. It was in this way, I feel sure, that the great fire originated.

There were quite a number of Federal prisoners confined in the suburbs of Columbia, who it was said, were fed on a quart of unsifted corn meal per day for over a year. Those who had not succumbed already to prison hardships and diet were released by the coming of Sherman's troops, and it goes without saying that many of these men were exceedingly revengeful. I saw a number of these recent prisoners during the fire prowling about the streets. I did not see them do any thing wrong. I am confidant it was these men who cut the hose of the engines that my men were operating. And it may have been these men who started the incipient fires that on such a windy night were soon flamed out of control. I talked to some of these men the next day, and while there is not proof that they either cut the hose or kept the fire going, I was then, and am still confident, that it was the revengeful ones among our own released prisoners who helped the fire along after it got started. There was, also, a tough gang of young bullies on the streets that night. These were residents of Columbia, and it is quite possible that much of the plunder they secured that night was secured by the light of fires kindled by their own hands. Several of this class was arrested. But as none of them were caught in the act, although some of them were gathered in near to fires that had just been kindled, but proof being lacking, they were discharged.

It was a fearful night to me and to all that witnessed the great fire and consequent destruction. Considerably over half the city was totally consumed, including all of the business portion and outside of this a large number of beautiful and costly residences. The women, of course, were wild with fright and many families fled in dismay from their homes with only such valuable articles as they could carry. It is simply out of the power of any one to depict the wild scene of that fire, and the desolation it produced. Loud crashes from the falling buildings were heard throughout the area and the light of the flames could have been seen for many miles away. A great many houses were saved by great exertion. I felt prouder than ever of the men I had the honor to command, when after it was hopeless to contend any longer with the fire, they turned their attention to helping the citizens, though they were enemies.

About the time the water gave out, I received an order to place my regiment on provost duty and to arrest every Federal soldier found on the streets after one o'clock. The various corps of Sherman's army had gone into camp around the city in the afternoon. When night came, hundreds of soldiers discovered the bright light of the fire that made everything as bright as day, they came into the town without orders or permission. Many of these men could not resist the temptation to imbibe "fire water" to so great an extent that they could scarcely navigate the streets as the night of gloom, disaster and destruction progressed. The order I received at about that hour was a difficult and unpleasant one to perform. The members of my own regiment had labored so unceasingly to stem the on-rushing tide of fire, that many of them were already exhausted when the unpleasant order was given, but every member of the Twelfth knew he had to obey. After some grumbling they took up the new duty and squads were sent out to patrol the streets. Precisely at the hour of one o'clock a number of companies started out on the duty. During the early part of the dreadful night, I had ridden past an enclosed piece of ground nearly a square in extent and as it was surrounded by a high board fence, I determined to use it as a guardhouse. I took possession of it at once, detailing a full company of the regiment to act as guards and to prevent egress for every man who was placed inside. I knew that there would be a good many men arrested under the order. I told the Captain and Lieutenant in command of the company to strictly obey the orders.

Very soon afterwards the company in charge became busy, and from then on until daybreak there was a steady stream of arrests, most of them in various stages of intoxication. As the daylight began to be seen, the streets were entirely cleared of stragglers and idlers, but what to do with the over four hundred that had been gathered in, I did not know. The majority of them had become sufficiently sober to feel the humiliation of arrest and begged me to turn them loose to go back to their respective commands. There were men of almost every rank from colonels down to corporals, and the private soldier, of course. I could easily perceive that no charges would be placed against any of them and there would be no court martials.

General Sherman and staff had taken possession of a large and handsome brick residence about a mile distant from the prison. I had visited the place in the earlier part of the long dreary night. There was a long flight of stone steps leading up to the front door of the residence. I concluded to march the men up to Sherman's headquarters for him to decide what should be done with them. Many of the arrested men had already begun to clamor for something to eat, and others for water. As I had no way to either feed or drink them and yet was very anxious to get rid of them, the plan to take them to Sherman was reached.

I marched the four hundred up to the front of the headquarters and the officers kept them in line till I could interview the General. After I had informed him of the situation, and the additional fact that the men were at that moment out in front, he went to the window and pulled back the curtain to view the men. I had already informed him that there were about four hundred of them and they were all anxious to return to their companies. The result was just as I had anticipated it would be. The General stepped out of the front door and from the height of the steps delivered a few scathing remarks over their unsoldierly conduct. He informed them that such a breach of discipline must never occur again. He then dismissed the whole party and ordered them to go at once to their respective commands. The crowd disbanded so quietly that I scarcely got an opportunity to speak to any of them, many of whom I knew. I returned to my headquarters where I received the order placing me in command of the provost duty of the city, and detailing the Twelfth regiment for guard duty with instructions for me to call on other regiments if more men were required.

I had not expected that the duties of my detail would prove so onerous as was the case. It was my duty to preserve order within the city limits, but I did not think the position should be one of acting as a mayor for the town also. I took up an office in a very convenient building that had escaped the conflagration, and strange to say it was in the business part of the town, most of which had been totally destroyed. Columbia was the place where all the Confederate money was printed as well as the cotton bonds that were so largely sold all over Europe. The bonds were backed up in some way by pledging the cotton crops of the South. Millions upon millions of dollars worth of Confederate money fell into the hands of the Federal army. It was not at all strange to come across private soldiers with their pockets full of Confederate notes ranging all the way from five dollars up to hundred-dollar bills, and some of them had a half-million on their persons. Many of these notes were just printed and still were unsigned, but there were many thousand of dollars that contained the official signature of the Secretary of the Treasury of The Confederate States of America. I, too, was well supplied with Confederate money to almost any amount that may suggest itself to the reader.

Nearly all of the forenoon, my time was taken up in receiving citizens of the town who had complaints of various kinds. Many of them asked that their homes be furnished with a guard. I treated all comers with politeness and kindness, though only in a few instances could I be of any special service in the face of a calamity of such huge dimensions. All at once while my office was crowded with visitors, two women, one a Negress and the other a rather handsome white woman, burst into the office, each one trying to be the first to speak. Their torn clothes showed very plainly that they had been pulling one another's hair on the outside. I judged, so for the reason that they had not been in my office for five minutes, when an altercation sprung up between them and they flew at one another as viciously as cats on the roof of a backyard. A soldier on duty in the office was compelled to use force to separate the two termagants. Peace having been restored, though many of my visitors had taken occasion to disappear, I proceeded to ascertain what the difficulty was. The Negress blurted out at the top of her voice that the white-trash woman owed her two hundred and fifty dollars—"in Confederate money," she added as a wind up. The white woman declared the "she-nigger-scrub" had stolen her silk dress when she left her house just before you Yankees come, and she had it in her hands now. The Negress called her a "liar" and another "set-to" would have occurred but for the soldier slipping between them. The Negress insisted that she didn't "steal nothin," nohow. The "white-trash woman" owed her that much money and she took de dress in part pay. "You did steal my dress and you know it! What is mo' I want it back and right off too." "Well, you kaant hev it! I'se got it and I'se gwoin' to keep hit!" Then another skirmish threatened and was prevented by the soldier on duty.

Having ascertained what the difficulty was, and thinking of the liberal amount of Confederate notes I had on my person, I asked the white woman what the dress was really worth. She replied by saying that it would easily bring two hundred-fifty in Confederate money. Then I asked the Negress if she would rather have two hundred-fifty in Confederate money than the dress? "No Suh I wouldn't," she snapped. "I'se got de dress now and she owed me dat much anyhow!" "But said I," you are taking the dress without the owner's consent as I perceive. Now, suppose you got three hundred in money, would you give the owner back a dress that is already hers?" "Oh cose I would for three hundred." "Well," said I, "give me the dress." She did so, and I counted her out three hundred dollars in the agreed upon money and handed the white woman the dress. A more grateful person I have seldom seen. As the Negress was leaving the room I called her back and laid an extra hundred dollars in her hand. Then, turning to the white woman, I presented her with a five hundred-dollar

Confederate note. I remarked to both of them as they were about to depart—"that's the way we Yankees deal justice, and prevent ill-feeling. Ain't you glad that the war is about over?" Both declared they were, and the incident was closed, both sides as happy as birds! In the streets that evening the story was repeatedly told as to how the Yankees "dealt out justice!"

Following the devastating fire, the once beautiful city presented a most heart-rending appearance. The business portion of the town was literally wiped off the face of the earth and many private residences were also destroyed. Little of the contents of the business houses were saved and in many of the beautiful private residences costly furniture, pianos with stools, it was said, made of solid silver, went up in the great conflagration, the silver stools melting down. The silver seeking the lowest level, of course, was picked up in fragments and in nuggets, just as soon as the foundations of the houses were cool enough for the curious to pick out the melted remnants. In fact, Columbia was the place where the wealthy Charleston people had sent much of their wealth, after the bombardment of their town began. There was much melted silver picked up in this way after the fire. To prove this it is only necessary for me to say that in evacuating the city, five or six days after the fire, my regiment bringing up the rear, we caught up with a soldier carrying a large tin bucket filled to the brim with melted scraps of silver, trudging along in the rear of the column. His hope to save it was that he might induce some teamster to carry it in his wagon for a share of the contents. I learned afterwards that he had to give this up as some of my men found the bucket and its precious contents abandoned at the side of the road, it being too heavy to carry.

The Fifteenth corps gave me a silver badge inscribed with, "The forty rounds in the cartridge box" that was made from the melted metal that had been picked out of the crevices of the sidewalk and the basement of a building that had once been a jewelry store. It was made in Washington City just after the Grand Review and presented to me by the officers of my regiment who had procured the silver from several of the soldiers who had carried it in their pockets and knapsacks. While on this subject I might add that from one of the Catholic churches a golden crucifix was taken that was said to weigh to the amount of seventeen thousand dollars, aside from the cost of making it. The theft was made known to Sherman, who, after the city was evacuated, halted the army and instituted a search. No one knew the halt was coming so that the thief could not have time to hide the image, but the perpetrators of the sacrilegious theft were never discovered.

Just previous to the breaking out of the war, South Carolina had been engaged in building a new, costly and spacious state house. The principal architect, I think, was an Englishman, and he was making his home in Columbia to supervise the construction of the building. The "bump of destruction" is very largely developed in the heads of some men, and the next day after the occupation of the city, I detected a soldier of this class engaged in knocking off the very beautiful carving of some of the capitals of the columns still on the ground. I severely reprimanded him for this wanton destruction, and in order to prevent any further diabolism of the kind, I established a guard over the building during the remainder of our stay. This so pleased the architect, who unknown to me, was standing by at the time, that he afterwards sought my acquaintance at my headquarters. He visited me every day and was profuse in his thanks for the course I had pursued in protecting the property. I found him to be a very pleasant gentleman and an agreeable companion.

I met another prominent man while in Columbia, a man who was well known in the North, William Gilmore Simms. He was a fine looking old gentleman with white hair and was a novelist of the time of Cooper. He founded his stories generally along the same line as the northern author. He contributed to Braham's Magazine and Godey's Lady's Book, prominent and widely read magazines in the later fifties and early sixties. On learning that I was a newspaperman at home, he, too, visited me every day. To me he admitted that the war was nearing its end, although he was sure that General Lee would fight till the last man was used up, or at least until it would be impossible to feed his army. He believed in the states' rights over and above government in all things. This belief was also supported by Governor Brown, as can be seen when he demanded that all Georgians serving with Lee should be sent home at once to defend their own state from Sherman's army. The majority of the Southern people believe implicitly in the proposition that the State was superior to the Nation, and that the allegiance of the people was first of all due to the State, then to the Nation.

But for the desolation cause by the great fire (and I insist upon the statement that the beginning of the vast conflagration could not be attributed to the Federal troops, for I was in a position to know, since I was at the head of the marching column and I saw that the depot building with their combustible contents were on fire as the Union troops marched down one of the principal streets leading to the central portion of he city) Sherman's army rather enjoyed the five or six days rest taken at that place. The citizens of the town did not lack for food, for all of them were fed by orders of General Sherman. The principal citizen of the town became somewhat alarmed over what might happen after the Federal forces abandoned Columbia. The people were concerned that the "tough element" of the city, mixed with the stragglers for the Confederate army might become unmanageable as soon as the town was evacuated by the Federals. Consequently, two to three hundred of the better class of citizens called on General Sherman in a body to talk with him on the subject, and for him to suggest some plan to prevent the lawless element from becoming a public danger. The subject was discussed in all of its phases.

Sherman proposed to issue to some one authorized by those present to receive them, three or four day's rations for all the citizens of the city, and at the same time to turn over to them three hundred muskets with an ample supply of ammunition. The citizens themselves could thus arrange for a body to act as a police corps, and would be placed in a condition to defend themselves and preserve order. The proposition was accepted. The muskets were given to an authorized person, and the rations were issued in a similar way, and stored in a convenient building. An armed guard was placed over the supplies before General Sherman withdrew his troops and proceeded on his way.

On the day the army withdrew from Columbia, I received an order for myself and regiment to remain until the very last of all the withdrawing troops, with a strict injunction for me to see that none of the stragglers of the army were left behind, as it would probably mean death to anyone who remained in the rear and fell into the hands of General Joe Wheeler's men or some of the vindictive citizens. On the strength of this order I sent a note to the commanding officer of every regiment and battery that had been camped within the limits of the city to see to it that when the withdrawal commenced all of the men were present. The beginning of the evacuation commenced at a fairly early hour in the forenoon of February 20, 1865, and continued until late in the afternoon, when my command bringing up the rear began to move.

I had taken all the precaution I could think of, for it was not only my duty to see that none of the Federal soldiers were left behind, but I had also to look out for an attack from the Confederate cavalry that was hovering near. The Twelfth regiment was formed in skirmish-line order—that is in single rank, and the men spread apart more or less widely as the conformation of the streets suggested. Each company was under the command of its Captain or the next officer in rank and each was assigned to a special street with orders to scan each side closely in search for stragglers. A detail of seventy-five or a hundred men was in reserve under my command. In this way we marched out of the city of Columbia in splendid order, and one and all scanning both sides of the street. Quite a number of men were picked up on the march, some from regiments that had been on the march for three or four hours. All of these were arrested and brought to me, where they were placed with the reserve force and an eye kept on them to prevent them from slipping away. Nothing serious occurred, and in departing, the rear guard of the army was not attacked, nor as far as I knew, did it leave a single man of Sherman's army behind.

I remember that on the street on which I passed out of Columbia was the very handsome home of General Wade Hampton. It was not only beautiful, but was a stately edifice occupying the center of a large, beautifully-sodded and well-kept lawn. Marble statues were interspersed among the trees and a wide stone pavement lead from the street up to the main entrance under a wide and very comfortable porch. In obedience to orders, an officer and four men had been guarding the property during the occupation of the city. These now joined my command in leaving the city. The officer guarding the house said to me: "Colonel, there are some works of art in the basement of the mansion that are worth seeing, and if you desire to do so I will show them to you. I have the run of the rear door to the basement." I jumped off my horse and went along with him. On entering the very large room, I was not only surprised but at first a little shocked, for my first impression was that I was in the presence of the dead. Sitting on tressels were six statues sculptured from the finest of Italian marble. They were so life-like in the face as to cause the shock referred to. They had been imported previous to the start of the war and were still enclosed in the original packing boards with only the coffin-like lid taken off and the faces of each were showing. They were about ten feet tall and very beautiful. General Hampton had purchased them to add to those on his lawn, but the war had interfered. The war checked many projects and ended many more for good.

I referred earlier to the oceans of Confederate money that fell into the hands of the Union soldiers on the taking of Columbia. Everybody had "stacks" of it, and on several occasions I saw the men use it to light their pipes or cigars. When the town was taken, a very large Palmetto flag floated from the top of what may be denominated "the treasury building," for it was from this edifice that Confederate money came. Having a peculiar look, distinct from the Confederate flag adopted by the Confederate congress following the beginning of the war, the flag especially attracted my attention. I sent Marsh Parks with a file of soldiers to take it down, and if possible to procure a garrison flag representing the "Stars and Stripes" to put in its place. The Palmetto flag was taken down but Parks was unable to find any other but a regimental flag, and this would not have been permissible to fly, so the building went without a flag during our stay. The large Palmetto flag was sent to Governor Morton at Indianapolis, and some years ago was still in the flag-room of the State House, where the tattered regimental flags of Indiana's regiments were stored.

That portion of the army that did not occupy Columbia had not been idle during the few days stay there. The work of destruction of railroads went on continually, east, west, and north. The left wing had been employed in rendering impassable the line of the Charleston and South Carolina Railroad. The Seventeenth corps had torn up many miles of what was known as the Greenville railroad. And the Fifteenth corps, whose troops had occupied Columbia, took good care to render impassable for many months the Columbia branch of the South Carolina road, including its passage through the city. While engaged in destroying the arsenal and removing the shells it contained, a terrible accident occurred by the carelessly handled shells. The accident shook all the remaining buildings in the city and some of the citizens were almost panic-stricken. The result was a Captain and a number of enlisted men were killed. Accidents of that kind were exceedingly few, yet they always caused a feeling of sadness to the survivors. A soldier takes his chance in losing his life in the roar and crash of battle, and anticipates death in that way, but he never counts on being killed by accident. Soldiers feelings are always more depressed when death comes to a comrade by the carelessness or negligence of others.

CHAPTER 17

Raid on Florence, South Carolina

"Forward was the word when day
Dawned upon the armed array.
"Fallen?" was the word when night
Closed upon the field of fight.
"Hurt, my boy?" "O, no! Not much!
Only got a little touch!"
"Wonder what the folks will say
When they hear the news today!"
—H. H. Vanmeter

None of the troops knew where they were going when they left Columbia nor did they care much. The right wing, of which the Fifteenth corps formed a part, moved directly northward from the South Carolina capital, and two days after leaving Columbia the Catawba River was reached. The left wing advanced as far north as Winsboro, where all of the army turned directly to the eastward. Guesses as to where the troops were going were numerous, but this last move led the troops to believe that the destination would be Wilmington or the coast. Heavy rains fell and the army was delayed for some time in effecting the crossing of streams.

General Joe E. Johnston, Sherman's old antagonist during the Atlanta campaign, had been placed in command of the Confederate forces that could in every conceivable way be collected to oppose the march of Sherman's army. He must have known he was playing a losing game on war's chessboard, yet it must have been some satisfaction to him to have President Jeff Davis appeal to him to take command of an army from which he had been displaced by General Hood in the preceding year.

The Seventeenth corps had moved rapidly forward and captured a town called Cheraw located on the Great Pedee River. Seventeen pieces of artillery had been abandoned by the enemy and fell into the hands of our troops. A short time after the capture of Cheraw, the Fifteenth corps reached the town. When the troops had gone into camp, I received an order from General Logan to take command of a body of cavalry and mounted infantry to make a raid on Florence, South Carolina. At Florence was one of the Confederate prison camps where several thousand Federals were confined. The written order directed me to be ready to start at eight o'clock on the following morning. As I had never had any thing to do with any other arm of the service save the infantry, I felt some reluctance in taking command of a body of mounted men. I went to my blankets earlier than usual in order to have a good night's sleep.

General Logan in person had informed me that, after reaching a village by the name of Society Hills, my command would consist of fifteen hundred mounted men. The village referred to had before the war been a very aristocratic place. The Twenty-seventh Missouri mounted infantry was nearby, and it was the intention for me to move with that body to Society Hills where the Seventh and Ninth Illinois cavalry were encamped. They had received orders through their commanding officer to place themselves under my orders for the purpose of making the raid. My orders also instructed me to pick up on the way to Society Hills all the mounted foragers I met. I gathered in many of these men, among whom I recall Jesse Perky was from Warsaw. He was the only man in the entire command that I knew; the rest were complete strangers. About eight o'clock on the morning of March 5, 1865, the troops were mustered for the move. General Logan came over from his headquarters to see the start made. The real object of the raid was the release of the Federal prisoners that were confined at Florence, South Carolina. Florence was estimated to be eighty miles distant, and my orders were to make all possible speed and to destroy on the way down all kinds of supplies that could be used by the Confederate armies, and to burn all the trestlework of the railroad that lay along the route of the march.

I found myself in a dilemma just as soon as I reached Society Hills, as my entire force consisted of just five hundred forty-six officers and men, including the foragers, instead of the thousand I had expected. I ascertained that the cavalry had been there for only a short time and, after feeding their horses, had gone in what was supposed to be the direction of the main Federal army. I hardly knew what course to pursue. I was a thousand men short of what the command was to be, as only a third of the fifteen hundred were present. I knew my own superior officers regarded the raid as an important one. As I rode past General Howard's headquarters, a few moments after the command began its move, he suggested to me to keep a close watch, for a message had just reached him that a force of the enemy consisting of mounted men and infantry were moving in the direction of Darlington. The disappointment in not finding the larger part of the force intended to make the raid on the prison-pens at Florence to me was great. I very much disliked returning without having accomplished any results, and I therefore resolved to make a reconnaissance in the direction of Darlington at any rate.

After coming to this determination I directed the troops to first feed their horses and themselves, as I intended to move in the direction of Darlington, and if a large force of Confederates was encountered to return to the main army. I counted on the demoralization of the Confederate troops due to their severe losses in recent days, to aid me in the raid. I was certain that if I fell upon the rear of a force of Confederate troops that they would in all probability conclude that it was the advance guard of Sherman's army proceeding to Charleston.

During the resting spell at Society Hills, I stopped at a very pleasant modern house in the suburbs of the little village. On entering the cottage I asked the very handsome middle-aged lady, who seemed to be the head of the family, whether she could supply the means for our cook to get us a dinner, adding that he had all the supplies he needed; all that was desired was a room. Very politely she replied by saying that everything at hand was at our disposal. So our cook was soon installed in the kitchen. My staff and I occupied the parlor, and I spent my time in looking over a large supply of pictures, autographs and books that lay on the center table. In examining a very handsomely bound specimen, I noticed that it was a gift to the lady of the house. The gift was dated at Florence, Italy. When the lady reappeared in the parlor I spoke to her about the book and its date. She at once replied by saying that her husband, during the administration of President Buchanan, had represented the United States in Italy. I found her to be one of the most intelligent ladies I had met in the South during the war. She said that her husband, then an officer in Lee's army, and from who she had not heard in a long time, returned with his family from Italy soon after the firing on Fort Sumter. They had reached the city of Charleston just before the blockade became rigid and dangerous for men who were as pronounced in his loyalty to the Southern cause as he was. I thought I detected a tone of regret all through her conversation as she lamented the war, its hardships, and especially the sundering of the ties that had so pleasantly bound friends previous to the attempt to make two nations out of one.

Dinner being over, I asked the lady what her charges were. She was almost offended to think that I thought she would charge anything, and replied by saying that I owed her nothing whatever, but afterwards added that if I felt like giving the servants anything I might do so, but that I and my friends were very welcome to what little service she had rendered. I called up all of the colored people, I think there were six of them in the house, and handed them five hundred dollars a piece. They were overjoyed and I could see that the lady of the house also was delighted. Before leaving the pleasant home and the kindly lady, I had my cook slip her a pound of coffee, and as he had no paper to put it into, he poured it into a large bowl and handed it to her. Tears came to her eyes.

After we had started and gone a quarter of a mile, a soldier of our own rode past, dangling before him a lady's very handsome gold watch and chain. Knowing that he must have captured it, and having seen such a one hanging on a nail in the parlor of the house where we had taken dinner, I at once took it from him. On ascertaining the facts, I put an officer in charge of the soldier to take him back to the house. The soldier was to give the watch back to the lady and to see that it again hung on the identical nail from which it was stolen, and to see that the young man did it with his own hands.

Following the brief stay at Society Hills the little command of five hundred forty-six, actual count, started about two in the afternoon for Darlington. The little band had not proceeded more than a couple of miles when the Captain from the advance guard, of about twenty men of the Twenty-seventh Missouri Mounted Infantry, sent word to me that he had come up to the rear guard of quite a force of the enemy. I rode rapidly forward with the man who had brought the information to see for myself the situation. The captain of the advance guard informed me that he was confident that there was infantry in the lead of the body of cavalry, judging by the tracks made by the soldiers' feet. These tracks were quite plain, even though they had been partially defaced by the feet of the horses that were acting as the rear guard of the enemy. If there was infantry in the Confederate party it was all the more necessary for me to observe greater caution. I remained with the advance guard until an open scope of country was reached that gave a view of the road the enemy was traveling for perhaps a couple of miles. Sure enough, a body of infantry could be plainly seen. The captain of the advance guard was certain that the enemy was aware of the pursuit. Although he had prevented his men from firing at the time when he first discovered the rear of the enemy, he was confident that they had been discovered from the accelerated speed the enemy adopted.

A short time afterwards the troops came to quite an extensive plantation, where a number of Negroes showed themselves in the large lawn that led up to the mansion. I had ordered the head of the column to halt so I could interrogate the colored people. They all said the enemy force was three times the size of my own. I also ascertained that the passing troops were firm in the belief that Sherman's army was coming by that road on its way to Charleston. I felt this belief would aid me greatly. After leaving the plantation I directed the Captain of the advance guard to push the enemy to a small extent as soon as he caught up with them. He was to endeavor to ascertain how large the force was and to do everything in his power to substantiate the belief of the enemy that the advance of General Sherman was really on the way to Charleston via Darlington and Florence. The advance frequently came in touch with the rear of the retreating enemy and finally shortly before dark they captured two prisoners. They were "pumped" of everything they knew. The troops camped at another large plantation so I could enter Darlington by daylight. I paroled the two prisoners, feeling sure that they would follow the retreating troops into Darlington and there repeat the fact that my force was the advance guard of Sherman's whole army going to Charleston.

The place where I stopped for the night was a beautiful plantation and was in better condition that any other I had seen for weeks. We were then in a region entirely free from the footsteps of marching armies of either side. No destruction of any kind whatever could be discovered. Every rail of the fences was in place as far the eye could reach, the scene was most peaceful. I placed the soldiers in camp, using the ten-acre lawn in front of he mansion for their resting ground. My self and limited staff took up quarters in the house after a proper guard had been established with the strictest orders to be watchful and careful. At this period of the war the men had learned to be vigilant on their own account, and it was easy for them to understand that watchfulness was a necessity. There must have been a hundred colored people on the place, all of them under a fearful state of excitement. The lady of the house had pointed out every old darkey who would be the one for me to see for anything I wanted. I called him to me and he informed me that there was not a white man on the plantation. I asked him if he could serve a good supper if I would furnish the bread and coffee? "Oh co'se we kin, massa. And it you'nms has got coffee hits sumthin' mo' dan we'se had for two year or mo'." I told him to get the "Old Mammie" to cook. I told him we would like to have fried chicken and either a few slices of ham or bacon. "Yes, sah," he said, "you shall have bofe, and chicken, too." And sue enough, within an hour myself and staff sat down to the best meal I had ever ate in the South during the wartime.

We gathered a good deal of information at this plantation. It was only four miles from Darlington, and I ascertained that the force we were pursuing was composed of a brigade of infantry and a regiment of cavalry. They were fleeing from Sherman's army and intended to push on through to Florence during the night. My orders were to destroy everything that could be used in sustaining the Confederate army, cotton, food of all kinds, roads and bridges, and this was done on the way. I asked General Logan why this might not be better done coming back? He replied by saying: "Colonel Williams there may be such a thing occur that you might not have time to do so on the return trip!" Already the troops assigned to the work had destroyed a few short trestles over ravines and had burned them down. They came to one that had just been built with new and green pine timber that would not burn. A detail was sent out to the cabins and farmhouses and all the axes were brought in and the men chopped it down.

At early daylight the bugle sounded and the command had breakfast. With my small force, I felt as though I was taking a very great risk in going forward where I was sure to meet an hourly increasing force of the enemy. I finally decided to go to Darlington at any rate, and there decide whether I would proceed the other ten miles to Florence or not. Following breakfast, I called the old man who had acted as the overseer to me and as I was still loaded with Confederate money, I gave him a thousand dollars to give to his mistress. I also gave him a half dozen five hundred bills to hand around to the colored people who had helped him to provide for us, and particularly to particularly to give the "Old Mammie" one of these bills. Then, in the way of a jest, I said to him: "Old man, you have been so kind to us that I guess I won't burn the house." The old man had spent every one of his sixty-five years on the plantation, and he replied: "Lawd God, massa, if you wants to buhn de old place down, don't stop on my account, "kase I don't keer!"

We left this plantation at an early hour and in the suburbs of Darlington, the command was halted to receive a delegation of citizens with the mayor and town council at the head. They had come to surrender the town. The mayor informed me that he had been chosen for the purpose and inquired for the head officer. A soldier pointed me out to him and he came forward and surrendered the town to me. I told him that Sherman's army was following—which was hardly true, for it was seventy miles distant and marching the other way—but I was solicitous to have all the people along the road to believe that my force was only the advance guard. And I told the mayor that I would have to destroy all supplies that could be used or was owned by the Confederate authorities. I expected to remain in Darlington but a short time. Proceeding to the central part of the town I was informed that there were about two hundred forty bales of cotton stored near the depot, a warehouse full of hams, shoulders, and side meat, and I directed that all of these should be destroyed under my orders. There was a very vicious Confederate newspaper in town and that office was also destroyed so that it could not sow any more seeds of discord against the Federal government. The troops moved forward to Florence and the prison pens.

Within a couple of miles of Florence the advance guard came suddenly came upon a couple of companies of Confederate troops. Their arms were stacked in the lawn of a very comfortable farmhouse. Word was sent to me, and taking about twenty-five men, I went forward. I saw that by letting down a fence, the Federal troops could, with a quick dash, get between the men and their stacked muskets. This was quickly done, and we had taken the two companies prisoners before they even knew there were any "Yankees" in the vicinity. From these prisoners we learned that Wilmington on the coast had been captured and that there was a portion of the Confederate troops that had escaped. They were so weary and worn out that it was scarcely necessary to place a guard over them. Consequently, I had an officer parole them on the spot, as I needed all my men for other use.

The prison-pens were some distance south of Florence, and the troops moved forward with all possible speed. In doing so, a number of Confederate soldiers were captured who informed us that on the morning of March 5th the Federal prisoners had been removed to Millen, Georgia.

And this proved to be a fact. In approaching the prison pens, however, the Confederates put up quite a fight, but as soon as I found that the prisoners had been removed, I withdrew my force. I had to go back through the town of Florence, where a force of Confederates were assembled in a much greater number than my own. We drove them into a big depot building which I had intended to burn, but before the torch could be lighted, an orderly came dashing up to me from the rear guard with a written note from his officer saying a big force of Confederates were disembarking from a train of cars! This would place my command between two fires and so I determined to fall back to Darlington. In making the rush on the prison pens, quite a number of Federal soldiers, half-starved, and some of them actually insane were picked up by the retreating soldiers. These men had escaped or wandered off into the nearby woods when the prisoners were being removed two days before. They were cared for, and the extra mules that had been captured were given to them to ride.

I was well aware that if we escaped from the large force of the enemy that now confronted us, it would be as a result of the belief that the main Federal army was not far away. However, we soon arrived at Darlington on our return, where I had determined to halt, so that the men could rest and the horses and mules could be fed. I was just getting up from my coffee when an orderly rode up with information that the enemy was forming in the outskirts of the town. The orderly had hardly gone before another came from the opposite direction with a similar report. Mounting my horse I rode out a short distance and sure enough the Confederates were forming clear around to the east and south sides of the town. "Boots and Saddles" were sounded and my command was at once mustered to continue the retreat.

In going to Florence, I had noticed that we crossed a deep and sluggish stream not far from where we had camped the night before. If I could make that stream and cross over, I could destroy the bridge and be comparatively safe. This plan was fully accomplished and the troops were so worn out that I let them rest. They were just getting comfortable when a picket-post sent word that the enemy was crossing the stream below the destroyed bridge. Word of the same kind soon came from up stream. It was out of the question for my small force to withstand the much larger force of the enemy. Very reluctantly I issued the order for the march to be resumed. A small squad of my command, that had been sent to destroy some railroad trestles, rejoined the command. I was relieved, for I thought they had been captured. It was considerably after dark when the troops resumed their return march, and it was not long until it was discovered that we were followed by a large force of the enemy. There was nothing left for us to do except to continue the march. At about three o'clock in the morning we reached a point where there was a flouring mill. The road crossed the stream on a bridge on top of the dam. Here I determined that the men must have a short rest and after seeing that every one of the command had passed over, I directed that the bridge should be destroyed. On the opposite side there was a cluster of houses and the soldiers occupied these for a few hours rest. I felt certain that the enemy could not easily cross the stream and felt quite secure.

At sunup an explosion that rattled the glass in the windows of the house occupied by myself and staff routed me out of my blankets. I felt sure that the enemy had attacked us with artillery, but this was not so. The enemy had followed us all of the way, but as we left early in the morning, it was my impression that they gave up the pursuit at that point, as we neither saw nor heard the enemy any more. The backward trip continued until late in the evening. The men and horses were totally worn out for they: had doubled eighty miles; fought a battle of four hours duration; had destroyed a depot of supplies at Darlington and Dove stations; burned and chopped down five hundred yards of rail road trestlework; burned over five hundred bales of cotton, fifteen cars and a warehouse filled with hams and bacon; brought back thirteen of our released prisoners and captured forty-five of the enemy. As I passed General O. O. Howard's headquarters he came out to the road and warmly welcomed us back. He said, "You had not been gone over a couple of hours before we learned that the cavalry that was to await your coming at Society Hills was not there, and that there was a force of four thousand Confederates directly south of your designated place of meeting. To tell the truth I never expected to hear from you or your small force, except as prisoners of war. I feel greatly relieved over your safe return." He was paying this compliment to the men, many of whom were sitting on their horses fast asleep.

After I had returned to my own regiment, the story of the explosion that aroused my small body of mounted men from their sleep while on the raid to Florence was told. As you will recall the windows in the building where we slept rattled so loudly and the shock was so great that I thought our pursers had brought up some artillery and had opened on the little town. The men declared that the explosion seemed to come from some distant place and pointed out that no injury had come to any of us, nor had there been a solid shot or shell thrown into the village. The men of my regiment related the story of the explosion, for they had been in the immediate vicinity and felt the force of the catastrophe, which had been a puzzle to my small command. It seemed, that on taking possession of Cheraw the troops that first reached the town captured a large amount of the munitions of war, which the enemy had abandoned. There were a few siege guns among the number of pieces of smaller artillery that fell into the Federals hands. Seven tons of powder had been shipped to Cheraw from Charleston previous to the fall of that city.

All the artillery, cartridges and loose powder was taken possession of by one of the ordnance officers who directed it destroyed for fear of some accident. Although the Pedee River flowed right past the town and the seven tons of powder could have been dumped into the stream, very thoughtlessly the entire quantity was thrown into a ravine in the suburbs. No notice had been given to the troops that were constantly arriving at Cheraw, and some of them went into camp, including the Twelfth, near this powder. The following morning while the men were cooking some of them found several pieces of this large-grained powder. This combustible material was quite thickly strewn by the ravine, but only scattered pieces were found where the men camped. Some of these were recklessly thrown into the mess-fires, doing no more harm than to blow the ashes about and scatter the coals and sticks.

It was never fully ascertained how the fire reached the great pile of powder at the bottom of the ravine where it had been so carelessly, thoughtlessly and almost criminally cast. The general conclusion was that, in playing with this very dangerous commodity in singled grains, it finally ignited the portion more thickly strewn and then reached the main body of explosive material. The deafening and powerful explosion that followed the instant ignition of seven tons of siege-gun powder was what myself and troops had heard on the morning of the preceding day, twenty-seven miles away. The explosion was a fearful thing. The bank of the ravine was quite steep on the side where the troops were camped and low on the other side. The steep walls of the bank no doubt saved many lives. The force of the explosion swept everything away on the low side. Several houses were moved several feet off their foundations. The air was filled with boards and splinters, and chimneys rolled off the roofs. Several building were totally destroyed by the fearful shock. Forty persons among the troops nearest to the ravine were killed and wounded. Twenty-one buildings were utterly destroyed and more than double that number was seriously damaged.

An investigation took place at once and was in progress at the time I reached my regiment. The way in which the fire was caused will be one of those secrets that, like the destruction of the Maine in the harbor of Havana, will never be truly know. The officer in charge of the disposition of the powder was placed under arrest, but nothing ever came of it to my knowledge.

Card 1

W | 12 | Ind.

Reuben Williams

Rank Col., 12 Reg't Indiana Infantry.

Appears on

Field and Staff Muster Roll

for May & June, 1864

Present or absent __Present__

Stoppage, $_____ 100 for _____

Due Gov't, $_____ 100 for _____

Valuation of horse, $_____ 100

Valuation of horse equipments, $_____ 100

Remarks: Commanding 1st Brig. 4th Div. 15 A.C.

Card 2

W | 12 | Ind.

Reub Williams

Rank Col., 12 Reg't Indiana Infantry.

Appears on

Field and Staff Muster Roll

for July & Aug., 1864

Present or absent __Present__

Stoppage, $_____ 100 for _____

Due Gov't, $_____ 100 for _____

Valuation of horse, $_____ 100

Valuation of horse equipments, $_____ 100

Remarks: Relieved from command 1 Brigade 4th Divis. 15th A.C. 3" August 1864.

Card 3

W | 12 | Ind.

Reuben Williams

Colonel, 12" Indiana Vols.

Appears on

General Order

No. 133, dated War Department, Adjutant General's Office, Aug 21, 1865.

Appointed to be

Brigadier General

BY BREVET

in the Volunteer Force, Army of the United States, for meritorious services during the war.

To date from March 13, 1865.

J. Cary
Copyist.

CHAPTER 18

March to Raleigh, North Carolina

This they have done for us, who slumber here—
    Awake, alive, though now so dumbly sleeping;
Spreading the board, but tasting not its cheer;
      Sowing, but never reaping;
          Building, but never sitting in the shade
          Of the strong mansion they have made:
Speaking their word of life with mighty tongue,
    But hearing not the echo, million-voiced
    Of brothers who rejoiced,
From all our rivers, vales and mountains flung.
    So take them, heroes of the songful past!
        Open your ranks, let every shining troop
        Its phantom banners droop,
    To hail earth's noblest martyrs, and her last.
       To take them, O Fatherland!
Who, dying conquered in Thy name;
    And, with a grateful hand,
Inscribe their deeds who took away Thy blame
Give, for their grandest all, Thine insufficient fame!
    Take them, O God! Our brave,
       The glad fulfillers of Thy dread decree;
    Who grasped the sword for peace and smote to save,
      And, dying here for freedom, died for Thee!
                    —Bayard Taylor

On the seventh of March the forward movement of the army was again resumed amid a dreary steadily falling rain. We reached Laurel Hill, North Carolina in the evening. The delay that had occurred at Cheraw had been caused by the lying of pontoon bridge across the Pedee. It is astonishing how quickly a pontoon bridge can be constructed. The pontoon train consists of a large number of boats allowed troops, artillery, teams, etc., to cross even fast running rivers. Often the pontoon corps built a bridge too quickly, for the weary, tired soldiers who would have enjoyed a longer rest. Very often when a stream was to be crossed, I would ride to the point selected and spend an hour or two in watching them with the deepest admiration for the speed at which the pontooniers performed their work.

As we entered North Carolina, the weather gave us no welcome. The rain had made the roads almost impassable. Very often I have sat on my horse watching the passage of a six-gun battery, and perceived that, while the ground would hold up the first gun carriage fairly well, the second one would cut deeper into the softened ground and then the third on would reach to a depth that the wheels in revolving would bring up a thin mortar, and the fourth one would reach the hub making it necessary to corduroy the road. The fourth gun would have to be lifted up until rails and poles could be placed underneath it. The last two guns had to wait until the pioneer corps could corduroy the road for passage. This was about the general run for a battery of artillery. For considerably more than seventy-five miles corduroy was built after leaving Columbia. All the rails on each side of the road were used for that purpose to the last splinter, but as it was a thinly settled region, there was always an insufficiency of these. The pioneer corps would then cut down pine trees of eight and ten inches in diameter split them in half and lay them down with the round sides up. Over three-fourths of those seventy-five miles were laid with split pine trees. The labor necessary for the passage of an army through such a country laid with the corduroy road was tremendous. In a earlier stage of the war all this labor would have to be done in the presence of the enemy, and the ax would frequently have to be laid down to take up the gun.

 This country was very thinly settled with a very quaint and peculiar people. It fell on my regiment to bring up the rear and on this particular day and night the "front" was probably thirty miles ahead with perhaps two hundred stalled wagons and batteries between the head of the army and its rear. The neighbors had come from perhaps ten miles around to see the sight of a passing army. The slow hours dragged along, and toward suppertime I asked the lady of the house where I was waiting for the march to resume, if she could get us some supper if I would furnish the food. The reply was in the affirmative and I had my own cook bring in a ham, two boiled chickens, crackers and coffee. The supper the woman prepared was fine indeed.

 As evening came on nearly all of her neighbors departed, promising to be back in the morning "meebe," so that by the time the supper was over only those who belonged at the dwelling were left. The trains must have been badly stuck at the front, I thought, for it was now approaching midnight and not an order or even a sign of movement in sight. My own command arranged themselves as best they could, and all that could do so in the unceasing drizzle dropped off to sleep. At about five o'clock in the morning there were some signs of life ahead and I hurried the breakfast, as I expected to be directed to move up in a short time. The woman at the head of the house did everything she could in helping to get breakfast. Just as the "mess" was ready to sit down, the order came to move up and to keep a close watch of the rear, as a couple of companies of Confederate cavalry was reported hanging about the rear of the moving army.

This news put new life into all of the officers and men, as they were anxious to be "on the go." The ambulance was loaded up with my headquarters "mess things, " and as I got on my horse and gave the command to march, I saw the old lady standing by me. I suspected that she probably did not have a bite of food left in the house, so I asked her if such was the case. With tears in her eyes she told me that everything eatable was gone, and she added what she ate with me last night was the first mouthful of food she had tasted for thirty hours. I called the cook, told him to give her the two hams that were yet remaining, all the chickens and whatever crackers the ambulance contained. When the cook piled the food out on the floor of the porch the woman said: "You hain't goin' to give all this to me, be ye?" "Every bit of it," I replied, "and I only wish it were more." At the words she dropped down on her knees and thanked me and then prayed to the good Lord to preserve my life, adding the hope that I might safely reach my home. The prayer was awkwardly worded, but every sentence came from her heart. Many of the soldiers were standing around and heard every word of it, and some of them took off their caps while the woman prayed.

The story of this North Carolina old lady did not end here. The woman was so impressed with my liberality towards her, that before leaving she requested me to write down my name and address on the flyleaf of a book she brought to me. I did so, using pencil, for the troops were just ready to start. Within three years after the war was over, I was surprised to receive a note from the husband of the woman of whom I have been speaking. Briefly, the bereaved husband announced that about a month previous his wife had died. After the war was over he had heard her speak of "Colonel Williams again and again, telling about your generosity in leaving her a sufficient amount of food to last her and her little family till more could be procured. She had done this so often and had so frequently pointed to your name and address in a book she kept that I have thought it more than right for me to tell you of her death. She many times told the story of the three days passing of the Federal army in early 1865, always ending up in relating to visiting neighbors and friend how that Yankee officer gave her all he had himself." He closed his missive with the remark that she was a good wife and mother. He ended by excusing himself for writing to me.

I answered the letter at once, and I related the incident only to show a feature of human nature that was not thought to exist between the two sections of the country, and yet one that was entertained in the breasts of many people, and that was gladness that the war was over. In the minds of many, both North and South, that it never should have been begun. The last point, however, was taken out the hands of the people to such an extent that nothing but a war could ever have settled that question. The war might have been stayed for awhile, but it could only have been done for a short time, and hence it is well that it is over. Now the two warring sections are becoming more and more friendly as the years rollaway, and as they recede, a more closely united nation than it ever was before the war will be the result if the people will only keep the demagogue from becoming the originator of mischief.

From the hour the army left Columbia, South Carolina, each of the various corps were followed by hundred of refugees consisting of both white and black people. Columbia has been a sort of gathering place for such whites as had escaped army service through the various means employed; lameness of limbs, invalidism, inability to hear—generally put; on loss of teeth, this disqualifying the person from biting a cartridge; loss of the forefinger on the right hand, this preventing the owner of such a hand from giving his service to his nation because he could not pull a trigger. The same kind of excuses were numerous up here in the North on the eve of every draft. Many escaped becoming soldiers by all these excuses. In the Confederacy they were cut down to a minimum, and hence this class were fewer than with us at home. All this kind, however were among the refugees, follow the army northward. Indeed, I found a squad of about twenty Spaniards, consisting of both men and women, provided with all sorts of vehicles, from a good old-fashioned family carriage, all the way down to a two-wheeled "gig" in use in the rear of the Fifteenth corps. The greatest body of camp followers was on foot. It seemed to us on the march that but few people of either color had remained at Columbia.

On this march I saw the first white slaves that I had ever come across till that time after the war begun. In fact, I saw this same family of white slaves while the army occupied Columbia, and afterwards came across them frequently on the march. They were so white that no one could believe that there was a trace of Negro blood in their veins. They were even redheaded and freckled faced, and when one of their number told me in Columbia that they were slaves I could not believe him, yet such was the fact. It was certainly a motley crowd that followed the triumphant Sherman northward. All these camp followers trudged through mud that was axle deep to wagons, unless the roads were corduroyed, and even the unevenness of the corduroying made them so rough that the jolting sometimes ended the career of a number of these vehicles.

The Fourteenth corps had the credit of the Federal army to first enter Fayetteville, North Carolina and as a body it is entitled to it as well, but in reality it was captured by the foragers of the army bringing themselves together from each of the corps. Foraging parties were usually made up of a detail of about two men from each company of a regiment, and each regimental detail was placed under the command of a commissioned officer, generally a Lieutenant. It was just such a body of men that first entered Fayetteville, although held by a pretty good size Confederate force—eight thousand, I heard it stated at the time. The Fourteenth corps was the first to enter the town, take possession of it and relieve the place from chaos to order. Fayetteville was a good-sized town, located on a large navigable river. After a march of over three hundred and fifty miles, the army opened communications with "the loved ones at home," as two steamers came up the river bringing the latest possible daily papers, but no mail in the way of letters. The returning steamboats took back thousands upon thousands of letters hastily written to friends "back in God's country." During all of this long march much damage had been done to the Confederacy by cutting off all its lines of communication, thus rendering it impossible to feed Lee's army.

Fayetteville had become a very important point for the confederacy. The United States government at the beginning of the war was in possession of the arsenal located at Harper's Ferry located at Virginia. Immediately after the breaking out of hostilities, all the valuable machinery—and it was very valuable, for the Federal government was very short of muskets—was taken to Fayetteville. The factory there was operated night and day in providing arms for the Confederate soldiers. It is hardly necessary to say that the arsenal there was most thoroughly destroyed. At this point all of the refugees and our own sick and disabled were sent by the boats to Wilmington. From the leaving of Savannah to the occupation of Fayetteville much had been accomplished towards ending the war. From the time that Sherman severed his connections with Atlanta and made "the march to the sea," thence up to Fayetteville, it was easy to see the doom of the Confederacy. The least informed man in all the army could feel in his bones that the long-sought end was nearing and might come at almost any day.

After resting several days at Fayetteville, permitting the horses and mules to recuperate after their toilsome labors through swamps and the horrible roads over which they had tugged wagons and guns, the army was once more set in motion. About the middle of March 1865, the left wing began moving in the direction of Raleigh, North Carolina, and the right wing taking a direction toward Goldsboro. The next day after the departure from Fayetteville, the left wing had a very brisk fight at Averysboro with the enemy's rear guard. In order to facilitate the movement of the Federal troops, all of the supply trains of each corps were left behind. The leading corps pressed forward, accompanied by the ordnance train only. In consequence of this movement on the part of General Sherman, the enemy was forced to fight in order to prevent his trains from falling into the hands of the Federals. Both sides engaged in this severe, though brief, contest suffered considerably and each side sustained, perhaps, a greater loss than had occurred from the period of leaving Savannah up to that time. The enemy however, while the fight was in progress, had put its trains in motion and had thus obtained its objective by saving the latter, but at a very heavy cost in killed and wounded. The threatened trains, while our army was checked, withdrew hastily from the Federal front and the pursuit was again resumed.

Following the contest referred to, the Twelfth was assigned to the duty of train guard, always an irksome detail to soldiers, who would rather be at the front even though bullets flew thick and fast, than to be governed by the slow progress of trains. It should be noted that there were two Generals Wood in the Fifteenth corps at the time. They were brothers from Ohio: General Charles R. Wood, commanding the division, and General William Wood, commanding the brigade to which my regiment was attached after reaching Savannah. The brigade had been put in charge of all the trains of the Fifteenth corps making probably a thousand or twelve hundred wagons. At places, after the first few leading wagons would pass over the roads they would simply become impassable, so the whole distance had to be corduroyed. The pioneer corps, generally composed of Negroes with white officers in command, labored unceasingly in reconstructing, or rather in breaking new roads, cutting down the green pine trees. I heard it stated at the time that from noon on one day till eight o'clock the next morning the heavy train had only moved eight miles. Every foot of the road had to be corduroyed in the manner already mentioned. The world at large can never know the amount of work performed in that portion of the country until reaching the South River. This stream crossed, the more serious part in the march seemed to have been overcome. The men, teams, drivers and members of the pontoon corps were utterly exhausted from the severity of their labors and from the want of rest and sleep. The roads had now become vastly improved—I use the words vastly improved only as a comparison with those roads that were now behind us—but even yet they were very far from being passable highways. Some idea can be formed of the labor performed when I state that at the time referred to it took five days of steady, unceasing work to make forty-five miles.

About this time the brigade was relieved from the arduous duty of guarding the trains. During all the previous day, the soldiers now being relieved had been hearing distant cannoning coming in the direction where we knew the left wing was marching and where a severe battle seemed to be in progress. The soldiers had been ordered forward, and every soldier brightened up in anticipation of a coming fight. Overworked as every one of them was, every musket mustered in the ranks when the call to "fall in" came to them. It was really wonderful to see the new life the soldiers took on by the orders they had received, and they broke out in cheers upon hearing the order. A soldier becomes a queer compound in time, and a very different man from what he was when he first enlisted.

The brigade was relieved from train-guarding duty in order to rush to the assistance of the Fourteenth Corps that was engaged in a severe battle. It was afterwards learned that the enemy had thrown a very heavy force upon the First division of that corps, which at first pressed the latter back, and for a time threatened disaster to the Federal army, scattered around as they were and engaged in road building. It was this first fierce attack upon this first division that Major Fred Boltz, of the Eighty-eighth Indiana, distinguished himself with such good effect that the advance of the Confederates was checked for a sufficient length of time to enable the entire division to form its line of battle. They held the enemy until the Second division of that corps could come up and take a part in what was proving the severest battle in what may be termed the "campaign for the two Carolinas." These two divisions of the Fourteenth held the enemy until a full division of the Twentieth corps—Hooker's former corps, but then commanded by General Slocum—came up as a support. The enemy was finally driven back with a heavy loss. Major Boltz was highly complimented for the bravery he displayed at the very onset of the fight as well as his splendid handling of the troops under his immediate command, small as it was, at the incipiency of the contest.

The indications pointed so plainly to the fact that General Joe Johnston—Sherman's Atlanta competitor—was again in full command of the confederate army from which he had been displaced by General Hood before the Atlanta campaign closed. Johnston's entire army was in front of the widely scattered Federal forces, and a great battle was in all probability being planned, so it was necessary for the Federal commander to concentrate his own forces in front of the Confederates. My regiment was hastened forward to assist, turning over the guarding of the trains to a division of the Seventeenth corps. General Wood's brigade, although it had labored for several days and nights in road building, and was at the hour the order came still busy at work, actually rejoiced at the night march they were directed to make. The men were directed to cook their supplies before starting, and at about eight o'clock, the night setting in quite dark, the troops set out for an all night march. The silver band, which the Twelfth had managed to keep through the war, and at one time was the only one left in the Fifteenth corps, played a march at the head of the brigade.

The regiment arrived in the rear of General Mower's division of the Seventeenth corps just as day was breaking. The civil engineer on General Hazen's staff, Ambrose Bierce, a brother of Augustus and Dime Bierce, who live near Warsaw, who was more familiarly known as "Brady" Bierce, said the distance traveled by the regiment was seventeen miles. Heavy skirmishing was in progress out in front when we arrived, but the men needed some rest and went into camp in the rear of General Mower's force. Soon they were dozing off to sleep to the rattle of the musketry of the two skirmish lines of the Federals and Confederates.

I cannot look back to those closing days of the war save with more than ordinary regret for those who were killed or died at that period. They had passed through many battles, skirmishes almost innumerable, dashes on picket posts and the constant danger to which the soldier is exposed at all times when the enemy is near. And at the same time they were never safe from the accidents of war, whether the enemy was near or not. It seemed to me that a life lost near the close of the war was so pitiful. The young man who had enlisted way back at the very beginning of the war, was yet called upon to lay down his life in the very closing days of the long-drawn-out struggle as a sacrifice. He was not to return to his home and loved ones; his waiting parents and perhaps one more dear than either father or mother, after his long absence. How much more pitiful would be the home-coming of the Confederate, who may not even have been given a furlough from the firing on Fort Sumter until he was given one by General Grant following General Lee's surrender at Appomattox! Many Confederates had no home to go to, and no friends to receive them after their long marches on foot. After the passing of four years of soldier life, it seemed all so uncalled for to have these men lay down their lives for a cause already lost. This feature of the great cost of the war comes home to me many times, even yet, and it is a mistake for any one to think that the Union soldier did not fully sympathize with the defeated Confederate veteran when the war was over.

On the morning following the all night march referred, the troops that had come up after a rest occupied some hastily improvised entrenchments. The re-enforcement's that had come up during the night consisted of many more than our division, and in consequence of the severe labor they had undergone followed by an all night march, were permitted to rest during the early part of the day. Knowing that General Mower's division of the Seventeenth corps intended to push the enemy in the early morning, Major Baldwin and myself of the Twelfth Indiana, had, during the night, determined to follow the attacking force. After a brief rest, we were up early and rode over to the point where we knew that preparations were in progress for Mower's division to push the enemy. It was well known that nearly all of the Confederate army was now in front of that of General Sherman. Sherman was determined, if possible, to bring on a general battle and if successful, of which General Sherman was very confident, to end the war right there so far as a victory would go, with Lee's army still confronting General Grant at Richmond and Petersburg, Virginia.

Major Baldwin and myself arrived a few moments before the skirmish line was directed to advance. Neither of us, of course, had any command, nor any business there, except that of curiosity. To prevent either of us from getting in the way, I notified the officer in charge of the skirmish line of our presence on the ground and asked his permission to accompany the advance, which was granted. The evening before, a Confederate division had been driven pell-mell over the ground on which the contemplated charge was to be made. It was only a short time after the bugle had sounded the advance of the skirmish line until we came up to and passed over the same ground that both the defeated and victorious troops had fought over only a few hours previously. Major Baldwin and I came across many of the dead of the last night's contest, nearly all of them being Confederates. In places the bodies of the dead were thickly strewn. The ugly feature of this strip of ground was that it was thickly covered with pine needles, which had caught fire. This material burns rapidly so it was not at all strange that we came across quite a number of the bodies of the enemy, who having first been wounded, had been burned to death by the on sweeping flames that had flashed across this battle-field. We passed several dead Confederates whose hands had been held above their faces where the excessive heat had cooked their fingers until they dropped and hung down from each joint. Two men were found who had at first been seriously wounded, but whose bodies were still squirming, although they were unconscious from the heat of the burning pine needles. Certainly and surely a "foughten field" is a horrible place to view. The skirmishers had just passed over this "stricken field," they having no leisure to observe its horrors, as they were busily engaged in compelling the Confederate line to fall back. While Major Baldwin and I had no special duties to perform, took occasion to look about us. I can most truthfully aver that the sight within view was horrible, ghastly, indeed, the dead ranging from the gray-headed veteran down to boys of fifteen or younger.

We kept fairly close to our skirmish line, which thus far had been a continuous advance. The Confederates had not been able to stay the oncoming skirmishers for a single moment, but fell back steadily before it. We were wondering why the Federals did not meet with a more stubborn resistance. All at once, however, there was a momentary check, then again a forward movement and then again a check. It seemed to myself and Baldwin, both of whom were well mounted, that we could see a number of mounted men in the rear of the Confederate skirmish line, but at the time we were uncertain. At any rate, the Confederate line had received re-enforcements of some kind, for quite suddenly the Federal line was brought to a standstill that lasted for several minutes. The rifle-fire of the enemy grew more fierce. I rode forward to see if I could discover the cause, but to no purpose. I perceived, however, that the enemy's fire was more vigorous, but the officer in command of the Federal skirmish line about that time had his bugler sound a charge. In obedience, the line pushed forward rapidly, the enemy retiring. By this time the Federal line was advancing so rapidly, and was using its "Springfields" so vigorously that the enemy retired before this fresh onset so rapidly that the pursuers could not keep up. The Federals could not know the lay of the land over which the enemy was retreating, and the little village of Bentonville lay on the opposite side of a small stream, the crossing of which partially caused the delay. While the re-enforcements were sent to assist in making the passage of the stream, and many Confederates waded the stream, the main body, however, assembled at and crossed the bridge then went into the little "tar and turpentine" town.

The little village of Bentonville had been for the past two days the headquarters of General Joe E. Johnston. While the Federal troops were coming up to occupy the village, the whole Confederate army was in full retreat. Major Baldwin and myself pushed into the town and were the first two horsemen into the village. A large building on one side of the only street in town had been taken as a Confederate hospital and we concluded to visit it. We found fully a hundred wounded men in the two good-sized rooms that were occupied, and among them several Union soldiers who had been brought in from the surrounding fighting field of the day before. In talking with the surgeon in charge of the hospital—he ranking as a major in the Confederate army just the same as was the case in the Federal organization—he told us that the Union soldiers were brought into Bentonville from the point where General Johnston's troops first engaged the Federal forces. The surgeon went on to talk about the incidents that had come under his view in the last two days, and that for forty hours neither he nor any of his assistants had been able to take even a short nap. All of the hospital attendants were completely worn out. Then very quietly he remarked to me that had the troops, with which I crossed the bridge in the edge of town, been pushed hard the war might have been ended right then and there. "For," he said, "General Johnston with thirteen other Generals were engaged in holding a 'council of war' in the building right across the street," pointing to it as he spoke.

Continuing his remarks he said: "When your troops got so near, General Hardee was compelled to send out his own mounted bodyguard to strengthen our skirmish line and thus hold the enemy in check until the men composing the council of war could gather their papers and have their servants and orderlies bring around their horses." This bodyguard was what Major Baldwin and myself saw when our own lines were brought to a stand, or at least checked. I have ever since lamented the fact that we were not possessed of the knowledge that the surgeon had given us a half-hour sooner. If we had known the situation we would have pushed the skirmish line "for all it was worth," in the hope of capturing such a crowd of prominent officers. Indeed, had fourteen Generals fallen into our hands, it might have ended the war a few weeks sooner than the end came, for it would have left all of that Confederate army without a head. We told the surgeon our side of the story and when we informed him of the slight check to General Mower's skirmish line he replied by saying: "That was the very time that the bodyguard of Hardee reached and re-enforced the skirmish line. I know because I saw them move out and heard General Hardee tell the Captain in command of the guard to hold the enemy back until General Johnston and the remainder of the officers could get started."

General Mower pushed his whole division forward behind the skirmishers that had taken the town of Bentonville. After this was done it was ascertained that had Mower's movement been supported, the only route by which the enemy could have secured their artillery and trains would have been closed to his retreat. General Johnston had gathered up every available body of troops at his command, but now that he had to give up his left to General Mower at Bentonville, he became alarmed for the safety of his army and hastily withdrew, taking the direction towards Raleigh. He crossed the Neuse River and destroyed all the bridges on his route. General Sherman's entire army was advanced to Bentonville, where he issued orders announcing the occupation of Goldsboro by General Schofield with the Army of the Ohio. The order also announced the close of the campaign, and the army was at once put in motion for Goldsboro, where it arrived on March 24th, 1865. On reaching that city, I find in an old order still in my possession, the disposition General Sherman made of his troops after reaching that old town. General Schofield, with the Twenty-third corps and a portion of the Twelfth, which had reached Newberne by sea, occupied the city and the fortified lines to the west with cavalry in his front several miles distant. The Army of Georgia, under the command of Major General Slocum, occupied the east, and General Terry, with two divisions each of the Twenty-fourth and Twenty-fifth corps held the line of the Neuse River. General Logan with the Fifteenth corps occupied the northeast, the entire force making perhaps eighty thousand men in all.

Bentonville was the last battle with General Sherman troops that had been involved in the Atlanta campaign. Before leaving what is known as the battle of Bentonville, I want to relate an incident that came under my eyes the next day after General Joe Johnston had held his council of war there. Just below the bridge that spanned the little stream that flowed past the village there had been stacked up on the high tank, a very large number of barrels of rosin (some of the citizens placed the number at two thousand and some at twenty-five hundred). Somehow or other the soldier had grown to like a fire, and wherever he stopped, or stood, there was likely to be seen fire and smoke. The one I am about to refer to was a great fire and a big smoke. Some one with no fear of shoulder straps in his make-up had set fire to this large number of barrels of rosin. The smoke from the fire was at times the equal of Vesuvius or Mt. Etna. The burning barrels of rosin produced a thick, black smoke. After the fire was well started, the melted rosin flowed down the embankment on the side where the barrels were stored and when the melted rosin struck the water in the little stream, it would instantly chill only to be again flowed over by succeeding torrents of rosin. This kept on until the stream fully forty feet wide was entirely bridged over. The men walked over the stream on ice made of rosin. On occasion this story had been disputed, but if it is in this instance, I have only to say the proof is at hand to assert it as truthful. After all there is nothing strange about it. If the rosin was melted, what else could it do but harden to its original state, when the flow, ever accumulating, struck cold water?

On arriving at Goldsboro, North Carolina, following a leisurely march to that place from the scene of the last battle at Bentonville, all the various corps composing General Sherman's army took up the location assigned them. The officers of the various commands were generally "West Pointers," of which the whole country may well be proud. The plan for the defense of Goldsboro was quite elaborate, and at the moment it was considered quite necessary too. The Confederate General Joe E. Johnston, with whatever forces he had left or could gather up, closed up on Goldsboro. Of course there was danger to General Sherman's army should General Lee conclude to give up the capital of the Confederacy, and by a rapid movement, join his forces with those General Joe Johnston in North Carolina. This would give him a force far garter than that possessed by General Sherman, and it was with this threatened movement in view that the plan for the defense of General Sherman's position at Goldsboro was on an elaborate scale. Several forts were planned of the broad-gauge sort, but if I remember correctly, none of them were ever completed. I remember hearing several discussions among the heads of the various corps on the subject. The idea seeming to prevail, that while General Lee might make an attempt with his Army of Northern Virginia to unite his forces with those of the Confederate General Johnston for the purpose of continuing a war that seemed to be closing on general principles, yet it was not at all probable, for the destitution of the country was so great that his army could not be fed when away from a railroad base. This view was so generally entertained that work on the elaborate plan of fortifications was never pushed. The subject was a favorite topic of conversation in the regimental camps. The verdict generally was decided that the Confederate army under Lee would be annihilated was he to attempt to make such a move.

Such was the situation during the time the Federal army occupied Goldsboro. The army received a large accumulation of mail here, and by way of Newborne on the coast, the soldiers flooded the mail sacks with missives for the "old folks at home." Of course the daily newspapers received here were some days behind their date, but they were just as eagerly pursued as though they were fresh from the press. It was always with great pleasure that the soldiers read the glowing accounts of the operations of General Sherman's army from the time he left Savannah until communications were again opened after arriving at Goldsboro. None pursued the praises bestowed upon General Sherman more eagerly than the officers and men whom he had commanded so long and so successfully. Sherman was the idol of this troops, and I think I would be perfectly safe in saying that no commander was ever so universally beloved as was "Uncle Billy", as his men delighted to call him. I only wish that the men he commanded could have heard him refer to his troops, as I did on one occasion at the Tremont Hotel in Chicago. With tears in his eyes he spoke of the men he had led from "Shiloh" clear through to the end, referring to them as the bravest and best soldiers that had ever fell to the lot of any man to lead and direct. As much as the old soldiers loved "Uncle Billy," it was returned to the fullest measure of his generous heart.

Resting for about three weeks at Goldsboro, the men composing the army thoroughly enjoyed the cessation from bridge building that had come to them after their wearisome tramp through the swamps of the two Carolinas. They were at last able to rest from the never ending corduroy building, the lifting of wagons bodily out of the mud and mire, the muscle-breaking effort required in doing the same thing for the gun of some battery that had buried itself over hub-deep into the soft soil in some river bottom. It is not at all strange that a three-week rest came as a godsend to the over-worked soldiers of Sherman's army as well as the good things they had to eat after their reconnection with "God's country" was once more established! Why, they at once began to "take on flesh," and had become, many of them, full grown men from the time they had enlisted until now. Then, too, all the indications pointed to the end of the war, for the entire seacoast from Fortress Monroe, clear around to Galveston, Texas, was in the hands of the Federals, with only an exception here and there. Hood's army, that General Sherman had left General "Pap" Thomas to take care of, had been driven out of Tennessee following the two brilliant engagements of Franklin and Nashville. And I must say the efficiency of the cavalry was never better shown than in the last year of the struggle.

General Philip Sheridan, following Missionary Ridge, had been taken from the Western army, where in the battle he had commanded a division of infantry in the Army of the Cumberland, and was transferred to the supreme command of all the cavalry and mounted infantry in the Army of the Potomac. It was very soon discovered that the right man to accomplish great feats had been found at last. Among the earliest of his successes was to recover the Shenandoah Valley, which up to the at time had been "the debatable ground" between the two armies, and was first in the hands of one and then the other until "Little Phil" gained the lead of all the mounted men of the Eastern army. After making the remark that he, "would make the valley so hot a place that a crow could not fly over it without taking along with it a haversack full of rations for the entire journey," right well did he keep his word, as the almost total annihilation of General Early's Confederate army most fully attested. Early in 1865, he swept down to Richmond, crossed the James River, and passing to Grant's left flank, he assisted to a great extent in the great triumph for the Union cause before

Petersburg. While Sherman was resting at Goldsboro, he was harassing the retreating foe, rendering his escape impossible.

General Stoneman, whose command went with Sherman clear through the Atlanta campaign, while the latter's troops were enjoying their well-earned rest at Goldsboro, was moving out upon the North Carolina railroad at Salisbury. General Kilpatrick was watching and occasionally picking up some of Wade Hampton's troops in our own vicinity. Early in the war the cavalry arm of the service was considered by many people, both in and out of the army as a costly branch of the service. The cavalry always referred to foot-soldiers by the nickname "dough-boys," a sobriquet well known in the regular army before the war, while the infantry nearly always jeered mounted men when their respective regiments met or passed one another on the road. Whatever happened during the earlier part of the war, and from the time that Sherman cut loose from Atlanta this arm of service, the eye and ear of the commanding general did most effective work and won high praise on every hand.

During the stay of the Federal troops at Goldsboro of three weeks, General Johnston's Confederate army fortified itself in position at a place called Smithfield. Both armies kept a close watch upon the other, and occasionally some skirmishing would take place, but both sides seemed not inclined to do no more than outpost firing. I took occasion one day, while this sort of conditions prevailed, to ride out to where the most advanced post of our army was on duty, ten or twelve miles, perhaps more, and came back in the evening. On the return trip, myself and my orderly, in an abrupt turn in the road, suddenly came upon a couple of men clad in Confederate gray. The meeting was so unexpected that both parties were somewhat surprised! I ordered them to halt and after pulling one of my Colt's revolvers from the holster, was instantly obeyed. In conversing with them they declared that their families lived about sixty miles below on the Neuse River and they had made up their minds to leave the army and go to their homes. I asked them if they had permission to do so. One of them spoke up and said they had not, but that anybody could see that the war was near its end and they had determined to quit, as two men would not count for much either way. "But," said I, "you are not the only two by any means that are deserting General Johnston's army, as our pickets report that a good many of the Confederates are deserting their colors." One of them hastened to say that he knew that many of the Confederate soldiers were very tired of the service and were leaving whenever an opportunity occurred, all of them believing that further fighting was useless. The Confederates were already defeated and there was no use to add more deaths to the thousands of lives already lost. I gave them what few crackers I had and bade them good-by, believing that the Union cause would not be in the least injured by the Confederates losing these two soldiers from their fighting force, even though both were able-bodied.

Along early in April, 1865, General Terry, who had joined General Sherman at Goldsboro with all his troops, having come up from Newberne on the coast was placed in charge of Goldsboro with orders to hold it as well as to keep open the line of communications back to Newberne while General Sherman's original force moved out toward Smithfield, where Johnston had gone into a fortified position. In this movement the histories show that General Schofield, with the Tenth and Twenty-third corps moved up on the south bank of the Neuse, thus becoming the right wing of General Sherman's army. General Slocum with the Twentieth, Hooker's old corps, held the center with General Howard on the right. The Fifteenth corps became the right of General Howard's command with General Charles R. Wood on the right of the corps and the Twelfth Indiana, the extreme right of the division to which it belonged. Before leaving Goldsboro, news had reached the western army of the fall of Richmond and Petersburg via Newborne. The report having come from the latter place was circulated by "word of mouth" instead of the usual way of sending it to the various headquarters officially and in writing. The report was disbelieved probably by a majority of those who heard it because news that came by the "grape vine" was generally so untruthful and sensational that the time came when all news received, whether true or false, was discredited. However, a dispatch received from General Carl Schurz, then at Newberne, on the evening of the first day out from Goldsboro confirmed the story. Even then many men would not credit it until late at night there came official information from Secretary of War Stanton, confirming the statement of the fall of both Petersburg and Richmond, the retreat of Lee, with General Grant in close pursuit with his entire army, and General Phil Sheridan with the cavalry, sure to head him off.

When the news of Grant's triumph over Lee was at last fully believed, the rejoicing of the soldiers could not be described. Officers and men simply went wild over the glad tidings. The doom of the Confederacy was sealed, the period of wounds and deaths, of prison pens, sacrifices and sufferings were nearly over. The rejoicing was very great, indeed. With Grant's pursuit of Lee and the gathering of gallant Phil Sheridan's wild riders in the latter's front, and hanging on to Lee's flank like the bull-dog fighter he was; Johnston's remnant of an army only a few miles away from Shermans "boys in blue"; the Confederate forces disintegrating by desertion and the abandoning of a hopeless cause; Old Pap Thomas with the heroes of Franklin and Nashville pushing his successful army into North Carolina from East Tennessee; the entire coast in possession of the Federal army and navy, it did not require the eye of a prophet to truthfully predict the nearness of the end and the glad shout of victory that would soon swell the breeze that had so steadily floated aloft the stars and stripes of which "Old Glory" is composed.

The news of the evacuation of Richmond and Petersburg by General Lee and his entire army, closely pursued by General Grant with the Army of the Potomac and Sheridan's wild riders in the advance, very greatly enthused General Sherman's entire force. Thus, in the advance from Goldsboro to Raleigh, the army was in such high spirits, firm in the belief that an the end of the war was not far distant, with home and the meeting of friends in the near future, that there was real danger that the elated Federals might, in the prevailing enthusiasm, lead to an attack upon the enemy too precipitately, before the front was intelligently examined. Confederate cavalry was in the front of the first division of the Fifteenth corps, and it has already been stated that the Twelfth Indiana occupied the extreme right of this division, and consequently that of the extreme right of the entire army. Some skirmishing occurred during the first day's march. Two companies of this regiment (I and K) along in the evening were deployed as skirmishers and drove the enemy from his camp. General Johnston withdrew his forces at Smithfield in the direction of Raleigh on the same morning the Federal advance left Goldsboro. It soon became fairly evident that the Confederate commander was not disposed to fight, and the prospect was before the Federals that there was to be another retreat and pursuit. It even seemed doubtful whether General Johnston would make the attempt to defend Raleigh, and after events proved that the surmises within the Federal army that he would not do so proved true, for his troops passed straight through the state capital where no defenses had been erected.

It was about this time that the news reached General Sherman's army that General Lee had surrendered the Confederate army of Virginia to General Grant at Appomattox. The prospects of peace by the end of the war was greatly accentuated by the reception of this great news. Every individual composing the army, from its highest officer all the way down to the humblest private in the rear rank, felt assured that the end was at hand. The desire to force the Confederate army under General Johnston to a like surrender was entertained to a very high degree, with the firm belief that if the Confederates could only be brought to a stand, General Johnston would follow the course pursued by General Lee by a surrender of the forces under his command.

In the march towards Raleigh, Wheeler's Confederate cavalry hovered about the flank and rear of the moving Federal troops. He never ventured to offer stubborn resistance, but impeded our advance by the destruction of bridges, and in picking up stragglers from the Union forces in the rear. It was thus that the bridge over Little River was destroyed at Folk's Church. The course he pursued at that point caused the destruction of the church itself, as it was torn down to obtain the necessary material to rebuild the bridge and thus allow the infantry to cross over that stream. It was along about this period of the march that John Sturman and Aaron Cutshall, both of them private soldiers in my regiment, were attacked in the rear of the column by a small party of Confederate cavalry. Cutshall was captured, but soon afterwards made his escape and rejoined his company. Sturman was a man without a shade of fear in his composition, and as reckless as he was brave. In the dash made by the squad of Confederate cavalry upon the two men, Sturman was so closely pursued that he was struck over the head with the butt end of a pistol, and although considerably stunned by the blow, he managed to retain his seat in his saddle. Being an infantry soldier he was armed with a musket, which was strapped over his shoulder, and not having time to remove it, he turned the muzzle backward without unslinging his gun and fired at random upon his foe behind. The ball from his musketry entered his pursuer's heart. He dropped lifeless from his horse, which kept on its course by the side of the one that Sturman was riding. This animal Sturman caught and brought in triumph into the camp of the Twelfth shortly afterwards. On returning to the spot soon afterwards where the Confederate trooper was killed, and in examining his person, several articles were found in his pockets that had belonged to John Clark, who had been missing for a few days and was thought to have been killed, but as it turned out had been taken prisoner and was soon exchanged. Cutshall, Sturman's comrade, also made his escape and found his way back to the regiment the same night.

Incidents such as the one described frequently occurred during the war. The same Sturman, while on a furlough two years before the above incident in his life, had been arrested for killing a man on a canal boat in Huntington, Indiana, in a fracas that was hostile to the prosecution of the war and those who were sustaining President Lincoln in his efforts to prevent the dissolution of the states. In the row that occurred there, the man Sturman killed was cheering for Jeff Davis and, having an old brass pistol on his person, he fired at him, mortally wounding him. Over and over again he told me afterwards that he really did not believe the pistol was loaded and he snapped the pistol at him more to scare him than anything else did. He was arrested and held in the Huntington county jail for several months, but through the mediation of Governor Morton, he was given permission to return to his regiment. During his absence he had been mustered as "held by civil authority" so that on his return, the paymaster counted him out all the money that was due him ever since he had been absent, amounting to a considerable sum. That, however, was not all of Sturman. Learning the time when the Twelfth was to be mustered out of the service at Indianapolis at the close of the war, the sheriff of Huntington County was promptly on hand to arrest Sturman just as soon as he became a private citizen. A prominent resident of Huntington "gave me the tip" and we resolved to circumvent his arrest. The sheriff very closely watched the pay table at Indianapolis, but I had arranged with the paymaster to hand the amount due to Sturman over to myself, the latter being in hiding at the

Bates House. As soon as I received the money I hastened with it to Sturman, and with quite a fair sum in his pocket, he left that same night for Kansas and thus escaped another siege of imprisonment.

I have already stated that General Johnston did not seem in the mood for fighting and passed on with the main body of his troops right though Raleigh, of course covering his rear with a cloud of cavalry. In approaching that little North Carolina City, my regiment had the honor of coming in contact with the Confederates for the last time. It was a mere skirmish, however, although there were one or two men killed by the sharp-shooting skirmishers of the Twelfth. The little affair occurred only a short distance out of Raleigh. The skirmishers in the lead very suddenly came upon a small body of Confederates in a strip of woods engaged in cooking their breakfasts. They were so completely taken by surprise, and so vigorously pushed that it was all they could do to mount their tethered horses and hurry out of musket range. I very well remember that on hearing the firing I galloped to the point, only to find the men of my regiment not only in possession of the camp the Confederates had occupied during the previous night, but all their cooking utensils as well, and their contents besides. There is no use of infantry pursuing fleeing cavalry, so I ordered a halt there and the men on the skirmish line fell to, and devoured the breakfast that the "Johnnies" were preparing, some of the skillets in which meat was frying being still standing over the coals. One of my soldiers possessed himself of a skillet that was full of fresh pork sausage, the "links" being about the size of what is known as "wienerwurst" at the present day. He presented me with a couple of links, which I ate on my horse, finding that portion of my breakfast a very palatable one. The sausage had, no doubt, been given to the Confederate soldiers by some one sympathizing with "the lost cause," or he may have "commandeered" it, as most soldiers on either side would have done. The main body of the army coming up, my regiment moved forward and was one of the very first to enter the city of Raleigh quite early in the morning of April 13, 1865.

The Confederates, having passed on through the place, halted about ten miles out of Raleigh. Sherman's forces also stopped at Raleigh and went into camp. Each camp took up a position suitable for defense. By the middle of the month of April all military operations had been suspended. Rumors began to fly that Johnston had surrendered. How wearily the hours wore away with no definite or reliable information being obtainable concerning the situation of affairs between the two armies. The next day it was known that there was a conference between the commanding Generals of the two armies, but what might be the outcome, the troops were in utter ignorance.

It was at this time, too, in the midst of the uncertainty caused by the negotiations referred to, and at an hour when one and all were so greatly rejoicing over the success that had crowned General Grant's strategic calculations, that the news came like a clap of thunder from a clear sky, falling on the hearts of the Union army like "the crack of doom" that President Lincoln had been assassinated! Indignation, sorrow and the cry for vengeance were heard on all sides. The shock was so terrible that it was one of the incidents of the war that could not be described. Every soul in that army of veterans was wounded as never before. Brave, strong men with ashen lips and tears streaming from their eyes refused to repeat the news to their comrades, it was so horrible. Many men tried to believe that the tale was not true; that the noble soul who for more than four years had borne the burdens of the nation until with sunken eyes and bowed head, he was but a broken image of the tall and erect Lincoln that entered the White House four years before in stalwart health and vigor, with only a few remaining years before him, should give up his almost saintly life to the assassin's bullet! After the first paroxysms of grief and deep regret, came the cry for vengeance and many an old and grizzled veteran with his yet tear-dimmed eyes, demanded to be led at once against the forces of General Johnston. Others insisted that the black flag should be raised and no quarter given! Such was the scene that followed the reception of the appalling news that so good a man as President Lincoln had perished from an assassin's bullet.

It was these threats for vengeance that led General Sherman to at once take measures for the protection of Raleigh and its people. It was but a short time until I received an order to place a portion of my regiment on provost duty in the heart of the city, and if it became necessary, to use the whole regiment. The portion was selected by companies and was immediately on duty in the down town part of the city. By night the entire regiment was called upon to do guard work and especially to keep a strict watch for incendiary fires. The aspect was, indeed, so threatening that after nightfall it was thought best to add two more regiments to this duty, so that the army would not be disgraced by the destruction of a town already in our possession. I was always glad that not a fire occurred during that night, although incipient flames were started at several points. Originally there was a good deal of Union sentiment in North Carolina, and this was especially the case where the state joined East Tennessee. Even in Raleigh, the proprietor and editor of the Daily Standard was arrested two or three times by the Jeff Davis government for criticizing army movements. Since negotiations were in progress between Sherman and Johnston, anything of a destructive kind that happened to Raleigh would have had a tendency to break off the negotiations. Fortunately, the next day new light had come to the soldiers who were crying for vengeance. They became more placable, and the whole army settled down in deep grief for the great loss that it and the nation had been called upon to sustain in the loss of so great and good a man as Abraham Lincoln.

All of the deep sorrow, grief and anger of which I have spoken followed a rumor, which, at first, one and all who heard it from the bottom of their hearts hoped that it was only an idle tale. It was hoped that further news would fail to confirm the crime committed, supposedly in the interest of the rebellion, while the Confederate army drew its last expiring gasp. The story seemed to many officers and men to be too wicked—hellishly wicked to be true, but, alas, the truthfulness of the news was confirmed by the official announcement of the terribly sad and shocking event by General Sherman, who had received a telegram from Secretary of War Stanton, dated the 17th of April. Deep grief with its attendant mourning for a man so beloved as Lincoln settled upon every soul who held him in such high esteem. There was one quite noticeable feature expressed by the citizens of Raleigh. Those of disunion tendencies, who had long despised their once honored citizen, Andrew Johnson, he once having lived in Raleigh for a short time, but now elevated through Lincoln's murder as the executive of the Nation by the foul crime, suddenly discovered that in Lincoln the South had lost a real and true friend. Like Pontius Pilate of old, they could scarcely find a sufficient number of washbowls in which to wash their hands of the foul crime that had been committed. No doubt it was true that, in the murder of Lincoln, the Southern States did lose the very man who was in the position to do more for the South than any man living at that moment. Many people believe, that had President Lincoln survived for a few years longer, the unification of the two sections would have come sooner than has been the case.

CHAPTER 19

At Raleigh

> All that to us thou art.
> Proud, patriotic air, bright flag unfurled,
> Thou wast to each brave heart
> Who for land's honor, life 'gainst treason hurled.
> O, very human they,
> Who richest gift to serve a country's need,
> They on her altar lay—
> The hearts of home that thro' the fray must bleed.
> Remembering all we owe
> To those who in the brunt of battle fell,
> Yet pity's tears will flow
> For love bereft whose woe not words might tell.
> You had, dear comrades ours,
> All to inspire brave men on bloody field;
> But while we scatter flowers
> We sorrow with the martyrs unrevealed.
> When war's smoke cleared away,
> O, eyes that looked in vain for faces loved!
> Our tend'rest thought today
> Are theirs who then earth's grief supremest proved.
> —Anonymous

The news of the assassination of President Lincoln came at a most inopportune time, to say nothing of the deep grief that it caused to the army and all its loyal supporters in the North. Negotiations between Generals Sherman and Johnston were in progress at the very movement that the terrible rumors of the President's death reached the army at Raleigh. Grave fears were held that the terrible calamity would put a stop to the convention then being held between the two leaders of the hostile armies still confronting each other. The first effects, as I have already stated, were almost a demand from Sherman's soldiers to be led at once against General Johnston's forces that were lying only eight miles distant. On all sides was heard this demand, often made by men whose eyes were filled with tears at the time. Shortly after the report of Lincoln's death, the announcement was made of the suspension of hostilities between the two armies. The agreement between these two officers was an assurance of the restoration of peace on equitable terms, and to make it binding only needed the approval of the chief executive of the United States. The document that had been decided upon, it was understood, was already on the way to Washington and without knowing just what the terms of surrender were, the troops under General Sherman were confident that it would be endorsed by the proper authorities at Washington. In the meantime, and while awaiting the answer to the agreement, the troops were placed in camps in and around Raleigh, pleasant locations being selected for the purpose, and thus Sherman's army was quietly awaiting the announcement of the final end of the great war.

Along in the latter part of April the news reached Raleigh that Generals Sherman's and Johnston's agreement had been disapproved by the Secretary of War, and, of course, with the sanction of the cabinet at Washington. General Grant had been directed to proceed to Raleigh with all possible dispatch, to either draw up new articles of agreement, or to recommence hostilities, after the two days' notice that had been agreed upon should elapse. In the meantime but very few of the troops, comparatively speaking, knew that Grant was in Raleigh. At that time all of the railroads had ceased running cars and the only means at hand for Grant was to use a fast flying dispatch boat, furnished him by the navy at Fortress Monroe. By the use of this boat he reached Newberne by sea, then ascended the Neuse River as far as Goldsboro, or at least the nearest point to that town and then proceeded to Raleigh on horseback.

General Grant reviewed General Sherman's army while in the city, a division at a time, but only one division each day. I undertake to say that but few soldiers were aware that these reviews were undertaken to cover up the very sudden appearance of General Grant, the head of the army, upon the scene, yet such was the fact. I gained this knowledge myself from overhearing Generals Grant, Sherman, and Logan conversing about the matter. It was surmised in the army that General Grant's presence in Raleigh might be misconstrued, and it was resolved to hold these reviews in order to cover up any wild guessing on the subject by the members of the army. In the meantime the negotiations between Generals Sherman and Johnston were renewed, and were proceeding quietly while General Grant was reviewing the troops in Raleigh. Sherman represented the Federal side and General Johnston for the collapsing Confederate cause. Such was the situation while Grant was in Raleigh, but the marching days of the Federals was nearly over. The second conference between the two officers led to a second acceptance of the terms on the part of General Johnston. General Sherman offered precisely the same conditions that General Robert E. Lee had accepted when he surrendered the Army of Northern Virginia to General Grant at Appomattox Court House.

The surrender of General Johnston's army, therefore, ended all hostilities between the two belligerent armies from the Potomac clear down to central Georgia, from the extreme northern part of Virginia, leaving only the forces under General Dick Taylor and those of General Kirby Smith to

At Raleigh,

be surrendered. It was not long until these two officers accepted the terms that had been accorded to Generals Lee and Johnston, and hence the war for the Union was ended.

During the reviews to which I have alluded, an incident came under my observation that may be worth relating. I have already stated that one division of troops was reviewed each day. That at least was the design at the start, but the remodeling and accepting of the terms which Grant had come down to re-negotiate with General Johnston brought about a change, hence, only three divisions passed in review before General Grant. Belonging to the first division of the Fifteenth corps as I did, and also of the First brigade of the First division, it fell to the lot of the troops composing this division to be reviewed on the first day. This gave me an opportunity to witness "the march past" of the two other divisions on the two succeeding days. Quite a lot of officers, myself among the number, occupied a balcony that stretched along the front of a business building on one of the principal streets in Raleigh. I was just in the act of going up to the balcony from the sidewalk to take that seat that had been provided for me, when I heard the emphatic remark from a citizen of the place, "What troops are these?" he asked, while he closely scanned the colors they carried and tried to read the name of the estate on the regimental colors. "That," said I, "is an East Tennessee regiment." "In God's name," he replied, "did East Tennessee fight on the Union side?" "Yes, sir," I replied, "and that," said I, "is only one regiment that you see. In all, cavalry, artillery and infantry, East Tennessee must have sent close to forty thousand men into the field, first and last, on the Union side, to say nothing of its superb body of scouts." He could not believe that whole regiments fought on the Union side. Individual enlistments he could understand, even squads of four or five, might have been the case, but here was an entire regiment carrying the Union and regimental colors with the name of that portion of the state from which they hailed boldly emblazoned on its regimental flag. He could scarcely believe what he had seen and with the remark, "Great God, it is no wonder that we were whipped when whole regiments in the South fought against us!" Had newspapers been circulated as freely in the South as they had been in the North, he might have known it. The news showed that East Tennessee was almost as faithful to the Union in point of numbers as was the same amount of territory in the loyal North. In the elections held to decide whether Tennessee should go out of the Union, or remain steadfast to the country and government, seven counties voted to remain by majorities of from one to three thousand, yet under Governor Isham G. Harris the state was swung over to the Confederacy very early in the war.

There was great criticism over the terms of the Sherman-Johnston settlement, for the surrender of the Confederate troops were not only adverse, but exceedingly severe, and much ill-feeling was engendered in consequence. The "Sherman-Johnston Conference" created no small amount of ill feeling in the North and some of the newspapers were exceedingly violent of the subject, and grave accusations were made against Sherman by the press. All the victories and successful campaigns made by Sherman counted for nothing in the way of severe criticism of the Northern press, and by members of Congress. Is it any wonder that Sherman—by whom the war was closed months sooner than it would otherwise have been by his sagacity, his fine generalship, his bravery in cutting loose from all aid of every kind and in the face of the most hostile opposition, plunged into the unknown "piney woods" of Georgia, neither knowing or caring very much where himself and his army came out—felt, and very keenly felt, the severe adverse criticisms that met him at Raleigh, when he had so much to his credit in bringing the war to a close? The officers and men of his command stood by General Sherman. They had served with the "grizzled old raider" so long that they had the utmost confidence in the man whose victorious banner they had followed.

The result of what had occurred and been accomplished within the last few days in the surrender and paroling of all of General Joe E. Johnston's body of Confederate troops following the example set them by General Lee at Appomattox, eventuated in a cessation of strife in all the insurgent states bordering on the shores that were washed by the waves of the broad Atlantic. Directly following the surrender of the forces under General Johnston, the Federal troops located in and around Raleigh were getting into trim for the march to Washington City to the Grand Review and at last home! How wonderful that last word fell on the listening ear of men who, from the day of their enlistment way back in 1861, until the hour that the word came to "fall in" for the "homeward march" had never had a furlough and consequently had never revisited the scenes of early childhood. It was the next march that would be in the direction that through all these years the heart of the "brave boy in blue" had yearned and centered—home!

When Sherman's army marched out from Raleigh on their way to Washington they carried nothing but their musket, unfilled cartridge box, a haversack for the soldier's own convenience, and that was all. With a liberality seldom known in an army, the men were directed to place their knapsacks and everything aside from what I have mentioned, into the wagons of their respective regiments, and hence it can be seen that they "traveled light." All of these preliminary arrangements having been made, it was well on towards the last of April, 1865, that Sherman's army once more "took to the road," this time with no enemy in front, no knapsack to carry, or well filled cartridge box tightly girdled around his waist, but everything of which it was possible to ease the man, was stowed in the regimental train. The war was over and all knew and felt it. Joy had settled down on the face of every marching man and officer, and it was in such a mood that the Fifteenth corps set their faces northward to

At Raleigh,

Washington, which thousands upon thousands of the "Western boys" had never seen.

Several days had been taken up in making preparations for the homeward bound trip. After the first day, I determined to view the country away from the regular line of march and detailed Joe R. Williams, the oldest living son of William Williams of Warsaw, to accompany me. When a road was discovered branching off from the main route, but leading in the same direction, we took it, believing it would lead past some sections of the country untouched by the war. This we soon found to be the case, for we had not gone five miles until we came to a region of country where at least some of the slaves were engaged at their spring work on several of the plantations. Every mile or two we met members of General Lee's paroled soldiers trudging their way to their far-away homes, which in some instances included Texas, and other Southern States west of the Mississippi River. Worn out and weary as these men were, and with a long journey on foot before them, I could not help but sympathize with them.

The contrast between the two armies was so great! The Federals, well fed as they had ever been, were on the way to their homes to be welcomed all along the line with cheering, shouting thousands and with victory perched upon their bullet-riddled banners. The Confederates on the other hand, many of them barefoot, and with bleeding feet, were on their way to far-off homes that, when they reached them, if they were able to stand the long and wearisome march, they would find in many cases their homes in ashes. The contrast between the home-comings was very great indeed, and we were only too glad that we had taken with us a fairly plentiful supply of "commissary stores" and therefore the means at hand to give these war-worn soldiers enough of food to last them for another day, and a spoonful of coffee each, enough to make a cup full apiece. Sometimes in a brief rest at the side of the road they would talk with us. They were genuinely relieved over the fact that at last the long drawn out war was over. We would part only to meet in the next mile or more another squad, a duplicate of the one just mentioned.

Continuing the practice of riding away from the regularly planned line of march for each of the different army corps, Joe Williams and myself, on one occasion, along about dinner time, rode up to one of the old-fashioned plantations houses. We concluded to ride up through the long and wide lawn that lead to the mansion and rest for a while on the big porch that covered the whole front of the great building. Dismounting we hitched our horses and walked up to the porch, and after sitting down awaited results. A colored boy, who had never before seen a Yankee in all his life, very timidly approached where we were sitting. I ascertained from him that the owner of the plantation was at home. I sent the colored lad to tell him that two strangers wanted to see him. Not long afterwards an old man, bowed with years, made his appearance and came slowly toward where we were sitting. I took him to be about seventy years of age. I told him who we were, adding that being somewhat tired of riding, we had taken the liberty to come up to his porch and rest ourselves for a short time. He replied by telling us that we were perfectly welcome, and requested us to remain as long as we felt like it. He was, I thought, a little nervous, and pretty soon he asked us if the report he had heard only the night before was true, that President Lincoln had been assassinated. It should be borne in mind that this was in Central North Carolina, and off the generally traveled lines of communication. Whenever news reached such a neighborhood, it came first as a rumor only to be confirmed by its truthfulness at a later period. Indeed, that was the way the news of Lincoln's assassination first came to Sherman's army itself. When I told the old man that the rumor of his death by the bullet of a murderer was true, he held up both hands and in the most touching manner said, "Oh, my God," then adding the remark, "The best friend the south had has been slain. What an awful calamity!"

To say that I was surprised at such remarks as these coming from an old man like him and so feelingly expressed astonished me greatly. The old gentleman then went on to say that from the first he was opposed to the secession of the states, and that he was known all through his neighborhood as a Union man. He was sincerely glad, he said, that the war was over, but he had most fervently hoped that the story of Lincoln's death would be contradicted by further reports. I listened to the old gentleman with my feelings all worked up over the sentiments that came from this old Southern gentleman, and when he went on to say that he had "watched the course pursued by President Lincoln all through the war, I thought I could see that he was an honest and a just man and the South had nothing to fear from a man like President Lincoln." In a tremulous voice, and with tears starting in his eyes, he once more repeated that it was a terrible blow to the South. I confess I listened to him almost with awe, his remarks were so impressively delivered. He insisted on us going in to dinner, but well aware of the fact that even the wealthiest people of that region had all they could do to secure sufficient food for themselves and their dependents to subsist upon, we declined, as our own supplies were amply sufficient.

Before leaving Raleigh, General Sherman had intended that the homeward march should be a leisurely one. His aim was to make it so easy that the men composing his army could even recuperate on the way. The troops were no sooner well on the way "homeward bound," than without anyone being especially chargeable, it became a race between the several corps as to which would arrive at Richmond first. The report having obtained credence, especially among the enlisted men, instead of being a leisurely march requiring fifteen days for the trip under the general's estimate, it was done in seven. In that time the troops marched one hundred and fifty-eight miles from the Neuse River at Raleigh. The army of the Tennessee reached Petersburg, Virginia, on the 29th of April 1865 and the Army of Georgia arrived later on the same day. During the march from Raleigh to Washington, all foraging of whatever kind was strictly forbidden. All the necessary supplies that were needed upon the way, and could be procured, were purchased and paid for by the Commissaries of Subsistence. The strictest of discipline was enforced on the way home, and the rights of property were as much respected. The desire of one and all was to impress the citizens residing along the line of march that, now the war was over, "commandeering" had been ended as well.

On reaching Petersburg, Virginia, the army halted for a day in order to give the marching men a rest, this scarcely being needed, owing to the great anxiety of the troops to push on to Washington, and—home! In addition to the rest, the opportunity was given the western army to view the numerous points of interest on the greatly extended field of Grant's operations in the surrounding and final capture of Lee's army. The next day, following the rest, the army pushed on to Manchester, a town lying directly across the James River from Richmond on the south, and between the two towns. The Federal army had already spanned the stream with a splendid pontoon bridge. General Sherman did not march with the army from Raleigh, but went down to Newberne on the coast, and then via Fortress Monroe and up the James River to Richmond in a dispatch boat. He was astonished to find that his army had beaten him on the trip, arriving at Richmond a day or two before the dispatch boat. General Halleck, who it will be remembered, was a military officer attached to the war office at Washington all through the war, had, previous to Sherman's arrival, issued an order proposing the review of General Sherman's army as it passed through Richmond, the Confederate capital. There was an intense feeling between General Sherman and Secretary of War Stanton, Halleck and other officers who had no experience in the field during the entire war, and on his arrival by boat, he at once countermanded the order for Halleck's review. Sherman made the remark at that time that he would "march his army around Richmond rather than suffer Halleck to review his troops," adding the remark that it was "a good deal like a visitor calling on his neighbor when he knew beforehand that the neighbor wasn't at home."

It was on the morning of the 13th of May that we crossed over the James River and marched through the streets of Richmond. The Twelfth Indiana Infantry was the last regiment of Sherman's army to tread the streets of the Confederate capitol. From that moment on the army traveled all the way to Washington over ground that had felt the tread of marching feet throughout the war. Almost every mile between the two cities in the four preceding years of war was the scene of either an exchange of shots between outposts, or a skirmish, or battle. It was a desolate region. After the first year, none of the great plantations had a crop of any kind grown, and one and all of them bore the impress of utter desolation. It must be remembered that war is terrible, and hundreds of old mansions, many of them possessed of deep historical interest of early colonial and revolutionary war days, were given over to the fire fiend and were so utterly destroyed that in some instances it would be difficult to find the exact spot on which they stood.

I remember that on the second day of the march out of Richmond, the army passed what had been an old-time plantation. Out in the fields were two white men still clad in confederate gray, with the emblems of their rank still on the collar and sleeves of their coats, showing that they were officers. They, with from ten to fifteen Negroes as helpers, were engaged in planting corn. This was only a short time after Lee's army had been paroled by General Grant, and these officers, freed from further military service, had gone to their former homes and were already at work endeavoring to raise a sufficient crop of various kinds to tide them over the coming winter. I perceived the value to the defeated Confederates, of the refusal by General Grant to take from General Lee's army the horses and mules, suggesting at the same time that they would become useful in helping to raise a crop, and though they were legitimate captures, all of the live stock of the Confederate army was left with the owners.

The march from Richmond to Alexandria passed over ground that had been the scenes of the most important battles. Often in passing through a forest of pine, the men frequently pointed out how the limbs of the trees were splintered and torn with shot and shell distinctly showing the fact that the woods had been the scene of a more or less severe skirmish or even a battle. A soldier standing near me pointed to a tree only a short distance away that had been hit with a solid shot at about the height of ten feet squarely in the middle of its body. The tree was split for a distance, I should guess, of about four feet below where it had been hit and six feet above. The cannon ball was still sticking on the further side of the tree. The trees of the forest were riddled with shot, shell and musketry bullets.

On the same evening the troops went into camp not far from the place alluded to, and after the tents were pitched (at this period of the war, tents had grown out of fashion and few officers used them, especially in fair weather) I discovered a hewed log house about a half mile distant. Smoke was coming out of the chimney, showing that it was occupied, so I resolved to visit it. On arriving there, I had an illustration of the "open hospitality" for which Virginians had been noted for the world over. On stepping into the house on the invitation to "walk in", I discovered two old people, both of them beyond seventy years, sitting on a bench. The room was entirely denuded of every article of furniture, that being neither table, chair nor a single thing of home convenience whatever. The two sat on the bench and requested me to take a seat at the other end. They had been out in the afternoon seeking wild strawberries had had secured a fairly good-sized cedar-staved bucket full of berries, which was sitting on the floor beside them. At once they invited me to eat some berries, but I declined, suspecting that the old people had better not be too liberal with their berries. I had noted when I came up to the house that there was not an outhouse of any kind whatever, not a rail or a fence of any kind visible for miles around. I came to the conclusion that the berries were about all the poor old people had to eat. They kept on insisting on my eating some of the berries, but still declining, I asked them finally if they were not in needy circumstances so far as food was concerned. Finally the old man acknowledged that until the wild strawberries began to ripen they were in a bad fix, but a Union soldier riding by had given them a couple of dozen crackers, and then the berries began to ripen. I could see a tear welling up in the eyes of the old lady, and I then insisted on knowing the facts in the case, and asked them to tell me if they were not nearly starving. The old lady at length replied that with the exception of the crackers given them by the soldier, they had had nothing else to eat but berries. And here were these two old people insisting on my eating a portion of the only food they had on earth!

I felt that I must do something for these two old people, so I mounted my horse and rode back to camp and supplied myself with a goodly portion of every kind of food my headquarters possessed. I took an orderly with me and a coffeepot, fearing that the old people, having so long been without the delicious beverage, might not even have anything in which to make it. I hastened back to the old couple, arriving the second time just as the sun went down. When I told them what I had for them and showed them the edibles, tears came into the eyes of both and the woman cried out, "James, didn't I tell you the Lord would not permit us to starve, now that the war is over?" They were profuse in their thanks, especially for the large amount of coffee I had left with them. Assuredly, I am a firm believer in "Virginia hospitality" from that day to this.

In due time Sherman's army arrived at Alexandria, Virginia. After the Bull Run battle fought on Sunday, July 21, 1861, I was in Washington, and from the rear steps of the capital building the Confederate flag could be seen flying from the top of a prominent house in Alexandria. It was on this historic ground of Alexandria that all of General Sherman's troops were encamped. The soldiers of both Grant and Sherman's armies were getting ready, more than four years after the firing on Fort Sumter, to be mustered out in the immediate vicinity of the first battle of the war.

AFFIDAVIT

I, Reuben Williams, a Col. & Bvt Brig Genl of Co. 12" Reg't Indiana Vols., being duly sworn, depose and say that I was commissioned as Captain and mustered into the service of the United States as such on the 27" day of May 1862; that I have served as Col. & Bvt Brig Genl in the 12" Reg't Ind. Vols., that I have never served in any other organization than the one mentioned, that during my term of service I have duly rendered complete and correct returns of all Ordnance Stores and Clothing, Camp and Garrison Equipage for which I was receipted, or became in any manner responsible, whether said Government property was captured from the enemy, duly invoiced to me, or came informally into my possession; that I have never had, and have not now in my possession, any such Stores, the property of the United States, for which I have not duly accounted in the manner prescribed by the Regulations governing the respective Departments; and that I am not indebted in any manner whatsoever to the United States.

Reub Williams
Col & Bvt Brig Genl
12 Warsaw Ind.

Sworn to and subscribed before me, this 17" day of January 1862, at Indianapolis, Indiana.

Chas. T. Murray
Notary Public Marion Co.
Ind.

CHAPTER 20

The Grand Review May 1865

Muffle the drums! See, the flag is furled!
Shouts of the battle have died away;
Over the fields where war's dust-cloud whirled
Peace and tranquility reign today.
Clashing of arms,
Wild bugle alarms,
Ne'er shall be heard where our heroes are sleeping.
Rest, soldier, rest,
While o'er thy breast
God's sacred watch-fires their vigil are keeping.
—A. E. Brininstool

For several days previous to the Grand Review the soldiers were engaged in getting ready for the event. Many regiments drew new clothes, and a spirit of emulation between the various regiments had seized upon both officers and men to make the best possible appearance on the two days of the review. All of the troops belonging to General Grant's command proper had been assembled in the vicinity of Washington previous to the arrival of General Sherman's command. It is said that when Grant's army was drawn out upon a single road to make the journey to Washington from Richmond and the surrounding region, that for fifty miles that road was spread over with men marching in regular order. Two days previous to the first day of the review, one of the newspapers of Washington, in giving its readers statistics for the assembled thousands, stated that the various batteries alone if drawn out upon a single road in regular marching order, with only the usual space between batteries and guns, would have reached from Washington to Richmond. There was no drilling of troops or much guard duty. Everybody was too glad and too happy, to require much discipline. The soldiers were mostly placed on their good behavior, and there was but little disorder of any kind. The soldiers spent their time hunting up their old friends of "before the war" days, and the visiting of one another went on every day.

The only cause for anxiety on the part of a number of the leading officers, came from the rivalry, and I may truthfully say, the jealousy, that existed between the two armies—the Eastern and Western. The only disorder that did come under my eye during the period of waiting for the review was a very vigorous fight between two squads of about twenty each, representing the two armies. The fight did not last a great while, but men on both sides came out of the squabble with black eyes and bloody noses. Very fortunately none of them were armed, or the affair would doubtless have ended with the report of both "killed and wounded." It was a strange thing for me to see men who had fought so valiantly in the same cause for four years permit mere rivalry to lead them into such a squabble that might have resulted in the taking of the life of the men who, within a few days would have had their discharge in their pockets and on their way home. Fortunately, as a general thing, the order prevailing where so many men had been assembled, was remarkably good.

A large number of ferryboats plied between the wharves of Alexandria and Washington, a distance of seven miles, and every day as well as far into the night, these boats were filled to their utmost capacity in carrying soldiers to and from the capital. Every one of the soldiers most fully enjoyed the liberty given them. Comparatively few of the soldiers of Sherman's department had ever before visited Washington, and for them the sightseeing was of more than ordinary interest. All of the public buildings, especially the capitol, conceded to be among the finest buildings of the world, were crowded to the limit with visitors. The unusual liberty given the soldiers in this particular case was very seldom betrayed. The men no doubt felt that an act so generous and so different from the usual army discipline that would permit but a few from each company to have passes for such a purpose, evidently felt themselves to be on their good behavior and conducted themselves as the gentlemen they instinctively were. The policemen of the city, too, no doubt had orders to make no arrests for trivial offenses, and as a consequence, there were few arrests made during the waiting days preceding the grand review.

It should be remembered that besides the assembling of the thousands upon thousands of soldiers at the capitol, there were also many thousands of the citizens of the United States who came to Washington to witness the grandest pageant of modern times, one that had never since been eclipsed in magnitude. Every state in the Union was represented, of course the far Western states being few in numbers, for in that day no Pacific railway spanned the continent, but from all other that were provided with railroads, they came in a never ending stream. Trains were constantly arriving filled to overflowing with the loyal people who had stood by President Lincoln in the most gigantic struggle that any man had ever been called upon to bear. It is likely that the beautiful city of Washington will never again see so large a number of patriotic visitors upon its streets as upon the occasion when the people gathered there to rejoice over the end of the war, and welcome the Western armies of Grant and Sherman.

It should be understood that not all was rejoicing, for down in the hearts of all of that immense aggregation of people, men and women, there was a tugging sorrow at the heart-strings of one and all that the one man who would have been most gladdened, the most dearly beloved Abraham

Lincoln, like Moses of old, could not look over into the promised land and see the end, the victorious end, and the happy culmination of all for which he had so constantly labored and suffered to save the Union from dissolution. The City of Washington on all its streets, from the palaces of the rich down to the lowliest cottage contained in the capitol and every other public building in the city, still wore its weeds of mourning over the death of the great and good man. How joyful would his heart have pulsed had he been there to witness the end for which no man ever before had labored to such an extent? Oh the pity of it all that he could not be present to rejoice with the people who had stood by him through his Herculean task! Hundreds of times I heard the remark from soldiers: "Oh, if Lincoln could only be here now!" I can only say, "Oh, had Lincoln only have lived to see the end, and to have witnessed the great rejoicing of his people, then the end would have been happier to one and all!"

Myself and the immediate friends around my headquarters spent much of the time on the ferry boats in going to Washington and in returning to Alexandria, making generally three or four trips a day. It was at Alexandria that Colonel Ellsworth, the commanding officer of the New York Fire Zouaves, lost his life very early in the war. His regiment wore the Zouave uniform, and as he was a master of tactics and drill, his regiment presented a very handsome appearance whenever it turned out. The Federals quite early in the war obtained possession of Alexandria and the Ellsworth Zouaves were among the first regiments to go into quarters in this old secession town. Ellsworth found a Confederate flag flying from the top of a hotel of which a man by the name of Jackson was the proprietor at the time. The following morning, after going into camp at that place, he directed Sergeant Bronson to take a squad of soldiers with him and go to the hotel and demand of the proprietor to haul down the flag. The Sergeant did so, and Jackson refused to lower the colors. By this time Colonel Ellsworth himself came on the scene and, going along with Sergeant Bronson and his detail, was proceeding up the stairway at the hotel, when Jackson suddenly appeared and shot the Colonel through the body, mortally wounding him. His death followed directly afterwards. The death of Colonel Ellsworth caused a great sensation and aroused the people all over the North to a wonderful extent. He was a very popular young man and in 1860, he as Captain of the Chicago Zouaves, toured the whole country giving exhibitions of the company that had advanced under his teachings to a remarkable degree of efficiency. His death caused a genuine sorrow throughout the entire North, and as he was one of the first officers to fall after the firing on Fort Sumter, the excitement produced over his death had the effect to send many, many young men into the army.

What a week it was just preceding the day fixed for the Grand Review! It was a week of hilarity and of keen enjoyment. The weather was as delightful as it could be, and the happy faces one met on every side tended to demonstrate the joyfulness that every one felt over the end of the long and bloody war. Not all the soldiers were idle, by any means, as many of them were quietly preparing surprises for "the march past," when the two days came that were required for the grand review. A couple of hours each day were needed to prepare the surprises. The "surprises" were as much as possible kept "under the rose," those instrumental in arranging them not desiring to have their plans exposed until they appeared in the march down Pennsylvania Avenue—a street one hundred and fifty feet wide and extending from the rear of the capitol building to the White House. Washington City is a place where one meets strangers on the streets from every section of the inhabitable globe, not even excepting unenlightened people from central Asia, interior Africa, Esquimaux from the Arctic Circle, Patagonians, South Sea Islanders, and even the chiefs of many tribes of Indians. These and many more can be seen from time to time walking the streets of the city in strange costumes and decorations in that barbaric manner that seems to be an inborn feature of the uncivilized nations, tribes and classes.

The Army of the Potomac, under the immediate command of General Meade, followed by the cavalry under General Sheridan, all—General Sherman's included—had preceded the troops under the latter to Washington. It was simply out of the question for so many troops to pass in review on a single day. It was decided by General Grant that the Army of the Potomac should be reviewed on the 23rd and that of General Sherman on the 24th of May 1865. Consequently the forces under General Meade, including the Army of the Potomac and the Army of the James, were directed to prepare for the great event. The troops composing these two great divisions of the army had never been compelled to make the long marches that those from the West had been called upon to perform. It was only fair to presume that they were superior in drill and all the duties of the soldier laid down in the tactics, than those who had put in so much of their time in long marches and in engaging in many skirmishes and battles, which left them no time to learn the niceties of military life. As the respective regiments, brigades, divisions and corps filed out into the upper end of that broad and handsome thoroughfare known as Pennsylvania Avenue, they presented a handsome appearance. Their company lines were so nicely adjusted and they marched in such perfect time that not even the slightest jog in the formation could be detected.

There being so large an army to be reviewed, it became necessary for each company to be "closed en' masse" in order to permit the passage of the troops past the reviewing stand in front of the White House on the same day. The closing up of the ranks by companies had to be done on both days, so great was the number of troops to be reviewed on each day. Of course, the sidewalks of Pennsylvania Avenue on each side were crowded to their utmost capacity with citizens intermingled with Sherman's soldiers, whose turn to "march past" would come on the morrow, May 24th. Hundred of Sherman's troops were in their camps trying on new suits of clothes, so that they too, could make a respectable appearance in new ones rather than appear in the ragged and tattered uniforms in which they had arrived at the nation's capital. Still others were engaged in getting the colored Pioneer corps, the ex-slaves, who had made the roads and built the bridges across hundred of streams, ready for the review. These colored pioneers, peculiar to the Western army, created quite a sensation, too, clad in new clothes as they were, and each carrying a shovel as a soldier would his musket "at right shoulder shift" in the grand parade of the next day. Then, too, at the insistence of some inventive genius, it had been resolved to represent "Sherman's Foragers", "bummers" they had come to be called by common consent, both in the army and out of it. The preparations for that feature required the procuring of many live chickens, several head of live sheep, sacks filled so as to represent sweet potatoes, and many other things that represent the kind of supplies the foragers would bring in to the hungry men of Sherman's army on the march from Atlanta to Savannah.

The 23rd of May passed with the troops composing the Army of the Potomac and that of "The James" marching past the reviewing stand from early morning until darkness had gathered. It was a great success in every particular. It was well into the night of the 23rd before the corps of Sherman's forces was silent, for there were many things to do in order for the officers and men to get ready to participate in the review the next day. The natural rivalry that had existed during all of the later years of the war had incited a desire on the part of the Westerners to eclipse, if possible, "the march past" of their Eastern brethren in arms, if not in marching, then in the novelty of the parade, and hence the preparations to which I have already alluded went on in the camps until after midnight. The generality of the troops knew nothing of this, and therefore, the vast majority of the Western army was as surprised and thoroughly enjoyed these novelties, as did the spectators, which lined both sides of Pennsylvania Avenue.

Sherman's army had been encamped in the region round about Alexandria ever since their arrival. On the morning of the 24th of May 1865, at a very early hour the troops under General Sherman's command crossed over the Potomac River on what was known as "Long Bridge." The starting point of the second day's review had been fixed for the head of Pennsylvania Avenue at the capital. These troops proceeded to their destination through the less known streets at an early hour, so as not to obstruct the reviewing street. The start had been fixed for precisely eight o'clock in the morning and the signal for the march to begin was three blank shots by the artillery on the capital grounds, two minutes apart. The troops were to then begin the march promptly after the third shot was fired.

I have already stated that spectators of the grand scene about to be enacted had been arriving for several days from every section of the country, and I heard it stated at the time that over fifteen thousand dollars had been expended in the purchase of flowers to decorate the passing troops. I know nothing as to the truthfulness of this statement, but I do know that my own regiment had been especially selected to lead the column on the second day's review and I had not moved a hundred feet into Pennsylvania Avenue, until my horse was covered from the saddle forward with great wreaths of flowers as large as the collar horses wear in harness. Bouquets were showered upon the moving men in endless profusion. All through the march on the great avenue, this shower of flowers continued. The crowds cheered the pioneer corps composed of ex-slaves, clad in their new uniforms and carrying their shovels and picks as a solder carries his gun. Well might these pioneer corps be cheered, too, for they were a very essential feature in Sherman's march from Atlanta to the sea and then northward to Washington. The four or five companies of foragers that brought up the rear of several of the divisions with their loads of live chickens, sheep, and calves, created a real furor. Wild applause was bestowed upon each of these odd illustrations of army life.

Like the formation of the Army of the Potomac, General Sherman's troops also moved in close order instead of by company fronts, the usual way laid down in the tactics. This was done in order that the great number in the line could pass the review stand before darkness ensued, which could not have been done had the troops been formed in the usual way. Even by forming in close order, the rear of the marching troops did not pass the reviewing stand until after darkness had settled upon the capital city. Owing to the fact, that with the exception of the commanding Generals with their respective staffs and body guards, my own regiment was the first infantry to pass the President and his cabinet and the commanding Generals occupying the stand, including all of the officials above a certain rank, and it thus happened that I witnessed the episode that occurred between General Sherman and Halleck. In such a military ceremony as that of a review, it is customary for the head of the army and his staff to occupy the extreme front of the troops to be reviewed. In arriving in front of the reviewing officers, in this case President Andrew Johnson, (though tears were shed because the deeply beloved Abraham Lincoln was not there to witness the end of the war) the officers at the head of the troops dismounts and takes his seat on the reviewing stand until after the troops under his immediate command pass by. At the grand review I am describing, this feature only extended to corps commanders in addition to General Sherman. My regiment was just passing, and as I was at the head of it, I could see General Sherman making his way forward on the stand in order to salute the President of the United States as his superior officer. This was done when Secretary Stanton, next in rank to the President, offered his hand to General Sherman, who at once turned away, refusing to take it. The adverse criticism Sherman had received from the

War Department following his treaty for the surrender of the Confederates under General Johnston created a very sore feeling on the part of General Sherman. This incident has been denied on the part of Stanton and his friends, but as I was a witness to the scene referred to, I take occasion to set it down as a downright positive fact that General Sherman did refuse to take the Secretary of War by the hand on that occasion, and although Mr. Stanton offered to shake hands, the General turned his back upon him. Many northern newspapers criticized General Sherman very severely over the fact that he granted too liberal terms to General Johnston and his army and not at all in accord with the views or the sentiments of the officials at Washington. Sherman laid the blame on the shoulders of Secretary of War Stanton, although the latter was wholly innocent, so far as the "lampooning" General Sherman received in the press.

Having the desire to see for myself the grand parade, immediately after passing the President's reviewing stand, I turned the command of the regiment over to the Lieutenant Colonel and rode back to the Willard Hotel, and after stabling my horse, I sought a position on a third-story balcony, where the whole line of march was in full view. On stepping through the window I was surprised to discover that it contained thirteen Confederate officers, who had sought the same place to inspect the soldiers as they passed. They were so interested in viewing the parade, and their attention was so wholly engrossed with the sight that they had not noticed my presence as the Western troops came down the avenue with that swinging step so noticeably different from the well-drilled veterans of he East. One of these Confederates, a brigadier general's mark on his coat collar, looking away up the two-mile line of troops, made the remark, as though it had been forced from him involuntarily, "Great God," said he, "we never could have whipped them in the world." And that seemed to be the sentiment of the entire party. Surely the Grand Review was a great event. All of the representatives of foreign governments, as well as consuls, who had gathered at Washington to witness the great parade, were almost carried away in the presence of those veterans of four years and were loud in their praises of such an army. These dignitaries from countries where the tread of soldiers was an every-day occurrence were enthusiastic over the wonderful sight.

The city of Washington was gaily decorated for the grand review. The authorities arranged it so that all of the emblems of mourning displayed upon every public building and private residences in the city as mark of sorrow over the death of the lamented President Lincoln were retained. The only addition to the displays of mourning, which were left hanging unless they were torn or frayed, was a lavish display of the American colors. The mourning drapery of black and white to which the Stars and Stripes were added to an extent never before known, gave the streets a gorgeous display.

In addition to the display on the streets, mottoes were also indulged in to a large extent. One motto was stretched all along the entire length of the capitol building itself, in letters as large as a small house contained the sentence, "The Only Debt the Nation Can Never Pay Is the One It Owes Its Citizen Soldiers." In answer to how the Nation has kept faith with the gallant men who saved it from destruction, it is only necessary to say that the records show the pension roll at the present time to be over a million. All, who participated in that grandest of all pageants at the close of the war and in the youthful vigor of young manhood, with muscles hardened by long marches and every day practice at the time, are now growing in years. The erect figures that paraded on Pennsylvania Avenue in May 1865 are becoming bent, their hair grizzled, and the elastic step with which they trod the handsomest street in the capital of the Nation has grown somewhat laggard. Every three months the pension enables the soldier to go around and pay every one who may have granted him credit to tide him through till pension day comes again! The pension received by the surviving soldier reminds one that it is like the dew of heaven, falling on all alike and benefiting every one it touches to a more or less extent.

I will relate here an incident that occurred on the first day of the grand review involving the late General George A. Custer, whose record during the Civil War was almost meteoric in his advancement as a soldier. He was a young man when he entered the army and was involved in the first battle of Bull Run. He was fresh from West Point at twenty-one; a brigadier general at twenty-three, a major general at twenty-four, and commander of a cavalry division, which in the preceding six months that brought with them the downfall of the Southern Confederacy, had taken one hundred and eleven guns from the enemy; sixty-five battle flags and over ten thousand prisoners of war, without losing a flag, or a gun, and without a single failure to capture whatever he and his troopers went for. Such was his record. At the review of the army of the Potomac General Custer's spirited horse ran away on Pennsylvania Avenue, in spite of the efforts of its rider, a peerless horseman, to restrain him. Custer's hat fell off during the stampede of his horse, and his long yellow curls floated back in the wind making a dashing romantic picture. General Custer was a man of superb physique and of magnificent strength. His devoted wife, who after the war remained with him in camp, was with him on the march as well as in bivouac. In her three books she told of the deathless romance of their married life on the frontier. She relates how in order to give an exhibition of his strength, on one occasion he rode up to her side, lifted her out of her saddle high in the air with his left arm, held her there for a moment, then gently replaced her on her horse. He frequently played many such pranks with the woman he adored, and Mrs. Custer's books read like pages from Sir Walter Scott's "Tales of the Crusades." On the plains General Custer was known to the Indians following the Civil War, as "the White Chief with the Yellow Hair," or still more frequently as "Long Hair," but by his own men of the gallant Seventh Cavalry as "Old Curly."

The review over, the next thing for the government to do was to transfer the members of that great army to their respective homes in the North. It is easy to see that transportation over the railways would be taxed to the uttermost to transfer so large a body of men to the capitals of the various states where most of the regiments were mustered into the army of the United States. While this was being arranged, orders were issued for an extra force of clerks to provide assistance to officers and men in every conceivable way. Mistakes were made in the field due to clerical blunders, not through any dishonesty or any attempt to "gouge" Uncle Sam, and they were made on occasions when it was impossible to rectify them. These blunders were soon made straight by the more experienced clerks in the various departments, and after a few hours' effort and explanations, were able to clear up whatever errors had been made in their reports. The officers were given a statement that all of his accounts were correct, and hence there was nothing more in the way to prevent him from drawing the full amount of pay due him whenever he found a paymaster. It was very wisely decided that the final payment should be made in the respective states from whence the soldier had enlisted. That way the last thing the soldier received from the government, as he was finally discharged at the various state capitals, was the money due him up to the last day of service. Many enlisted men, who had been charged with a lost or mislaid gun, by making a full statement of the manner in which it had been lost, and the amount that had been taken from his monthly allowance, had the price of the gun restored to him, and a check given him for the amount—eighteen dollars, if I remember correctly. I aided many soldiers in this manner for several days following the grand review and my men and officers had cause to be grateful to the generous government for the clerical aid furnished them in this way.

I had a case in hand of my own which will explain the situation in settling accounts. Immediately after the battle of Richmond, Kentucky, I filed my claim for the price of the horse that I lost in the engagement. As nearly all officers were "strapped" on reaching Washington, the great majority of them were in need of some money as almost a necessity, and therefore, I thought I would look up my claim and see how it stood. It was numbered between six and seven thousand, the odd number being forgotten. I had employed John Paul Jones, of Lagrange, Indiana, to prosecute my claim for the lost horse directly after the battle in September 1862. Now, all I had to do was to revoke the power-of-attorney given by me to Mr. Jones, when the case was at once lifted up to number one. Within two hours afterwards I had a check for one hundred-fifty dollars, twenty dollars less than I had paid for the animal just a week before the battle. Out of this I sent a check to Mr. Jones for twenty-five dollars, leaving me just one hundred and a quarter!

It can readily be seen how generous was the act of the government in providing officers and clerks who were directed to do everything in their power to straighten up the accounts of all who applied. Left to run through the various departments through which all claims against the government have to go, I would not have received pay for the horse under two years. In fact it was about that long afterward I received a note from a Washington officer, stating that my claim had been allowed, he having just reached it in the regular course, and requiring that length of time to reach it in the regular order of doing business with the inevitable "red tape" that surrounded it.

One and all very pleasantly spent the time intervening between the close of the grand review and the date fixed for the departure of the Indiana troops. The joy so prevalent over the conclusion of the war continued. It would have been difficult in those closing days of the month of May to have met or found any one on the streets whose face was not wreathed in smiles, causes by the cessation of hostilities and the preparations necessary for the departure of the troops to their homes. When a sufficient number of cars had been procured over the Baltimore and Ohio railroad, I received an order placing me in command of the Eighty-eighth, One Hundredth, and Twelfth Indiana regiments, to which two more were added after receiving the order in a second note to that effect. The train was made up in sections and we were to go to Parkersburg, West Virginia, where steamboats would be furnished us to proceed down the Ohio River to Lawrenceburg, Indiana, where we were again to entrain for Indianapolis, there to receive pay and turn over whatever property that belonged to the government that the various regiments still possessed.

It is hardly necessary to state that all of the troops, from necessity were compelled to ride in freight cars, passenger cars being entirely out of the question, for it must be remembered that every railroad in the East was engaged in the same way, transporting the disbanded army to all the states in the North, Northwest and Northeast at the same time. I have always thought that it was owing to the scarcity of cars that the government officials selected for my command the Ohio River route for the homeward journey. By using steamboats the railroad cars could be used elsewhere. Whatever may have been the cause, it was the pleasantest trip that our soldier-days ever knew throughout the four years' service. The weather was all that could be desired, ideal, in fact, and in the leafy month of June, the days were proverbially delightful.

The fleet of six boats took five days in making the trip. Plentiful supplies were on board of each boat, and these included the full army rations, while the facilities for making coffee were of the best. My own regiment had selected a very handsome boat called "The Forest Rose," the steamer being as handsome as her name was poetic. At all of the towns and on either side, not matter whether it was Ohio or Kentucky, the fleet presenting a very gay appearance on the beautiful Ohio River. We were received with cheers and the waving of flags and handkerchiefs. The wharves were usually crowded to their utmost capacity to witness the passage of the brigade. In several instances free lunches of homemade sandwiches were sent on board, carried by handsomely dressed young ladies. None of the knights returning from the crusades in Palestine in "the old days" received such ovations, as did the homeward bound veterans as they floated down "La Belle Reverie" in those early June days of 1865.

At Cincinnati the fleet stopped for about an hour and the correspondents of the old Cincinnati Gazette and the Daily Commercial sent their representatives aboard the various boats composing the fleet. The incident was written up in splendid style and given to the public through the columns of these journals. The news of the arrival was conveyed to the firesides of the homes of hundreds of the veterans aboard the boats more than a week before the "returning braves" reached them in person. Within two hours after leaving Cincinnati, the fleet reached its destination at Lawrenceburg. The disembarking troops went into camp to await the cars that were to carry them to Indianapolis.

The command only stayed at Lawrenceburg for about three hours until they boarded the train for Indianapolis. The citizens of Indianapolis had a regular committee appointed to receive all the returning veterans from any regiment. It was a grand reception. Speeches were delivered in front of the Old State House Square to the returning soldiers, and listened to by the thousands of their friends who had gathered there to welcome home fathers, brothers, husbands, and lovers. All listened to the touching words of the Governor as he alluded to the valiant services they had performed. He spoke with great feeling of those absent ones who never again would receive a welcome from mortal hands, they having laid down their lives for the country they loved on many a "foughten field."

After the reception which was such a joyous welcome, coupled as it was with sadness and lamentation for those who would return no more, all attention of the officers was given to the final muster-out rolls. This was no small matter, for four copies had to be made out, one for the Adjutant-General of the State; two for the War Department at Washington, and one for the officer in charge of each of the various companies that were to receive their final discharge. It should be remembered, too, that in the muster-out of a regiment, the name of every man who had ever belonged to it from first to last had to be taken up and accounted for in the marginal notes. The whole number of the Twelfth was well up into fourteen hundred. When a full regiment was one thousand and forty, it can be seen that the clerical work for each company was no light piece of work. All this had to be done, however, before a cent of pay could be drawn by officers or men. It required about four days after the reception to complete the lists. When these were all examined and found correct, the paymasters were on hand to turn over to officer and men every dollar that was due them. They bid the comrades, with whom they had shared the hardships of war, bivouac and battle, march and skirmish, advance and rear guard duties, and all that goes to make up the life of a soldier in wartime, a touching good-bye, and hastened to the bosom of their family. The "goodbyes" that were spoken brought tears to many eyes. Attachments had been formed during the period the regiment had been together that could only be severed by the hand of the "grim-reaper", and many farewells and handclasps were made for the last time. Many of those who had been together for all these years were never more to meet again on earth.

Previous to the final disbanding of the Twelfth Indiana Regiment at Indianapolis, I issued a "farewell address" to the men I had commanded from the date of the battle of Richmond, Kentucky in 1862 to the final muster-out in Indianapolis on June 19, 1865. This "farewell order" I had printed in a form suitable for framing, and each surviving member was given a copy before he left for his home. I therefore reproduce it here as a fitting ending to my wartime memories.

INDIANAPOLIS, INDIANA, June 19, 1865,

Officers and Soldiers:

Your commanding officer addresses you for the last time as an organization. In a few more hours the Twelfth Indiana will live in history alone. Its members, the heroes of many a hard fought field, will soon have separated, to gladden, by their presence, the firesides of the homes from which they have been so long absent. Your commander embraces the opportunity, before we separate, to pay tribute to the devotion with which you have served your country during the long and bloody struggle from which we have just emerged. Your conduct upon many bloody fields attests the high regard you have borne the "starry banner"—the emblem of our nationality. Your return to your state with Richmond, Kentucky, Vicksburg, Jackson, Mississippi, Mission Ridge, Resaca, Dallas, New Hope Church, Kennesaw Mountain, Nickajack Creek, Atlanta, 20th, 21st, 22nd, and 28th July, Jonesboro, Savannah, Griswoldville, Columbia, and Charles, South Carolina, Bentonville, and Raleigh inscribed upon your colors. The blood of six hundred of your comrades defines the manner in which the Twelfth regiment conducted itself upon these fields.

For more than four years your Regiment had had an existence. Many of you have been present during the entire period, and all of you have fought under the same battle-scarred colors for three long years. You have numbered over thirteen hundred men in all, who have marched with you to battle. Nine hundred of your number today do not answer to the call of the roll. The bones of three hundred of these may be found in Kentucky, Tennessee, Missouri, Arkansas, Louisiana, Mississippi, Alabama, Georgia, the two Carolinas, and Virginia. Your feet have pressed the soil of every Southern State save two (Texas and Florida). You have fought upwards of twenty distinct and bloody engagements, and have, in the same time, with knapsacks upon your backs and guns upon your shoulders, marched upwards of six thousand miles. Your first bloody act in the great rebellion was the part sustained by you in the battle of Richmond, Kentucky. You went into the field at early morn; throughout the entire day you were engaged. No soldiers ever fought better than you did. Thirty killed and one hundred and forty-three wounded speaks for the gallantry with which your services were rendered on that memorable day. It was there that you lost your lamented commander, Colonel William H. Link, who fell gloriously in the heat of battle. From this ill-fated field, you visited the valley of the Mississippi, and were attached to the grand old army of the Southwest. With it you did your duty at Vicksburg and Jackson, Mississippi. At a later day you hurried with Sherman to the relief of the beleaguered army at Chattanooga. You arrived there hungry, tired, ragged and barefoot. No rest was allowed you. The battle of Missionary Ridge was fought and won, and the army of General Bragg driven in rout from that stronghold, though mother earth drank blood from more than a hundred of your comrades.

Then followed the long and toilsome mid-winter campaign to Knoxville, which you accomplished without rations, sufficient clothing, and scores of your number barefoot. Your commander recollects well of many of your number encasing their bleeding feet in strips of rawhide to protect them from the snow and ice and sharp pointed rocks which met you at every step. Again with the Fifteenth Corps, under the glorious Logan, you participated in the great Atlanta campaign. You opened the ball at Resaca, being the first regiment engaged, losing fifty-eight in killed and wounded. From this time until the fall of Atlanta you were scarcely ever out of reach of the enemy's fire. Your losses during the campaign numbered two hundred and forty killed and wounded. Soon again you were on the warpath, accompanying General Sherman on his "March to the Sea," participating in the battle of Griswoldville, and were frequently under fire during the march and upon the occupation of Savannah. The grand triumphal march of this army from Savannah to Columbia, South Carolina from thence to Raleigh and Washington City, is so well known as to render comment useless.

While at Washington, you had the honor of leading General Sherman's great army in the grandest review ever held upon this continent, where, by your soldierly appearance, you elicited the praise of thousands and ten of thousands of spectators who had crowded thither from every part of our county to welcome your arrival. Many of your gallant officers are numbered with the dead. The memory of Colonel W. H. Link, Captains Avaline, Beeson, Peoples, Anderson and Huston, and Lieutenants Day, Wescott, Waters, Weaver, and Kirkpatrick, who have given their lives to their country, will ever be revered. I would gladly mention the names of every man of your number who has fallen in this harvest of death, had I the statistics at hand. My sympathies shall ever be enlisted in behalf of the gallant officers and men who have been disabled from wounds received in action. Among those of this class are Chaplain Gage, Quartermaster McClellan, Adjutant Bond, Captains Price and Bowman, and Lieutenants Blackwell and O'Shaughnessy, all of whom have received severe and dangerous wounds while in the line of duty.

During these years of service you have by your strict observance of the duties of a soldier, acquired a reputation second to no regiment from our State. The State of Indiana, its officials, your friends and relatives have much reason to be proud of you. The cordial and hearty support that both officers and men have given me at all times and places has been most satisfactory. I shall, in after years, look back with real pleasure to the three years that I was connected with this regiment, as its commanding officer. Hoping that you all may prove as good citizens as you have heretofore been brave and faithful soldiers, and that peace and prosperity will ever be your lot, I am, your obedient servant.

        REUB WILLIAMS,
        Brevet Brigadier General U.S.A.

Official: MARSH H. PARKS,
    Acting Assistant Adjunct General

EPILOGUE

    Among our fallen soldiers
        And with the nation's heroes
    They brought him o'er the deep,
        They laid him down to sleep,
    A starry flag above him
        And on the simple stone
    That marked his final bivouac
        The single word, "Unknown."

    Perchance a mother watches,
        Her eyes with weeping dim,
    Or sweetheart waits the postman
        In vain for news of him,
    While snow of winter freezes
        And April violets thrust
    Sweet blossoms through the grasses
        Above his nameless dust.
                —Late War Verses

    The reader of today, in all probability, has never thought that the march of an army could be traced through the country by the graves it leaves behind, yet such is the fact. Many men lost their lives to the "advance guard", in the skirmishes and in the many battles of the war. Even when there was no enemy in the immediate front, deaths occurred on the march from illness or previous wounds. All the regiments of the Union armies were supplied with ambulances for the purpose of carrying the sick and disabled. When the wounded soldiers died in the wagons their remains were interred by the roadside, if in the country, or if near a town, they were buried in "God's Acre,"—the cemetery. Directly following the war the government had provided for the gathering of the remains of the fallen in cemeteries, the grounds for which were purchased and set apart for the purpose. Not only was re-interment for those who perished in the holy cause to preserve the Union, but also for those who had lost their lives while fighting against the government. And where is the Federal soldier today who would have it otherwise? In all cases the graves of the dead were marked as well as could be done at the time that death came. Very often this was rudely done, and sometimes so hastily that the name of the soldier was dimly penciled on a fragment of cracker box or a bit of board from a cartridge box. Great pains have been taken since the war in gathering the remains to ascertain the correct names of those whose remains were to be interred in the government cemeteries. The cemeteries were generally located near where some great battle had been fought. When it was impossible to decipher the names, the remains were gathered and located in a body in a section of the grounds, and labeled "unknown."

Those who have visited Arlington cemetery at Washington City have no doubt been deeply touched when they came to view that portion of the ground dedicated to "The Unknown Dead." I am not certain as to the number of dead who lie there just as tenderly cared for by the government as those whose names are known, but I think it is thirteen thousand. No one can tell how these men died for the cause so dear to us all, but to the parents how sad it must have been to feel that the boy they sent to defend his country lies in an unknown grave. This must have been in the thoughts of the members of Congress that passed the law providing for government cemeteries at or near the great battlefields. Nothing done better fitted the coming peace than the act providing for the cemeteries, Federal and Confederate alike, and the keeping of them in order by a great patriotic, liberal-hearted, magnanimous people. If we are to be the great nation that the world predicts, the Civil War must be counted as fairly won and those who fought for a separate government just as freely forgiven. That has been my view from the hour that the "Stars and Bars" went down at Appomattox.

Following the war, for a good many years, parents searched for the spot where their sons were buried; wives searching for husbands, sisters for brothers, children for fathers. Many families gave more than one son as the price of the newly cemented Union. Fortunately, after many of the battles, the comrades of the killed had so marked the graves of their tentmates that they could be identified. No other government has displayed a more touching generosity in providing cemeteries and gathering up and identifying the dead of both friend and foe in the great war for a united country. It makes one proud and grateful that he is a citizen of such a magnanimous nation.

In speaking of the government cemeteries, I am reminded that Decoration Day was just observed. A large number of this community (Warsaw, Indiana) braved the inclement weather to honor those who gave their lives for the Union, and I rejoice that such was the case. Not many years ago, apparently, a certain portion of our people seemed to desire to make it a holiday—a day on which to meet to play baseball and football and at one or two places to have horse racing. I am glad to perceive that the attempt to make it a free holiday did not "take" with the people. To the tottering old mother and father, whose son went down in that fearful deathgrapple at Shiloh; or who laid down his young life on the bloody field of Chickamauga; or it might have been while scaling rock-ribbed Lookout Mountain at the time "Old Glory" broke out its beautiful folds just "above the clouds"; or in the battle of Missionary Ridge, the day is so sacred that it almost seems a sacrilege to them to introduce a horse race. It is a great offence to the fathers and mothers, dear relatives, and to the surviving soldiers to introduce common diversions on a day so deeply sunk in the hearts of the people by the trials and tribulations though which the country had passed. Decoration Day was established as an anniversary to remember the "loved and lost", and should always remain so.

As the years come and go it seems to me that the minds of the survivors of "the great war" more and more drift back to the exciting days through which so many of them, in the heyday of youth or more vigorous young manhood, passed their younger years. What great, grand days they were when a whole nation arose in its might to preserve its own life! The great majority of each regiment was composed of young men in the first flush of entering upon man's estate, and how patriotic and true were they all, whether young or old. The principles included, too, besides the saving of the Nation's life, those that appealed to the purest and best in manhood. It is no wonder that the veteran of the War for the Union, as he becomes gray headed from advancing age that his thoughts should turn back to that period when he felt the call to assist in saving the country from destruction, a cause that appealed to him as a personal matter. How true and how lasting were the friendships formed at that early period in the lives of most men composing the Union army; and I am not the one to deny the same feeling to those who were opposed to us on many a bloody field. Mistaken they were, as many of them now freely admit, yet they were as brave men as ever fired a musket on a "stricken field". The friendships formed during the war have been as lasting as the rocks.

The day is not so very far distant when the survivors of the Civil War will become, like angels' visits, "few and far between." A new generation has grown up since the grand review, which was held in Washington in May 1865, and the veteran is no longer in the majority in any assemblage. It is not at all strange to find in a crowd of grown-up people those who know less about the war than the small boy of eight or ten years of age did a quarter of a century ago. All this goes to show that the period covered by the four years of that mighty contest are rapidly receding, and the next generation will know as little about it as all of us do at the present moment of the Mexican war. Thus history is rapidly made but soon forgotten. There is one thing, however, to keep the army and the tread of its mighty hosts in remembrance, and that is the literature founded on the Civil War period, as well as its numerous histories. These will remain with the people of this country and will be preserved in public as well as private libraries.

> The battered saber breathes of time
>   When fields were won and lost;
> The empty sleeve in silence tells
>   How much the victory cost.
> Behold the heroes mustered out
>   They sleep in glade and glen,
> On mountain-top, by river side—
>   Four hundred thousand men!
>
> The silky grass is long and green
>   Upon the rampart old,
> The farmer turns the rusted shell
>   Up from the dewy mold;
> And war no longer shakes the skies
>   That smite above the South;
> The robin woos his sweetheart in
>   The cannon's brazen mouth.
>   —T. C. Harbaugh

*   *   *   *   *

General Williams passed away in Warsaw at 1 a.m. on Sunday, January 15, 1905. At his death, General Williams knew all those about him and called them by name. He was rational and talked to those at his bedside, until almost an instant before the last breath left him. He told his watchers he was in no pain. The end came as peaceful as the sleep of a little child, so easily did the spark of life pass out. The funeral of General Williams was held at his residence on Wednesday, January 18, 1905. During the service, from two to four o'clock, business in Warsaw was suspended, all the business houses, as a mark of respect to the memory of the deceased, closing their doors[1].

The Kosciusko Post, No. 114, G. A. R. of Warsaw[2] adopted the following resolutions on the death of General Williams:

WARSAW, IND., Jan 20, 1905
To the Officers and Members of Kosciusko Post,
No. 114, G. A. R.:

---

[1] Williams, Logan H., To the Memory of General Reub Williams, Kosciusko County Historical Society, Warsaw, Indiana

[2] Williams, Logan H., To the Memory of General Reub Williams, Kosciusko County Historical Society, Warsaw, Indiana

Epilogue

"Comrades: your committee to whom was assigned the duty of preparing a memorial on the death of our comrade, General Reub Williams, would submit the following for your approval, to the memory of our deceased comrade:

"General Reub Williams was born August 16,1831, in Tiffin, Ohio; died at his home in Warsaw, Indiana, January 15, 1905.

"Thus it is written of the two all-important events in the lives of all men, rich and poor, high and low, learned and unlearned. Whatever station in life between these two periods may be our lot, whether performing the lowliest duties of the life we live or occupying the exalted position of the statesman, all must pass through the gates of entry and exit. Our comrade has passed through the gate and it is not the province of man to judge the seventy-four years that lies between. That is in the hands of an All-Wise and loving Father who judges with mercy; but it is not only the privilege but the duty of his comrades and neighbors at this time, when the last gate has been closed upon the disappearing form, in retrospect, to look back over the record left and take therefrom the best of that record for our future guidance and loving remembrance.

"That record left by our comrade is that of an upright citizen—of strict integrity, honesty of purpose, a kind and affectionate husband and father. As a defender of his country from 1861-1865, his record is a most honorable one. That is now a part of the history of the state he loved so well. What more can be said? He has lived his life and is gone. His country, his state, his county and the city of his home have profited because of that life. It is fitting that his comrades of Kosciusko Post, No. 114, Grand Army of the Republic, should express their sympathy to the wife of his youth, who shared the sunshine and shadows of his life, and the sons whose childhood was made happy through his love and in their mature years have shared the pleasures and cares incident to a business life with him; therefore, be it

"*Resolved*, That Kosciusko Post, No. 114, G. A. R., in regular meeting assembled, does hereby extend to Mrs. Williams and the children of our departed comrade our most heartfelt sympathy and wish it was in our power to do or say something to lighten their grief. In our helpless condition we can only look to our Heavenly Father, who alone can comfort the widow and fatherless and who was never appealed to in vain."

Charles W. Scott
S. D. Hathaway
J. S. Neely,
Committee

And from Companies I and F:

"The following resolutions were passed by Companies I and F, of the Twelfth Indiana Infantry, in respect to their deceased comrade, General Williams. For years these two companies of the Twelfth Indiana Regiment have held annual reunions, and the deceased was always an active participant in the gatherings:

"Whereas, Death has claimed another member of Companies I and F, General Reub Williams, therefore, be it

"*Resolved*, That in the death of General Reub Williams we realize that we have lost one of our active and faithful members, having at all times the interest of the companies in view, wise and prudent in conference and in discussing matters pertaining to the good of Companies I and F. We deeply mourn his loss, but trust that it is his gain.

"*Resolved*, That we tender to his afflicted family our heartfelt sympathy in this, their day of greatest bereavement, and commend them to the love of our most merciful Father in heaven, believing that if invoked His tender compassion will assuage the grief of their stricken hearts."

W. H. H. Bennett
L. L. Lamkin
John A. Peterson,
Committee[3]

Reverend D. R. Lucas, department commander of the Indiana G. A. R., came from Indianapolis in response to a request of General Williams some years ago to say a few words over his body if death should claim him first. Rev. Lucas's and General Williams's friendship was born at a period that tried men's souls. Rev. Lucas said[4]:

"It is with a sad heart that I come today to speak a few words by the coffin of my friend. I come not as a minister of the gospel, not as an orator, with a fulsome eulogy, but as a friend to lay a flower, the tribute of my friendship, upon his casket. In speaking once of the end that must come, sooner or later, to us all, he said: 'When I go hence I would like to have you or Chaplain Gage say a few words, for you know more of my life than any one else.' In harmony with the request I come here to say a few things of the life of this man. My acquaintance with him began in the days of the Civil War, when we met at Memphis in the autumn of 1862, where

---

[3] Williams, Logan H., <u>To the Memory of General Reub Williams</u>, Kosciusko County Historical Society, Warsaw, Indiana

[4] Williams, Logan H., <u>To the Memory of General Reub Williams</u>, Kosciusko County Historical Society, Warsaw, Indiana

Epilogue

he was serving as Colonel of the Twelfth, Indiana, and I was chaplain of the Ninety-ninth Indiana. Our regiments from the time to the close of the war were always in the same division and marched and fought side by side. Since the war I have attended with him many of the reunions of the Twelfth Indiana, and he would always say to me at our soldier gatherings: 'I am not a speechmaker, and I have appointed Chaplain Lucas to make my speeches for me,' and so here today, surrounded by his comrades of the old regiment, I come to say what I believe he would have me say, for it is the profound faith of my heart that he remembers us as we remember him. He knows what I say, and also I must speak as in his presence. The only solution of the problem of human life, the only outcome of it possible, it seems to me, is the fact that death does not end all, that our comrade has only changed to another place, where he still thinks and hopes and loves. He is still in the hands of the Great All-Father, who is too wise to err, too good to be unkind, too just to deal unjustly with any of his creatures. His ways are omniscient and His mercy endureth forever. No word that I can say will help or harm this friend of mine.

"With these comrades around me, I can say that General Williams was a brave man. I have seen him where none but a brave man could ever stay. Comrades of the Twelfth Indiana and all other members of regiments here assembled, your commander is now with General Logan and the comrades on the other side. The boys who died at Missionary Ridge, who fell at Atlanta and along the way are with us today. They passed from our sight in the strife of battle, but have never passed from our hearts, and the Father of us all, who notes the sparrow's fall and hears the cry of the wingless ravens, will gather them all with us on the eternal camping ground; for they, as well as our comrades here, have, as was said of the dying Garfield, 'felt upon their wasted brows the breath of the eternal morning.'

"So, comrades, bear him away to his rest, where 'over him will bend the arching sky as it did in great love when he lay down weary with the march, or on the battlefield for an hour of sleep. As he was then, so he is still—in the hands of the Heavenly Father. 'God giveth His beloved sleep.'

"And now, my comrade, General Williams, I have stood by the coffin over which is spread the flag you loved so well; I have said what I believe you would have me say. I have given you the tribute of my friendship; I have done all that I can, and so I bid thee farewell. When the snows of winter fall upon thy grave and the flowers of summer blossom on thy tomb, may thy soul be in peace."

The following lines were read at the closing of the funeral by Rev. D. H. Guild, pastor of the Warsaw Methodist Episcopal Church. They had been clipped from a newspaper by General Williams and pinned to a leaf of the book containing his biography. The clipping itself failed to give the name of the author, and it is probable that General Williams never knew it. It is a coincidence, however, that Rev. Lucas himself penned the lines so applicable to the character of the man at the side of whose casket he came to say a few words.

> To lay my wreath upon this comrade's bier
>   I come, for I would find a humble place,
> Among the mourners as they gather here,
>   His many deeds of honest worth to trace.
>
> He was a man that men of honor trust,
>   Faithful in good or ill and to the end.
> To conscience true and seeking to be just,
>   A man that men are proud to call a friend.
>
> He would not shine with those called debonair;
>   He felt contempt for shams, for well he knew
> That roughest garb might cover diamond fair
>   And homely form encase a heart most true.
>
> He had no miser thirst for glittering gold,
>   For fame no fever that men call him great,
> But in that wiser, better class enrolled
>   That love their God, their country, home and state.
>
> He loved his comrades with a steadfast heart,
>   And bore their sorrows as a partner true;
> With tongue and pen he bore a loyal part
>   In honor of the men who wore the royal blue.
>
> His work is done; no more with voice or pen
>   For right he'll join the conflict and the strife,
> But his example speaks to living men
>   The story of an honest, upright life.
>
> And so we say farewell; the end has come;
>   By faith, though dead, he speaketh to us yet:
> Be true to God, to country and to home;
>   His voice, 'Lest we forget, lest we forget.'"

General Reub Williams was laid to rest in Oakwood cemetery in Warsaw, Indiana, by members of his old regiment— the Twelfth Indiana

Bibliography

a. <u>The Northern Indianian</u>, January 8, 1903 thru July 21, 1904
   <u>Warsaw Daily Times</u>, January 3, 1903 thru July 16, 1904

b. Reid, George I., <u>Encyclopedia of Biography of Indiana</u>, Century Company, Chicago, 1895

1. "Gone To His Reward", <u>The Northern Indianian</u>, January 19, 1905, p. 1

2. Williams, Logan H., <u>To the Memory of General Reub Williams</u>, Kosciusko County Historical Society, Warsaw, Indiana

3. Williams, Logan H., <u>To the Memory of General Reub Williams</u>, Kosciusko County Historical Society, Warsaw, Indiana

4. Williams, Logan H., <u>To the Memory of General Reub Williams</u>, Kosciusko County Historical Society, Warsaw, Indiana

United States Civil War Records

Pages 30, 56, 130, 164, 210. 224, 238, 258, Military Records File, Kosciusko County Historical Society, Warsaw, Indiana

Photographs

Page 1   Reub Williams working at his writing chair, 1903, <u>Warsaw Times-Union Souvenir Edition</u>, July 3, 1954, Kosciusko County Historical Society, Warsaw, Indiana

Page 174   Reub Williams as Captain in 1862, Photo File, Kosciusko County Historical Society, Warsaw, Indiana

Page 311   Portrait Reub Williams, <u>Warsaw Times-Union Souvenir Edition</u>, July 3, 1954, Kosciusko County Historical Society, Warsaw, Indiana

Index

Abercrombie, ___ 50
Andersonville 31, 36, 203
Ashby, ___ 16,19,20
Aveline, Frank 121
Baker, Myron 189
Baldwin, ___ 98,100,104-108, 124,
  140,152,203-204, 239-240, 266-268
Banks, N. P. 12,16,26-27,49,51
Barber, Lucius 190, Miss ___ 190-191
Battle Above the Clouds 118
Baylor, ___ 20-25
Beauregard, ___ 5, 11,111,234
Bee, ___ 25
Belknap, ___, 197
Belle Isle 31
Bennett, Thomas 213
Benton Barracks 87, 90-91
Bierce, Ambrose 265, Augustus 265
  Dime 265
Big Ben 123, 229
Big Shanty 165-166
Blackwell, ___, 302
Blair, Frank P. 125,132,163
Boltz, Fred 265
Bond, Jared D. 121, Stephen 55
Boone, Daniel 71
Boughter, Samuel 52, 54, 61, 66, 188
Bowles, William 214
Bowman,___ 302
Bragg, Braxton 54, 73, 110, 114, 121-
  124, 143, 301
Bronson, ___ 291
Brown, John 5, 101, Gov. 204, 245
Brownlow 44
Buchanan, James 5, 9, 226, 251
Buckner, Simon 9
Buell, Don Carlos 73
Burnett, Henry L. 213-214
Burnside, ___ 113-114, 125-127
Butler, Ben 12
Camp, Chase 66, 91, 1126,
  Morton 10,74-78, 160, 215
  Sherman 79, 109-110, Sullivan 10
Carrington, Henry B. 214, 225
Chalmers, ___ 80
Chapman, C. W. 13, 189

Chicago, Illinois 27, 79, 122, 136, 191,
  271, 291
Chickamauga Creek 117-118, 124
Childs, George 49
Chipman, Silas 54
Cincinnati, Ohio 54, 57, 65-74, 85, 208,
  213, 216-217, 299
Cincinnati Commercial 59
Clark, John 275
Cleburn, Pat 198
Coggswell, ___ 40
Colfax, Schuyler 33,36,49
Colgrove, Silas 213
Congaree Creek 235
Conner, John B. 79-80
Corse, John M. 152, 303
Cruft, Charles 54, 57, 73, 75
Custer, George A. 139, 296, Mrs.
  George 296
Cutshall, Arron 274-275
Daily, Janet 94, 139
Davis, Abram 200, Charles F. 200,
  Jeff C., 117, 177, 189, Jefferson 15,
  37, 43, 117, 155, 170, 204, 249, 275,
  277 Theodore R. 132, 184
DeGrass, ___ 182-183
DeHart, Richard 213
DeNyce, Edwin 216
DeVilliers, Charles A. 37-39, 61
Dodd, Harrison H. 214
Dodge, Gen. 145, 153, J. B. 7, 213
Draper, ___ 16
Early, Gen. 271
Elkhart, Indiana 98
Ellsworth, ___ 291
Ely, ___ 39-40
Ewing, Hugh 76, 117, 124, 140
Flowers, Henry 103, 133, 159
Floyd, ___ 9
Flynn, Pat 102
Fort, Donelson 9, 36, 41, 169, Henry 34,
  36, Loomis 93-96, McAlister 216,
  Monroe 38, 41, 44, 47, 271, 280, 285,
  Pickering 80, 86, Pillow 80, Sumter
  5-6, 9, 233-234, 251, 266, 287, 291,
  Wagner 87
Fort Wayne, Indiana 61, 190-191

Index

Franklin, Horace 171-172, 232
Frazer, James 228
Funk, Joseph A. 52
Gage, M. D. 76-77, 120, 132, 153, 302, 308
Gallagher, A.P. 6, 13
Garrard, ___ 192
Gettysburg 87
Gibbs, ___ 31
Goodnow, James A. 85, 94, 151, 203, 205-206
Goodwin, ___ 236
Gramman,___ 33
Grant, Ulysses S. 49, 80-86, 96-99, 102, 112, 117-118, 121, 125, 132-135, 142, 144, 163, 169, 197, 206, 266, 271, 273-276, 280-281, 285-292
Great Pedee River 149
Greathouse, ___ 178,
Halleck, ___ 134, 207-208, 285, 294
Hamlin Dan 51
Hampton, Wade, 230-233, 246, 272
Hard Tack 128, 141, 148, 229, 239
Hardee, ___ 197, 200, 233-234, 268
Hardee's Tactics 6, 38
Harker, ___ 169
Harper's Ferry 10, 12-13, 49-51, 263
Harper's Weekly 132, 184
Harris, Isham G. 281, W. C. 40, 48-50
Harrow, W. 140-141, 147, 150-152, 156, 159-161, 168, 180-181, 183, 193, 203
Hazzard, Lemuel 17, 52
Heath, Albert 98, 123, 213
Heffren, Horace 214-215
Hicks, ___ 12
Hood, ___ 17, 176-177, 180,-181, 185, 187, 189, 192, 196-197, 199, 201-207, 234, 249, 265, 271
Hooker, Joseph 113, 117-118, 144, 153-155, 160-163, 170, 176-177, 208, 216-217, 265, 273
Horry, ___ 232-233
Horsey, Stephen 214
Hovey, Alvin P. 214
Howard, ___ 154, 250, 256, 273
Hubbard, Alonzo 54
Hubler, Henry C. 6-7, 13, 16-17, 19-20 Oliver 17, Thomas 217

Hueston, ___ 63
Humphreys, Andrew J. 214-215 George 13
Huntington, Indiana 214, 275
Illinois Infantry 7th 250, 9th 89, 250, 26th 120, 141, 144-145, 154, 156, 180, 184, 188, 40th 178, 90th 97, 101, 120, 122, 137, 143-144, 181, 183, 100th 89
Indiana Infantry 6th 93, 9th 76, 11th 40, 14th 140, 16th 51, 20th 31, 35th 77, 48th 118, 74th 52, 167, 189, 198, 88th 265, 99th 106, 309, 100th 97-98, 101, 120-121, 132, 144, 173, 213, 101st 25
Indiana Conspirators 203, 211-213
Iowa Battery 123, 155, 159, 166
Jack-ass Battery 58
Jackson, Andrew 44, 127, 278, 294 Stonewall 16, 20-27, 50
James River 31, 46, 271, 295
Johnson, Albert 111, Andrew 44, 127-128, 278, 294
Johnston, Joe E. 97-99, 102, 149-150, 153-157, 165, 167, 170, 176, 249, 265, 268-274, 276-277, 279-282, 295
Jones, John Paul 297
Kempton,___ 67-72, 84-86, 94
Kentucky Jeans 13
Kentucky Brigade 234-235
Key to Vicksburg 99
Kilpatrick, ___ 147, 149-150, 272
Kimball, Nate 50
Kirkpatrick, Gen. 144, 192, Lieu. 302
Knights of the Golden Circle 191, 211-215
Lagrange, Indiana 101, 297
Lane, Jim 5
Lee, Fitzhugh 201, Henry 40, Robert E. 51, 142, 157, 199, 201, 204, 213, 225, 233, 245, 251, 263, 266, 270, 273-274, 280-286, S. D. 201
Leedy, J. K., Dr. 189-190
Lenfestey, ___ 80
Libby Prison 27, 33, 35-37, 40, 46, 55
Lincoln, Abraham 5-7, 9, 37, 51, 53, 87, 140, 206, 209, 212, 227, 275, 277-279, 284, 290-291, 294-295

Index

Link, Colonel William H. 13, 53-54, 58-61, 64, 66, 301-302
Logan, John A. 39, 132, 135, 139, 144-147, 149-153, 155, 157, 159-162, 168, 171, 178-180, 186, 188-189, 207-208, 227, 249-250, 253, 269, 280, 301, 309
Longstreet, ___ 113, 125, 127
Loomis, John Mason 119, 122, 136, 140-142
Lucas, Rev, D.R. 308-310, Thomas J. 213
Lynch's Creek 232
Manson, Mahlon D. 57, 62-68
Marmaduke, ___ 87
Marsh, ___ 82-84, 86, 90
Marion, Francis 231, 233
Mason and Dixon's Line 8, 17
McCarty, Larry 143, 149
McClellan, George, 44, 213, 227, Quartermaster 81-82, 84, 302
McClure, ___ 122
McConnell, Nate B 17
McCook, Gen. 169
McCulloch, John 59
McDowell, ___ 169
McGoffin, ___ 7
McGruder, ___ 38-39
McGuire, James 17
McLane, William E. 213
McPherson, ___ 42, 142, 144-145, 159, 171, 178-181, 186
Meade, George G. 292
Merriman, Jacob 54, 60
Metcalf, ___ 58-71
Michigan Infantry 15th 187
Milice, Andrew 6-7, 13, 114-115
Mililtary Commission 203, 208, 213
Milligan, L. P. 214
Mississippi River 76, 80-81, 90, 93, 96-97, 126, 199, 218, 283, 301
Morphine 96
Morton, O.P., 7-10, 13, 51, 54, 64, 66, 74-76, 108, 212, 215, 247, 275
Mosby's Guerillas 51
Mower, Gen. 265-266, 268-269

Mule, Army 58, 108, 113, 138, 143, 155, 229, 231, 286
Murphey, Dennis 61
Murray, Charles D. 213
Negro Soldier 87, 264
Nelson, Gen. 57, 60, 66, George 146
Noble, Laz 13
Neuse River 269, 272, 280, 284
O'Mara, Timothy 122
O'Shaughnessy, ___ 302
Ohio Infantry 7th 124, 11th 37, 39, 46th 141-142, 159
Old Glory 118, 172, 273, 304
Oliver, ___ 17, 187
Orphans 8, 61
Osterhaus, ___ 117, 150, 159
Oswego, Indiana 183
Palmetto Flag 247
Pancoast, ___ 34, 40, 44, 46
Park, Gen. 99, 105, 107
Parks, Lawrence 183, Marsh H. 73-74, 191, 193, 231, 247, 302
Parrott, ___ 101, 120-121
Peoples, Thomas 152-153, 302
Perce, B.F. 153
Pemberton, ___ 96, 100
Perky, Jesse 250
Pitman, Ben 213
Plymouth, Indiana 217
Pontoon Bridges 117-118, 124, 136, 259, 285
Potomac River 15, 18, 20, 23, 25-26, 28, 49, 280
Potomac, Army of 34, 44, 51, 86, 113, 134, 140, 271, 274, 292-294, 296
Preston, ___ 26
Price, ___ 302
Quimby, ___ 86
Quinine 96
Richhart, Robert 17, 41
Rifle Belgian 10, 226, Enfield 226, Harpers' Ferry 226, Springfield 10, 18-19, 141, 149, 173, 226, 267
Robins, Timothy 18
Rooker, ___ 80
Rosecrans, ___ 110, 112

Index

Runyan, John N. 167
Ryan, Dick 77-78
Ryan, James 220
Schofield, ___ 142, 144, 153, 269, 273
Schurz, Carl, 273
Scrip 32-33
Shaffer, William 193
Shepard, Resin 15-17
Sheridan, Philip 139, 271, 273-274, 282
Sherman, William T. 76, 80-81, 93, 97, 100, 102, 105-106, 111-137, 140, 143-144, 150, 153-155, 158-170, 175-177, 185, 187, 190-192, 196-198, 201-209, 216, 219-228, 230, 232-235, 240-247, 249, 251-254, 262-266, 269-295, 301
Sherman's Foragers 293
Simms, William Gilmore 171, 245
Slocum, Gen. 203, 265, 269, 273
Smith, Kirby 54, 57, 64, 70-71, 73, 75, 78, 280, Morgan L. 153, 182, 186 William Sooy 96, 105-106
Sons of Temperance Hall 23, 25
South Bend, Indiana 49
Spooner, Benjamin 213
Stanton, ___ 273, 278, 285, 294-295
Steamer, Ajax 216-218, 225, Dunbar 118, Forest Rose 71-72, 298, George Washington 47, Maria Demming 93, Mellville 216-217
Stevens, Ambrose A. 213
Stone, ___ 236
Stoneman, Gen. 144, 192, 272
Stuart, Owen 122
Sturman, John 274-276
Sutler 82-83, 190
Swamp Fox, see Marion, Francis
Tamany Regiment 40
Taylor, , Dick, 234, 280, Gen. 203, B.F. 191-192, Zachary 234
Terry, Gen. 269, 273
Terrill, ___ 8
Theodore, the cook 148, 155
Thomas, George 144, 155, 160, 176, 207-208, 271, 273
Tithing Sack 233
Toombses 8
Twiggs 32
Vallandigham, ___ 227

Van Doran 82-85
Vanskike, David 193
Vassal, ___ 35
Vicksburg 76, 80, 83-84, 87, 96-102 109-111, 136, 140, 142, 144, 163, 169, 180, 199, 300-301
Walcott, Charles 316
Walker, John C. 214
Wallace, John M. 12-13, Lew 9-10, 40, 57, 72,
Warsaw, Indiana 6, 13, 33, 41, 50, 52, 61, 73, 167, 183, 188-189, 191, 198, 200-201, 213, 217, 226, 228, 250, 265, 283, 304, 306
Washburn, ___ 80-81
Wass, Ancil D. 213
Weaver, Col. 145-147, Henry 183, 302
Webster, Ed H. 52, 54, 149, Gen. 218
Wells, Samuel 52
Wescot, Henry 17, 19, 65, 302
Wheeler, Joe, 230, 232-233, 246, 274
Wildman, ___ 25
Williams, Joe R 283, Mrs. Reub 33, 307, William 6, 283
Winder 31
Wises 8
Wood, Charles R. 237, 264, 273, Ed 118, William B. 221-222, William, Gen. 264
Wool, Gen. 47-48
Wright House 52
Yanceys 8
Yates, Dick 39, 102
Yazoo River 97
Zouave 11, 291

ABOUT THE AUTHOR

Sally Coplen Hogan has always been interested in the Civil War and is delighted to be able to bring the story of General Reub Williams's involvement in the greatest conflict this nation has endured to those everywhere who share her interest. She has done extensive research into the life of Reub Williams and believes him to be one of the driving forces behind the early development of the city of Warsaw.

Sally received her Bachelor of Science degree from Ball State University, Muncie, Indiana in the field of Elementary Education. She is an active member in the Kosciusko County Historical Society where she maintains the membership records. Sally has had articles published in national magazines and has written and directed historical plays about the history of Kosciusko County. She served as chairwoman for the June 2004 Warsaw Sesquicentennial and wrote a series of nineteen historical articles for the two local papers leading up to the Sesquicentennial Celebration.

Sally is a songwriter, member of the Warsaw Evangelical Presbyterian Church, and vice president of The Resource Development Group LLC of Warsaw, Indiana. Widowed in 1991, she remarried in 1997 and resides in Warsaw with her husband, Jerry. In their combined family, they have six grown children, four grandchildren, and a German Shepherd named Archie.

www.ingramcontent.com/pod-product-compliance
Lightning Source LLC
Chambersburg PA
CBHW051036160426
43193CB00010B/967